PROHIBITION IN KANSAS

PROHIBITION IN KANSAS
A History

Robert Smith Bader

UNIVERSITY PRESS OF KANSAS

To the people of Kansas
Who have struggled heroically
And not without success
With the eternal question

Published by the University Press of Kansas (Lawrence, Kansas 66045),
which was organized by the Kansas Board of Regents and is operated and funded
by Emporia State University, Fort Hays State University, Kansas State
University, Pittsburg State University, the University of Kansas, and Wichita
State University

Library of Congress Cataloging in Publication Data

Bader, Robert Smith, 1925–
    Prohibition in Kansas.
    Bibliography: p.
    Includes index.
    1. Prohibition—Kansas—History. 2. Liquor laws—
Kansas. I. Title.
HV5090.K2B34 1986   363.4'1'09781   86-231
ISBN 0-7006-0298-4
ISBN 0-7006-0299-2 (pbk.)

Printed in the United States of America
10 9 8 7 6 5 4 3 2 1

Contents

List of Illustrations, Figures, and Tables

ILLUSTRATIONS

FIGURES

TABLES

Preface

THE CONCERN OF HUMAN BEINGS with alcohol-induced behavior undoubtedly coincides with their use of alcohol as a beverage. Legal restrictions on the sale and consumption of alcoholic beverages and formal sanctions against excessive drinking have existed at least since the Babylonian Code of Hammurabi, which dates from 1700 B.C. In the United States the organized temperance movement is nearly as old as the nation itself. Over the decades the anti-alcohol crusade has attracted to its standard literally millions of Americans, including some of the most zealous reformers the nation has ever produced. Their efforts culminated in 1920 in the adoption of an amendment to the Federal constitution which banned the manufacture, sale, and importation of all intoxicating liquor.

After a fourteen-year trial, the nation rejected the "noble experiment." For three decades following repeal in 1933, historians and journalists portrayed prohibition and prohibitionists largely in deprecatory and derisive terms. Prohibition was depicted as a cruel joke; prohibitionists were portrayed as cranks and freaks on the outer margins of society. In social conquests, as in military ones, the victors write the history, at least for a time.

In the early 1960s, emerging from the long, deep "shadow" of repeal, historians began to approach the temperance movement in a more mature and balanced fashion, according it the same serious attention as a popular reform as, say, progressivism or populism. A leader of the modern phase, Jack S. Blocker, Jr., has characterized it as an attempt "to understand the passage of the Eighteenth Amendment [prohibition] rather than to justify the Twenty-first [repeal]." Understanding the temperance movement is important, Blocker says, "because of the ways in which prohibitionists were like other Americans, not because of the ways in which they were different."[1]

In no region of the nation has the question of liquor control been of more consuming or enduring interest than in Kansas. The issue has been under continuous, and usually heated, public discussion throughout the state's history.

Kansas is one of the very few states that have had extensive experience with prohibition as a public policy in both the pre- and post-Volstead periods.

Not unexpectedly, primary materials on state prohibition offer riches to satisfy the demands of the most dedicated researcher. But it is surprising to find that secondary work is almost nonexistent. What we know, or think that we know, about the Kansas events has largely been gleaned from passing comments in nontemperance studies of the state or from references to Kansas in histories of the national temperance movement. Kansas prohibition has lain as a massive lump in the collective digestive tract—unexamined, undigested, unassimilated.

This book covers nearly one hundred years of state history, beginning in the 1850s. It is a broadly interpretive, narrative social history with detailed analyses at selected points. Events in Topeka have been frequently taken as representative for the state, both because it is the capital city and because both wet and dry voices were heard there persistently and with approximately equal volume. The Kansas story has been embedded in the national matrix as appropriate. Women played a critical role in the state temperance movement and have been so recognized in both nineteenth- and twentieth-century events. While the coverage has been reasonably broad, this study can hardly lay claim to exhaustiveness, since a lengthy article or monograph on prohibition lies buried in the archives for nearly every one of the state's 105 counties. A conscientious effort has been made to produce a "balanced" account, though "balance" may lie largely in the eye of the beholder on such an emotional and multifaceted topic.

The Kansas experience brims with irony, pathos, and tension. The last stems in large part from the conflicting demands of the state's storied individualism and of her reform-generated desire to curb the liquor traffic. Kansans characteristically seem inclined, oftentimes even anxious, to believe the worst about themselves, their heritage, and their traditions. Given the national disrepute into which prohibition fell after 1933, it has served the Kansas predilection for apology and diffidence almost perfectly. Perhaps a systematic examination of the record will correct the astigmatism that has resulted from over fifty years of looking through the dark glasses of repeal. In the most sanguine view, the work may be helpful in constructing a more "usable past" for the state and her people.

MY GRATITUDE IS EXTENDED to Katie Armitage, Douglas Bader, Vernon Branson, Phyllis Couch, Don Conrad, Jeff Freeman, Prusilla Hancock, Bob Haywood, Larry Hinton, James McHenry, Jr., Don McCoy, Connie Menninger, Tim Miller, John Ripley, Mary Rowland, Norman Saul, Virginia Seaver, Homer Socolofsky, Lloyd Sponholtz, Ron Wasserstein, Hal Wert, and all the others who helped to make the research easier and more complete. My most sincere thanks go to the staffs of the Kansas State Historical Society and of the Kansas Collection, the Government Documents Library, and the History Department of the University of Kansas. Generous support for the work was provided by the

University of Missouri–St. Louis. A special thanks to my family and most especially to my wife, Joan Larson Bader, for her patience, her interest, and her encouragement. No sooner had the poor woman heard the last Ronald Finney story than the prohibition ''deluge'' began.

1
Prologue

With hope and sincerity, the prohibitionists looked forward to a world free of
alcohol and, by that magic panacea, free also from want and crime and sin, a sort of
millennial Kansas afloat on a nirvana of pure water.
—Andrew Sinclair, *Prohibition: The Era of Excess*

IT WAS LATE AUGUST of 1879, at Bismarck Grove, two miles northeast of
Lawrence, Kansas. The occasion was the National Temperance Camp Meeting,
organized by the newly formed Kansas State Temperance Union (KSTU).
Bismarck Grove was the high-water mark of temperance activity in Kansas to
that time and one of the most notable social gatherings in the history of the state.
During its eventful twelve-day course the camp meeting would attract nearly one
hundred thousand people, more than 10 percent of the entire population of
Kansas.

Six months earlier the legislature had passed a resolution to submit to a vote
of the people in November 1880 an amendment to the state constitution which
would prohibit the manufacture and sale of all intoxicating liquor. By the late
1870s only three states in the nation had statewide prohibition, and in each of
them it was statutory, not constitutional. No state had ever written prohibition
into its constitution; indeed, no state had ever voted on such a proposition.
Bismarck Grove would serve as the kickoff for an intense yearlong campaign for
this first-ever amendment. "The eyes of the whole people," Governor John St.
John exclaimed, "are turned toward Kansas."[1]

Lying peacefully on the flood plain of the Kansas River, the grove's
magnificent site was dominated by fine old elms and a picturesque pond covering
several acres. So attractive was the setting that one visitor was prompted to
wonder why anyone would want to travel all that distance just to see Colorado
mountains. Recent improvements to the property by its owner, the Kansas
Pacific Railway (soon to be reorganized as the Union Pacific), included walks,

1

drives, fountains, gas lights, and dining halls. The *pièce de résistance,* an octagonal-shaped tabernacle which seated five thousand, stood proudly at the edge of the woods on a low rise of ground which would soon become known as Prohibition Ridge.

Several hundred neat white tents punctuated the landscape, providing a temporary home for over one thousand enthusiasts. A few oversized tents, serving as headquarters for the temperance organizations, sported banners "of every hue," adding to the festive air of the scene. In the southeast quadrant such exotic attractions as the petrified man, the fat lady, and the Chinese juggler competed with the "privilege" stands for the customer's dimes. The latter beckoned enticingly with their array of photographic booths, shooting galleries, and lemonade criers. Liquor, it was whispered, could be had "if you knew where to buy it"—thus the incipient stages of an enduring Kansas theme.

The idea of a meeting national in scope developed during the heyday of "boosterism," a community mind set that required everyone to become acutely sensitive to the outsider's view. With the state's population rapidly expanding, "growth" had become fully synonymous with "progress" in the collective psyche, as it remains yet today. Both the Kansas Pacific and the city of Lawrence (population 8,500) appreciated the immigrational possibilities inherent in promoting the camp meeting and in presenting a thriving image to the outside world. A Lawrence newspaper suggested that the town's citizens pile sand at strategic locations on their property, so as to produce for unsuspecting visitors an appearance of vigorous building activity. In spite of such zeal and though the meeting had been advertised in the East and in the Midwest, the "national" encampment drew primarily from Kansas and emphasized Kansas themes.

The sea of humanity—both the converted and the curious—came by omnibus, express wagon, private carriage, on horseback, and on foot. Reduced railway fares proved so popular that special trains had to be scheduled from Leavenworth, Kansas City, and Topeka. These trains "poured out their living freight by multitudes from early morn till dewey eve." Despite one report of a pocketbook snatching, the crowds comported themselves in an orderly and good-natured manner. A dearth of hitching posts seems to have been the most serious logistical complaint. As for the motives of the attendees, most observers agreed with a description of a Sunday crowd as full of zeal for a good cause, eager to see its temperance champions, and desirous "to spend the sacred day in such a manner as to best promote the wellfare and happiness of the community, the state of Kansas and the human race."[2]

A hard rain, which dampened the opening-day ceremonies, came as no surprise to the participants. That temperance meetings brought rain had become a frequently confirmed maxim in eastern Kansas. Water, measuring as much as three inches in some places, flooded many tents, but spirits remained high, buoyed up by witticisms about the remarkable ability of drys to endure the inexpedience of cold water. One of the damp and bedraggled faithful was

SECOND
GRAND NATIONAL
TEMPERANCE
CAMP MEETING
AT
BISMARCK GROVE,
August 14 to August 26, 1879
On Kansas Pacific Railway, near the City of Lawrence,
KANSAS!

Under the auspices of the Kansas State Temperance Union and the National Christian Temperance Union.

Gov. J. P. St. JOHN, Topeka, Kansas,
Pre't Kansas State Temperance Union.
MRS. M. B. SMITH, Topeka, Kansas,
Pre't Woman's Christian Temperance Union of Kansas.
J. S. WILSON, Lawrence, Kansas,
Grand Templar, United Order of Ancient Templars of Kansas.

FRANCIS MURPHY, { Address until August 30th }, Lawrence, Kansas,
Pre't National Christian Temperance Union.
ALBERT GRIFFIN, Manhattan, Kansas,
Chief Leader Temperance Volunteers of Kansas.
L. J. LYMAN, Manhattan, Kansas,
Grand Worthy Patriarch, Sons of Temperance of Kansas.

J. R. DETWILER, Osage Mission, Kansas,
Grand Worthy Chief Templar, Independent Order of Good Templars of Kansas.

A flier announcing the National Temperance Camp Meeting in 1879 (courtesy of the Bourquin Collection, Kansas Collection, University of Kansas).

observed, "seemingly quite happy," wading around in the mud, picking up wet sticks for her morning fire.[3] The state's leading German-language newspaper, the Leavenworth *Freie Presse,* no friend of temperance, scoffed that the outpouring of the heavens undoubtedly came as a divine answer to the prayers of the "water fools."

But after these initial meteorological problems, the skies cleared, and the crowds increased proportionately. Before each day's program, family groups strolled leisurely on the newly installed walkways, listening appreciatively to stirring numbers by the Abilene Hook and Ladder Band or the St. Marys Silver Coronet Band. Interspersed between platform speakers, gospel singers kept the emotional pitch high, though in a different key. One singer's "pure sweet voice"

The audience gathers for a session at the National Temperance Camp Meeting at Bismarck Grove, near Lawrence, in 1878 (courtesy of the Kansas State Historical Society, Topeka).

rendered "Where Is My Wandering Boy To-Night?" so movingly that "many an eye paid the tribute of tears" to both singer and song.[4]

Some assemblies generated a great deal of audience participation, bestowing a decidedly revivalistic tone on the meeting. At one afternoon session a "love feast" featured spontaneous five-minute temperance orations, which came "thick and fast." The speakers' words were punctuated at intervals by the opening phrases of hymns, which arose as unstudied responses from the moved audience. Such events might be followed by pledge signing en masse: "Old men, young men, and boys, old ladies, young ladies, and girls, all walked forward and signed the pledge amid singing, shouting, crying for joy, and the shaking of hands. The most intense enthusiasm prevailed, and everybody seemed in the happiest of moods."[5] Despite such fervor the crowds remained parsimonious, as Kansas temperance workers were to discover and rediscover down through the years. One of the largest days at Bismarck, with a crowd estimated at twelve thousand, produced a freewill offering of only $36.15.

Although the auxiliary events proved attractive, the principal interest centered at the speakers' rostrum, where the unitary temperance message was delivered in as wide a variety of styles as the diverse backgrounds of the lecturers. Featured speakers, noted for their prowess at the lectern, came from such disparate parts of the nation as Brooklyn, New York, and Bourbon County, Kentucky. A black minister from a Methodist church in Mississippi told of the Negro experience. Four Indian chiefs from the Indian Territory pleaded (through interpreters) for the whites' help in "knocking down the glass." On some days a specific ethnic group presented a program, as did a Swedish temperance organization. Speakers echoed the common temperance theme of the day as they denounced "the twin evils" of slavery and intemperance. The same gallant people who had rid the nation of the one curse, they assured their audience, would soon cleanse it of the other.

On one day the Woman's Christian Temperance Union (WCTU) had charge of the program. The WCTU, which had been organized on a statewide basis only the year before, would come to play a large role in the temperance affairs of Kansas. The crowd heard from Amanda Way, a tall, lanky "motherly looking" evangelist and WCTU leader. With her face radiating "charity and love," she spoke in "most eloquent and convincing words" of the "great and good fight." The sixty-four-year-old Drusilla Wilson ("an ideal grandmotherly sort of woman") joined Way on the platform. A pioneer of the Kansas temperance movement, Wilson was elected president of the WCTU at Bismarck. A reporter wrote admiringly that she "speaks plainly and carries conviction of truth with every word. Her facts were true and her arguments unanswerable."[6]

On another day the Independent Order of Good Templars (IOGT) was in charge. A semisecret fraternal organization whose core idea was abstinence from intoxicating liquor, it admitted both sexes and all races to membership. During the previous winter it had played a key role in pressuring the legislature to pass the amendment resolution. The IOGT was led by J. R. Detwiler, a young implement dealer from Osage Mission (St. Paul) who could claim more credit for legislative acceptance of the amendment than any other person. J. Ellen Foster, an Iowa lawyer who was prominent in the national WCTU, also spoke for the Good Templars. Foster declared that of all the states, Kansas, which had been "radical since its birth," should be sound on the question. Her closing remarks about young boys and liquor were so moving that they "brought tears to the eyes of every lady in the house."[7]

The denouement of the encampment came on Sunday August 24, when a crowd estimated at twenty-five thousand swarmed over the grounds. Many ministers in eastern Kansas canceled regular services (at the request of the WCTU) so that their congregations could attend the "grand glorification day." The great mass of humanity crowded into every nook and cranny of the grove; the rapid filling of the tabernacle, "crowded to suffocation," necessitated the frantic organization of overflow meetings. The magnetism of the two most powerful temperance speakers of the era drew the huge throng to the grove. In John P. St. John and Francis Murphy, the men and women of Kansas heard from the platform that day the country's foremost exponents of legal suasion and moral suasion respectively.

St. John had been elected governor just nine months before, emerging from the Republican Convention as a surprise nominee. Tall and handsome, with his striking appearance highlighted by the largest mustache west of the Mississippi, he had become the favorite son of the temperance element and its most eloquent spokesman. In 1878 the crusader-politician had helped to organize the KSTU and was currently serving as its president.

Spending as much time at the camp meeting as his official duties would allow, the governor circulated cheerfully among the crowds, infusing "the tired and weary workers for reform with new courage and energy."[8] After scriptural readings and prayers, Francis Murphy himself introduced St. John to the expectant crowd. No state had ever elected a governor, Murphy said, who wore the badge of total abstinence so proudly or so publicly. With his usual strong voice and commanding presence, the governor stressed the importance of the passage of the amendment in overcoming the evils of the alcohol traffic and stressed the nonpartisan nature of the amendment: "It is in no sense a political question. All parties should unite in this cause for God and humanity."[9]

The forty-three-year-old Murphy had been born in Ireland of Catholic parents and, as a teen-ager, had immigrated without his family to New York City. There he had quickly fallen into a life of dissipation as a habitué of the city's numerous saloons. A hopeless drunk by 1870, he had been converted to Methodism and had signed the pledge in that year. He soon became noted as a raconteur *par excellence,* and in the early 1870s he had founded the nationwide temperance movement that bore his name. The blue ribbon served as the identifying badge of its multitudinous pledge signers.

The Murphy Movement had had a profound impact on Kansas in 1877/78, building a moral-suasion base from which the political rocket of prohibition could be launched. A stoutly built man with a rich brogue and "a pleasant cast of countenance," Murphy had his audience alternately laughing and crying as he drolly recounted his own degradation and subsequent victory over it. Murphy's magic lay in "a sort of peculiar, confidential, and cordial way of speaking which makes every one of his hearers feel that he is speaking to him personally and that every word he says is designed to do him good."[10] Kansas loved nothing more than a redeemed sinner, the poets tell us, so Kansas loved Francis Murphy with all her heart.

Two days later the camp meeting officially closed. Everyone proclaimed it a grand success, and planning began immediately for another encampment the following year. The temperance faithful dispersed to their homes with renewed vigor and determination for the upcoming battle to place the principle of prohibition in the organic law of the state.

SUCH PROFOUND TEMPERANCE SENTIMENT, of course, did not originate with the Murphy Movement, nor did it spring *de novo* from the fertile prairie soil. Rather, its antecedents are to be found deeply rooted in the religious, scientific, economic, social, and political matrices of the first decades of the new nation.[11]

During the colonial period of American history, alcoholic beverages were regarded almost universally as the "good creature of God." Tradition held that alcohol, in whatever form, would effectively reduce fatigue, sustain hard labor, and buffer the extremes of heat and cold. It was viewed as an aid to digestion, a nutritious dietary supplement, and a potent medication for everything from the common cold and influenza to external infections and snakebites. Disadvantages that were associated with drinking, clearly perceived or only dimly imagined, dwarfed into insignificance when compared to the lengthy catalog of its virtues.

Given such a limited comprehension of alcohol and its physiological and psychological effects, it is not surprising that nearly everyone drank some, and some a great deal. Farmers placed jugs of rum in the fields for their hired hands; shopkeepers included liquor rations as part of the week's wages for their employees. In New England villages the town bell tolled at 11 A.M. and 4 P.M., signaling a work break for an alcoholic drink, which was usually supplied by the employer. At public and private celebrations, including ministerial ordinations, the rum, whiskey, wine, cider, and beer flowed freely. Since water was often of doubtful purity and was held in low esteem among the available potables in any event, a great deal of drinking took place in the home at mealtime—morning, noon, and night.

Women and children partook freely, though not nearly so freely as the adult males. This largely unrestrained pattern of usage, driven by both ignorance and practicality, led to the highest per capita consumption of alcohol in the history of the republic. From 1770 to 1830 (reliable data are not available before this period) the adult population (aged fifteen and older) annually consumed the equivalent of six to seven gallons of absolute alcohol per capita (compared to less than three gallons in 1980).

Throughout the colonial and early national periods the constraints on public and private drinking, such as they were, came primarily from societal norms and community controls, acting through informal, extralegal channels. Drunkenness was a legal crime in all the colonies, though the punishment that was meted out was often lenient. The most severe strictures came from New England, where the Puritans, though not teetotalers, considered drunkenness a major sin, to be dealt with harshly; on occasion they even forced an inebriate to wear a scarlet *D*. Prohibition laws of the period applied only to Indians, slaves, servants, chronic drunkards, and to the Sabbath, and frequently even these laws were enforced laxly or were circumvented easily. The free white adult male had only to face an occasional quixotic restriction, such as the Connecticut law that limited drinking by townspeople in taverns to one hour per day, since taverns existed principally for the convenience of travelers.

The first American organization, either religious or secular, that formally condemned alcoholic beverages was the Society of Friends, which discouraged the public use of distilled spirits as early as 1706 and by the 1780s was opposing all use of spirits. The Methodists represented the only other sect in America to raise its voice during the eighteenth century. In the 1780s, under the ardent leadership of their founder, John Wesley, they took a stand similar to that of the Quakers.

The first serious scientific challenge to the "good creature of God" view of alcohol came from Dr. Benjamin Rush, a Philadelphia physician who served as surgeon general of the Continental Army and was a signer of the Declaration of Independence. The best-known physician of his day, Rush summarized his state-of-the-art conclusions in an essay that called into serious question the concept of alcohol as an unmitigated good. His insights included the first recognition in America that chronic inebriation was a distinct and progressive disease. However, he limited his attack to distilled spirits, recommending wine and beer as part of the recovery program for drunkards. Although the essay had little impact on the public's perception of alcohol when published in 1784, it exercised in pamphlet form a profound influence on the next generation of physicians and reformers. By 1850, 170,000 copies had been distributed.

One of those who were influenced by Rush's message was the Reverend Lyman Beecher, a Congregational minister in New England and one of the most prominent clerics of the early nineteenth century. From his pulpit, Beecher delivered "thunderous" sermons against the evils of alcohol, culminating in 1825 in his famous *Six Sermons on the Nature, Occasions, Signs, Evils and Remedy of Intemperance*. In published form they soon rivaled Rush's essay in their impact among the middle and upper classes.

The religious and scientific arguments were buttressed by growing concerns from the commercial sector regarding the inefficiencies of intemperance in the marketplace and an increasing awareness of the civic necessity for sobriety in the young republic. These intersecting influences, but especially the religious one, led to the organization of the first temperance societies in New England and New York State during the period 1800 to 1815. In 1826, local and state societies coalesced into the first national society, the American Temperance Society. By the mid 1830s this organization claimed one million members in over six thousand local societies, concentrated chiefly in New England and New York.

Initially the pledge of the national society required abstinence only from distilled spirits (the "short pledge"). After a decade of debate and soul-searching, the reformers altered the pledge in 1836 to call for abstinence from all intoxicating liquor (the "long pledge"). Henceforth, fermented beverages with alcoholic content in the range of 4 to 20 percent (beer, ale, cider, wine) would be proscribed by the movement, as well as distilled products with approximately 50 percent (such as rum, whiskey, gin, brandy). By this time the word *temperance* had been appropriated by the anti-alcohol movement, just as *drinking* had earlier become restricted to alcoholic beverages. *Temperance* as moderation had mutated to a generic term for the activities of the movement. In late-nineteenth-century Kansas, temperance would be defined as moderation in all things beneficial and abstinence from all things harmful. Alcohol, of course, fell into the latter category.

A typical leader of the ante-bellum temperance movement was likely to be a Congregationalist or a Presbyterian, a Federalist, and well above average on the socioeconomic scale. Joseph Gusfield has portrayed such a leader as a status-conscious conservative, a victim of the ongoing "republican revolution" who was clinging desperately to the last vestiges of a fading influence. But more-recent and more-detailed studies, such as those by Ian Tyrrell and Robert Hampel, conclude that the typical leader was a progressive, change-oriented achiever, serious about the alcohol problem and less anxious about status than were those who opposed the movement. Many were well-to-do and influential men who had an optimistic and perfectionistic outlook and were eager to change the moral world as they had already changed the material one. Drink, they felt, was an "unnatural influence" which delayed the ultimate victory of "Cold-Water,—Capital,—Enterprise,—Industry,—Morals,—and Religion."[12]

A representative example of such "gentlemen of property and standing" was Ichabod Washburn, a self-made Massachusetts manufacturer and a major benefactor of Washburn College in Topeka. The son of a sea captain, Washburn amassed a fortune from a wire-manufacturing concern which United States Steel later absorbed. A Congregationalist deacon and the secretary of a local temperance society, Washburn sought "to provide for the spiritual as well as material needs of his employees."[13] The title of his 1868 autobiography sums up his life as he saw it: *Autobiography and Memorials of Ichabod Washburn, Showing How a Great Business Was Developed and Large Wealth Acquired for the Uses of Benevolence.*

Men joined the ante-bellum movement for a wide variety of reasons: a genuine concern for the alcohol problem by the most idealistic, a pious hope for greater self-discipline by alcoholics, an earnest desire for greater worker efficiency by employers, and an urgent need for an image of respectability by young men on the way up. However, women joined for reasons that were uniquely their own.

The "cult of domesticity" had increasingly restricted woman's sphere to the concerns of home and family. Since the central interest of the temperance movement related so intimately to the hearth, women could participate in this public reform and still keep safely within their assigned sphere of influence. Many thousands of women, typically from the middle class, did join the temperance crusade, often accounting for more than one-half of the membership of the local societies. However, they rarely held leadership positions or influenced policy. Women—like children—the age dictated, were better seen than heard. Even so, many leaders of the embryonic women's-rights movement—for example, Lucy Stone, Susan B. Anthony, and Elizabeth Cady Stanton—gained their first public experience in the temperance movement and its sister reform, the antislavery crusade.

The rise of the temperance movement coincided with a religious revival, or series of revivals, known collectively as the Second Great Awakening (1800–30). It swept from New England villages westward through New York and Ohio to camp meetings in rural Kentucky. This great sustained outburst of religious enthusiasm, which added large numbers of converts to the church rolls, had been wrought by a change in theological thought that carried profound consequences for the incipient temperance movement.

The Congregationalism of the Puritans embraced the Calvinist doctrine of predestination, whereby only the Elect, predetermined by God, would realize salvation. All others, regardless of their earthly behavior, faced eternal damnation. By the early nineteenth century the grip that this harsh doctrine had on the minds of the leading theologians had begun to relax. The prolific "harvester of souls," the Reverend Charles G. Finney, and other charismatic, often itinerant preachers began to espouse the more-appealing and democratic doctrine of Arminianism. That is, everyone could obtain eternal salvation through the conversion experience, namely, by a direct confrontation with Christ. Continuing moral behavior would be interpreted as a sign, or proof, of conversion and salvation. According to this view, man was a perfectable spiritual organism; the responsibility for the ultimate fate of each individual rested solely with that individual.

The implications for the temperance movement were at once simplistic and enormous. An individual's primary purpose in his earthly journey, in this view, was to gain eternal salvation. The befuddled, rum-soaked mind of the habitual drunkard patently lay beyond the reach of God's saving grace. Intemperance diminished man's moral sense and his self-control, hardened his heart, and inflamed his sexual passions. Even moderate drinking dulled reality and fogged the mind, separating a man from his God. A social drinker might well be on the road to perdition; abstinence marked the only safe and sure course to salvation.

Not all churches saw the matter in the same light. Support for the temperance cause came chiefly from those in the evangelical-pietistical tradition, namely, the Methodists, Baptists, Congregationalists, Presbyterians, Disciples of Christ, Scandinavian Lutherans, and Quakers. With their strong revivalistic traditions, these faiths emphasized the individual's personal relationship with God, along with an attendant church structure that was relatively weak. They expected their members to exhibit signs of redemption through moral behavior, and they considered even mild forms of intemperance sinful. For them, the group norm was total abstinence.

Another group of churches did not enter into the temperance movement with any enthusiasm, generally remaining cool or even hostile to it. Although of diverse theologies, these liturgical denominations—notably the Roman Catholic, Episcopalian, German Lutheran, and Jewish ones—stressed the church community, with its rituals, creeds, and tighter authority. Suspicious of revivals and their associated emotionalism, these groups held that "proper belief" was more important than "proper behavior" and that insubordination or heresy was a greater sin than intemperance. For the liturgicals, moderate drinking was the group norm.

The religious dichotomy carried with it strong ethnic and political correlates. The pietists came principally from the so-called Old Stock (English, Welsh, Scotch, Scotch-Irish, Scandinavian), who became predominantly Republican during the second half of the nineteenth century. The liturgicals included many Irish, German, and Eastern European immigrants of the middle and latter part of the nineteenth century, who typically were, or soon became, Democrats.

AN EVENT IN A BALTIMORE TAVERN in 1840 interrupted a temporary lull in anti-alcohol activity and led to the establishment of a second major tradition in American temperance. A half dozen artisans, confirmed drinkers all, inspired by a temperance lecture that two of them attended as a lark, signed an abstinence pledge and proceeded to organize the Washington Temperance Society (in honor of the first president). Dedicated to the reform of others who had drinking problems, the movement spread rapidly. By mid decade an estimated six hundred thousand had taken the pledge under its auspices.

The new movement differed from the established, or Lyman Beecher, tradition in a number of important respects. Most obviously, it drew more heavily from the working and artisan classes, though it included many from the middle class as well. About 10 percent of its membership admitted to having serious drinking problems, a group that was almost never represented or even welcome in the regular societies. The drinkers and the nondrinkers, the churched and the unchurched, the working class and the professional class, the rich and the poor—all flocked to the meetings.

And what meetings they were. A temperance-society meeting had often been a rather staid affair, where proper ladies and gentlemen gathered to listen to an arid lecture on the evils of intemperance. Not so with the Washingtonians. Their emotional, sometimes rowdy activities included temperance picnics (the Fourth of July became a specialty), fairs, parades, songfests, concerts, and melodramatic theater (with King Alcohol as the Evil One). Many of these social innovations became permanently incorporated into the continuing temperance crusade. The most important departure from the older tradition was the "experience" meeting, at which reformed men "witnessed" by describing in lurid detail the depths of their degradation and the destructive impact of Demon Rum on their innocent families. Some of the more talented speakers went on national tour, and at least two of them became famous.

Auxiliary Martha Washington Societies for women quickly developed and soon approached the men's organizations in size and commitment. Many of the women came from the working class, often being the wives of members of the male organization. The new organization gave women another socially acceptable public vehicle and something more. For the first time in the temperance movement, it gave them an opportunity for leadership positions on the platform and in the meeting room. Since few women were known to drink to excess, the women's activities devolved largely on reforming the men and on aiding their impoverished families.

Initially, the established, clerically dominated movement welcomed the Washingtonians for bringing new life and interest to the cause. Soon, however, tensions and jealousies developed both within the new movement and between it and the older societies. The latter began to fear that the Washingtonians, with their different tactics and priorities, might take over the entire temperance movement. The clerics felt that their leadership was being threatened, since the Washingtonians often found formal theology irrelevant to their problems and the ministers' preachy style and moralistic tone irksome.

After the initial euphoria had passed, the young movement began to experience the classic signs of organizational stress: members failed to pay dues and to attend meetings; committees malfunctioned; and personality conflicts increased in frequency. It struggled futilely to fill a reform niche alongside the traditional movement. But the absence of a strong organizational structure— another sharp contrast with the highly organized regulars—proved so damaging that the Washingtonians, as such, had passed from the scene by the mid 1840s.

However, two fraternal organizations that were destined to play important roles in the national temperance crusade arose from the ashes of the movement. The Sons of Temperance, founded in 1842, grew to a quarter of a million by

1849, to become the largest temperance organization in the Washingtonian tradition in the ante-bellum period. After the Civil War, its popularity waned, and it never became important in Kansas. In 1851 the group that would become critical for Kansas—the Independent Order of Good Templars—organized in New York State. Its major growth would be in the post-bellum period, when it reached a membership of about 735,000.

THE TEMPERANCE MOVEMENT underwent a major change in philosophy during the 1830s as it shifted its emphasis from moral suasion of the individual to legal suasion of the community. If alcohol and the traffic that it spawned represented unmitigated evils, the legal advocates argued, then government was wrong to wrap it in a cloak of respectability by licensing it in any manner whatsoever. In an 1842 speech, Abraham Lincoln, a dedicated member of the Sons of Temperance, argued that the harmful effects of alcohol came not "from the abuse of a very good thing" but from "the use of a bad thing."[14] "Moral suasion for those that have hearts to feel its force," the enthusiasts exclaimed, "and legal suasion for those that have not."[15] Not everyone, even among those in the movement, agreed; the Washingtonians, especially, tended to discourage the political approach. The skeptics claimed that legal coercion was "a device to make the constable a substitute for the teacher and the preacher."[16]

A licensing system had been in place since colonial times. Its primary purpose had been to generate revenue; its secondary purpose had been to regulate; moral considerations hardly entered the matter at all. But if the state could license for the public weal, it could prohibit for the same reason. The prohibition of the sale of intoxicants began at the local level in the early 1830s, as spontaneous developments in isolated townships and municipalities in New England. Initially encompassing only ardent spirits, by the late 1840s it included beer and wine as well. The local-option or no-license campaigns grew until the focus shifted to the county level and, finally, to the entire state. The first halting effort at a statewide ban came in 1838, when Massachusetts passed a "fifteen gallon" law, which forbade the sale of spirits in anything less than fifteen-gallon lots. Enterprising saloonists skirted the law by advertising a peek at a "striped pig" for six cents, which privilege included also a free glass of whiskey. From this humble nomenclatural beginning came the "blind pig," the "blind tiger," and other zoological marvels.

Political temperance culminated in Maine in 1851 in the first enforceable statewide prohibitory law. Due chiefly to the indefatigable zeal of Neal Dow, "the Prophet of Prohibition," the Maine Law prohibited the manufacture and sale of all intoxicating liquor and included stringent enforcement provisions. It did provide for the sale of liquor for medicinal and mechanical purposes through state-appointed agents. A "Maine Law" fire soon blazed across the Northeast and the Midwest, engulfing by 1855 all of New England, New York, Indiana, Michigan, and Iowa, among others. The measure nearly passed in Pennsylvania,

Ohio, Illinois, and Wisconsin. These fourteen states would contribute approximately 70 percent of the native-born immigrants who came to Kansas during the nineteenth century.[17]

As the irrepressible wave passed through its successive stages, cresting in statewide prohibition, the drinking habits of at least the northern section of the country changed dramatically. Strongly influenced by the prevailing temperance sentiment, the better-trained physicians prescribed much less alcohol for their patients, and the public consumed far less liquor for its gratification. Consumption of absolute alcohol per annum per capita of the drinking-age population, which had ranged between six and seven gallons during the period 1770 to 1830, dropped to five by 1835, to three by 1840, and to two by 1850. Patently, the status of liquor in the public mind had changed significantly from the "good creature of God" era. And just as clearly, moral and legal suasion could markedly affect consumption, a fact that was sometimes overlooked in the twentieth century.

What had once been a simple social custom would become increasingly complex as the years wore on. Whether one drank and how much and how one thought or felt that the state should deal with the problem, if at all, would henceforth become matters of considerable social and political moment. When the Territory of Kansas was opened to hopeful settlers in 1854, the Maine Law had become a national public question second only to the slavery controversy.[18]

2
Prelude

We are all anxious for the freedom of Kansas. Resolved that the curse of Slavery shall never enter its borders. That these fair, green prairies shall never echo to the groans of a bondsman. . . . Do we forget the bondage of body and mind by the demon intemperance? . . . We are pleased to see that . . . our young men are . . . waging war against whisky barrels and their kindred relatives. . . . We may hope that . . . our influence will extend all the country round, and . . . Kansas will be free, Free, not only from the withering blight of Slavery, but the equally blighting curse of Intemperance.

—*Prairie Star* (Topeka), 1857

Kansas loves a man without blame and without blemish, of pure and spotless character—true. But . . . Kansas loved one thing even more: a sinner who has been saved, a brand from the burning.

—Paul I. Wellman

KANSAS WAS POPULATED during the territorial period by Free Staters eager for economic opportunity and anxious for the ascendancy of their sociopolitical ideology and by southerners eager and anxious for precisely the same things. The Free Staters, who came almost exclusively from the "Maine Law" states with their New England–inspired temperance tradition, soon dominated the scene numerically. By 1858 the political issue in the territory no longer remained in doubt.

Although the slavery question overshadowed all else, the regulation of liquor received a great deal of attention in the new territory. The spiritual and intellectual nucleus of the Free State movement, the New England Emigrant Aid Company, offered four specific reasons for its venture: freedom, religion, education, and temperance. A company circular, sent to all New England clergy in 1855, asserted that "the traffic in intoxicating liquor scarcely exists in any one of the towns founded with the Company's assistance [Lawrence, Topeka,

15

Osawatomie, Manhattan, Wabaunsee, Burlington] and any attempt to introduce it will be resisted by their citizens."[1]

Several of the "Yankee" towns incorporated Maine Law principles in their organic laws. The constitution of the Lawrence Town Association forbade the sale of all intoxicating liquor within the city limits. A clause in the deed of sale of town lots conveyed the restriction to future owners: the lots were to be forfeited if the prohibition was violated. Maine Law prohibition carried seventy-four to one in a city election in July 1855.

The bylaws of the Topeka Town Association, which were adopted in March 1855, banned the sale or purchase of spirituous liquor on property deeded by the association. A conveyance clause was included in the deed of sale. Liquor that was used for medical, mechanical, or sacramental purposes was excepted. No elections on the issue were held, but at the first recorded public picnic in May 1855, the Maine Law was toasted (with nonalcoholic beverages, we may assume). Real-estate restrictions were also incorporated into the town-company bylaws of Emporia, Ottawa, Baldwin, Quindaro, Pomona, and, later, Hutchinson, Russell, and several western-Kansas towns along the Union Pacific.[2]

Although greatly outnumbered by men in the pioneer communities, women who were on the scene soon made their presence felt. Mrs. Sam Wood, the wife of a prominent Free Stater, sounded an enduring keynote in October 1854 on the occasion of Territorial Governor Andrew Reeder's first visit to Lawrence. A forlorn but hopeful village of "frugal board and tented homes," filled with "unshaved, weatherbeaten, yet noble countenances," Lawrence entertained the governor at a festive dinner at the Pioneer Boarding House. Mrs. Wood responded to a toast to the ladies of Lawrence "in an eloquent . . . and womanly style": "Woman's sphere is wherever there is a wrong to make right, a tear to wipe away, a good work to carry forward. And 'tis here to guard our beautiful State from the invasion of wrong, oppression, intemperance, and all that tends to debase and demoralize mankind. Yes, Kansas must and will feel that woman has an influence, and that influence on the side of God and truth."[3]

Women soon took collective action on the temperance question. Fifty-six ladies from Topeka petitioned the Free State Legislature in March 1856, calling for immediate laws "to prevent the manufacture and importation for sale or use as a beverage . . . of any distilled or malt liquors." In their memorial they argued that one of the chief obstacles to effective liquor regulation in the older states had been hoary tradition, "entrenched behind the bulwark of law." But in Kansas "everything is new . . . we are laying the foundation of a new society." Ninety Lawrence women presented the same petition two days later. John Brown, Jr., presented both petitions to the house, which referred them to the Committee on Vice and Immorality, but no further action was taken.[4]

Not all of the activity associated with temperance was orderly and lawful. Both men and women resorted to extralegal measures in direct response to violations of the local prohibitory laws. Covert selling of liquor had increasingly resulted in violent behavior, including the state's first murder, in November 1854. Lawrence, "a temperance, moral and reformatory community," saw the most dramatic retaliatory activity. In the summer of 1856, not long after the sack of the town by the Missouri "border ruffians," a dozen of the leading women, led by Mrs. Sam Wood and Miss Sue Spencer, a young Quaker schoolteacher, formed a vigilante committee. Armed with "axes, hatchets, and hammers, or whatever they could best use for the purpose," they marched determinedly to a log-cabin saloon and spilled every drop of liquor that they could find in bottles, casks, and barrels. After a second attack, liquor selling dropped dramatically, only to reemerge full blown toward the end of the year.[5]

In late December, in a "densely crowded" schoolroom, agitated citizens heard several temperance speakers, including Charles Robinson, head of the Free State government, deplore the situation. The leading voice of the Free Staters, the *Herald of Freedom,* which was almost as fervent about liquor as about slavery, tried to prod the community into action: "Whoever brings liquor here to sell . . . is looked upon as an enemy to the city—an enemy to the public— and as an enemy to God. . . . Any man who aids to make drunkards . . . should be looked upon as a thief of character, a robber of virtue, and . . . a destroyer of life."[6]

In late January 1857 the ladies, "ever foremost in all good works," took action. No less than forty women, protected on the flanks by their menfolk, began a "tour of inspection" of the groggeries, armed with hatchets and other implements of war. Much mayhem was wreaked on the offending establishments, but the town's view of the matter fell a good deal short of the unanimity that was implied by the 1855 vote on prohibition. In midafternoon a group of "ruffians" returned from nearby Franklin with half a barrel of whiskey. "With a red flag flying, . . . the liquor was then paraded through town; a noisy, yelling rabble followed in its trail." Members of the local temperance society, lauding the ladies for performing "a great public service," refused henceforth to trade with merchants who dealt in liquor and condemned those who rented to dealers in "liquid fire and distilled damnation." An election in February affirmed the Maine Law by a vote of 110 to 11.[7]

In May 1855 a group organized to enforce the Topeka Town Association's ban on the sale of ardent spirits, "peaceably, if we can; forcibly if we must." On July 4, several irate male citizens demanded that a notorious violator surrender his stock. To their surprise he said that he would if they would pay for it. They quickly agreed, knocked in the whiskey barrel heads, and ignited the contents. That provided the principal fireworks at Topeka's first Fourth of July celebration. Two years later a spontaneous mob of some one hundred "prominent and respectable citizens" took violent action under leadership that included John Ritchie, a major benefactor of Washburn College. Ritchie and his compatriots, "with the entire approval of the ladies," attacked several stores that were known to be in the business and destroyed $1,500 worth of liquor in two hours of hectic action.[8]

At Centropolis (Franklin County), Mary Still, a teen-age daughter of the Methodist minister, in company with three women friends, broke into a saloon while the owner was in court successfully defending a charge of selling liquor illegally. When he surveyed the damage, the dismayed saloon keeper locked the doors and gave up the business; no replacement appeared for at least ten years. Similar incidents during the territorial and early statehood periods occurred at Big Springs (Douglas County), Quindaro (Wyandotte County), Oskaloosa (Jefferson County), and Mound City (Linn County).[9]

These isolated and often spontaneous outbreaks of violence represented a species of direct-action frontier justice aimed at the alcohol traffic. Kansas would not see such concentrated demonstrations again for more than forty years. The sale of liquor typically diminished after the incidents, but it inevitably returned, and in increasing volume, as the communities focused on the national political issues and the Civil War that ensued. Of course, some settlers, particularly those of southern persuasion, did not want temperance in any form.

AT A VERY EARLY DATE the public mind came to associate temperance with the Free State cause and, conversely, liquor with the southerners. The northern press, both in Kansas and in the East, promoted that linkage, and the southerners did not often bother to deny it. For example, Sara T. D. Robinson, the wife of the Free State governor and the best-known woman in the territory, described the Missourians as "whiskey-drinking, degraded, foul-mouthed marauders." The *New York Tribune* in 1857 published a composite portrait of the border ruffians, in which it alleged that "their chief occupation is loafing around whisky shops, squirting tobacco juice and whittling with a dull jack knife. They drink whiskey for a living, and sleep on dry goods boxes. . . . They are 'down on' schools, churches, and printing offices and revel in ignorance and filth."[10]

Even though the proslavery partisans enjoyed a clear majority among the qualified voters of the territory during 1854/55, Missourians "invaded" Kansas several times on election days during that period. The white ribbon did not make its first symbolic appearance in Kansas on the blouse of a member of the WCTU, but in the buttonhole of a Missourian who was identifying himself to his compatriots on election day.

These brief political pilgrimages, composed of young males who were not at all adverse to combining pleasure with business, were infamous for their drunkenness and violence. Missourians who financed the "vandal hordes" became alarmed at the increasing size of the electoral bill, money that went "for whiskey and for the buying of votes." The largest such incursion occurred in March 1855, when the territory served as unwilling host for "an unkempt, sun-dried . . . mob of five thousand men with guns upon their shoulders, revolvers stuffing their belts, bowie-knives protruding from their boot-tops, and generous rations of whiskey in the wagons.''[11]

The most organized attempt to establish a southern colony in Kansas served to reinforce the intemperate image of the southerners. In November 1855 an Alabama lawyer, Jefferson Buford, issued a call for three hundred "industrious, sober" men to plant the southern idea in Kansas. By the next April the patriotic call had attracted nearly four hundred volunteers, sanguinely described by their leader as "a superior class of young men, quiet, gentlemanly, temperate." But sensing possible trouble ahead, Buford cautioned his restless band to abstain from liquor and to conduct themselves like southern gentlemen. At the Mobile embarkation point, every man was "armed" with a Bible that was supplied by the churches, a symbolic answer to the prolific shipment of Sharps rifles ("Beecher Bibles") to the Free Staters.

Far removed from the restraining influences of the home, the Bible-toting young men soon proved to be more than Buford could handle. They made their first impression in the friendly environs of Westport (Kansas City), Missouri. "The people of Westport were glad to see Buford's men come," a citizen recalled; "they were doubly glad when they went away." The Alabamans never bothered to take claims, preferring instead to roam the countryside, living a life of "dissipation" with their "too-hospitable friends" in Kansas and Missouri. A leading southern newspaper accused them of degenerating into a mob of irresponsible revelers who knew or cared little for plowing or sowing. Within a few months, less than fifty remained in the territory. Later that year the frustrated Buford made an abortive second attempt to plant a colony. Now a practical prohibitionist, he required prospective emigrants to swear to obey orders and to abstain from liquor "so long as necessary."[12]

Liquor became intimately associated in the Free State mind with two of the most inflammatory proslavery acts of the territorial period. The sack of Lawrence constituted the most violent action of either side up to that time. On "the day after," 22 May 1856, an English journalist, Thomas Gladstone, happened upon the returning ruffians in a Kansas City hotel and recorded his impressions in a book that was avidly read in the North. The returnees, he wrote, were "still reeking with the dust and smoke of Lawrence, wearing the most savage looks, and giving utterance to the most horrible imprecations and blasphemies. . . . [I looked] at these groups of drunken, bellowing, blood-thirsty demons, who crowded around the bar of the hotel, shouting for drink."[13]

In April 1858 the Jayhawker chieftain of southeast Kansas, James Montgomery, led twenty men on a raid of a proslavery settlement, Trading Post, in Linn County. Their prime targets included a "Pro-slavery Doggery" and its three barrels of whiskey, which they destroyed. A month later, in a retaliatory action near Trading Post, a band of border ruffians murdered five Free Staters and left six others for dead, an event known as the Marais de Cygnes massacre, which was memorialized by John Greenleaf Whittier.[14]

These events and others, especially Quantrill's Raid of 1863, served to plant the temperance flag firmly on the Free State side of the question. Some evidence suggests that the "Secesh" opened saloons with a considerably higher frequency than did their Yankee neighbors. Whether southerners actually drank more or were more prone to violence when they did so remains unknown. There is no indication, for example, that John Brown and his friends had been drinking on that dark night on Pottawatomie Creek when they whacked five of their innocent neighbors into oblivion. But the association between temperance and the Free State cause remained firm and carried over into the postwar period. "Temperance and Freedom go hand in hand," the *Herald of Freedom* proclaimed, "while whisky and slavery are fit companions."[15]

GIVEN THE FACT that the proslavery "bogus" legislature produced it, the first territory-wide law regulating the sale of intoxicants was a remarkably stringent one. Passed by lopsided majorities in August 1855, the bill was entitled "An Act to restrain dram shops and taverns, and to regulate the sale of intoxicating liquor." It did not come "bodily from the Missouri Statutes," as has been alleged; no Missouri law of the period came close to being so stringent.

The act provided for a local-option vote every two years to determine whether any liquor licenses at all should be granted within the voting unit, that is, the incorporated town or rural township. If the proposition received a majority vote of the qualified electors (males), a successful applicant for a license had to present a petition, signed by a majority of the householders (males) of the unit, recommending said applicant. The law also prescribed penalties for selling without a license, on Sundays, and to Indians and to slaves without the slave owner's consent.[16]

The legislature of the sister territory of Nebraska, which had a Democratic majority, passed a short-lived Maine Law in 1855. In Kansas the 1855 legislature received only one petition (which had only a few signatures) praying for the passage of a prohibitory law. The lack of interest by the temperance-inclined citizens stemmed from the fact that the Free Staters chose to ignore the "bogus" legislature as much as they could with impunity. Under these peculiar circumstances they concentrated their antiliquor efforts at the local level.[17]

The 1855 legislature met at Shawnee Methodist Mission, and though ample room was available at the site, most of its members chose to board at Westport, Missouri, a few miles to the east. The reason is not difficult to ascertain. The United States Government forbade the selling of liquor to the Indians, so the area had no open saloons. Therefore, the mission, as a domicile, was "not wholly satisfactory to those who needed stimulation produced by the spirit of corn."[18]

The dramshop act appeared to be so satisfactory on paper that even the *Herald of Freedom*, which never wittingly uttered a syllable in praise of the proslavery crowd, could find nothing in it to criticize. The problem, of course, lay in its enforcement. Little evidence has been found that either of its principal provisions—namely, for elections and petitions—was enforced with any regularity during the tension-filled days of 1855 through 1858.[19]

The 1859 legislature, firmly under Free State control, amended the dramshop act in several significant ways. The major changes were in the wet direction, reflecting the diminished vigor of the Maine Law movement under the prevailing quasi-military conditions. The legislators dropped the local-option vote and exempted towns of one thousand or more from the petition provision. This exemption marked the first sign of an urban/rural schism that would grow wider and deeper as the state developed. The new law provided that an injured wife or child could seek civil recovery against anyone who sold liquor to an intoxicated person, habitual or otherwise. Adding a quixotic touch, another section made it unlawful to sell liquor to "any married man against the known wishes of his wife." That potential disturber of domestic tranquility did not produce any known legal action during the nine years of its fitful life.[20]

During the late 1850s there was a flurry of activity with regard to a constitutional convention, culminating in 1859 in the Wyandotte Convention, which wrote the document that became the state's organic law. Delegate John Ritchie, fully recovered from the bruises incurred in the 1857 Topeka saloon riot, introduced a resolution that granted the legislature the specific constitutional power "to prohibit the introduction, manufacture or sale of spiritous liquors." Subsequent discussion on a similar proposal failed to elicit sufficient support, and the section was withdrawn. Thus, when Kansas became a state in 1861, its constitution made no reference to intoxicating liquor, though the grand event itself did give everyone in the reform-conscious territory an opportunity to turn over a new leaf. The *Leavenworth Herald* was jubilant: "Everybody is 'clothed in the panoply' of freshly formed resolve—no more tobacco is to be used—no more whisky will be consumed—vice and immorality are at a heavy discount. Hurrah for the State of Kansas!"[21]

The legislature of 1867 submitted a constitutional amendment for woman suffrage to a vote of the people (the first such vote in the nation) and amended the dramshop act in two important ways. It repealed the provision that exempted towns of one thousand or more from the petition requirement and made a fundamental change in the petition section itself. Henceforth, an applicant for a license would have to present to the local governing body a petition signed by a majority of the adult residents, "both male and female," of the township or ward. The amendment added legal authority to the unofficial influence heretofore exerted by women. In liquor matters, from this time forward, "she was considered practically a voter." The amendment raised the possibility that much of the state might become legally dry, since women, it was thought, would be reluctant to sign license petitions. The legislature also passed a bill prohibiting the sale of intoxicating liquor in the unorganized counties of the state.[22]

The dry victory was short-lived, however. A good deal of pressure developed during 1867, especially from the growing German community, to modify the most restrictive provisions of the law. In 1868, under the leadership of George W. Glick, an Atchison attorney, the wets gained what they wanted most: the exemption of cities of the first and second classes (those with populations over two thousand) from the petition provision of the act. The legislators, 75 percent of whom had emigrated from Maine Law territory, did retain the provision that allowed females to sign the petition and did prohibit the sale of liquor to minors, without parental consent, for the first time. They also continued the ban on the sale of liquor to Indians, but exempted those who had become citizens.[23]

The liquor industry exercised a great deal of political clout nationally during the last third of the nineteenth century. The saloon itself became a frequent meeting place for political parties; the "Knight of the White Apron," the saloon keeper, had an unrivaled daily opportunity for crystallizing support for his candidates and issues. While awaiting the completion of the east wing of the Statehouse, the 1868 legislature met in a nondescript building located on lower Kansas Avenue. The legislators found themselves tightly sandwiched in between two drinking establishments, a position that was not incompatible with their subsequent modifications of the dramshop act.

On the north, a somewhat coarse, frontier-style groggery catered largely to the working class. It was heated by "a large, square box-stove" on which water was warmed for making "whisky slings." Directly to the south of the state building an imposing two-story brick structure, the Senate Saloon, literally and figuratively cast its shadow on the legislature. Much more impressive than the tottery structure that housed the affairs of state, the "temple of Bacchus" included among its "elegant appointments" several "rude works of art" and gaming rooms for the "sporting fraternity." The saloon, of course, furnished an all-too-tempting opportunity for the legislators "to while away their leisure hours . . . , drowning their sorrows and celebrating their triumphs."[24] And to contemplate amendments to the dramshop act.

DURING THE 1860s and the 1870s the young and growing state seemed to be awash with liquor, especially in the more primitive or pioneer communities. Towns of the third class (population 250 to 2,000) and the rural townships were often legally dry, due to the petition requirement of the law. But many scofflaws operated without a license and frequently violated the bans against selling on the Sabbath and to minors and habitual drunkards. And in the larger towns the liquor flowed freely, both legally and illegally. In the early 1870s, with a population of four hundred thousand, Kansas had two distilleries, forty-six breweries, and sixteen hundred federal permits to sell at retail.

Some towns were said to be "ablaze with drunkenness." In LeRoy (Coffey County) during the late 1850s, observers reported (with a degree of exaggeration that remains indeterminate) that "the whole town was drunk." During a two-year period in the early 1860s a Council Grove merchant who supplied the Santa Fe Road trade sold $12,000 worth of whiskey and only $15.20 worth of Bibles.

The Lawrence brewery owned by John Walruff, who later became a prominent antiprohibitionist. During the 1870s it was the largest in the state (courtesy of the Kansas State Historical Society, Topeka).

Girard in 1870, two years after its founding, had one saloon for each nine dwellings. Coffeyville, adjacent to the Indian Territory and on a cattle trail for a time, had its main thoroughfare renamed Red Hot Street. Filled "with lewd women of the most beastly type," the dance halls and saloons flourished as "revelry, debaucheries and criminalities ran riot." At Baxter Springs, a "tough place" in the southeast corner, the Quapaw Indians, as well as the white settlers, found a ready supply of liquor. During its cattle-trade period of the late 1860s, saloons "of the most violent character" thrived while the town enjoyed "one continuous state of uproar, night and day."[25]

As the railroads extended their lines to the west, a succession of towns served as the railhead for cattle that were being herded up from Texas. From 1867 to 1885, Abilene, Hays, Newton, Ellsworth, Wichita, Caldwell, and Dodge City served the cow-town function in approximately that order. The saloons that they spawned became renowned in story and verse as symbols of western violence and disorder. In its rawest state in the pioneer communities, the saloon consisted simply of a plank resting on two barrels in a tent or dugout. Several months later the drinking emporium could be found occupying a long, narrow, dimly lit room, sporting a modest bar and emitting a memorable odor— an unforgettable blend of liquor, tobacco, straw, horses, and kerosene. As the town matured, it might be fortunate enough to attract a showplace saloon, such as Abilene's Alamo or Dodge City's Saratoga. There, one could find proudly displayed a magnificent mahogany bar, a splendid mirror, which would cover one wall, and a naughty reproduction of nude ladies at the bath, which would cover most of another.

As Robert Dykstra has demonstrated, the social history of a cow town passed through successive and predictable phases. In the initial stages of development, typically when the cattle trade was at its height, the town comprised from 250 to 400 males, mostly young and single, for every 100 females. With the advent of the young males came a demand for prostitution, gambling, and saloons. The town, in effect, became "wide open."

During this phase the forces of secular factionalism dominated the local political scene. Gambling and prostitution, though illegal, were licensed for the revenue they would bring. The town struggled under the conflicting demands of the "sin" industries and those of law and order. In some instances, as in Wichita, an attempt was made to segregate the rowdiness from the rest of the town. The "respectable" element often had at least an indirect economic stake in the entertainments and was loath to press reform measures in any radical fashion. Under these discouraging circumstances, would-be reformers had to take what they could get. In Wichita in 1875, for example, a local religious revival sparked a campaign that led to the mayor, a liquor dealer, being replaced by his reform-sponsored successor, a saloon owner.

As married women arrived on the scene in numbers, churches became firmly established, and the community's sensitivity to the more blatant excesses of the "wicked town" increased markedly. Gambling and prostitution were driven underground, a position formerly occupied only by reformers. Antiliquor sentiment manifested itself through increases in the liquor license fee to the $500 maximum and through limitations on the number of licenses the town would grant. With the end of the cattle trade in sight, the standpatters lost their economic arguments, and the reformers became more aggressive. An effective political coalition began to form among the evangelicals, the feminists, and the drys.

When the cattle trade ended, the physical as well as the moral face of the community changed. "One by one these barbaric domiciles are being remodeled into fit places for good society," Newton's reformer-editor wrote in 1873 about the town's former saloons. But the former cattle towns exhibited little overt prohibition sentiment until the 1880 amendment campaign. One of the towns, Caldwell, did carry the amendment, but its cow-town phase came after 1880. The western half of the state continued to lag behind the more settled east in temperance sentiment, at least through the early 1880s.[26]

LOCAL TEMPERANCE SOCIETIES appeared early in the territorial experience. During the winter of 1855/56, Topeka and Lawrence both had organizations composed of the "most worthy and influential" citizens. A year later, the women of Topeka's Philomathic Literary Society produced a weekly journal, the *Prairie Star,* which often featured temperance poems and sketches. Statewide organization did not develop as long as the temperance activity remained scattered and focused at the local level.

The central figure in the movement that led to a statewide organization was Dr. Amory Hunting, a Massachusetts-born physician who removed to Manhattan in 1854. He chaired the 1855 Big Springs meeting that gave birth to the Free State party and participated in the Topeka and Wyandotte constitutional conventions. A fervent Congregationalist and Washingtonian, Hunting had to channel his temperance work into nonoral avenues because he had suffered for years from a lingual cancer. The first organization that went beyond the local level was formed in Hunting's rustic cabin in April 1856. Members of the Central Kansas Total Abstinence Society named their host as president and filled several offices of the society with ministers. The society sponsored two memorials to the legislature—one for each sex—calling for a prohibitory law.

During the late 1850s, several attempts to organize a state society failed. However, Dr. Hunting and the Ministerial Alliance of the Protestant Churches, with the Congregational Church in the van, continued to urge the matter. Success finally crowned labor, and on 18 April 1861, during the first session of the state legislature, the State Temperance Society came into being. The lieutenant governor, Joseph P. Root (1861–63), was elected president, and Hunting became one of fifteen male vice-presidents. Women were welcome as members but did not hold leadership positions.

Some biographical material is available for twenty-four men who were closely identified with the founding and earliest development of the society. Among these were eleven ministers, four physicians, and a scattering of lawyers, businessmen, and holders of positions of public trust. Nearly all were Republicans, and all were extensively involved in public affairs (almost half served in the Wyandotte Convention or in the state legislature). They came to Kansas primarily from New England or the New England "belt" (New York, Pennsylvania, Ohio) and were active in the evangelical denominations. As a group, these "gentlemen of property and standing" represented the Kansas equivalent of the temperance leadership of New England and New York during the 1820s.

At the first annual meeting of the society, a series of resolutions was debated and approved by the membership. The society recommended total abstinence as "one test of membership," expected the "Ministers of the Gospel" to take "immediate steps" to organize auxiliary societies, asserted that the sale of liquor "should be put upon a par with other crimes," and urged that all friends of temperance "labor for the enactment of a law, prohibiting the sale of all alcoholic drinks . . . in our state."[27]

The society met only sporadically during the war years but met more regularly during the postwar period. The president in 1866/67, the Reverend

Hugh Dunn Fisher, a Methodist minister, enlivened the annual meeting by moving to memorialize the legislature to submit a constitutional amendment on prohibition to a public vote. His motion represents the first recorded public instance of such action in Kansas. After a vigorous debate, it lost by a small margin, though all the women who were present voted for it.

During the 1870s the society frequently petitioned the legislature for amendments to the dramshop act, often meeting in Topeka during the legislative session to make their influence more direct and personal. They called for prohibition, but being realists, they were willing to settle for less. What they concentrated their energies upon continued to elude them: repeal of the immunity of the towns of the first and second classes from the petition requirement. Throughout this period the house, in which there was greater rural influence, received temperance legislation more favorably than did the senate, in which the towns held disproportionate representation. In 1872 and 1874 the bill to repeal town immunity passed the house but failed in the senate after a good deal of political maneuvering. In 1876 the perfunctory bill to repeal was amended to prohibit all selling of liquor within the state. To the surprise of nearly everyone, it passed the house by a vote of 55 to 38, though it failed to come to a vote in the senate.

The State Temperance Society continued to function as the central organization of the dry movement into the late 1870s. During this period it often called for woman suffrage (Susan B. Anthony addressed it during the 1867 campaign). As the decade wore on, the organization languished, though its leadership continued to be as distinguished as that of the founding group. Increasingly, other associations and alliances filled the temperance reform niche; by 1877 the state society had become completely moribund.[28]

The most organized opposition to the aims of the temperance society came from the German-American community, which was concentrated in the river towns of Leavenworth and Atchison. Although general resolutions against temperance laws had been passed in the 1860s, the antitemperance state meeting that convened in January 1872 was the first to fight specific changes in the dramshop law. Many strangers of "unmistakable German appearance and accent" appeared unexpectedly on the streets of Topeka. John Walruff, a prominent Lawrence brewer, chaired the meeting. Fully one-half of the 119 "respectable appearing, sober" delegates came from Leavenworth.

As the first order of business, the convention had to settle on a language. The delegates received favorably a proposal that only German be spoken but later adopted a compromise permitting both German and English. The convention heard Col. Charles R. Jennison, the "terror and scourge" of the border counties during the late war, declare that it should "demand" that the legislature make no change at all in the dramshop law. The delegates, most of whom were still staunch Republicans, wholeheartedly agreed and urged the legislators to stand fast against attempts by "fanatics" to pass laws encroaching upon the "rights and liberties" of the citizens.[29]

THE OTHER MAJOR TEMPERANCE ORGANIZATION that was active in the two decades following statehood was the Independent Order of Good Templars. A semisecret fraternal society in the Washingtonian tradition, it offered a family-oriented social life that was attractive both to townspeople and to farmers. The Good Templars readily acknowledged the centrality of religion, declaring that "the Gospel of Christ is the substance of all reform." Striving to make "a proper impression" on young Kansas while public sentiment was still forming, they organized the first Kansas lodge at Iowa Point (Doniphan County) in July 1856. Other early local chapters included Lawrence, where in 1858 the lodge sponsored a Fourth of July temperance picnic that was attended by three thousand (the event actually occurred on July 3, since July 4 fell on a Sunday).

The Grand Lodge grew from nine active lodges and a few hundred members in 1860 to over two hundred lodges and seventy-five hundred members in 1878/79 (see table 2.1). As the eastern half of the state filled up with farm families during the 1870s, the Good Templars adapted to the rural milieu and kept pace in membership. At least 70 percent of its lodges were located in farm villages or in the countryside. It was not uncommon for completely rural townships, with populations of five hundred to one thousand, to support a lodge

TABLE 2.1
MEMBERSHIP IN THE GRAND LODGE OF KANSAS,
INDEPENDENT ORDER OF GOOD TEMPLARS, 1861–83

Year	Number of Lodges	Membership
1861	19	700
1868	39	1,574
1870	95	3,772
1873	63	2,328
1874	96	3,829
1875	130	4,533
1876	152	5,569
1877	166	6,458
1878	193	7,498
1879	207	6,867
1880	185	6,538
1881	141	3,785
1882	73	2,217
1883	38	1,211

Source: Annual Proceedings of the Independent Order of Good Templars, Grand Lodge of Kansas.
Note: The membership grew rapidly during the 1870s but declined sharply after the prohibitory amendment was passed in 1880.

with a membership of fifty or more. For example, Kanwaka Township in Douglas County organized lodge number 202 in 1871 and reported that it had sixty-five members among a population of only 870 in 1878. But after the vote on the prohibition amendment, the statewide membership declined precipitously. Kanwaka forfeited its charter in 1882.

Although the rank and file came chiefly from the rural sector, the fraternal leadership was, or came to be, not unlike that of the State Temperance Society, except that it also included women. From its inception the IOGT had been open to women, though men typically dominated the leadership positions. Of the eleven officers of the Grand Lodge in 1860, three were women (one married, two unmarried), a higher percentage than usual and one that the Kansas lodge would sustain in the ensuing years. The male-to-female ratio among the membership tended to be about two to one.

The first meeting of the Grand Lodge urged the national lodge to adopt a satisfactory ritual and "thereby settle the vexed question which has nearly destroyed our organization." Another vexed question concerned the pledge to abstain from all intoxicating liquor, a membership requirement. Was the pledge binding for life? After a heated discussion, the members voted two to one in the negative. Unfortunately, the national order later voted in the affirmative.[30]

Each year the Grand Lodge approved a list of questions to be debated within the local lodges. Not as reserved as the traditional temperance societies, the Good Templars discussed the questions with a great deal of vim and vigor, approaching rowdiness on occasion. During the late 1860s the questions included: Is sweet cider intoxicating? Are we "intemperate" in advocating temperance? Is a stringent license system preferable to a prohibitory law? Is it advisable for temperance men of all parties to unite to support a temperance ticket?[31]

The last question proved to be especially fruitful. In 1873 the Grand Lodge endorsed a report of the Political Action Committee that recommended the formation, outside of the order, of "a distinct prohibitory political party." After the Temperance party had been organized in 1874, the Grand Lodge was urged to support "this waif upon the vast sea of political ambition and desire."

Not everyone felt comfortable with the proposed endorsement of the political offspring by its fraternal sire. The grand worthy chief templar, John B. Campbell, urged that any endorsement by the order should be considered only as nonbinding "fraternal advice." The order existed, he reminded the delegates, "to educate public sentiment through moral and social agencies up to that point where it shall acquire and sustain the most radical demands of the temperance reform." After vigorous debate, the Grand Lodge approved in 1874, and reaffirmed in 1876, a resolution that members should use their influence to elect the Temperance party's ticket.

In stimulating the birth of a political party, the Grand Lodge only followed the shining example of the national organization. Although the Good Templars derived from the Washingtonians, where moral suasion was king and political activism was suspect, they did not hesitate to promote both. In the late 1860s the national IOGT urged the formation of a national political party based on prohibition principles. In 1869, at a convention that was liberally attended by Good Templars, the national Prohibition party came into being. It fielded its first presidential ticket in 1872 and has continued to do so down to the present day. Several of its nontemperance reform proposals—for example, woman suffrage, a federal income tax, and the direct election of United States senators—were later endorsed by the major parties and were incorporated into the United States Constitution.[32]

The proximate cause of the Kansas Temperance party was a convention called in August 1874 to promote "the needs" of the temperance movement. Chaired by J. Jay Buck, an Emporia attorney who was prominent in the IOGT, the one hundred delegates included ministers and lawyers predominantly, with a sprinkling of physicians, politicians, newspapermen, and postmasters. In background and standing, they approximated the group that had founded the State Temperance Society, but they also included women. Though only a minority were women, Amanda Way and Drusilla Wilson did crucial work on the three-person Resolutions Committee.

Some of the most zealous delegates wanted to organize a political party then and there, but the more moderate Republican majority, reluctant to discard so summarily their ancient faith, voted to await the outcome of the Republican Convention, which was only a week away. That convention renominated Governor Thomas Osborn, a notorious drinker, but it resolved against drunkenness, favoring legislation "as experience shall show to be the most effectual in destroying this evil." Mild as that appeared, it represented the first formal recognition of the temperance question by a political party in Kansas.

The temperance zealots indignantly rejected the Republican sop and met in September at a Leavenworth Methodist church to organize the Temperance party. Many of the delegates came from "primaries" that were called by ministers or local temperance societies. The party platform called for "the civil and political equality of all men and women," "improvement of our system of common schools," public assistance to the victims of "the grasshoppers and drouth," and "the legal prohibition of the manufacture, importation and sale, as a beverage, of all intoxicating liquors." The state ticket included Mrs. M. J. Sharon, of Marion County, for superintendent of public instruction, the first woman to be nominated to a state office by a Kansas political party. But the temperance vote remained solidly in the Republican column. W. K. Marshall, the Temperance party's gubernatorial candidate, received 2,227 votes, about 3 percent of the total cast in the 1874 election.[33]

EVANGELICAL RELIGION represented the most important single factor in the temperance matrix. Indirectly through each temperance organization and directly through the churches, religion served as the *sine qua non* for the Kansas movement throughout its history. No organized temperance activity existed that was not informed and inspired by the Christian message. The evangelical-pietistical denominations, with their heavy emphasis on individual salvation mediated through moral behavior, championed the cause. Through moral suasion, they urged total abstinence for their individual members and, through legal suasion, prohibition for the collective community.

The evangelicals were in the field early and often. At the first meeting of the Kansas-Nebraska Conference of the Methodist Episcopal Church in 1856, the delegates resolved: "We give king alcohol no quarters within our bounds." In 1861 the Kansas Methodist Conference declared: "Christians should carry their temperance principles to the ballot box." A year later it called for "a judicious prohibitory law in the place of the present license law." True to their New England heritage, the Congregationalists labeled the traffic "a crime" in 1862 and resolved that state law "should recognize it as such and should prohibit it." During the two decades after statehood, the Presbyterians, Baptists, Disciples of Christ, Scandinavian Lutherans, United Brethren, and Friends all took similar stands against intemperance and the liquor traffic.[34]

Prior to the 1870s, public temperance activity had been isolated, scattered, and essentially exogenous in nature. That is, the pioneer settlers had responded to local events in small groups with whatever ideological and psychological equipment they had brought with them to Kansas. Though that local response could at times be intense, the broader community did not experience it, often did not even learn of it, and therefore could not share it. The temperance movement had yet to experience the broad, passionate, and cohesive events that so firmly knit together the Free State political community in the 1850s. The first such endogenous event, on a modest scale, occurred in 1872.

During the first five months of that year, an internationally known Presbyterian evangelist, the Reverend Edward Payson Hammond, held a series of revival meetings in the larger towns of eastern Kansas. The revivals, conducted chiefly in Leavenworth, Atchison, Lawrence, Topeka, and Fort Scott, held the public's attention for months. By the conclusion of the meetings in May, some twenty-eight hundred Kansans had been converted.

As always, the revivals carried a major temperance dimension. The converts visited saloons and houses of ill repute to dissuade the inhabitants from their sinful ways. On occasion the peaceful mission of the faithful produced violence. In Topeka, when the Reverend E. O. Taylor led a group into a saloon to hold a prayer meeting, a bloody fight broke out, and three of the participants were arrested. In Atchison, several teams of young children visited the saloons on Commercial Street and sang religious hymns in them to the discomfited patrons before departing. A few years later, a Presbyterian historian noted that "in general . . . there has been no time of wide-spread religious interest when the foundations of society were stirred to their depths. . . . But Kansas has by no means been left unblessed.''[35]

The next endogenous event proved to be broader in scale, a Kansas manifestation of a national phenomenon. Dr. Diocletian Lewis, who was an ardent advocate of physical education for women and was the inventor of the bean bag, gave a temperance lecture on 23 December 1873 in Hillsboro, Ohio. Lewis related the story of how, years before, his mother and a few friends had persuaded a saloon keeper to close his shop by persistently praying in the saloon. The homeopathic physician had given much the same lecture for twenty years on some three hundred different occasions without significant issue. However, on this particular night in Hillsboro, it led to momentous events, becoming yet another tantalizing monument to indeterminacy in matters historical.

Bands of praying and hymn-singing middle-class women soon visited saloons across Ohio, the Midwest, and the East. For most, it represented their first public "statement"; and for all, it was a unique experience that they had been ill prepared for by their families and society. It took, therefore, an uncommon amount of courage to face a hostile saloon keeper and a jeering crowd of raucous men. But before the "Woman's Crusade" had fully spent its course, a few months later, at least 912 towns in 31 states and territories had witnessed some version of the phenomenon. The temporary closing of hundreds of saloons did not constitute its most lasting product. In November 1874 a few hundred of the erstwhile crusaders organized the Woman's Christian Temperance Union.[36]

The impact of the Woman's Crusade in Kansas was substantial, involving upwards of a score of the larger towns. But activity in Kansas dwarfed in comparison with that in Ohio, the movement's epicenter, where 144 communities produced praying bands. The crusade came to Kansas in the latter part of February 1874 and peaked about a month later. It spread slowly at first, a fact that puzzled the *Topeka Commonwealth,* because Kansas, it said, "is very susceptible to any reformatory contagion." And when agitation did develop, it didn't always result in visitation.

In Topeka, on February 26, the Ladies Temperance Society warned the saloonists, via individual postcards, to abandon their evil enterprises by March 9. If they did not do so, the cards said, the women would visit them and "invoke the aid and blessing of almighty God to so enlighten your mind that you may . . . forever quit your present wicked business." But the appointed day came and went, and no visitation occurred. Well-attended daily prayer meetings rotated among the evangelical churches, a total-abstinence pledge circulated around town, and politically inclined groups organized to reflect on the temperance dimension of the upcoming city elections. But no praying bands came forth.[37]

In March the women of Lawrence organized the Ladies Temperance Association and elected Drusilla Wilson, who had only recently arrived in the community, as their president. At a "grand temperance meeting" in Plymouth

Congregational Church, twelve hundred townspeople listened avidly to the importunities of Wilson, Professor Francis Snow (who was later appointed as chancellor of Kansas University), and Dudley C. Haskell (soon to become congressman of the district). From daily prayer meetings, bands of twenty or so determined women sallied forth to visit the town's saloons. Drusilla Wilson, clad in the traditional Quaker garb of bonnet and shawl, led them on their visits, on which they encountered men "whose jeering and coarse brutal laughs struck terror to our hearts."[38]

The most sustained activity took place in Leavenworth, the state's largest city and arguably the most rum soaked. In early March about twenty women, escorted by as many men, marched to the Saratoga Saloon, the most magnificent drinking and gaming house in Leavenworth, perhaps in all of Kansas. They were denied admission by the proprietor, Col. Charles R. Jennison, who pompously declared that he couldn't have his business interfered with, because he was "frequently called on to aid charities and churches."

A few days later, in an evident change of heart, Jennison spruced up his saloon, turned the "naughty" pictures to the wall, and generally made the emporium look like a religious tabernacle. When the women didn't appear at the designated hour, he sent a hasty note saying that he looked forward to their visit and would they please make it at 4:30 P.M. At that hour, two hundred nervous women, "representing the best families in the city," met and cautiously decided to perfect their organization before venturing forth to such places as the Saratoga.

A few days later, saloon visiting commenced when nine women invaded a restaurant-saloon. Picking up momentum, the women scheduled two or more visitations for every day of the week. They received cooperation from black women, but the few Jewish women declined to participate. On one occasion, twenty-two women formed a long line at the bar of a German beer saloon. The line, however, was not long enough. At each end of the even-longer bar the beer was dispensed "vigorously" while the raiders held devotionals and attempted to coax the patrons into signing the pledge.

The mercurial Jennison continued to keep the crusaders off balance. His biographer has described the old Jayhawker as a Jekyll-and-Hyde personality in which "the thief and the apostle lived as amicable neighbors in a completely harmonious unity." When the praying band finally paid a second visit, Jennison once again denied them entry and then, suddenly, produced a Bible and piously started reading scripture to the startled would-be raiders.

Several days later, over two thousand of the curious heard Jennison, "the prince of thieves, gamblers and rowdies," deliver a temperance lecture at the invitation of the local temperance alliance. He wanted very much to cooperate with the ladies in the war against intemperance, he said, yet if they refused his help, he would resist them, but "with such gallantry and courtesy as no gentlemen forgets in the presence of a modest and worthy womanhood."[39]

Although he was an eccentric, Jennison's cavalier attitude toward the crusaders undoubtedly was shared by many of the more "respectable" men of the state.

The temperance fervor in Fort Scott became especially intense, adding an entirely new dimension to the crusade. The movement was led by Miss Amanda Way, an itinerant Methodist minister and a national officer of the Good Templars. Described as a "feminine Abraham Lincoln," due to her stature and angular physiognomy, Way publicly debated the merits of the crusade with some local businessmen, but she seemed to be unable to carry the crowd with her. Many people opposed the crusade and its tactics, preferring instead "the exercise of wholesome, restraining influences" in the home. The *Fort Scott Monitor,* however, saw Way "as an earnest, honest woman intent on accomplishing good for her sex and for humanity." The women began to hold daily prayer meetings in mid March and soon announced that they awaited "directions from the Lord to begin the crusade."

The Capitol Saloon advertised free lunches, as saloons of the period frequently did. On March 21 a dozen women escorted a crowd of twenty-one "ragged, forlorn and unkempt children" into the saloon, some of them "unreasonably dirty and all bearing the stamp of poverty and hardship." Several of the urchins, the offspring of drunken parents, were accompanied by their mothers, who, "in wretched appearance, were quite the equals of their unfortunate offspring." With all the women kneeling, Way offered up "a long, earnest and fervent prayer for the proprietors, and the rum sellers generally." Heavier drinking than usual was reported amid "the strangest scene ever witnessed in Fort Scott."[40]

A Baxter Springs minister puckishly suggested that perhaps praying bands of men should visit millinery shops that "vie with the rumseller in destroying the peace of families." To which the *Kansas City* (Missouri) *Times* replied: "A core of praying men in good practice can be picked up in very few towns outside Kansas."[41]

Measured in terms of saloon closures, the crusade must be considered a failure both in Kansas and in the nation. And the sole reported act of violence only temporarily discomfited its target. At Burlingame (Osage County) the wives of two drunkards left their more timid sisters at a crusader prayer meeting to take a hatchet to the windows and glassware of Schuyler's Saloon.

The generation of a heightened public awareness of the excesses of the liquor traffic was a more lasting impact of the Woman's Crusade. In Fort Scott, Girard, Ottawa, Emporia, Manhattan, Junction City, Abilene, and several other moderate-sized towns, the increased sensitivity translated immediately into dry victories in the spring elections. The concerned citizenry elected city councils and other local officials who were pledged to a temperance program. That translated into no licenses in the larger towns and stricter enforcement of the dramshop act in the third-class towns and rural townships.[42]

THE MURPHY MOVEMENT burst onto the national scene in the mid 1870s, at a time when temperance forces generally were in retreat. Most of the gains of the heady days of the Maine Law movement had been lost during and after the war. The liquor industry itself had become a more formidable foe after it had organized nationally in 1862 as a result of the federal taxation on alcoholic beverages, a wartime measure that became a permanent source of revenue. Aside from the short-lived Woman's Crusade, few successes and low morale marked the temperance trail during the Reconstruction Era.

Called Gospel Temperance by its founder, Francis Murphy, the movement emphasized the power of Christ to change lives. Its pledge card featured the famous Lincolnian phrase "With malice toward none and charity for all." Solidly in the Washingtonian tradition, its charitable impulse extended even to those who were engaged in the traffic, the *bête noir* of the traditional societies. The message of brotherly love and Christian hope, delivered by its charismatic and good-humored leader, attracted over forty thousand pledge signers in Pittsburgh, Pennsylvania, in 1876/77. The crusade quickly spread throughout the Northeast and the upper Midwest, and eventually to England and Scotland. By the mid 1880s, after its force had been fully spent, an estimated three to ten million souls had signed the Murphy pledge and had worn the blue-ribbon badge.[43]

Amanda Way, under the auspices of the Good Templars, initiated the Kansas campaign in June of 1877. She began a three-months' tour at Hutchinson, where she garnered five hundred pledges. John B. Campbell, head of the Good Templars and Fort Scott's postmaster-turned-newspaperman, took to the field in July, with impressive results. Campbell's most important contribution, however, came in September, when he induced the former head of the Indiana Good Templars, E. B. Reynolds, to join the Kansas campaign. Blessed with "a keen eye and a powerful voice," Reynolds was "clear, logical, fiery and magnetic" on the platform.

Soon the pledge rolls began to swell at a phenomenal rate. The cities produced the greatest numbers: Wichita—2,500; Lawrence—2,000; Leavenworth—1,800; Atchison—1,500; Wyandotte—1,200. In the middling-sized towns the numbers were smaller, but the proportion was higher: Manhattan—1,400; Beloit—1,000; Paola—1,000; Chetopa—600; Eureka—500; Osage Mission—480. In places where the excitement reached fever pitch, such as Tonganoxie (Leavenworth County) and Pleasanton (Linn County), the reported number of pledge signers among the men, women, and children nearly equaled the entire population.

The rural areas, where meetings were held in schoolhouses or churches, also caught a virulent case of the revival fever. Farmers and townspeople, abstainers and hard drinkers, rich and poor, young and old—all proudly donned "the bonny badge of blue." The estimated total of pledge signers, after the crusade had ended by the summer of 1878, came to an astounding two hundred thousand, about one-fourth of the state's total population.[44] Even if that total were to be reduced by a factor of two, the numbers remain impressive.

In addition to the handful of paid lecturers, many people of some prominence took to the stump for the movement. The annalist D. W. Wilder cynically noted that "the people heard this [Murphy] gospel gladly and the lawyers and politicians went with the crowd." Governor George T. Anthony, a Quaker by birth whose temperate habits were well known, headed the list. The governor "pitched into" the Germans for their stubborn opposition to the temperance crusade and urged them to become "Americanized." John P. St. John, a lawyer from Olathe who was on his way to the governor's chair, joined the crusade with his characteristic gusto, "doing more work for the cause than a regiment of ordinary talkers." A partial list of other notables who were visible in the movement includes Alfred H. Horton, chief justice of the Kansas Supreme Court (1876–95); George R. Peck, United States district attorney and later chief counsel for the Santa Fe Railroad; P. I. Bonebrake, state auditor (1876–83); A. L. Williams and A. M. F. Randolph, former attorneys general (1871–75 and 1875–77, respectively); and Balie P. Waggener, a devout Democrat and Atchison attorney who would later become chief counsel for the Missouri Pacific Railroad.[45]

Though the Murphy Movement urged change only through the vehicle of moral suasion and did not verbally abuse the saloonists, it did not wholly escape public opposition. That opposition stemmed largely, and not unexpectedly, from the German community, which feared the movement less for what it was than for what it might become. The *Freie Presse* accused the blue-ribbon workers of being avaricious, vain in manner, and "liars and cheats." Only "miserable weaklings," it declared, would need the twin crutches of a written pledge and a blue badge in order to practice moderation.

The Murphy revival as such had disappeared by late spring of 1878. It left in its wake a few temperance-inclined city councils, a large number of no-license towns, and broad areas that were devoid of open saloons. For example, in all of Crawford County, a hotbed of antitemperance activity in the twentieth century, no licensed saloons remained open by May. In the matter of closing saloons, either through direct pressure on the saloonists or indirectly through the town councils, the Murphy Crusade succeeded to a much greater extent than did the Woman's Crusade, though that was not its avowed purpose.[46]

The Murphy Movement lifted the state to an even greater sensitivity to the dangers of alcohol and left it with a burning desire to do something about it. But the sentiment, though sincere and profound, remained unfocused and aimless; no concrete agenda suggested itself to discharge the moralistic energy. By the fall of 1878, eastern Kansas had become a 200-mile-square tinder, awaiting the igniting spark. That would come from a surprising quarter and, ironically, would be materially abetted by those who were most ardently dedicated to snuffing it out.

3

The Amendment

It is a matter of public history that between the submission and the vote . . . this proposition . . . was the subject of a warm and heated canvass throughout the entire state.

—Kansas Supreme Court

I like whisky too well . . . so I will vote to put it where I can't get it.

—A Brown County voter

THE MURPHY MOVEMENT produced its first long-term effect when temperance leaders issued a call to all interested parties for a general convention at Olathe on 14 May 1878. "We believe there has never existed in our State such an all pervading interest in this subject, as at the present time." The "multitudes" demand a program to reduce "the evils of intemperance," the leaders declared. The call conveyed no specific plan of action, only immediacy: "We must do something. The responsibility is upon us; we cannot remain inactive and be guiltless."

The convention delegates organized the Kansas Temperance Union, an umbrella type of confederation to which all other temperance societies were made auxiliary. Every local society, lodge, and church was invited to send two delegates to the annual meetings. Incorporated in October 1879 as the Kansas State Temperance Union (KSTU), the organization would play a central role in state temperance affairs for nearly forty years. The KSTU functionally replaced the State Temperance Society, which had virtually ceased to exist by the mid 1870s.

Considering the elevated level of temperance fever, it is a curious fact that the convention took no definitive position on antiliquor legislation, past, present, or future. The delegates, predominately Republican, took a firm (and very negative) stand only on a third-party temperance ticket. The organization did not press for prohibition, constitutional or otherwise, at this time. A month later the

36

society's attention focused on planning for the first of four successive national temperance camp meetings at Bismarck Grove.

Leadership in the new organization fell into the Lyman Beecher conservative tradition. It remained largely what it had been in the defunct society: substantial young-to-middle-aged males from the middle and upper-middle levels of the socioeconomic spectrum, who were motivated by religious, social, commercial, and health concerns, in approximately that order. It broadly overlapped both the leadership of the Good Templars and the founders of the Temperance party. The Olathe convention elected newspaperman Albert Griffin of Manhattan as its vice-president and lawyer John St. John as its president.[1]

John Pierce St. John was born in Indiana in 1833 to parents who were in reduced circumstances. The St. Johns were of Connecticut stock and Huguenot ancestry. John had only limited schooling, earning his own way at an early age. His father (and as a result, the entire family) suffered from a severe drinking problem. Devoted to his mother, the Congregationalist son promised her that he would never drink and that he would fight the traffic with all his energy. He would keep both promises fully throughout his eventful life. After knocking around at odd jobs while living with relatives in Illinois, he migrated to California in 1852, where he panned for gold and fought the Modoc Indians. In 1859 he returned to Illinois and began to practice law. While serving two ninety-day hitches in the Union Army during the Civil War, he rose to the rank of lieutenant colonel.

St. John arrived in Olathe in 1869 with a reputation as a staunch Republican and as an ardent admirer of Gen. Ulysses S. Grant, whose pro-alcohol tendencies evidently did not disquiet the young lawyer. Though not noted as an especially profound thinker, St. John quickly became respected around Olathe as a keen reasoner who was especially ingenious in oral argument. He began to speak for the temperance cause soon after his arrival in Kansas, and by the early 1870s, he had become known in this interest outside of Johnson County. By 1876 he had become sufficiently visible in temperance circles to be offered the top spot on the ticket by the Temperance party. St. John shrewdly "accepted," on the express condition "of its ratification by the Republican State Convention." The ruffled Temperance party made other plans.

St. John's salient characteristics included a commanding appearance, an easy manner, a boundless energy, and a fervent, indefatigable devotion to the cause—all of which served him well on the platform, which was his most natural habitat. After attending a temperance meeting led by St. John, one admirer wrote: "He is a perfect type of manhood . . . fine looking and exceedingly intelligent, with a keen, piercing eye for the detection of wrong, kindling with holy indignation against injustice and cruelty and melting in tenderness and pity for the wronged. A man you know you can trust, when you . . . gaze into the depths of those clear blue eyes, that indicate truth and fidelity."[2]

Governor John Pierce St. John (courtesy of the Kansas State Historical Society, Topeka).

St. John also possessed all the instincts and behaviors that are normally found in a successful politician. He began his political career in 1873 as a state senator. During his legislative tenure he led the dry forces in their perennial attempt to amend the dramshop act. After declining renomination for the senate in 1874 and the Temperance party's offer in 1876, he became a contender for the Republican gubernatorial nomination that fall. But he delivered his support to the winner, George T. Anthony, a cousin of Susan B. and Daniel R. Anthony, on the seventh ballot.[3]

Three months after being elected to the most prestigious position in Kansas temperance in May 1878, St. John received the Republican nomination for governor. The two events are not causally linked to the extent that has been commonly assumed by historians. John A. Martin, a former Free State leader and the publisher of the influential *Atchison Champion,* mounted a serious challenge to the renomination of Anthony who, though able, often appeared cold and arrogant to the public. Of some one hundred newspapers that had declared themselves by late summer, seventy-two supported Martin; nineteen, Anthony; and only three, St. John. But Anthony, despairing of victory in a deadlocked convention, delivered enough support on the seventeenth ballot to nominate St. John, who had been running a hopeless third.

St. John's antiliquor reputation did not hurt him in his political quest, but it failed to distinguish him clearly from the other two candidates, both of whom carried strong temperance credentials. In any event the electorate considered temperance a nonpartisan social issue and a political question only in a general and vague sense. The Republican platform made only the most perfunctory bow to temperance, taking a less ardent position even than its stand against drunkenness in 1874.

On the hustings, St. John emphasized monetary policy (the campaign's chief issue), Republican principles, and the greatness of Kansas, on occasion waving the "bloody shirt" or recommending suffrage for women. Temperance became an issue only in the German community, which viewed with considerable angst the prospect of having a cold-water champion, the leader of the *"Wassernarren"* (water fools), become the next governor. But the Republican leaders soothed the Teutonic anxieties by assuring the Germans that St. John's antiliquor views represented only his "private" opinions. Before predominantly German audiences, St. John stoutly defended his "private" principles—that is, his teetotalism—declaring that if "they wanted a drunken Governor they must elect some one else."[4]

St. John did not advocate prohibition in his political speeches that autumn. The Kansas people did not elect him to lead a temperance crusade, with or without prohibition. As an issue of moment in the 1878 campaign, temperance did not exist. The tinder had yet to find its spark.

DURING THE FALL of 1877 the Good Templars placed on the agenda for local discussion the question of prohibition ("the principle itself, and also the best means of securing it"). At Osage Mission, in Neosho County, which was a Good Templar stronghold and hotbed of Murphyism, the discussion proved to be especially fruitful. One member, J. R. Detwiler, found the subject endlessly fascinating and proceeded to explore its several ramifications.

Joshua Rollins Detwiler, when two years of age, had been adopted in Illinois as a "poor, penniless, orphan boy" by a Protestant minister who had fourteen children of his own. In 1854, when J. R. was four, the family removed to Shawnee County, where it crowded into its first Kansas home, a tattered, weatherbeaten tent. Instilled with temperance principles by his father and his Sunday School teacher, P. I. Bonebrake, the state auditor (1876–83), the young man moved to Osage Mission and went into business for himself when he reached his majority. Endowed with an abundance of energy and zeal, Detwiler was the kind who "made things go when he took a hand." He soon became a successful dealer in grain, farm machinery, and sewing machines. He joined the Good Templars and, at the age of twenty-three, became secretary of the local temperance society. By 1878 he had become a leader in the Neosho County Good Templars, though he was hardly known beyond the county line.[5]

When some of Detwiler's friends told him that the Kansas Constitution forbade prohibition, the young businessman began a study of the document. He found no such restriction, but his search piqued his interest in the constitution. If prohibition was a measure so devoutly to be desired, why not write it into the state's organic law? Several aspects of this idea-in-embryo seemed attractive. Since the whole people would vote on such an amendment, it would be much more democratic than a legislative enactment. A public vote also would defuse a favorite wet argument—namely, that liquor legislation was too often more prescriptive than descriptive, that is, it ran ahead of popular sentiment. If the majority of the voters did want prohibition in their constitution, it should be enforceable. If not, perhaps the question was premature.

As a young state, unhampered by a long tradition of domination by the liquor traffic, Kansas should be willing to try a novel approach, to create something new under the sun. Of course, it would be difficult to gain the required two-thirds approval of both legislative houses, but what was difficult to put in the constitution would also be difficult to take out. The excited Detwiler took his bright, shiny idea to Fort Scott in October 1878, to share it with the Good Templars at their annual convention.[6]

The session of the Grand Lodge that Detwiler found at Fort Scott burst to overflowing with enthusiasm for the cause. The grand worthy secretary warned: "We are now approaching a crisis. Our State is making a mighty effort to free itself from the terrible thraldom of intemperance." John B. Campbell, the grand worthy chief templar, said to the delegates: "The field is now fully ripe, and it is only needed that we thrust in the sickles and garner in a golden harvest. . . . Let us then be glad and rejoice, giving God all the glory, and go forth with stronger resolves than ever before to work in the Master's vineyard."[7]

The report of the Political Action Committee struck a note for independence, giving us also an excellent example of nineteenth-century temperance rhetoric:

> Whereas, it is the opinion of your Committee that the Temperance question is *the issue* before the American people today, before which all others pale into insignificance; that our Nation receives blood-money from a murderous traffic; that the Nation groans and staggers under the weight of the rum fiend, while murder,

red-handed, raises the cross-bones above its slain victims, and the gallows stands, like the Inquisition of old, to receive its prey, while wife, child and mother starve in their wretched abodes, or are found cold in death, struck down by rum-cursed fathers and husbands; therefore,

Resolved, That we pledge ourselves to no party which gives uncertain sound upon this question.[8]

Amanda Way, who at one time or another held nearly all of the major offices in the Grand Lodge, directed the convention toward a more specific goal. "I have done all I could to increase the army of Blue Ribbons in Kansas," the veteran evangelist said, "but wherever I have gone, teaching the beautiful doctrine of total abstinence, . . . I have kept the doctrine of prohibition constantly before the people, as the grand ultimatum of all temperance effort."[9]

Given the tenor of the meeting, Detwiler found no difficulty in selling either his idea or himself. The session adopted a resolution to petition the legislature to submit a constitutional amendment "prohibiting the importation, sale and manufacture of intoxicating liquors." It also gave authority to its chief executive to appoint a committee to draw up the petition and send it to the 193 local lodges, with their 7,498 members, for public circulation. And as grand worthy chief templar, to oversee this momentous undertaking, they elected the twenty-eight-year-old Joshua Rollins Detwiler.[10]

Copies of the petition were circulated within each county, to be signed by voters (males only) and returned to Detwiler on or before 23 January 1879. The double-columned petition ran to sixty feet when glued together. Detwiler remained coy about the total number of names that the "monster petition" contained. From surviving fragments, an estimate of thirty-three hundred has been made, an impressive number of adult males but not so large as some other petitions, both wet and dry, for amendments to the dramshop act earlier in the decade. Detwiler later claimed that the appeal could have had thirty thousand names, "but with the comparatively few names we actually had, it required no little engineering to accomplish our purpose. We carried our point and did not make a single false statement."

Detwiler went to Topeka on January 24 and "day after day hovered around the State House showing the petition and urging its claims upon the attention of members." He copied the entire petition, one for each legislative body ("This was a big job, but we worked almost day and night"). Although many of the legislators were sound on temperance, few had any understanding of constitutional prohibition. To help in the educational effort, Detwiler appeared before the House Temperance Committee and received what he considered to be a favorable hearing.[11]

A few days after his arrival in the capital, Detwiler visited Noah C. McFarland, a well-known fifty-seven-year-old lawyer who was active in the anti-alcohol movement. As a Presbyterian elder, a Republican, a Scotch-Irishman, and a professional man who was active in public affairs, McFarland fit perfectly the archetype of temperance leaders of the period. In 1881 this "Abe Lincoln style of man" became the first Kansan to head a federal bureau when he was appointed commissioner of the United States Land Office in Washington, D.C.

Detwiler asked McFarland to help him draw up a prohibitory amendment. The twenty-one words that McFarland drafted, without the change of a jot or a tittle, subsequently became a part of the Kansas Constitution for sixty-eight years: "The manufacture and sale of intoxicating liquors shall be forever prohibited in the State, except for medical, scientific and mechanical purposes."[12]

IN HIS JANUARY MESSAGE to the legislature, Governor St. John discussed at some length the question of temperance legislation. "I am clearly of the opinion," the crusader said, "that no greater blessing could be conferred by you upon the people . . . than to absolutely and forever prohibit the manufacture, importation, and sale of intoxicating liquors as a beverage." But in the very next sentence the crusader retired in favor of the politician. The latter voiced the concerns of many that a "prohibitory law could not, or at least would not, be enforced, and that any law that cannot be, or is not, enforced, is worse than no law at all."

Pulled in diametrically opposite directions by his two overriding passions, the governor resolved his dilemma by feebly calling only for repeal of the dramshop proviso that excused towns over two thousand from the petition requirements. He proposed nothing new, only what had been unsuccessfully sought by temperance advocates since 1868.[13] Many of these advocates must have been keenly disappointed that the charismatic crusader-politician had failed to focus the white-hot sentiment of the people on more advanced antiliquor legislation.

The legislature received a flurry of petitions and letters from their constituents, the great majority of whom urged the temperance side of the question. The KSTU, as well as several churches, specifically supported St. John's recommendation, rather than the much more radical Good Templar proposal. The legislature itself, especially the house, exhibited strong dry propensities, both in its personal habits and its public actions. Without realizing the full scope of the change, the people had elected a large number of representatives who were prepared to support strong dry legislation (the senate had been elected in 1876, before the Murphy phenomenon). The assemblage impressed a Lawrence paper: "The legislators this year look better than they used to. . . . They drink much less whiskey. What whiskey they do drink is of much better quality. . . . They are less like 'dumb cattle driven.' They vote with more intelligence, and hence with more independence."[14]

The level of temperance sentiment combined with the failure of leadership to produce a plethora of temperance bills in the senate and in the house. The senate's survivor, introduced by John T. Bradley of Council Grove, went well beyond St. John's recommendation. Bradley's bill required two-thirds, rather than a simple majority, of the residents of a township or ward to sign a license petition and repealed the exclusion of cities from the petition provision. Both sides concentrated on this harsh bill, which would have meant virtual prohibition if rigidly enforced. After several days of consideration in mid February, the senators stood nineteen to eighteen in favor, with three wavering in the balance. When two of the latter began to lean in the dry direction, the now-desperate wets looked elsewhere for a solution to their problem.[15]

They found it, or thought that they had, in the constitutional-amendment proposal. Detwiler had taken the McFarland draft to a friendly senator who had introduced it on February 8 as a senate joint resolution. It had been assigned to a committee, where, despite Detwiler's best efforts, it seemed destined to "sleep the sleep that knows no wakening." But on the day when the Bradley bill came up for final vote, an antitemperance senator, upon the urging of a liquor lobbyist, moved that the joint resolution be substituted for Bradley's bill.[16]

The course for the wets seemed clear. Determined to defeat Bradley's measure, they gambled that the joint resolution would not receive a two-thirds vote in the house and that even if it should, it would be defeated in the popular referendum. For the drys the issue was more complex. They had almost certain victory at hand in the Bradley bill. To give that up for the long-shot amendment seemed unwise, but a vote against prohibition might not be fully understood by the home folks. For those who were firmly planted on the fence, one feature of Detwiler's proposal, the referendum, seemed especially attractive: the matter was too important for mere politicians, so let the people decide. The motion to substitute passed 21 to 17, with most of the leading drys voting in the negative.[17] Both sides had underestimated the latent strength of the temperance movement.

The house voted on the evening of March 5, before a gallery that was jammed with excited spectators. Several wives of members attended, urging their husbands "to rally for home protection." The ironic turn of events had resolved St. John's personal conflict. Now freed from his nearly crippling ambivalence, he enthusiastically buttonholed legislators on the floor, putting in one last word for the amendment ("I was governor but I couldn't keep out of the fight"). The vote was expected to be extremely close, with 86 needed to pass the resolution (there were 129 members in the house). The final tally showed 88 yeas, 31 nays, and 10 absent or not voting.[18]

From the vote that night, a legend grew that the wife of one of the members prevailed upon him to change his vote, a grand event that saved the day and ultimately brought prohibition to Kansas. In its fully inflated form, as developed by Frances Willard, president of the national WCTU, the legend passed into the standard hagiography of the national temperance movement. After relating that the initial roll call found the temperance side one vote short, Willard hit her stride:

But look, a woman, gentle, modest, sweet, advances from the crowd. What, is she going down that aisle, where woman never trod before . . . ? Yea, verily, and every eye follows her with intense interest, and the throng is strangely still as she goes straight to her husband, takes his big hands in her little ones, lifts her dark eyes to his face, and speaks these thrilling words: "My darling, for my sake, for the sake of our sweet home, for Kansas' sake and God's, I beseech you change your vote." When lo! upon the silence broke a man's deep voice: "Mr. Speaker . . . I wish to change my vote from no to aye!" How loud rang out the cheers of men: how fell the rain of women's tears, for love had conquered, as it always will, at last, . . . So Kansas leads the van, and one little woman saved the day.[19]

George W. Greever, a Democrat from rural Wyandotte County, usually voted with the wets; and he did change his vote that night. The forty-eight-year-old prosperous farmer had taken the twenty-five-year-old Margaret Virginia Newland as his bride on the previous Christmas Day. ("He had just married her and was foolish about her.") A schoolteacher and a Methodist who was later active in the WCTU, Margaret Greever was considered a "temperance crank" by the opposition. She did attend the session and evidently successfully beseeched her husband to switch his vote. The critical nature of Greever's action has been widely credited in the temperance literature, in the public press, and in modern state histories.[20] Just what impact did the switch have, and how critical was it to the outcome?

Several members changed their votes during the roll call, amid a great deal of confusion on the floor. When the proponents fell several votes short, they passed a "Call of the House" and directed the sergeant at arms to bring in recalcitrant members. Over the next couple of hours this produced eight votes— five yeas and three nays. Only when it was fully satisfied that the issue had carried did the dry leadership suspend the call. Seven representatives of unknown sentiment still cowered in their offices, cravenly awaiting the knock of the sergeant at arms.

St. John, who loved a good story, created and sustained the legend and almost certainly served as Frances Willard's source for her version. He met with the Greevers on the next day to extend his congratulations, and in later years he criticized the press for disputing "the facts" of the case.[21] Although the incident did not determine the political issue, it furnishes a potent symbol of the social relationship between the sexes in the late nineteenth century, the woman on her knees beseeching her man to vote "right" to protect the home and family.

Legislative opposition to the amendment centered in those districts that would remain strongholds of antiprohibitionist sentiment throughout the nineteenth century. The border counties, with their concentration of Catholic, German, and Democratic voters, constituted the bulwark of the opposition. House members from four counties in the northeast corner (Brown, Doniphan, Atchison, Leavenworth) gave all sixteen of their votes in opposition and thereby furnished more than half of the negative total. Religious and ethnic influences dominated the political, as can be seen in these solid counties, where nine

Republicans joined five Democrats and two Greenbackers to produce the unanimity.

Since the religious and ethnic elements carried a political correlate, the legislative vote as a whole showed marked party divergence. Sixty-three of eighty Republicans (79 percent) and seventeen of twenty Greenbackers (85 percent), many of whom were former Republicans, but only seven of eighteen Democrats (39 percent) voted for the amendment. The only Democrat from a Missouri River county to support the amendment was (Mrs.) Greever. A statistical test of the voting patterns of the three political parties yields a very significant chi-square value (P < .005). Several areas, only sparsely populated in 1879, that would vigorously oppose prohibition in later years gave mixed support for the amendment: Bourbon (three yeas, one nay), Crawford-Cherokee (four yeas, one absent), Sedgwick (one yea, one nay), Saline (one yea), Ellis (one nay), Ford (one nay).[22]

In his insightful interpretation of the American prohibition experience, *Deliver Us from Evil,* Norman H. Clark has attempted to explain the coming of prohibition to Kansas. In the late 1870s, he claims, "nowhere in the nation was there a more disorderly society than Kansas—disorder from the bloody turmoil before the war, from the war itself, the coming of railroads, the migration of tens of thousands . . . and disorder inflamed by raiders, jayhawkers, bank robbers, cowtown revelries, farm failure, and farmers' protests." A more realistic description of the state's settled portion is that of an optimistic and prideful agrarian society enjoying a developing prosperity which subsequently became a "boom." Had the society been under intense economic, political, or military pressure, it would have been much less likely to have taken up such a radical social reform.

During the 1870s, what had been a strongly agrarian society became even more so. During that decade the state's population increased from 364,000 to 996,000 (174 percent), the Kansas equivalent of the California gold rush. But despite such an influx, the proportion of those who lived in towns of 2,000 or more actually dropped from 14 percent to 12 percent. In eastern and central Kansas, scores of townships in which organized communities were virtually nonexistent reported populations of five hundred to twelve hundred in 1880. In an average political township of about fifty sections (or fifty square miles), such density meant, on the average, a family of four per quarter section—or virtually fence-to-fence yeomen farmers.

As hopeful families by the thousands moved onto their homesteads during the decade, the proportion of males in their twenties dropped by 23 percent. With the farm family replacing the young single male as the dominant element in the social profile, the per capita consumption of alcoholic beverages undoubtedly dropped during the 1870s.[23] While, of course, "disorderliness" was not unknown, it hardly qualifies as the predominant characteristic of 1880 Kansas. Kansans voted for prohibition to maintain an orderly society, not to attain it.

OF THE THIRTEEN STATES that passed Maine Laws during the period 1851 to 1855, eight had lost them by 1863 through repeal or adverse court decisions or had had them modified by exempting wine and beer. After Connecticut (1872) and Massachusetts (1875) repealed their laws, the tattered remnant of the "first wave" of prohibition included only Maine, Vermont, and New Hampshire. "Retreat and defeat" characterized attempts to pass temperance legislation during the 1870s as the liquor interests significantly increased their political power. The Kansas events, then, represented the most encouraging sign on the national scene for the drys since the mid 1850s. The nation watched closely as the campaign developed, the temperance forces hopeful that a second wave might be initiated which would crest in national prohibition.[24]

While Kansas would be the first to vote on constitutional prohibition, the idea itself was not new. Michigan (1850) and Ohio (1851) had adopted amendments to their constitutions which prohibited liquor licensing. A semantic nicety negated enforcement: retail liquor outlets operated on a levied "tax," rather than on the proscribed license "fee." A few states in the ante-bellum Northeast had considered constitutional prohibition, and New York's legislature very nearly passed it. State law required that a constitutional amendment be passed by two successive assemblies. Such a resolution passed in 1860, but the attack on Fort Sumpter turned the attention of the next assembly to more pressing matters, and the amendment died.[25]

A month after the 1879 camp meeting at Bismarck Grove, the KSTU convened in Topeka to plan for the campaign. Though the union had reelected St. John as its president, coordination of the campaign work devolved upon A. M. Richardson, a Congregational minister from Lawrence, who was a Temperance party stalwart. As vice-president and "general agent," he directed the often-hectic operations and made Lawrence the nerve center of the proamendment campaign.

Richardson and his indefatigable co-workers organized "prohibition clubs" in all the cities and towns, and in most of the hamlets and crossroads as well, nearly one thousand in all. They coined the slogan "Vote as you pray" and distributed over one hundred thousand pages of literature, as well as ten thousand free copies of their newspaper. Richardson supervised the work of some twenty lecturers who were in the field at one time or another, including several from out of state. And to support the prodigious undertaking they struggled with the ever-present problem of financing.[26]

Though $8,500 was pledged in monthly subscriptions, the Temperance Union received only $1,900 in cash from this source. Less than $500 came in from out of state. The drys' total expenditures for the campaign did not exceed $5,000. A resolution passed at the August 1880 meeting at Bismarck Grove prescribed a thorough canvass of eastern Kansas "by ladies who shall personally solicit donations from the friends of temperance." But during the final critical weeks, funds became so scarce that some lecturers had to be withdrawn. A few

James A. Troutman (courtesy of the Kansas State Historical Society, Topeka).

of the most effective, however, such as Drusilla Wilson and John St. John, continued on an unpaid basis as they had from the beginning. One disgusted solicitor, James A. Troutman, summed up the vexing financial problem: "We have a great many men in Kansas who will ride forty miles, or even walk that far to make a temperance speech, full of doubtful logic and questionable rhetoric, who cannot be induced by any known process to give a dollar to the cause. They believe in free speech, free literature, free temperance, and expect to reform the world by the sweat of their jaws."[27]

The twenty-five-year-old Jimmie Troutman interrupted a promising Topeka law practice in November 1879 to move to Lawrence and devote full time to the *Kansas Temperance Palladium.* For the next year it became the official temperance organ. Always partisan and occasionally surly, it took on all comers under the leadership of its feisty editor. "Its weekly reports," Richardson said at the end of the campaign, "have been our war bulletins, nerving us for the conflict."

The first issue of the "free, fearless and aggressive" *Palladium* sounded the campaign keynote: "We address you in reference to the greatest social and moral evil that ever cursed a civilized people—an evil, so wide-spread, gigantic and powerful, that it can [only] be subdued and removed by the united, persistent and prayerful efforts of all friends of God and humanity. . . . Its only claim to respectability is found in the sanction of law. Yet legal license can never lessen the turpitude nor change the moral character of a traffic fraught with such terrible evils."[28]

The drys worked in close harmony throughout the campaign, though one serious breach in the ranks did occur late in the season. Former Governor Charles Robinson, his wife, Sara, and their neighbors petitioned the Douglas County commissioners to issue a beer license for a Lawrence fair. Annie L. Diggs, who later became prominent in the Populist movement, circulated a counter petition. One of those who appeared before the commissioners to plead the wets' case was John H. Rice, a member of the Executive Committee of the KSTU. Rice also held a position with the Fair Association, which had received a handsome offer for the privilege of selling beer on the grounds.

The temperance camp bitterly denounced Rice, who, it said, had urged the beer license while "clad in the livery of heaven." "Were he possessed of as much manhood as Judas Iscariot," Troutman raved in the *Palladium,* "he would hang himself." Opting to resign from the KSTU rather than take Troutman's advice, Rice lashed back at "the little mean corrupt ring of fanatics" who led the KSTU. The fair lost its beer license, but the temperance cause came close to losing much more.[29]

The WCTU was organized on a statewide basis at the 1878 camp meeting at Bismarck Grove. The omnipresent Amanda Way chaired the meeting, which was held in a tent. At the August 1879 meeting, the little band elected Drusilla Wilson, the Quaker minister, as their president. A "born prohibitionist," Drusilla and her husband, Jonathan, had emigrated from Indiana in 1871 after a lifetime of service in Freedman's and Indian schools. They settled initially in Atchison County so as to be near their son, Joseph C., who was well on his way to becoming a power in Republican state politics.

Drusilla Wilson had begun to question the efficacy of moral suasion as a result of her experience in the Woman's Crusade. "Women saw it was

Drusilla Wilson (courtesy of the Kansas State Historical Society, Topeka).

inconsistent for our fathers and brothers and husbands to make laws protecting [the traffic], and the women follow in the wake pleading with the men thus licensed to quit the business. . . . We must have prohibition instead of license.'' Henceforth, Drusilla used moral suasion in urging men to use legal suasion.[30]

After she was elected president of the WCTU, the pietistic woman, who later became known as the ''spiritual mother'' of Kansas prohibition, made a critical decision, significant both for herself and for her organization. Instead of supervising the development of the embryonic WCTU organization, Wilson elected to further the amendment cause in a very different manner. Over the next twelve months the hardy, strong-willed sixty-four year old, accompanied by her seventy-year-old husband, traveled some three thousand miles in a horse-drawn carriage, speaking for the amendment.

Under the auspices of the KSTU, not of the WCTU, and without remuneration from either source, she gave more than three hundred public lectures and dozens of talks to church groups across the state. Working the rural schoolhouses and village churches, they kept to the backroads, avoiding the railroad towns to which temperance workers tended to gravitate. Near the end of the year she began to wonder, as had some of her colleagues, if perhaps she had not made an error in judgment. She fervently hoped that Frances Willard would understand. But if error it was, it had been "of the head and not the heart."[31]

Drusilla Wilson believed strongly in the dignity and equality of women. Doing her "Master's work" gave her "sweet peace," yet she could hurl a well-directed barb at the men when the occasion demanded. After a debate had been scheduled between herself and the prominent lawyer Sam Wood, who was known for his rough-and-tumble tactics at the podium, he suggested that it might be advisable to substitute a man. "I told him," she said, "that it was a woman who was challenged, and a woman would debate the question."

Wilson never let the men forget that the women had been denied the right to vote in the referendum ("And, now, our brothers, as you've taken this right on you alone. . . ."). In March, after she had been working the icy, muddy backroads all winter, she impishly suggested in her newspaper column that since "spring is close, gentlemen will [now] feel safe to venture the exposure and may leave [the] railroads." As election day approached, she proposed that since women already had the privilege "of begging men to do right and of cooking good dinners for [them] . . . , they should feed [them] into good humor on election day, and then coax them to vote for the women's side of the question."[32]

The best-known American woman of the last quarter of the nineteenth century, the WCTU's President Frances Willard, came to Kansas to speak for the amendment in the spring of 1880. In May at Lawrence, the chancellor of Kansas University introduced her to "one of the largest crowds in history." The *Palladium* found her of "pleasing appearance and address, . . . producing the conviction that she is a cultured lady." But it seemed to be most taken by the astounding fact that her female voice carried to all parts of the large auditorium. The *Lawrence Journal* said that she was "the best lady orator we have ever heard. . . . Her arguements and illustrations were plain and simple, yet she was at times truly eloquent."[33]

Having started it all, the Good Templars were in the prohibition fight to the finish. ("Its adoption will be our victory, and its failure our defeat.") The order flourished, though it continued to meet some coolness from business and professional men, including ministers, who thought the IOGT appealed chiefly to the young and "those in the humbler walks of life." Some prescient members expressed concern that victory for the amendment might sharply reduce the need for their organization. But the more optimistic saw a brighter future: "We have the moral suasion of the ribbon movements, we are just as religious as the Woman's Christian Temperance Union, we educate the young, reform the old, and teach the voter his duty."[34]

During his year as chief templar, J. R. Detwiler traveled 3,700 miles by rail and 660 miles on horseback in support of the amendment. He published two influential pamphlets on prohibition and started the *Temperance Banner,* which became a major voice in the campaign. He encouraged local lodges to hold social affairs to pay for campaign literature—every Sunday at 4 P.M. if possible, and if not, "at any other hour convenient for the Christian people to attend." Detwiler declined another term in office, though he assured his brothers and sisters that he loved the Good Templars because "it reaches as low as humanity falls and as high as Heaven itself."[35]

The most indefatigable worker who carried the Good Templar standard was Amanda M. Way. A native of Indiana, she had been active in antislavery and temperance societies in the ante-bellum era and had helped to found the first women's rights association in Indiana in 1851. In 1869 she had been a delegate to the organizing convention of the national Prohibition party. Though a birthright Quaker, she became a licensed Methodist preacher in 1871, and a year later she joined a small colony of Quakers at Pleasanton (Linn County), Kansas. Gentle and quiet, though strong and dedicated, she held high office in all three of the major Kansas temperance organizations.

During 1880 she organized prohibition clubs and held temperance picnics for the IOGT and the KSTU, and she either spoke or preached on a few hundred occasions, sometimes as often as three times a day. Although widely respected, even loved, by her co-workers, as an unmarried female she had entered the male sphere and therefore had to pay the price. For example, in one town the public learned of her upcoming lecture in these words: "Tonight a hen will try to crow."[36] Amanda undoubtedly just smiled sweetly and then proceeded to crow loudly.

THE ANTIAMENDMENT FORCES recovered from their dismay at the house's passage of the joint resolution to discover that the drys would present a much more difficult target than they had imagined. Respectable people generally, including many who were not associated with the temperance movement, held the saloon in contempt for its brazen defiance of regulatory laws, its corrupting influence in politics, and its demoralizing effect on the home. Even the Kansas free-thought radicals of the Liberal League, Moses Harman type, supported prohibition because they believed alcohol to be "a primary cause of social ills."[37]

The drys clearly held the "higher" ground, which was as important for social as for military battles. How could one defend the liberty to drink but not defend the pariah of the age, the saloon, and not attack the most sacred of cows, the home and family? And the wets lacked precisely that which made the drys so formidable: a zealous core of dedicated workers who had no direct economic stake in the outcome. The wets found that it was much easier to take a drink than to do battle against those who were "clad in the livery of heaven."

The antiamendment position was not without its strengths, however. Many Kansans hesitated to give up their "right" to liquor, whether they personally exercised that right daily or never. Since the question was not just prohibition, but constitutional prohibition, legal confusion reigned. Capitalizing on the fear of the unknown, the wets raised numerous judicial questions, and the drys found themselves with a monumental task of education. The wets upheld the status quo in appeals to the conservative-minded, of which the state had its full complement. Raising the specter of the proposal's adverse economic impact proved to be an effective strategy in the young, vulnerable state. An antitemperance tradition, albeit limited in scope and duration, had developed within the state, especially in the German community. And the wets hoped to tap into the abundant resources of the national liquor organizations.

The first organizational sign appeared in November 1879, when a protective union of Topeka merchants formed and called for a state convention. That convention met in Topeka in January and organized as the People's Grand Protective Union (PGPU). Those who were associated with the liquor industry in some capacity, many of whom were of German extraction, completely dominated the convention. Robert W. Ludington, the liquor dealer who had urged that the amendment be substituted for the Bradley bill, chaired the meeting.

The delegates resolved against the amendment as unprecedented, unenforceable, going beyond public sentiment, and permitting the manufacture and sale of liquor totally unrestrained by law. A curious document, the PGPU Constitution included these, and only these, four organizational purposes: "to preserve and strengthen those kind and fraternal feelings which should bind together in one common brotherhood the whole human family," "to make those feelings efficient in works of kindness," "to furnish material aid and assistance to our members," "to maintain true allegiance to the United States of America."[38]

A month later the chief voice of the wets, the *Kansas State Journal* (Topeka), reported that every part of the state warmly welcomed the PGPU as it organized its subordinate unions. The organization was meeting with "grand success," the paper said, in its fight against the "fanatical efforts that will be made against our free American citizenship." In the summer a small delegation, which included Ludington and John Walruff, the Lawrence brewer, went East to solicit funds from the larger brewers and distillers. The PGPU reportedly had a goal of $100,000 at the outset of the campaign. The drys loved to speculate on the magnitude of the campaign fund. St. John later claimed that the wets had spent $150,000. The actual amount, though not known, was probably much less than half of St. John's estimate.[39]

The PGPU proved to be embarrassingly ineffective and was ultimately a liability for those working against the amendment. Liquor dealers and saloonists, the wets learned to their dismay, cannot effectively lead a public campaign in regard to liquor policy. By September some of the antiamendment newspapers openly acknowledged that the PGPU was doing more harm than good. They called on it to discharge the "disreputable characters" in its employ and to give the lead to men who had no personal stake in the outcome.[40] However, by then, most of the damage had already been done.

The most visible protagonist of the antiamendment cause was Charles Robinson. He represented the type of respected, disinterested public figure that the wets so badly needed in numbers. Since serving as the state's first governor (1861–63), Robinson had lived as a gentleman farmer on his extensive landholdings near Lawrence but had continued to be very active in public affairs. A Republican during his gubernatorial term, he became a prime mover in most of the third-party economic movements throughout the remainder of the nineteenth century and even ran as a Democrat before he died in 1894.

Robinson's position on the amendment came as a surprise to his Kansas public. A lifelong teetotaler, he had championed the temperance cause on numerous occasions since his arrival in 1854 as an agent of the New England Emigrant Aid Company. In his 1856 gubernatorial message to the Free State Legislature, he had branded the liquor traffic "an unmitigated evil." As a state senator in 1879, he had voted for the amendment—so that the people might express themselves, he said. As late as September 1879 he had been elected president of the Liberal League at a convention that had endorsed prohibition. Four months later he helped to organize the PGPU. The drys always claimed that Robinson switched sides when he perceived a real or imaginary political advantage; Robinson always denied it.[41]

Robinson fired his first shot in March in a long, well-reasoned letter to a Lawrence newspaper and continued to send lengthy epistles to newspapers throughout the campaign. Though he gave a number of spirited speeches and debated some of the temperance leading lights, he reached the most people through the newspapers. He argued that the Maine Laws had proved ineffective—that prohibition wouldn't prohibit. Adoption of the amendment would be "the greatest calamity that could befall our State and a blow against temperance that we could not recover from for long years if at all."[42]

Taking advantage of the public's perplexity about the legal aspects of the issue, though perhaps as honestly confused as they, Robinson introduced into the campaign one of its most controversial dimensions. He held that under the amendment, anyone could sell for the three exempted purposes (medical, scientific, mechanical) and that the legislature would be powerless to prevent it. Prohibition would bring less control than the dramshop law, and "free"—that is, unregulated—whiskey would reign. He further claimed that regulatory laws would require a two-thirds vote in the legislature in order to be passed.

In May, Robinson sent a circular letter to several dozen prominent lawyers, soliciting their opinions. The responses of the great majority shared his view of the prospects for "free whiskey." But a brilliant young Topeka lawyer, Gasper Christopher Clemens, and several other attorneys whom the drys managed to identify, took sharp exception to the legal position of Robinson and his supporters. Robinson, himself a physician, had once asserted that "for $25 [you] could hire any lawyer in Douglas County to give an opinion upon any side of any question."[43]

Robinson made another original contribution to the debate, which was more sound than his legal opinions, though not so widely discussed. He took a philosophical position against prohibition, advancing arguments that were similar to those advocating political liberty. He contended that prohibition contradicted God's plan for the universe, since by eliminating choice, it eliminated free agency. Man became reduced to a mechanical, soulless being, devoid of virtue and character. Prohibitionists, he advised, could better advance the temperance cause by advocating education in the proper use of liquor, rather than legislation to forbid it.[44]

By late spring the public had heard all of the major arguments that each side had to offer. Believing beverage alcohol to be the major social curse of the age, comparable in sinfulness to slavery, the drys held that the state should remove the thin veneer of respectability bestowed on the traffic through the dramshop act. Because it was all too seldom enforced, that act needed to be scrapped. The traffic represented a dire and growing threat to the home and to free, popular government. If the amendment were adopted, crime, disease, poverty, and taxes would be substantially reduced. Riding an anticipated wave of prosperity, Kansas would become "a beacon light leading her sister states to the . . . harbor of safety and sunshine."

In sum, the drys argued from the traditional temperance premises of science, religion, law, and economics. J. R. Detwiler touched on all four when he asserted that adoption was "reasonable, right, just and profitable." Ironically, Charles Robinson had said almost precisely the same thing in 1856, when he had declared that the use of liquor impaired the "health, morals, good order and prosperity" of society.[45]

Encroachment on personal liberty represented the most potent argument of those who opposed the amendment. Prohibition would take the state into the area of sumptuary law, dictating what the people could eat or drink. The drys, reluctantly acknowledging that liquor had "a deep-seated hold upon the affections of many good citizens," countered that personal liberty had to be subordinated to the public good. Thus the key liquor issue resolved itself into the eternal conflict between community and individual rights.

The wets saw enforcement of the dramshop act as adequate and held that that law essentially conferred local option on communities through the petition provision. Prohibition, they claimed, would reduce revenues and increase taxes. It would retard immigration and stimulate emigration, especially with respect to the German community. Land values would plummet as immigration declined and the alcohol market for grain contracted. Since the drys had avoided including a ban on liquor importation in the amendment, a temperance victory would bring increased business to towns that bordered on Kansas, particularly Kansas City, Missouri. Turning the dry argument for "innovation" on its head, the wets held that the unprecedented constitutional "bedamnment" was a foolish and unnecessary experiment. Prohibition, they predicted, would bring personal animosity, expensive litigation, and "party commotion."[46] These three predictions all proved to be brutally accurate; the last would be especially painful for the Republicans.

DURING THE MAINE LAW ERA, political parties "trimmed" as much as possible to avoid a forthright stand on the politically explosive liquor question. Generally the Whigs, and later the Republicans, gave the most consistent support to the temperance position. Even so, in five of the thirteen prohibition states, Democratically controlled legislatures had passed the law, including the flagship commonwealth of Maine.[47] In Kansas the Free State territorial experience had reinforced the Republican predilection for the temperance position. But as a party, it had gone no further than to pass a resolve against drunkenness and to bask in the somewhat undeserved reputation of being "sound" on the question.

From every side echoed the righteous cry that the referendum was, and should remain, nonpartisan. The proamendment Republicans, a majority within a majority, seemed to be content not to press for a formal endorsement, given the internecine row that they would ignite and the public support that they enjoyed from the leading state officers, especially the governor. The more vulnerable wet Republicans, a substantial minority within the majority, and the Democrats, a not-very-substantial minority, happily seconded the nonpartisan position. Thus, none of the parties addressed the question in its 1880 platform. In all but the formalities, however, nonpartisanship was a fiction.[48]

The man who urged the nonpartisan nature of the amendment more often than anyone else and, by so doing, made it ever less so was Governor St. John. The governor had become the most sparkling jewel in the temperance crown. Giving upwards of two hundred impassioned speeches to audiences in nearly every county of the state, he often drew the largest and most enthusiastic crowds ever assembled there. Though most of these speeches came on Saturday nights and Sundays, the opposition accused the tireless governor of improperly using his time and the prestige of his office. But his supporters thought it a rare and beautiful sight to see a politician "squaring himself and striking stalwart blows for what his conscience teaches him is right, irrespective of . . . his own political success."[49]

The fact that St. John campaigned for renomination at the same time that he canvassed for the amendment dulled the nonpartisan claims a good deal. In both of these endeavors he met the vigorous opposition of the wet Republicans as well as the Democrats. He was variously labeled as "an ass," an "idiot boy," "Moses" St. John, "John Petered St. John," and the leader of the "temperance snakes." His prominent role in aiding the exodusters to settle in Kansas had already earned him the epithet of "Nigger-lover." The leading wet Republican paper, the *Kansas State Journal* (Topeka), called prohibition a "tyrannical law" and declared that St. John was full of "twaddle and bosh of no ordinary kind." But after he had easily captured the renomination in September, the paper loyally ran his name at the top of its masthead.[50]

The most unkind cuts came from his "friends," as they always do. Albert Griffin, vice-president of the KSTU, epitomized the type of temperance mainstay who had long worked the Kansas vineyard but who chafed at the dual publicity accorded to St. John as a crusader and as a politician. A native New Yorker of New England stock, Griffin had come to Kansas in 1856, at the age of twenty-two. In 1869 he started to publish the *Manhattan Nationalist* ("An Advocate of Purity, and Progressive in All Things") and soon became a leading figure in the temperance movement and a committed woman suffragist. He supported John A. Martin in 1878 and considered St. John to be no more important than a hundred others as a temperance worker before he was elected.

St. John's supporters repeatedly asserted that he "risked political annihilation for the sake of his principles." But Griffin and others felt that St. John had gained politically, and knew that he would, by being closely identified with the amendment. Griffin had harsh words for those who had been "so blinded as to believe that St. John is himself the amendment, or something a shade holier or more important." The governor contributed to this image with utterances such as "one man and God is a majority," leaving no doubt about whom he considered to be in holy alliance with the Almighty. Griffin also saw the governor as being "sadly deficient in executive ability" and "intellectually, a decidedly lightweight." In spite of these grave reservations, he also nimbly hopped on St. John's bandwagon after he was renominated.[51]

INITIALLY, BOTH SIDES considered that the chances for the amendment's being adopted were no better than "fighting," but as the months passed, it became apparent, even without a scientific poll, that the proposition was generating a great deal of support, some expected and some not. Early in the campaign the largest evangelical denomination, the Methodists, left no doubt where they stood: "Let Governor St. John count on this division of his army, equipped and drilled, waiting for orders." The other evangelical churches all

Albert Griffin (courtesy of the Kansas State Historical Society, Topeka).

enthusiastically declared for prohibition during the campaign—not surprising, but nonetheless welcome, support for the drys.[52]

Somewhat unexpectedly, about two hundred newspapers came out for the amendment, with only fifty being opposed and sixty not declaring themselves. Newspaper opposition centered in the dailies of the large towns: the *Topeka State Journal, Topeka Commonwealth, Leavenworth Times, Atchison Champion, Atchison Globe, Wichita Eagle,* and the German-language *Leavenworth Freie*

Presse. Broad newspaper support was augmented in June by the public schoolteachers who, in convention assembled, resolved unanimously to "heartily" endorse the amendment.[53]

With the exoduster immigration of the late 1870s, blacks became a potentially greater political force. Mary E. Griffith, a vice-president of the Ohio WCTU, removed to Leavenworth and organized twelve Good Templar lodges among the blacks, but she affiliated them with the rival International Order, rather than with the Independent Order. Charles M. Langston (the maternal grandfather of Langston Hughes) chaired a Colored Men's Convention in April, which encouraged southern blacks to immigrate to Kansas, particularly those "whose educational and financial conditions are more favorable." The convention resolved to support prohibition, regarding it "as a measure calculated to aid in the progress and elevation of our race." Several delegates opposed the resolution, fearing that its adoption might hurt the Republican party.[54]

The results of the spring municipal elections brought additional encouragement to the drys. With women being active in the canvass, several towns of the second class elected temperance tickets. Since the larger towns were the strongholds of antiamendment sentiment, the prospects for the latter darkened appreciably. For the first time, many observers, not just the hard-core faithful, began to see the passage of the amendment as a distinct possibility.[55]

By late summer the PGPU had lost much of its steam, but the drys continued their work unabated. "The State [is] ablaze with enthusiasm," a worker remarked in September. During the closing weeks, as many as one hundred temperance rallies were held daily, some of which were all-day affairs of grand proportions.[56]

A rally at Sabetha (Nemaha County) may be taken as typical of the genre. An exuberant crowd, swollen by a large influx from the adjacent counties, participated in the daylong festivities. The celebration began in the morning with a street parade "a half-mile in length," featuring the local temperance societies, whose brilliant banners and badges made "an imposing spectacle." The principal speaker, the nationally prominent Iowa lawyer J. Ellen Foster, "completely captivated" her audience with a talk "full of strength, force and pathos." Several area ministers followed Foster to the podium. In the afternoon she spoke to the children, who were called forward and talked to "as only Mrs. Foster can." In the evening a mass meeting, "packed to overflowing," convened in the largest hall in town. The crowd of townspeople and farmers heard Foster ("never weary of well doing") speak for the third time. It was "truly a grand day for the faithful workers [which] cheered them to greater activity and . . . did much for the cause."[57]

The uniqueness of the campaign attracted several outstanding "foreign" speakers, such as Francis Murphy and Frances Willard, and captured the attention of the entire nation as well. "All America is watching this struggle . . . with anxious hearts," an Iowa paper said. "The battle in Kansas," declared the

National Temperance Advocate, "is the battle of the nation." Kansans themselves self-consciously recognized the importance of the outcome to the larger community: "Remember the eyes of the world are upon us, and Kansas expects every man and woman to do their duty."[58]

The women of Kansas performed critical work for the amendment. "What would the work be without the women?" St. John asked rhetorically. As Drusilla Wilson had recommended, they advanced the "woman's side" of the question by using moral suasion to urge men to use legal suasion. Without their informal influence in the home and their organized activity abroad, the amendment would have failed. In effect, women voted by proxy through their male relatives and neighbors. The campaign stands as a classic example of the transformation of sociopolitical energy from informal influence to formal authority. And women presented an almost solid front. No woman campaigned against the amendment, and only a tiny minority—the wives of saloonists and a few free spirits such as Sara Robinson—identified themselves in any public fashion with the pro-liquor position.

The success of the amendment hinged to a great extent upon the work of women as individuals and as volunteers in the churches and in the sundry temperance organizations. Several historians, however, have grossly exaggerated the role that the state WCTU played in the campaign. In a recent account the white ribboners had become, by 1880, "the most powerful special interest lobby" in the state.[59]

President Drusilla Wilson's decision to canvass the state personally, rather than to direct a broad organizational effort for the WCTU, severely limited its influence. Of the three dozen or so nominal local unions that "existed" in 1880, only seven paid their state dues, and only eight sent representatives to the annual meeting in August, which approved the first "Plan of Work." In that plan they resolved to "work, pray, watch, . . . talk, sing, serve lunches, make boquets, do anything and everything *right* to secure ballots of men, each one of which is more precious than gold." The small band proceeded to do just that, but the WCTU remained a weak, struggling organization in Kansas for another five years.[60]

At its convention a few weeks before the election, the KSTU recognized the essential role of women. The male-dominated federation (75 percent of the delegates were men) was anxious to enlist the help of the women in their new public roles but was equally anxious that the women not neglect their traditional duties in the process. The union "earnestly requested" the women of Kansas to "so arrange their domestic work" on election day that they might be available "to lend their powerful aid" at the polls.

Women responded to the appeal in large numbers on November 2, providing free lunches at the polls for everyone, friend and foe alike, and lending their "powerful aid" in every conceivable manner. In some of the larger towns they convened at a church early in the morning, prayed and sang hymns, and then proceeded to the polls in a body.[61] And the evidence has yet to be unearthed that any man either suffered from an inadequate supper or volunteered to help with the "domestic work."

The amendment carried 92,302 to 84,304, by a margin of 7,998 votes, or 4.5 percent of the total. Since the drys had been confidently predicting a 30,000 to 60,000 majority, the final margin came as something of a disappointment. The amendment carried in fifty-three counties but did not in twenty-seven (see app. A). The voting pattern closely followed the house vote on the amendment. Religious, ethnic, political, urban, and geographical factors can be identified. Counties tended to vote dry if they had a strong presence of evangelical churches, Old Stock ethnicity, Republican politics, small-to-moderate-sized towns, and an "interior" position removed from the Missouri border. Many of the driest counties are found clustered in the south-central region. They include the banner temperance county, Cowley (with a 79 percent dry vote), and Lyon (73), McPherson (70), Elk (69), Sumner (67), and Butler (66) counties.

Those counties that voted against the amendment tended to have a significant Roman Catholic and/or German Lutheran influence; German, Irish, or Eastern European ethnicity; Democratic politics; a large urban center; and a border position across from Missouri or out in the untamed west. Ford County (Dodge City), still in its "cowboy" phase, produced the smallest proportion of dry votes (20 percent); it was followed by Leavenworth (28), Doniphan (28), Atchison (30), Barton (32), and Wyandotte (33) counties. Counties that would later rebel against the amendment included Cherokee (55), Crawford (53), and Sedgwick (52), all of which approved it, and Ellis (43) and Bourbon (42), which did not. Shawnee County carried the amendment with a 56 percent majority.[62]

Correlation coefficients have been calculated for the dry vote, by county, and for several independent variables: the turnout (percentage of eligible voters who voted), nativity (percentage of native-born voters), density (percentage living outside of townships of 2,000 or more), politics (percentage of Republican plus Greenback-Labor votes), and denomination (percentage of evangelicals among the total who belonged to churches). The coefficients (all positive) are turnout, .12; nativity, .19; density, .19; politics, .43; and denomination, .51 (see app. B). The manifest difference between politics and denomination undoubtedly underestimates the importance of the latter due to the impreciseness of the religious data for 1880.[63]

The election cast additional light on Clark's "disorderliness" hypothesis. Only 9.8 percent of the total vote came from west of a line described by the western edges of Jewell, Ellsworth, Reno, and Harper counties, a line that bisects the state into two almost equal halves (see fig. 3.1). The average dry percentage of the twenty-one counties west of the line is 50, lower, though not significantly so, than that of the fifty-nine counties east of the line (53). The only significant east-west differences are in voter turnout (79 percent in the east, 61 percent in the west) and in the percentage of rural voters (75 percent in the east,

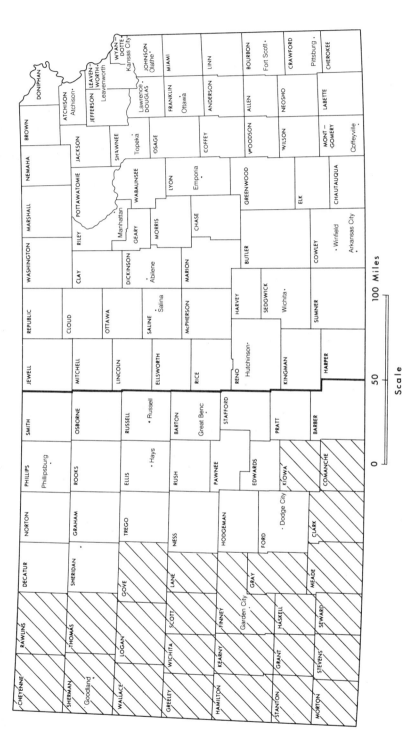

Fig. 3.1. The twenty-one counties west of the bisecting line accounted for only 9.8 percent of the total vote on the prohibition referendum in 1880. Counties that had not been organized by 1880 are indicated by crosshatching.

99 percent in the west). If the disorderliness concept had any validity, the western counties should have voted considerably drier, not wetter, than those in the east. Dodge City, arguably the most disorderly spot in Kansas, had the wettest sentiment in the state.

For years after the election, speculation centered around the unknown desires of those who had voted in the election but not on the amendment. While 176,606 voted on the proposition, 201,277 cast ballots for president. The wets charged that most of the 24,671 unrecorded voters came from wet counties and intended to vote against prohibition but were too confused to do so. A statistical correlation between the percentage who voted dry and the percentage who voted on the amendment yields a positive but statistically insignificant coefficient. That is, among those who went to the polls, the tendency to abstain from voting on the amendment is not significantly associated with the temperance proclivity of the county.[64]

Young Kansas had created something new under the heavens—constitutional prohibition. The tradition of reform, rooted in the Free State fervor of the territorial period, had been nurtured by the New England–inspired evangelical temperance movement. The Hammond revival and the Woman's Crusade had further sensitized the population to alcohol-related problems. The Murphy Movement had left a tinderbox to which the Good Templars had applied the spark. Miscalculation by antitemperance politicians represented the fortuitous element, which is omnipresent in historical cause-and-effect chains. Dedication to the cause and old-fashioned hard work capped the campaign with victory for the drys. But much remained unknown and unresolved. The amendment now needed a law to explicate it and a people to enforce it.

4
The Auspicious Eighties

Kansas has always managed to keep herself prominent before the Nation and the world. She has the reputation of never doing things by half—either for good or evil. . . . Kansas would rather be talked about adversely than not at all, and the louder the better.

—C. B. Schmidt, Santa Fe's European agent

Another objection to the amendment and the law is it develops and brings to the front a class of hypocrites, spies, detectives, liars and informers, the most loathsome and offensive class of vermin, that can possibly afflict the body politic.

—A Topeka Democrat

Kansas is the mausoleum of the saloon, the sepulchre of its vices, the tomb of its iniquities.

—James A. Troutman

A LAW TO IMPLEMENT the amendment became the first priority of the 1881 legislature. In his message to the people's representatives, Governor St. John reminded them of their awesome responsibility: "We now look to the future, not forgetting that it was here on our soil where the first blow was given that finally resulted in the emancipation of a race from slavery. We have now determined upon a second emancipation, which shall free not only the body but the soul of man. Now, as in the past, the civilized world watches Kansas, and anxiously awaits the result."[1]

A subcommittee of the Senate Temperance Committee, chaired by Alfred Washburn Benson, drafted the bill. Descended from Massachusetts stock on both sides of his family and reared in western New York, Benson had immigrated after serving in the war and had opened a law office in Ottawa in 1869. In 1878 he had been elected mayor on a dry platform. Before his public career ended, he served as a United States senator (1906/7) and as a justice of the Kansas Supreme Court (1907–15).[2]

63

With two other lawyers, Benson drafted the act, which was not a copy of other legislation but was an original bill, produced after weeks of arduous work. The bill had relatively easy going in both houses, considering the interest and emotion attached to it. The drys, in a comfortable majority, defeated an amendment that would have excluded from the law any wine made from grapes and any cider made from apples that had been grown in the state. An amendment that would have excluded sacramental wine also lost, though the attorney general later ruled that only the sale, not the use, of such fermented beverages was prohibited. Representative Bob Wright of Dodge City whimsically moved to exclude from the provisions of the act all of Kansas west of the 100th meridian, claiming that the people in those parts had special need for snakebite medicine. He even threatened secession, but promised that if his territory were excluded, "harmony will again prevail upon the border . . . and future generations of cowboys will arise and call you blessed."[3]

Some of the more extreme drys, led by the Reverend Pardee Butler, an Atchison minister of the Disciples of Christ and a Free State hero, pressed for a harsher law that would have a strong central enforcement authority. Primary responsibility for enforcement would be vested in a temperance commissioner, who would oversee the operations of a statewide constabulary. But St. John was cool to the idea and was enthusiastic about the Benson bill, which met his criteria of a "plain, positive and stringent" law. He signed the bill on February 19, in a "solemn and impressive" ceremony that was witnessed by "an admiring crowd," which included several women "of the old femining stand-bye." A few days later the women suffered a humiliating defeat when the house, "after considerable amusement and some earnestness," voted down a resolution that would have resubmitted a woman-suffrage amendment to the male voters.[4]

A tough law that would become even more so in the ensuing years, the Benson Act provided for sale to the public for the three excepted purposes with, and only with, a druggists' permit. The probate judge issued such permits, at his discretion, after the applicant had submitted a petition signed by twelve (male) citizens certifying that he was of "good moral character," lawfully engaged in the drug business, and had posted a $2,500 bond. The druggist could sell for medical purposes only upon presentation of a physician's written prescription. The law required the druggist to keep a record of such sales, which record would have to show "the names and residence of all purchasers of such liquors, the kind and quantity sold, [and] the purpose for which sold. . . . The record so kept [should] be open to the inspection of the public at all reasonable times during business hours."[5] Thus began a pastime for some Kansans that later rivaled in popularity listening in on the party telephone line.

Since selling for medical purposes quickly became the largest loophole in the law, the physician assumed a central role in dispensing liquor with which neither he nor the general public felt comfortable. The contemporary medical community recommended intoxicating liquor for a wide range of illnesses, so that many legitimate transactions occurred under the law. But the possibility of abuse by either physician or patient was there and was sometimes realized. The provision that chafed the physicians the most required them to file with the probate judge every five years a sworn affidavit that they would prescribe liquor only "in cases of actual sickness" and would "faithfully keep, observe and perform all the requirements . . . regulating the sale and use of intoxicating liquors." Most physicians deeply resented the oath as impugning their professional honor and dignity, so they often ignored the requirement. They soon began to apply pressure to end the unwelcome "physicians' era."

Although every law official carried some obligation for enforcement, the principal responsibility devolved upon the county attorney. He would remain in the stellar enforcement role through the years, though his burden was lightened somewhat by a fee of $25 per conviction. Penalties for violation of the law, including selling without a permit, ranged from $100 to $500 in fines or (not *and*) thirty to ninety days in the county jail. The law provided for civil action against places, as well as criminal action against persons. Places that a court found to be making, selling, bartering, or giving away intoxicating liquor could be declared "common nuisances" and shut up, the nuisance thereby abated.[6]

The Benson Law applied to "intoxicating liquor," but it did not sharply define that to which it applied. An opinion by the state's supreme court in June 1881 established guidelines that would be followed by the court, with only two significant changes (in 1914 and 1933), as long as the constitution included a prohibitory clause. Writing for the court, Justice David Brewer identified three classes of alcohol-containing liquids. Those intended as beverages—such as whiskey, gin, brandy, wine, and beer—were fully covered by the law. A second category, which included liquids not intended as beverages—such as toilet articles, extracts, varnishes, and medical compounds whose formulae appeared in the U.S. dispensatory—were not covered by the law. The third category included the very popular patent medicines, such as tonics, cordials, bitters, and syrups. Here the court threw up its hands and held that the total factual circumstances as determined in each individual case by a local jury would be binding.[7]

WHEN THE LAW went into effect on 1 May 1881, the temperance forces were both quietly confident and excitedly expectant. Most of them shared the sanguine outlook of the Senate Temperance Committee, which had said it was "unwilling to believe that any laws of the State reasonable in their provision, and sanctioned by the constitution, will long remain inoperative in any part of the State." Even before the effective date, Governor St. John noted the improved social climate as saloon keepers moved out and "sober, industrious, energetic" families moved in.[8]

The approach of the effective date ushered in a "period of uncertainty"— uncertainty as to the role of the physicians and druggists, the rigor of enforcement, the public's tolerance of violations, and the constitutionality of the law itself. The apprehensive public flooded the newspapers with lengthy letters to the editor, which feebly illuminated some obscure point or excoriated the wets or the drys for their foolishness and stupidity. The associate editor of the *Atchison Champion,* Noble Prentis, called for a moratorium on all drinking, a ban that was designed to save the state "from cant, humbug, slander, professional reformers, hired apostles, and another fool Legislature of Kansas. . . . It would shut off a Niagra of slushy communications to the newspapers[,] for the . . . tormented editor then could tell the contributers to imitate the guzzlers and 'dry up.' "[9]

Soon after May 1, both the wets and the drys began to claim that their worst fears, or fondest hopes, were being realized. In the most accurate statement of the day, one that would remain valid for sixty-eight years, an observer noted that Kansas had adopted prohibition, but with what success "would be stated differently by different individuals." Both sides did agree that it had caused "more rows than any theme that Kansas was ever called upon to discuss, if we except the slavery question." The KSTU soon claimed that "no law in the State [was] more rigorously enforced than the prohibitory liquor law." St. John said that "the evidence of the success of prohibition is to be found every where throughout our state." But John A. Martin's antiprohibitionist *Atchison Champion* declared that the commonwealth, at least in the larger towns, was "in a state of anarchy, lawlessness, and revolt against the Constitution and the laws."[10]

Within a few weeks the major outlines of the picture came into sharper focus. In the smaller towns and rural districts the law was "honestly obeyed and enforced," and the open saloon virtually disappeared. Liquor was decidedly more difficult to obtain than under the dramshop law. But in the larger towns, saloons ran wide open in flagrant defiance of the law. The persisting pattern of differential enforcement along an urban/rural axis firmly established itself from the beginning.

Although the overwhelming majority of Kansans lived in small towns or rural areas in 1880, the urban minority soon began to grow relative to the state as a whole. In 1870, 14 percent of the population lived in the eight towns with more than two thousand people. The percentage changed to 12 (in twenty-three towns) by 1880, to 21 (in fifty towns) by 1890, to 24 (in fifty-one towns) by 1900, and to 31 (in sixty-seven towns) by 1910. In 1880, Leavenworth, Atchison, and Topeka were the only cities of the first class, with populations slightly in excess of fifteen thousand.[11] The major enforcement problems of the reform amendment would center here.

Leavenworth became the most celebrated symbol of urban defiance in nineteenth-century Kansas. Located on the Missouri River and with a large German Catholic population, the state's largest city openly flouted the law after the effective date. Toward the end of June a lecturer-organizer for the KSTU,

Frank Sibley, came to town. A mining engineer and a Prohibition party official from New York who had come west for the amendment campaign, Sibley selected three among some fifty saloons and then filed information that led to the arrest of the proprietors.

On the next day the incensed saloonists physically attacked Sibley in three separate street incidents. Badly beaten, he was carried to the rear of a store by friends, while an angry crowd milled menacingly in front. Fortunately, the building had a back door, through which he was spirited to the police station, where he was held for protection against the howling mob. The first effort at law enforcement ended so disastrously that another attempt was not made until 1884, when Col. Charles R. Jennison, the temperance speaker and saloonist, was arrested. But a jury of his peers, not surprisingly, could not be impaneled, so he was released.[12]

Disturbed by the Sibley incident, St. John angrily declared that the state would "suppress rebellion against the constitution and laws in Kansas, as the general government did in South Carolina." Disregarding the counsel of friends who were concerned about his personal safety, he delivered himself of a fiery speech in Leavenworth a few weeks later, in which he threatened to enforce the law at the point of the bayonet if necessary. In December he issued an unprecedented gubernatorial proclamation, which offered monetary rewards to those who would supply information leading to the conviction of law violators or to the removal of nonfunctioning officials. He singled out officers in Leavenworth, Atchison, Wyandotte, Topeka, and Dodge City as the worst offenders. Especially in the named cities the proclamation received a good deal of attention but almost no response.[13]

A somewhat more sedate city than Leavenworth, Atchison approached the prohibition aggravation in a more dignified fashion, though it started out in the Leavenworth mold. In June, St. John gave a scolding speech to the citizens, following which a "rotten-egging" threat resulted in his being furnished a police escort to the city limits. A period of more than two years of tranquillity followed, but it threatened to become disturbed when some local temperance "cranks" filed information for the arrest of seventeen saloonists. A dozen prominent citizens issued a call to the business and professional sector for an emergency meeting "to consult the best interests of the city, which are threatened by certain proceedings now pending, which tend to destroy the unity and general harmony of this community."

At the meeting, which was chaired by the former proslavery champion B. F. Stringfellow, the civic leaders decried the economic impact of a dry crusade. A "prohibition war" could only result in the "calamity" of trade diversion, driving away "some of our most substantial and prosperous business houses." A petition that soon circulated around town, signed by "nineteen twentieths" of the businessmen, urged the county attorney to move slowly against the law violators. That obedient public servant was only too happy to oblige.[14] No strife, no bloodshed, no enforcement.

In wet cities such as Leavenworth, Atchison, and Wyandotte and in dry towns such as Emporia, Ottawa, and Winfield, public sentiment and the reflected behavior of the elected officials ran strongly to one pole or the other. No doubt could be entertained about the dominant local sentiment. But in Topeka, both sides had strong and vocal representation in nearly equal proportions. Reflecting the ambivalence of the state and the tension generated thereby, Topeka continued to be a seat of contention as well as government for twenty-five years. Both wets and drys strove mightily to "capture" the capital city because of its prized symbolism for the state as a whole.

Agitation in the capital began in perfect symmetry. In mid July the antiprohibition partisans held a mass meeting of some three thousand to denounce the Benson Law. Featured speakers included Charles Robinson, Sam Wood, and Cyrus K. Holliday, a founder of Topeka and of the Santa Fe Railway. Holliday complained about the adverse economic impact of prohibition and about the strife that it had caused, which had "set the people by the ears in every locality." Two days later a large gathering of drys, meeting in front of the Methodist Church, heard St. John describe Robinson and Wood as "political chiggers starting festering sores in the body-politic wherever fastening."[15]

Shortly after the Benson Law went into effect, Topeka's City Council authorized the licensing of establishments that sold "German mineral water." The ordinance served as a thinly veiled invitation to liquor establishments. Once a month each saloon dutifully paid its $50 "fine" for operating without said license. The more than thirty functioning saloons produced $20,000 for the city treasury annually. In most of the larger towns, with minor variations, this basic pattern lent a patina of legality to that which was illegal. In Fort Scott, for example, "the ordinance was prohibition, but the private interpetation by the mayor . . . was license."[16]

After nearly eighteen months of such legal chicanery, a mass meeting in Topeka led to the Committee of Fifty, which was composed of many of the town's leading citizens. Fed up with trying to "coax" men to be loyal to the constitution, the committee decided to take legal action. It petitioned the Kansas Supreme Court to oust the mayor from office because of his persistent licensing of saloons. Although the drys had frequently denounced him as the "pliant tool of the whiskey ring," the mayor found an unexpected friend in the governor's office. The young man ought to be given a second chance, St. John said, because he had "an excellent Christian mother who would come to grief if her son was impeached." The mayor, it turns out, was none other than Joseph C. Wilson, the beloved son of Drusilla Wilson.[17]

The committee changed its mind, but Wilson didn't mend his ways. A few months later the committee reinstated the legal cause against the mayor and also brought proceedings to oust the City of Topeka from assuming legal powers—

that is, the licensing of saloons—that it did not possess. The Kansas Supreme Court upheld the latter petition, declaring that the city had gone beyond its granted powers "to encourage an illegal business." The court ruled, however, that the mayor had not forfeited his office, since "mere misconduct" was not sufficient cause for ousting him. The question became moot a few days later when Wilson suddenly resigned due to "ill health." "During his administration," the drys said, "he has covered a formerly good name with infamy."[18]

Other schemes surfaced for a time in Topeka in an attempt to fill the void. The short-lived Idaho Mining and Prospecting Company sold shares for twenty-five cents, which included a drink set up by a "company officer." The officers were said to be busy well into the night "issuing stock." But nineteenth-century Topeka would never again see quasi-legalized saloons, though a drink was never difficult to find.[19]

THE MOST INTENSE and organized opposition to prohibition centered in the unassimilated ethnic communities, especially those of Germanic origin. In 1880, German-speaking Kansans made up a small but vocal 3.9 percent of the total population, and Germans accounted for 25 percent of the state's total of foreign-born. The totals included the recent arrivals, mostly Catholics, who had settled in the west-central county of Ellis, and the Mennonites, who had populated the south-central counties of Harvey, Marion, and McPherson. Both groups strongly opposed woman suffrage, but the Mennonites soon began to vote Republican and enthusiastically support the temperance cause. Only about 43 percent of them voted dry in 1880, but by the twentieth century that level of support had nearly doubled. The Germans in Ellis County came to Kansas as Republicans, as did those who settled in the Missouri River counties, but chiefly as a result of the temperance issue, "they shut their eyes and vote the Democratic ticket." Only about 10 percent of the Catholics in Ellis County supported the amendment in 1880.[20]

The Germans worried not only about the threat to their beer supply but also about the adverse impact that prohibition might have on immigration. German newspapers in Missouri had begun to paint a desert-dry picture of Kansas for their European brethren, hoping thereby to deflect the immigrant tide. C. B. Schmidt, the European agent for the Santa Fe Railroad, who had been instrumental in bringing the Mennonites to Kansas, wrote bitter public letters in which he decried the effects of prohibition on German immigration. A few months after prohibition became the law, if not the fact, of the land, the German Immigration Society formed in Atchison. Its purpose was to promote immigration and to "relieve the State of its false theories caused by fanatical legislation." But in some other areas of Europe—for example, the Netherlands—dry Kansas was lauded for its enhanced attraction to immigrants.[21]

Pardee Butler, minister of the Atchison Christian Church, who had been accused of developing "political hysteria whenever he thinks or dreams" of

Germans, wrote an open letter to them, chiding them for always being on the losing side of the question and urging them to get on the right side. A member of Atchison's German community responded, admitting that many saloon keepers were Germans but decrying a law that made a man a criminal for serving his friends a glass of wine or cider made on his own farm. "The German-Americans despise a drunkard," he said, "yet they despise the hypocrite more."[22]

Some Germans turned the ambivalent milieu to their advantage with a nimbleness that would do a veteran politician proud. A publisher in Ellis County put out a four-page paper in 1882, the first two pages in English, the last two in German. "We hear that a new saloon is to be built soon on the old Krueger corner," page one tells us, "May the gods forbid." On page four we find: "A reliable source tells us that a new tavern will be opened here soon. Let's hope that we can get a big glass of beer at half price."[23]

Not all of the communities that had a northern-European ethnic composition were hostile to prohibition. The Swedes of the Lindsborg area (McPherson County) included some of prohibition's most ardent friends. As one venerable pioneer stated: "We lived it till it became the law of the state." Mostly Scandinavian Lutherans, the Swedes had held many church-sponsored temperance meetings during the campaign to generate enthusiasm for the amendment. Preelection ardor became postelection vigilance. Some of the town's elders took turns visiting the local drugstores to count the number of patent-medicine bottles displayed in the windows. If the number was less than on the preceding day, the self-appointed guardian of public morality would immediately enter and demand an accounting from the flustered owner. The druggists soon learned to replace quickly a sold item with a new bottle.[24]

As time passed, the discrete ethnic communities became increasingly assimilated into the Anglo-Saxon mainstream. The educative aspects of the law were subtle, pervasive, powerful, and enduring. The younger generation grew up in a very different milieu from that experienced by their elders. Where the parents had been reared in intimate daily association with a *Biergarten* in Munich or Stuttgart or western Russia, the children might grow to adulthood in Kansas without seeing an open saloon. Formal, organized opposition by the German community ended well before the nineteenth century did, though many individuals continued to oppose prohibition and to serve as prime customers for the clandestine joint or the bootlegger.[25] By the early twentieth century, organized ethnic opposition to prohibition had shifted to a different area and a different people.

Many of the most far-reaching temperance victories in the 1880s over the beer-loving Germans and other wets occurred in the courtroom. In 1881 the Kansas Supreme Court found the amendment and the Benson Law constitutional in all respects. Over the next several years the drys scored a number of other significant victories in the supreme court, involving sundry aspects of the law. The floodgates had opened on liquor-related legislation, and the courts at all levels threatened to become swamped. During the 1870s the supreme court considered a total of eighteen liquor-related cases, an average of less than two per year. For the five years beginning in 1882, the high court rendered opinions in sixty-four cases, an average of thirteen a year. In the more specific rulings of the higher court, which often related to procedural questions of enforcement, the state was upheld about 60 percent of the time.[26]

The most important dry victories came in the United States Supreme Court. In 1884 the Kansas Supreme Court ousted John Foster, the county attorney of Saline County, for refusing to perform his sworn duty. In a petition "numerously signed" by citizens of the county, Foster, "a frequenter and patron" of saloons, had been accused of "willfully and persistently" violating his oath by refusing to prosecute under the Benson Law. On appeal, the United States Supreme Court validated the state's procedure for removal from office and held that the prohibitory law was not repugnant to the federal constitution. The latter question, the court said, "is now no longer open in this court."[27]

The 1887 decision in *Mugler* v. *Kansas* became not only essential for enforcement in Kansas but a national landmark in temperance legislation as well. A Salina brewer, Peter Mugler, had been charged with having illegally manufactured intoxicating liquor and with having maintained a common nuisance. The state closed his brewery in a civil proceeding, without a jury trial. Mugler argued that his business had been illegally enjoined and that his property had been confiscated without compensation in violation of the Fourteenth Amendment. The United States Brewers' Association financed the appeal of the adverse decision by the Kansas Supreme Court. An attempt was made by the Kansas liquor interests to delay the federal decision until after the 1884 state election, though the efficacy of those efforts is still not known.

The *Mugler* decision by the United States Supreme Court reaffirmed the validity of the Kansas amendment and of the Benson Law as "fairly adopted to the end of protecting the community against the evils which result from excessive use of ardent spirits." The Court ruled that the prohibitory laws could be enforced against breweries and distilleries without compensating them for their property and that the state's right to abate a nuisance without a jury trial was in harmony with the settled principles of equity jurisprudence. The court gave a strong boost to prohibitionists everywhere when it declared that "we cannot shut out of view the fact, . . . that the public health, the public morals, and the public safety, may be endangered by the general use of intoxicating drinks; nor the fact, . . . that the idleness, disorder, pauperism, and crime existing in the country are, in some degree at least, traceable to this evil."[28]

IN FEBRUARY 1882 the *Topeka Capital* began to agitate for a third term for Governor St. John. Other papers quickly picked up the refrain. They pointed with pride to his skillful handling of the massive black immigration from the South, his rapid suppression of the red threat on the western border, and his humane treatment of the white victims of the severe drought. His administration had been scandal free, and he had become the champion advertiser of the state to the national audience. But above all else, he had been tried and found true on prohibition enforcement. Until the ultimate success of the law was assured, why risk a change of leadership?[29]

The unprecedented third term represented a major liability for the governor. The overt or covert defection of many in his own party proved to be as harmful. Wet Republicans opposed the "temperance warrior," but so also did others who held no strong antiprohibition convictions. Many anti-St. John Republicans had difficulty in resolving the core ambivalence that they found in the governor's character. He had to be either a crusader or a politician, they reasoned; he couldn't with sincerity be both. They came to conclude that he must be solely motivated by political ambition and, therefore, that he was a gigantic fraud.

Those who shared these feelings mocked the "senior member of the firm of St. John and God" and his prohibition "hobby." They envied the immense popularity that he enjoyed with the temperance crowd, which included an army of adoring women. They scoffed at his national reputation as a crusader, now second only to that of the venerable Neal Dow, author of the Maine Law. Though St. John had brought Kansas far more favorable publicity than had any of his predecessors or contemporaries, his detractors renewed their charge that he should have spent more time in Topeka minding his official duties. Both a dedicated crusader and a dynamic politician, St. John simply worked harder and longer than had his predecessors in fulfilling the dual roles.[30]

Politicians such as United States Senator John J. Ingalls (1873–91) had special cause for concern about St. John's candidacy. After another term as governor, St. John would be an attractive alternative when Ingalls came up for reelection in 1885. Cautiously venturing during the campaign that perhaps prohibition was a mistake, Ingalls was one of the leaders of an anti-St. John faction which met secretly after the Republican Convention to plot the defeat of the incumbent. Though the two were never "on cordial terms," political protocol demanded that the United States senator introduce the gubernatorial candidate at a mammoth rally the day before the election. Ingalls said: "Whatever might be the opinion of men . . . about the peculiar views of Gov. St. John concerning matters which are by some claimed to belong to the domain of morals rather than politics, he had been fearless, he had been faithful, he had been cleanly."[31]

The "peculiar views" of St. John had been adopted as a major plank in the 1882 platform of the Republican party. Going beyond a perfunctory enforcement stance, the delegates declared that they were "unqualifiedly" in favor of the principle of prohibition. The overpowered opposition maintained a sullen silence. The temperance enthusiasm spilled over to woman suffrage, which was also endorsed, though only after brisk opposition led by John A. Martin. The party had embraced two major, and controversial, social reforms in its formal statement to the people. Three weeks later the Democratic platform described the Republicans as "ambitious demagogues, unprincipled adventurers and sham reformers." It labeled the Benson Law, with its "unwise oppression and tyrannical provisions," a failure and called for the resubmission of the question.[32] Thus the temperance battle was cleanly joined, or so it seemed.

The Democrats nominated the Atchison railroad lawyer and stockman George Washington Glick. A respected public figure for two decades, Glick had been the legislative leader of the antitemperance forces since the late 1860s. Charles Robinson became the candidate of the Greenback-Labor party, one of the spiritual antecedents of the Populists. Although Robinson's well-known position on prohibition encouraged the drys to portray him as the "champion of the whiskey ring," he stuck closely to economic issues, emphasizing the allegedly prorailroad views of the governor.[33]

If Robinson said little about prohibition, Glick talked about little else. Glick said that prohibition gave employment to "busybodies" and the "meddlesome." The only thing it prohibited, he said, was "thousands" of Europeans (by that he meant especially Germans) from immigrating to Kansas. Personally a teetotaler, Glick said he favored moral suasion "of the old Washingtonian method." As for enforcement, he declared that "no man with a spark of manhood or honor in him would inform on another who had sold him intoxicating liquor." The topic that upset Glick and his fellow Democrats almost as much as temperance was the specter of the woman's vote. The Republicans, Glick lamented, by declaring for woman suffrage, had "dragged our mothers and sisters into this political damnation."[34]

During the campaign the prohibitionists received a boost from an unexpected quarter, and the public gained an insight into wet strategy when the press obtained a copy of a letter written by John Walruff to a fellow brewer. For years, Walruff, the most prominent brewer in Kansas, had been the leading figure in the antitemperance movement and had become, for the drys, the most despised symbol of resistance to prohibition. When the adverse *Mugler* decision came down in 1887, Walruff quit Kansas permanently after years of intermittent exile during which he and his sons were "hounded worse than murderers or horsethieves." "I have fought the fanatics for six long years," he said; "their hatred toward me is unbounded."[35]

Written on the stationery of the Lawrence Chemical Works, Manufacturers of the Celebrated Stomach Invigorator, Walruff's letter advised his troubled friend to cease selling beer and "go somewheres" while court was in session. He urged him to make retailing "arrangements" with the city council if possible and, if arrested, to get the sheriff on his side to ensure "at least one juror . . . who will hang the jury untill dooms day." Reinforcing the opinion of many wets, and drys as well, Walruff wrote that "if we beat St. John, then the back bone of prohibition is broken." Above all else, he urged that the liquor interests support anti–St. John men "first, last and all the time." Treating the letter like a direct message from the devil, the St. John camp delighted in sharing it with the general public.[36]

In the campaign, St. John spoke primarily on prohibition, with an occasional reference to woman suffrage and railroad regulation. With a plank about prohibition in both party platforms, all semblance of nonpartisanship disappeared; the fusion of St. John and prohibition in the public mind seemed complete. His opponents called him "a demogogue, a fanatic, a cheap politician," and worse. But his supporters saw him as a persecuted hero, defending the good, the beautiful, and the true. Even Albert Griffin, who had been so slow in warming to the governor, admitted that St. John had "much more real nobility of soul than we have given him credit for." And the spellbinder had not lost his magic on the stump. After a political rally in October an observer wrote: "It is wonderful and beyond comprehension the power of a man for the right, whose soul is ablaze from the coals on the alter [sic] of the Most High. When old men and young men, women and children, all are seen wiping away the tears that flowed in quick succession, there is power, there is eloquence, and it is the eloquence of truth, of the right, of humanity."[37]

In the election that followed the bitterly contested race, Glick received 83,232 votes; St. John, 75,158; and Robinson, 20,898. Had the people repudiated prohibition so soon after adopting the amendment? The entire Republican state ticket, running on the prohibition platform, had been comfortably elected except for the top position. More importantly for the future of prohibition, a group of temperance-minded legislators and county attorneys had also been elected. Factors peculiar to St. John—namely, public opposition generated by the third-term issue and personal animosity toward him within the Republican ranks—were largely responsible for his defeat, with an assist from the railroad issue and woman suffrage.[38]

Liquor flowed freely at the Glick "jollification" as the victors celebrated the hard-earned election of Kansas' first Democratic governor. Wiping away bitter tears at the defeat of their idol, temperance leaders called for renewed faith and increased pledge-signing activity. St. John himself took the defeat stoically. "A thousand St. Johns may go down in the fight for prohibition," he said, "but the principle will still live."[39]

A CHASTENED KANSAS State Temperance Union gathered in Topeka in early January 1883 to keep a watchful eye on the legislature and to chart its own future course. Nearly all of the delegates represented churches, Sunday Schools, or the WCTU. ("The clerical and female element was noticeably prominent.") Nevertheless, for nearly two hours the convention debated the propriety of having the union formally recognize "the power of the Lord Jesus Christ." The motion eventually lost because the majority felt that temperance support should be drawn "from all sects and creeds."[40]

The union's chief concern stemmed from the legislative message of the new governor. Glick had told the legislators that "a body of people do not change their habits, customs, sentiments, opinions, and modes of life, which they do not admit or believe to be bad, at the behests of would-be reformers, or even constitutions or statutes." He recommended that the question be resubmitted to the people at the earliest opportunity, a position that some observers claimed was the principal reason for his election. But both houses soundly trounced resubmission resolutions, and so the temperance folk breathed easier.[41]

Despite the legislative defeat a good deal of clamor for repeal developed during the summer. The resubmissionists argued that the rifts within the Republican party, within communities, and even within homes could only be healed by another vote on the question. Since the law appeared to be unenforceable in the cities, the principal difference between license and prohibition, they said, was that under the former, local option was exercised lawfully but under the latter, unlawfully. Above all else they were sick of the hypocrisy of "temperance tickets" that were filled with men who drank. Referring to a local slate proposed by the *Topeka Capital,* the *Topeka State Journal* claimed: "One end of its ticket is in the church, the other in a whisky barrel. Such a ticket is past praying for. God would not be able to reconcile their prayers with their practices in time for the election."[42]

The undaunted prohibitionists called for stricter enforcement, declaring a war of "absolute extermination" against the liquor traffic. On occasion the resubmissionist rhetoric got under the skin of some of the more volatile drys. After a state meeting of the "nullifyers," a Winfield ardent labeled the gathering "a crime against Kansas, an impudent, brazen and infamous piece of treason, and everyone of the miserable and disloyal whelps and whipper-snappers . . . ought to be sent to the penitentiary."[43] Clearly the time had not yet arrived for a meeting of the minds on the question.

The 1884 Republican Convention adopted another strong prohibition plank and rejected by nearly five to one a resubmissionist proposal to endorse a constitutional convention. It also condemned Glick for his policy of lax law enforcement, including the too-liberal issuance of pardons to those convicted of liquor infractions.

The most celebrated case involved six saloon keepers from Salina, including Peter Mugler. When news of the pardons reached the town, an impromptu parade marched up the main street, with the six men and the ousted county attorney, John Foster, in the positions of honor. Foster held aloft an American flag, which a local newspaper said had never been seen "at the head of a more disgraceful looking body of men." A protest meeting a few days later, which filled the opera house to overflowing, strongly condemned the governor's action. The *Topeka Capital* concluded that "the law is defeated, justice is defeated, the people outraged by an ignorant, obstinate and malicious usurper."[44]

In 1884 the Republicans nominated John A. Martin, who had been waiting for the call not very patiently since the mid 1870s. Though he had been a fervent antiprohibitionist, he swore that he would uphold the law if he were elected. Somewhat surprisingly, the dry Republicans found that declaration acceptable. When most of the anti–St. John men quietly returned to the fold, Glick's chances for a second term were doomed.[45]

AFTER YEARS OF BEING COURTED by the Prohibition party, John St. John finally allowed himself to be seduced in 1884. Undoubtedly pushed by the personal attacks of Republicans during the 1882 campaign, but also pulled by the opportunity of a national platform from which to espouse his consuming cause, St. John made himself available after the Republican National Convention. When that assemblage rudely rejected Frances Willard's plea for a plank on constitutional prohibition, the lifelong Republican left his party. A month later he accepted, with some reluctance, the nomination of the Prohibition party for president of the United States of America.

To Kansas Republicans the defection demonstrated that "in a moment of foolish pride," St. John had left the high road of unselfish devotion to a moral principle to satisfy an unquenchable political ambition. The presidential nomination occasioned no state pride, only shame that the former Republican governor would accept "an empty and hopeless nomination, the only purpose of which is to secure the defeat of the Republican ticket." Though the Prohibition party had attracted votes primarily from Republican ranks since it had fielded its first national ticket in 1872, there seemed to be little cause for concern. The party had never polled more than ten thousand votes in a national election, even with the renowned Neal Dow at the head of its ticket.[46]

St. John concentrated his efforts in the Northeast, especially in New York State, where he hoped to hold the balance of power between James G. Blaine, the Republican nominee, and Grover Cleveland, the Democrat. St. John was the target of a good deal of personal abuse during the campaign, including two attempts by would-be assassins. Kansas Republicans tried futilely to lure him back to his home state, where he could do less damage than in the East. His tireless efforts had raised sufficient concern by October to cause a group of New York "temperance Republicans" to request that he withdraw. He polled 150,369 votes nationally, including 25,016 in New York, which Blaine lost by only 1,149. Had Blaine carried New York, the Republicans would have retained the presidency.[47]

Astounded at the improbable turn of events that had cost them the White House for the first time in the postwar era, the Republicans were beside themselves with anger. Rarely in American history has a defeated politician absorbed more vitriol than St. John did after the 1884 election. Though other factors could be identified as contributing to the defeat, the Republicans were in no mood to wait for a multivariate analysis. In over one hundred towns across the United States the traitor was burned or hanged in effigy. The national press was pitiless in its attack. "We have not a very exalted opinion of Judas," fumed the *St. Louis Globe Democrat,* "but there were some good points about him, and he was in every respect superior to the brainless and mercenary sneak from Kansas."[48]

Building on the residual hostility from 1882, the reaction in Kansas was the most intense. The hate mail poured in; numerous towns held "effigy picnics." A Topeka partisan, Patrick H. Coney, achieved momentary national fame when he mounted a wooden box to make a scathing attack on St. John before a spirited Kansas Avenue crowd of three thousand while an effigy swung silently from a telegraph pole nearby. "I am sorry that the original of the effegy was not burned instead of the effegy," wrote one of Coney's admirers. "St. John is hated," Albert Griffin reported, because "hundreds of thousands . . . believe he is a hypocritical scoundrel, who has used a glorious cause to advance his own personal ends." "The ultra and insatiable prohibitionists," lamented Senator Ingalls, "with an ingratitude equaled only by their fatuity, made Glick Governor of Kansas and Cleveland President of the United States."[49]

In the election the temperance faction in Kansas remained loyal to the Republican party. St. John received only 4,495 votes, gaining almost no support beyond the hard-core third-party partisans. (It represented, however, about the same percentage of the total vote as in New York.) Two weeks after the election, delegates gathered for the annual convention of the KSTU, which had become uncharacteristically subdued since St. John's defeat in 1882. ("Is it dead, poor thing, or merely sleeping?") St. John made an appearance but was received coolly as he settled himself "within a circle of female friends." The convention promptly passed a resolution lauding the Republicans and condemning the Democratic and Prohibition parties. When St. John took the floor to defend the latter, hisses and catcalls filled the hall. The KSTU and its first president and original hero parted company for many years thereafter.[50]

St. John suffered one other, and more lasting, indignity at the hands of the vengeful Republicans. They continued to carefully nurture their hatred, the more pious even suggesting that the name of the fourth book of the New Testament should be changed. Since that project seemed to lie beyond their secular reach, they did what they could. In the halcyon days of 1881 the legislature had honored the popular governor by naming a new northwestern county for him. A bill introduced in the 1885 session proposed changing the county's name to Jennison. If it had been successful, that alteration would have merely shifted the honor from one temperance champion to another.[51]

During John A. Martin's second term in 1887 the evil deed was done, and St. John County became Logan County in honor of the recently deceased John A. Logan, a Civil War general who had been Blaine's 1884 running mate. The speaker of the house, whose name has disappeared into oblivion, gave the bill his unalloyed blessing: "I would to God that the name of St. John could be obliterated from Kansas history.'' The grand irony of the substitution derives from the fact that Logan had an ante-bellum record as a ''bitter'' opponent of Negro freedom and the Maine Law. As a Democratic legislator in Illinois, he had guided through the 1853 session a bill that made it illegal to aid and abet the immigration of free Negroes into the state. St. John had been arrested under ''Logan's law'' in Illinois in 1862 for befriending a homeless Negro boy.[52] The Free State of Kansas had made an interesting change in its political landscape.

Determined that the national party should never again be embarrassed on the temperance issue, a group of Kansas Republicans, led by Albert Griffin, organized the National Anti-Saloon Republican Movement in 1885. In Chicago in 1886, Griffin chaired a national antisaloon convention, whose chief goal was to pressure the Republicans into adopting in 1888 a platform ''of uncompromising hostility to the saloon.'' The thirty-man Kansas delegation to Chicago was composed of many of the leading political and business figures of the 1880s. The Executive Committee that the convention appointed included Theodore Roosevelt, who was then in his Dakota cowboy phase.

Despite the best efforts of Griffin and his committee the 1888 convention insipidly called only for ''all wise and well-directed efforts for the promotion of temperance and morality.'' Some credit accrued to the movement for preventing the reelection of President Cleveland, but the ''radical Kansas basis'' was clearly ''too advanced'' for a majority in the national party. As a war-horse of the party explained, the Kansas movement ''was irresponsible and irregular, . . . and the practical politicians were not disposed to encourage a factional, loosely connected, sentimental, and unauthoritative organization.''[53]

After the collapse of his movement and after nearly two decades as a zealous prohibition leader, Albert Griffin had a change of heart. By the late 1890s he had become as ardent a champion of moral suasion only as he had formerly been of legal action.[54] His defection represented one of the very few major personnel losses that the prohibitionists experienced during the nineteenth century.

KANSAS' MOST EMINENT HISTORIAN, James C. Malin, once wrote an article entitled ''Was Governor John A. Martin a Prohibitionist?'' Malin explored Martin's transformation from an avowed antiprohibitionist, at the outset of his first term, to an apparently avid prohibitionist a year or so later. Malin answered his own question in the affirmative, though he stressed Martin's devotion to the Republican party rather than to the social ideology.[55] Actually, Martin had significantly altered his staunch antiprohibitionist position of 1879–82 more than a year before he gained the long-coveted gubernatorial chair in 1885.

During the winter of 1883/84 Martin's newspaper, the *Atchison Champion*, had changed its antiprohibitionist stance sufficiently to catch the watchful eye of Albert Griffin. In January 1884 Griffin wrote that the tone was ''so changed as to indicate that Mr. Martin is unwilling that the great struggle for humanity shall end without his having done some good work on the right side.'' At about this time, however, Martin began to wonder if perhaps he had not gone too far, at least for Atchison, whose boasted defiance of the law, the drys said, was ''a vulgar byword and stench in the state.''

The *Champion* had published an editorial lamentation of the alcohol-induced death of one of the town's more prominent young men. ''There are more prohibitionists in Atchison this morning,'' it said, than ''before this sad ending of what promised to be a bright, useful and honored life.'' This seemed innocent enough,'but ominous rumblings sounded in the wet community, and the rival newspaper blasted the editorial as being too prohibitionist in tone. The apprehensive publisher then polled several dozen townsfolk to find, to his relief, that most agreed that the piece had properly spoken out in defense of ''the rights of home and family.'' By May, Martin had become sufficiently emboldened to advise Atchison saloonists to accept the inevitable and to take up other, and more honorable, occupations. By June he had declared that he did not favor resubmission and would not run on a platform that included it.[56]

Martin completed his ''conversion'' in the Statehouse and came to embrace prohibition warmly. The journalist Tom McNeal, who knew many Kansas governors intimately, said that Martin had become ''one of the most intense prohibitionists I ever saw.'' If the metamorphosis was genuine, it was also politically expedient. By mid decade the resubmissionist threat had been beaten back, and prohibition appeared to be permanently entrenched as the policy of Martin's cherished party and the law of his beloved state. When the public came to demand more rigid enforcement of the law, Martin responded promptly and with vigor. At the start of his second term he declared that his ''one ambition'' was to close every ''open saloon within the limits of the state of Kansas.''[57]

The legislature did what it could to help Martin realize his ambition. Based in part on bills drafted by the KSTU, in 1885 and 1887 the legislature passed a number of important new acts and amendments to the Benson Law. For the incorrigible cities, the Police Government Act gave the governor discretionary power to appoint police commissioners in those cities in which the liquor law was being flouted. A new law resuscitated the grand-jury system, which had been moribund for over twenty years. Opponents denounced the system as ''secret, sneaking, cowardly, inquisitorial, mean, vicious [and] thoroughly bad.'' To make sure that the right citizens got on the juries in the larger towns, a new law authorized the appointment of jury commissioners. They selected, from the list of qualified voters, prospective jurors ''possessed of fair character and approved integrity.''[58] No saloonists need apply.

The WCTU lobbied successfully for several bills of special interest to women. Henceforth, pharmacists would be required to obtain, on their permit petitions, the signatures of twenty-five women of the community, as well as of twenty-five men. Effective in 1886, instruction in physiology and hygiene, ''with special reference to the effects of alcohol stimulants,'' became mandatory in the public schools. Most importantly, and with decided implications for local law enforcement, women were permitted to vote in municipal elections beginning in April 1887.[59]

Acceding to pressure from the rural and religious communities, the legislature exempted from the law home-produced wine and cider and the sale of communion wine. All the other amendments to the Benson Law, however, were in the dry direction. The "era of the physician" ended as responsibility for selling for medical purposes passed solely to the pharmacists. To place that group on a more professional basis and to reduce the abuses, an act "to prevent incompetent or unauthorized persons from engaging in the practice of pharmacy" was passed. It created a state board, which was charged with examining and licensing pharmacists.

Other amendments to the liquor code changed the punishment for violating it from fine *or* jail to fine *and* jail; introduced search-and-seizure provisions; stiffened the nuisance-abatement section with an injunction provision; and increased the county attorney's enforcement powers. Private citizens were permitted to retain an attorney to assist in the prosecution of specific violations; suits could not be dismissed unilaterally by the county attorney before the court had heard arguments from the special counsel. And should the county attorney prove negligent, the new law charged the attorney general with full enforcement responsibilities within said county.[60]

THE NEW AND AWESOME responsibility that devolved on the office of attorney general would prove to be a political boon for some incumbents, a headache for many, and a greatly increased work load for all. Attorney General Simeon Briggs Bradford (1885–89), a descendant of the Puritan leader Governor William Bradford, became the first to function under the new circumstances. Bradford, a thirty-seven-year-old native of Ohio, had formerly served as county attorney of Osage County.[61] He brought to his work all the zeal of his famous forebear.

Bradford's first serious challenge came in June 1885 from the western frontier, where Dodge City remained as the last and most unregenerate of the cow towns. A visitor described Dodge as the "rendezvous of all the unemployed scallawagism in seven states. Her principal business is polygamy without the sanction of religion, her code of morals is the honor of thieves, and decency she knows not." Another put the matter more succinctly, if less grammatically, by cogently observing that "Francis Murphy don't live in Dodge."[62]

The furor was touched off by Albert Griffin, who, as a KSTU organizer, had delivered a well-attended temperance lecture at the Methodist Church and had organized a local temperance society. When he found ten saloons running wide open, he filed information against the sellers with the county attorney. When the latter refused to act, Griffin complained to Bradford, who assigned an assistant attorney general, A. B. Jetmore, to the case.

A few days later, Griffin, accompanied by Jetmore, returned to Dodge City, only to be met by a well-armed crowd of some three hundred who "seemed evil disposed." For the remainder of the day and well into the night, the well-lubricated mob ran wild, especially seeking out and assaulting the "offensive citizens" who had previously shown temperance proclivities. Since the sheriff and the county attorney had conveniently absented themselves for the day, Bat Masterson, the town's most popular citizen, had to protect Griffin and Jetmore from the vengeful mob. Griffin hurriedly advised Bradford "not to institute proceedings . . . until [you have] force enough . . . to render a massacre of peaceful citizens improbable." But the undersheriff soothingly assured everyone that the officers knew that this was "simply a little drunken spree of the boys, hence they did not interfere." Besides, Bat Masterson was in the crowd "and knowing this, they entertained no fears of there being any trouble, for they knew Bat would hold things level."[63]

Bradford himself went out to survey the scene of rebellion a week later. Met by a friendly crowd and generally well treated, he quickly discovered that the women of the WCTU represented the "backbone" of the temperance movement. "They discussed the question quite fully with me," he said, "and I found their views to be much more practical and sensible than those of many of the men." The district judge advised Bradford that a little patience would solve the problem, since Dodge City would soon become extinct as a cattle and cowboy center. Bradford took the advice, and within a year or so, Dodge City assumed the same peaceful mien as the other erstwhile wild-and-woolly cow towns.[64]

As the public increasingly called for law enforcement in the cities, the attorney general, with the governor's blessing, responded energetically. In early 1886 Bradford began "paying his respects" to the several dozen saloons of Atchison. Finding an "unbiased" jury in a wet town such as Atchison had become an almost insurmountable problem. But Bradford closed nearly all the saloons within a month, taking advantage of the 1885 law that had provided for civil-court injunctions to abate nuisances. When he attempted to apply the same remedy to Leavenworth, the district judge held that the defendant was entitled to a jury trial. Injunction cases against brewers in Lawrence (Walruff) and Atchison (Ziebold and Hagelin) ended up in federal court on petition of the defendants. But the issues were resolved satisfactorily for the state in 1887 when the United States Supreme Court handed down the *Mugler* decision.

Bradford then moved against the 218 saloons (his figure) in Leavenworth and claimed to have closed down all but some 10 percent of them, which remained to do a clandestine business "in some dark alley, garret or cellar." Proceedings to oust the city from licensing saloons proved successful, as the Supreme Court simply affirmed its decision in the 1883 Topeka case. Bradford also took action against the sheriff and the county attorney, forcing the latter to resign. In consultation with Governor Martin, police commissioners were appointed for Leavenworth and, subsequently, for Wyandotte (Kansas City) and Wichita as well. By 1889 an attorney who specialized in defending liquor-law violators, Lucien Baker (U.S. senator from 1895 to 1901), was declaring that there weren't "ten places in Leavenworth in which whiskey or beer can be obtained." A year later, another leading antiprohibitionist, Daniel R. Anthony, admitted that all the open saloons had been closed.

While this vigorous activity in behalf of law enforcement earned the attorney general the plaudits of the steadily growing temperance community, it also drew the ire of the "whisky faction." Many letters threatened bodily harm to the attorney general and his associates. Skull and crossbones signs, daggers, and coffins often adorned the bottoms of unsigned epistles. The lives of Bradford's assistant in Atchison County and of members of his family were endangered when a keg of powder exploded under their home.[65]

With the attorney general's office fully enmeshed in enforcement, it had to respond to a flood tide of letters from Kansans who were concerned about the liquor question. Bradford's zealous successor, Lyman Beecher Kellogg of Emporia (1889–91), felt the full impact of the deluge. A metropolitan police commissioner complained of a sheriff who released his liquor-law violators on election day (some of whom were "very much under the influence") to work for the Democratic ticket. Another police commissioner kept Kellogg up to date on his personal circumstance ("I have been giving them the hot end of the poker [but] I do not want to be slaughtered by these Hell Hounds in this way"). An antiprohibitionist lawyer felt that Kellogg had overestimated the degree of local law violation: "I am satisfied that you have been wrongfully informed as to the number of joints in this city"; but that Kellogg had underestimated the strength of the temperance sentiment: "We have more cranks to the acre and more spies, than any other city in the State."[66]

Many angry correspondents complained about the failure of their county attorneys to do their sworn duty. The writers usually offered only scant and obscure evidence of violations, which often had never been presented to the county attorneys. The latter countered that they had less than the full support of the "moral part of the community." In one case a seller, who had been arrested on twelve counts, had suddenly turned "very pious" and had joined the church. When the minister and the congregation had pleaded for mercy, the county attorney reduced the charge to one count. Several months later the minister complained about the county attorney and cited this case as evidence that the official was soft on violators.[67]

Petitions often called for the assignment to a county of an assistant attorney general to enforce the law. In one instance, Kellogg wrote to a state legislator who had signed a petition a few months earlier asking if he still felt that such action was called for. The representative responded that the need for outside help had passed since "at this time . . . [we are] as clear of Joints as a new England town of the most puritan class." In fact, he had forgotten all about the

"portition": "it must have been gotten up during the setting of the legislature
. . . as at that time I with lots of other members signed most everything in shape
of portitions presented thinking that no attention would ever be paid to them and
many times never read them [.] of course it was Rong and should not hav been
don."[68]

Two female officers of a local "Temperance Suffrage association" spoke to
a common problem when they wrote for help in closing the local saloon, which
masqueraded as a drugstore. The local officers had become mute, since a "drink
of whisky will close their mouths more affectually than a court plaster." "A man
that is known to be a habitual drunkard," they said, "can go in and sign any
persons name to the Statement no mater if he lives a thousands miles from here
and get liquor. Now please let us hear from you immediately or feel the affect of
your Power."[69]

THE CONSTITUTIONAL EXCEPTION for medical purposes posed one of the
largest law-enforcement problems. It remained a concern for nearly thirty years,
until a latter-day legislature applied the "final solution" to the drugstore
problem. Physicians had been so unhappy with the oath requirement in the
Benson Law that two years after it went into effect, no physician in Douglas
County had complied with that provision. A year later, "much the larger
number of physicians" in the state were still ignoring the law.

In his 1885 message, Governor Martin suggested changes in the law so as
not "to annoy or embarrass the members of an honored and honorable
profession . . . with vexatious restrictions, . . . oaths and forms." The legislature proceeded to lift entirely from the physicians the responsibility for
administering the medical provision and to place it squarely upon the broad
shoulders of the pharmacists.[70]

The amended law dispensed with the physician's oath and with the need for
a physician's prescription for medicinal purposes. It permitted druggists to sell
only on a written statement made by the applicant, which named the disease to be
treated and the amount and kind of liquor desired. The prescription became both
unnecessary and insufficient. Why did the KSTU recommend and why did a dry-
controlled legislature pass an amendment that required what appeared to be a
ridiculous self-diagnosis and seemed to be no clear improvement over the former
law?

The change came largely as a response to the pressure of the physicians and
of the more liberal minded, who felt that more "freedom of action" was needed
in obtaining medicinal liquor. It came at a time when factional disputes were
sundering the medical profession and when public confidence was declining
sharply due to the failure of such traditional practices as bloodletting and
purging. Moreover, physicians of the period did prescribe beverage alcohol for a
wide variety of illnesses, including digestive disorders, debility, and some
fevers.[71]

The reputation of druggists had been none too savory before prohibition. One of the arguments for the prohibitory amendment had been that it would "lift druggists . . . from being a race of outlaws to the place of lawful gentlemen." But after five years of prohibition, Attorney General Bradford stated that "if a large percentage of the persons now in the business were restricted to the limits of the county jail the communities in which they live would be better off." The Pharmacy Act of 1885 helped, as did the more restrictive qualifications mandated in an 1887 amendment to it, but the problem remained, even increased, as the sale of intoxicants made pharmacy an ever-more-lucrative economic venture. For most druggists it meant several hundred dollars a year in additional income, and for a few it meant a good deal more than that. An Arkansas City druggist, for example, cleared over $4,000 from the sale of liquor in 1885.[72]

The probate judges, upon whose discretion so much of the effectiveness of this section of the law depended, also had an economic interest in the volume of sales, at least for a few years. An 1887 amendment geared their fees from the liquor statements to the size of the county's population and limited to $1,000 per annum the amount to be obtained from this source. Before this, the judges had been receiving five cents for every statement filed by the druggists, which could produce as much as the governor's salary ($300 per month) in the most profitable cases. During 1886 the judges averaged $1,956 per person from this source, approximately doubling their regular salary, which had been considered adequate by itself. "Such conditions," the WCTU wisely noted, "do not make it easy for men to do right and hard for them to do wrong."[73]

One can reconstruct in broad outline the effect of the 1885 law on the behavior of the general population. Those who wanted to stay religiously within the law continued to obtain a physician's prescription before they would sign the druggist's statement. The law-abiding, but slightly less scrupulous, citizen filled out a statement whenever he had a legitimate need. But for those whose urges took them on an extralegal course, the simple expedient of listing a disease, real or imaginary, and signing one's own (or another person's) name to a printed form proved all too attractive.

The medical loophole conveniently widened just as the saloons were being driven out of business or underground, as joints, by Bradford and Kellogg. Drugstore sales tended to fluctuate inversely with the availability of joints, serving as a crude barometer of the pressure on the illegal outlets. For example, during a period of adversity for Topeka's joints in the late 1890s, monthly sales in drugstores rose from sixteen hundred to seven thousand over a period of three months. However, the effect on the total consumption of liquor of what amounted to the substitution of the open drugstore for the open saloon was decidedly negative. An 1885 calculation estimated that drugstore consumption in Topeka was about one-seventh of that associated with the banished saloon.[74]

The prodigious talent of Kansans for inventing diseases for the druggist's statement has passed into the treasured folklore of the state. That purchasers did offer a wide variety of ailments is supported by the 1886 statements of nineteen Osage County druggists, which listed over two hundred specific conditions. A tabulation of the statements from two Topeka drugstores in 1892/93 is presented in table 4.1

TABLE 4.1

DISEASES CLAIMED BY PURCHASERS OF ALCOHOLIC BEVERAGES
IN TWO SHAWNEE COUNTY DRUGSTORES IN 1892/93

Disease	Number
Colds	29
Indigestion, dyspepsia	27
Malaria, chills	26
Debility	12
Diarrhea	11
Lung, bronchial trouble	10
Rheumatism	8
Cramps	7
Bathing	7
Nervousness	5
Biliousness	5
Kidneys, bladder	4
Weakness	4
Mechanical purposes	4
Colic	3
Asthma	3
Flu	3
Other	11

Source: KSHS, Manuscript Department. The average quantity per sale was slightly less than one pint.

Twenty-five reasons were advanced for the 179 sales, with five (colds, indigestion, malaria, debility, and diarrhea) accounting for 59 percent of the total. The most popular ailments with the public were those for which physicians commonly prescribed beverage alcohol. In one instance the customer evidently changed her mind on the spot, scratching out "rheumatism" and inserting "putting up pickles." The amount per sale varied from six quarts to one-half pint, with the latter accounting for 49 percent of the total. The average is slightly less than one pint per sale. Whiskey accounted for 70 percent of the sales; beer, 13 percent; and alcohol, wine, and gin, the remainder.

An 1887 analysis of 1,172 sales in a "town of 4,000" by the State Board of Health reveals a similar picture. The same five conditions headed the list, accounting for 77 percent of the total. Beer (40 percent) and whiskey (36 percent) were the most requested remedies. Although women traditionally consulted physicians more often than men did, 93 percent of the drugstore requests came from men.[75]

For the general edification of the community, newspapers sometimes published the monthly pharmacists' report, which included the names of the purchasers and the kind and amount of liquor purchased. A Ness City (Ness County) publisher, who was a member of the Prohibition party, enlightened his community in this manner in 1885. Most of the purchasers took the publication of their names good-naturedly enough, worrying only (though with faulty arithmetic) that when the editor had inadvertently doubled the medicinal alcohol purchased, the people would expect "to find [our] condition 50 percent better than it really is." Some disgruntled customers didn't take the publicity so light-heartedly, however, for a few weeks later the publisher found that his type had been dumped in the local lake.[76]

When it became apparent that liquor wasn't as freely available as formerly, Kansas began to be flooded with patent medicines and other potables under a variety of names and guises. The Kansas Supreme Court had placed such beverages in the "third" category, that is, local juries were expected to render decisions on a case-by-case basis. The beverages that imitated weak beer, such as malt and hop tea, had a low alcoholic content, though their purveyors claimed that they had none at all. But the patent medicines typically contained from 15 to 45 percent alcohol. The famous cure-all for female complaints, Lydia Pinkham's Vegetable Compound, contained over 18 percent alcohol, about the same as that of wine.[77] Those vigilant old Swedes in Lindsborg had good cause for concern.

With the effectiveness of many standard medical treatments in question, the people had turned increasingly to patent medicines for relief. The value of such nostrums consumed by the American public rose from $3 million in 1860 to $75 million at the turn of the century. Though only one in five applications was accepted, the government granted over five hundred new patents for medicines in the 1880s. Only the labels, trademarks, and advertising copy were registered; the ingredients remained a deep, dark secret from competitors and the public alike. The lucrative business came to furnish a sizeable portion of the advertising budget of newspapers, the tawdry, gassy ads often taking up a large fraction of even the front page.

Almost every pharmacist made up special concoctions for his customers, but the biggest sellers were the nationally advertised brands. Prickly Ash Bitters ("cures laziness by cleansing the liver"), Boschee's German Syrup ("three doses will relieve any case"), Paine's Celery Compound ("no remedy ever accomplished so much good"), and a host of other panaceas promised cures for everything from pimples and flatulency to rheumatism and heart disease. And sometimes they lived up to their extravagant claims. Who can doubt that Parker's Ginger Tonic, which had an alcoholic content of 42 percent and was liberally laced with morphine, could deliver on its promise to bring sweet peace to the entire family: "The nursing mother . . . finds her strength and nerves restored by its use, while the mother's comfort . . . is imparted through the milk to her babe, making the little one happy, cheerful, free from pain, and disposed to refreshing sleep."[78]

A SURVEY OF COUNTY ATTORNEYS, which was made by the KSTU twenty months after the prohibition law went into effect, produced responses from sixty-six of the eighty-one organized counties. Of the 972 liquor cases that commenced in district and justice-of-the-peace courts, 75 percent resulted in convictions, 13 percent in acquittals, and 12 percent in hung juries. For 1884 the attorney general reported a 79 percent conviction rate, and by 1888 that had risen to 85 percent. For 1885, 44 percent of all convictions were for violation of the liquor statutes. The KSTU survey identified 708 saloons in the reporting counties prior to 1 May 1881; the statewide total was estimated at approximately 1,200. The survey reported an (underestimated) 313 saloons in December 1882, with twenty-five of the reporting counties being completely devoid of saloons. In 1886 the attorney general reported open saloons in only ten counties, and in early 1889 he announced that "the saloon has been banished from Kansas soil."

The number who held federal liquor stamps, a somewhat doubtful barometer of enforcement and consumption, plummeted from one per 674 persons in the period 1881–84, to one per 1,001 in 1886, one per 1,829 in 1887, and one per 2,220 in 1888. The 1888 figure was the lowest in the nation. Distilleries decreased in number from four in 1880 to one in 1889. The number of breweries dropped from thirty-nine in 1880 to seventeen in 1884 to three in 1889. The production of the distilleries and breweries (in 1889, 752 gallons and 8,290 barrels, respectively) went primarily for medicinal purposes through the drugstores. Estimates of consumption relative to the 1880 level varied from a grossly optimistic 1 percent through the 10 percent, claimed by Governor Martin and Attorney General Bradford, to 25 percent, claimed by the less sanguine. Ninety of the ninety-six probate judges who were surveyed in 1889 estimated consumption at 5 to 50 percent of the preprohibition level.[79]

In early 1890, Attorney General Kellogg systematically surveyed the county attorneys in regard to law enforcement and temperance sentiment in their counties. Their replies yield a composite picture of conditions at the close of the decade. Though the responses varied somewhat, they typically reported enforcement as being good to excellent. Many noted that the liquor law was enforced in the same way as other criminal laws. Obtaining juries that would convict on the evidence did not present a major problem in most locales. "It is no longer necessary here to select juries from any particular class of citizens," one respondent wrote, "as juries which are composed of persons of all political and religious faiths, whether prohibitionists or anti-prohibitionists, seem to deem themselves in duty bound to convict persons who sell liquor, where the evidence satisfactorily shows them to be guilty."

As a foreshadowing of events to come, the economically depressed western counties seemed to be preoccupied with their growing financial problems and consequently were little concerned with liquor-law enforcement. The cities, especially Leavenworth and Wichita, continued to make rigid enforcement difficult. Some bootlegging had developed in the counties bordering Nebraska and Missouri. But the great majority of the respondents reported that their situation had significantly improved over what it had been three to five years earlier. Consumption, such as it was, came principally from the drugstores, legal "foreign" importations, a few back-alley joints, and the furtive bootleggers. A composite estimate of public sentiment on the resubmission question placed the dry majority at from 60 to 70 percent.[80]

Additional evidence that resubmissionist sentiment was low and waning is found in the fact that the Democrats failed to call for repeal in 1888, and the legislators failed to file a resubmission bill in 1889, the first such omissions of the decade. As a result of elections in 1888 and 1889, the drys claimed the support of 153 of 165 legislators, 92 of 106 county attorneys, and 90 of 106 probate judges. "A large majority of Kansas people consider the saloon a sort of small-pox eruption," said the prominent Topeka attorney Charles S. Gleed; "Why should we want it reinstated?" Governor Lyman U. Humphrey (1889–93) administered the *coup de grâce* in his message to the 1889 legislature: "As an issue in Kansas politics, resubmission is as dead as slavery."[81]

At the conclusion of his second term, Governor Martin declared that "this State is, today, the most temperate, orderly, sober community of people in the civilized world." A year later, at their annual convention, fourteen hundred teachers echoed the governor's words when they grandly declared that prohibition had "elevated Kansas to a plane of civilization never reached by any people in the history of the world." A state senator from Mound City, Joel Moody, rhapsodized about the effects wrought by prohibition: "The old den has had the sunlight of righteous indignation let into it; the spigot has dropped out of the bung-hole; the bar-tender has left the State, or gone to work; the old rum-blossomed covey are bleaching out in the sunlight and soft rains of Kansas; and the wives of heretofore drunkards are singing their songs of praise, and their little girls once more wear new gowns and stick posies in their hair in honor of prohibition in Kansas."[82]

Although the cold facts hardly justified their more extravagant rhetoric, the prohibitionists had much to be grateful for and, apparently, much to anticipate as the new decade opened. The higher courts had affirmed the amendment and the law in all important particulars. A number of public figures, headed by Governor Martin, had converted to the cause. The prohibitionists had promised prosperity, and prosperity there was: the great rollicking boom of the eighties that brought broad smiles of confidence to even the most skeptical. The incidence of crime, pauperism, and drunkenness had decreased, at least somewhat, as the prohibitionists had predicted it would. And the open saloon had been banished from the land.[83]

From the confusion and defiance of the St. John period and from the inaction and recalcitrance of the Glick administration, support for the law and enforcement of it had steadily increased. If the state had been ill prepared for the new and radical policy in 1881, it had grown to embrace the policy fondly by the end of the decade. The aggressive prohibitionists had seized the momentum; the wet sector had been forced into sullen retreat. The relatively dry condition came in no small measure from the indefatigable work of the women, most particularly those who wore the white ribbon of the WCTU.

5

For God and Home and Native Land

The bonnets are on the increase, and . . . there is a great deal of determination in the bonnets.

—Kansas Woman's Christian Temperance Union

Municipal suffrage for women and prohibition send from the State the white-aproned gentry, and bring in return hundreds of thousands of white-aproned women, whose thanks go heavenward that Kansas, ever first in all good works, has produced the manhood that is proud to go on record in favor of banishing the rum fiend from the State, and giving woman the enfranchisement her position as man's better half demands.

—*Lyndon* (Osage County) *Journal*

WOMEN HAD BEEN CONTRIBUTORS to the temperance reform since its antebellum inception, though largely in a secondary role. By the 1870s a large pool of educated middle-class, Old Stock evangelical women stood anxious to participate in the cause in a more meaningful fashion. By this period, as Ruth Bordin has emphasized, women of the middle class had a significantly reduced economic role outside the home. For the first time they could devote most of their energies to child rearing and other domestic duties. Increased educational opportunities and a halving of the birth rate during the nineteenth century led them to an enhanced interest in the quality of life in the home and the impact of alcohol thereon.

The Woman's Christian Temperance Union was born in Cleveland in November 1874, delivered by midwives who had participated in the Woman's Crusade. The erstwhile crusaders wanted a national temperance organization that would make permanent "the grand work of the last few months." The convention adopted a constitution which had been drawn up by a committee headed by J. Ellen Foster, the Iowa lawyer and sometime visitor to Kansas. The organization was ecumenical from the outset, drawing broadly from the evangelical Protestant denominations. But the Methodists represented by far the largest minority among both the membership and the leadership. And of the inspirational fount there could be no doubt. "You have no need to be reminded," the presiding officer said, "that this is simply and only a religious movement."

Such an assemblage would have been impossible in the not-very-distant past, the delegates were told. Formerly, woman had been "no more than a slave to man," but the long-overdue change had been wrought by the "power of God." The convention adopted rules that excluded all males from active membership (debating, voting, office holding), though they could affiliate as honorary members. It adopted the white-ribbon badge, a total-abstinence pledge that was not unlike the Murphy pledge, and a motto that delineated their priorities: "For God and Home and Native Land."[1]

The WCTU got off to a sluggish start in Kansas, which lagged behind even her sister state Nebraska. Amanda Way attended the 1875 national convention and, as the Kansas "vice-president," accepted the responsibility for developing a state apparatus. But she became deeply involved with the Good Templars and the Murphy Movement and consequently did nothing to develop a statewide WCTU organization. A scattering of local unions did form in the larger towns, but these isolates hardly differed from ladies temperance societies that had been common in Kansas for two decades. Finally, in a tent at Bismarck Grove in September 1878, a state organization was brought into being.

For the first two years of its existence the incipient organization melted more or less indistinguishably into the general cauldron of proamendment activity. Only four local unions paid state dues in 1879, and only seven in 1880; in the latter year the state treasury received the grand total of $42.43. President Drusilla Wilson's (1879–82) decision to forego effective state organization in order to canvass directly for the amendment caused concern not only at national headquarters but also much closer to home.

In June 1880, Laura B. Fields of Leavenworth, who would become the third state president (1882–84), shared her anxiety with Frances Willard: "Our vice-presidents have done so little during the year, and Mrs. Wilson has been almost wholly engaged in work for the Kansas State Union [KSTU]. I regret to see . . . that she is again lecturing for the K.S.U. I hoped she would give the entire remaining time to the women's work. We must have different officers next year—a President whose heart is in the work above all other kinds. . . . This should have been a year of unusual activity in our work, for our peculiar situation demands it."[2]

In the fall of 1879, Wilson proudly reported to the national convention that "bright, young Kansas," with her upcoming vote on the amendment, was already "far in advance of her older sisters" and earnestly sought the convention's "fervent prayers" for her success. The 1880 convention bid "God-speed to Kansas as the pioneer in this grand endeavor" and moved that election day be observed as a "day of prayer" for Kansas.[3] But the most valuable contribution that the national organization made to the campaign was its illustrious president, Frances Willard. After a speech by Willard in Leavenworth, one of her admirers put her thoughts on paper, affording us an insight into the impact of the Willard charisma upon others:

> Well, Miss Willard "came and saw and conquered," and this is the feeling of the whole community. We can have but a meagre conception of what her power is by reading about it, or hearing of it from others; we must see and know her to understand just what she is. . . . Not a fault could be found with a single utterance she made, and the unanimous verdict from the most cultured and refined to the lowest in the audience, was that the lecture was in all respects perfect. As for our women, she left us all in a state of perfect infatuation. When I think of her and all the wonderful good she is doing my heart warms and glows, and I feel almost a reverent admiration for her. . . . And I pray that God will preserve her health and prolong her days of usefulness, for verily there is, in all the world, but one *Frances Willard.*[4]

In common with the other temperance organizations, the WCTU suffered from the slump in interest that followed the passage of the amendment. Many felt that temperance organizations were no longer needed, now that prohibition had been written into the state's fundamental law. After 1880 a number of local chapters simply ceased to exist. Only sixteen chapters appear in the treasurer's report of 1881, and as late as 1883 only twenty-five unions were active, a smaller number than the nominal total of 1879.[5]

"Distant whisperings" wafted in from the East in 1882 that the beloved national president was "distressed" about the state of the Kansas union. Outgoing President Wilson admitted that the organization was "not in complete working order as in the Eastern States." In 1884, President Fields said that the state union had been "almost swallowed up" by the amendment work which had been carried on "mainly by men." A lagging WCTU, she said, came as a surprise to outsiders, since Kansas had become the banner prohibition state. On yet-another sensitive topic she asserted that Kansas temperance money went largely to the KSTU, "leaving the crumbs to . . . the W.C.T.U."[6]

An issue that almost rent asunder the young organization stemmed from St. John's decision to leave the Republican party. He had become almost literally *Saint* John to the adoring women, and his popularity had remained high with them even after his bitter defeat in 1882. Most of the women were Republicans, or more accurately, they were married to men who were. But an increasing number, seen as "a dangerous element" by their Republican sisters, had followed the lead of Frances Willard and the national convention and had endorsed the Prohibition party. When St. John defected, bitter conflict ensued within the ranks of the state union.

President Fields and the Executive Committee recommended to the 1884 convention that it endorse the Republican state ticket but that it remain neutral at the national level, a concession to the "radicals," which they expected would be sufficient. But the convention rejected the national recommendation and resolved to support St. John. When the Democrats won the presidency, the more irate Republicans put the WCTU high on their list of culprits. "Christian republicans" became violent to their "frail but devoted wives," and threats of burning the WCTU women "in effigy" filled the air. When some people even accused the WCTU of being the chief agent of the Republican defeat, the indignant women acidly responded that no woman had voted in the election and few ever expected to during their lifetimes.[7]

The battle lines were firmly drawn at the 1885 state convention. When the president read the political resolution that pledged cooperation with the Republican party as long as it continued to be "the unswerving exponent" of prohibition, a "breathless silence" descended on the delegates. Sensing the need for a tension-reducing interlude, the president called for two minutes of silent prayer. After that pause the discussion "waxed furious, many ladies speaking pro and con, [and when] the storm was at its height, the very air was blue." The resolution passed by a comfortable margin, affirming the majority view that the state Republican party continued to be the true friend of prohibition.

Many members left the ranks, however, upset about the bitter contention and convinced that the WCTU should take no political stand at all. The controversy scarred and sensitized the union for years. Subsequent conventions deleted all reference to the Republican party and resolved only to succor any parties that "openly and unequivocally" supported the rigid enforcement of prohibition. Years later the leadership was still exhorting the members to avoid subjects that tended "to annoy others, or provoke unpleasant discussion." But die-hard Republicans continued to show irritation at the alleged role of the WCTU in the St. John campaign of 1884 and dismay at the persisting endorsements of the Prohibition party by the national conventions.[8]

THE DISTRESS of the state union at the specter of conflict stemmed largely from its religious nature. From its inception it had been characterized by "a peculiar religious earnestness." "Our Union was born of prayer," declared the first president, Mrs. M. B. Smith (1878/79), "and must be nourished by its power." At the tiny 1880 annual meeting at Bismarck Grove, four of the eight delegates who reported for local unions were wives of ministers; and they reported to a Quaker minister, President Drusilla Wilson.[9]

Although they derived their spiritual sustenance from the Christian message, the self-described "exceedingly timid" women had not organized to exchange devotionals or to debate the number of angels that could dance on the head of a pin. Watching their fathers, brothers, husbands, and, eventually, their sons march off each day to the manly and meaningful spheres of commerce and politics, they ached for some small influence in the world of affairs. Like their sisters of the ante-bellum era, they found a release for their pent-up sociopolitical energies in the temperance movement, an activity that kept them, at least initially, within their assigned sphere of domesticity.[10]

The women of the union channeled their vitality and dedication into practical pursuits. President Smith set the tone in 1878/79, when she established a coffee room in Topeka which served over four thousand meals in nine months to the victims of alcohol abuse. The women gave a high priority to newspaper columns, recognizing that "a world of good" could be accomplished through favorable publicity. In the early years they gained access only to the smaller, generally weekly, papers. But by 1890, in most of the state's leading dailies, they had established columns in which they could share their concerns.[11]

Advocacy of temperance in the 1880s began to take on a female hue so fully that a Kansas male could become suspect if he did not continually reaffirm his manliness while espousing "the woman's side" of the question. The wets called prohibition "effete" and called prohibitionists "human capons." Prohibition, they said, was a fad led by "half-baked preachers and senile old ladies." The wets did their utmost to keep the image of "short-haired women and long-haired men" before the public. The drys reacted with strained praise for their own, such as "manly," or, risking redundancy, paid the ultimate tribute to a colleague with "a manly man." St. John once heard, from an exasperated male constituent, that support of prohibition was "very good work for the women to be engaged in, but it's poor business for the Governor of a State."[12]

A state WCTU convention grew to become a social, religious, and political event of considerable moment. A meeting in a Baptist church in Ottawa provides some flavor of the character of the WCTU in the late nineteenth century. The church sanctuary stood resplendent, festively decorated with autumn leaves, white mums, Kansas sunflowers, and American flags, with small bunches of evergreens scattered here and there, proudly sporting knots of white ribbon. To the right of the pulpit, which was draped with white lilies, stood an easel, which lovingly held the portrait of the "sainted leader," Frances Willard. To the left a wooden table groaned with temperance books and pamphlets for distribution to the delegates. Scattered about the cavernous room were the colorful banners and mottoes ("Agitate, Educate, Organize") of the many local unions.

The proceedings opened with a spirited rendering of "Onward Christian Soldiers." A "quiet, restful" consecration service, conducted by the Quaker minister Mary Sibbitt, followed; the devotionals closed with an ardent prayer. The tone then changed abruptly as the resolute delegates settled down to serious, consequential, and secular business. Before the four-day meeting adjourned, the delegates had greeted, with an enthusiastic "Chautauqua salute," their special guest, Anna Gordon, private secretary to Frances Willard, and had listened to a special program put on by no less than "one thousand" Ottawa school-children.[13]

The WCTU of LeRoy (Coffey County) celebrates Temperance Day in the early twentieth century.

As the populace belatedly began to realize that the liquor law would not enforce itself and that public sentiment would play a critical role in that enforcement, the WCTU began to grow in strength and influence. By 1884 it had become sufficiently potent that a worried politician confided to a newspaper reporter that it was "much stronger than anybody knew."[14] But the politician anticipated the future more accurately than he described the present. The organization developed significantly under President Fields, but the catalyst that would explode the combustible mixture of energy and dedication had yet to occupy the president's chair.

FANNY H. RASTALL brought a badly needed business sense and superb administrative skills to the young organization. During her tenure as president (1884–91) the WCTU grew rapidly in effectiveness and power, ushering in a truly "golden era." A small woman with a squarish, "good face," which suggested a latent strength, she had married John E. Rastall in Milwaukee in 1868. A few years later they had moved to Kansas, where he became publisher of the *Burlingame Chronicle* and a prominent prohibitionist. "Strong-minded she certainly is," an observer said; "she is also soft-voiced, gentle, self-possessed and dignified in manner and convincing in argument."

Her talents first attracted the attention of the statewide membership during her years as corresponding secretary (1881–84). Initially she was so timid at the rostrum that she could make a public presentation only "with great difficulty." But she overcame her platform terror to develop into one of the movement's most reasoned and dynamic speakers—in great demand in Kansas and, later, throughout the region. She became the first Kansas woman to gain any prominence in the national organization. "One of the best executive officers" Kansas ever had left her state stewardship after seven eventful years to become the business manager of the national WCTU publishing enterprise in Chicago.[15]

As corresponding secretary, Rastall had doggedly urged the value of good record keeping and full, accurate, and timely reporting. Though despairing at times, she eventually impressed upon the membership the need for systematic reporting of their activities, lest their light remain hidden under the biblical bushel. Most responded with the requested details, though a few wrote only that while they were not "ousting any druggists or breaking any beer bottles," they felt they were "doing some good."[16] As president, she continued her efforts to perfect a businesslike organization and to graft onto the Kansas agenda Frances Willard's "Do Everything" policy.

The national president promoted a policy that directed the union's energies into a wide range of temperance-related activities, organized into some forty departments, each one headed by a national superintendent. The Kansas union had maintained only six departments as late as 1883, but under Rastall's leadership that grew to thirty-two by 1890. And the annual reports of the state superintendents soon reflected the thoroughness and earnestness of their president.

Twenty-five local unions, with 750 dues-paying members in 1883, expanded by 1891 to 148 locals, with 2,234 active members (and 428 honorary male members), organized along congressional district lines. The state treasury had only $14.25 on hand in 1879, but a decade later it could report that it handled over $11,000 annually, from which it paid a small stipend to a few of the top officers. In 1886 the union began publishing a monthly newspaper, *Our Messenger,* which filled a long-felt need for regular communication among the members.[17]

Rastall came into office shortly before Governor Martin and Attorney General Bradford assumed their duties in the Statehouse. The growth of the WCTU both contributed to and profited from the renaissance of temperance sentiment that Martin and Bradford triggered in the last half of the decade. During the early years of her tenure, Rastall railed against the laxity of law enforcement that would permit open saloons in the cities and the border counties. An avid supporter of the Prohibition party, she had no qualms about publicly accusing the Republican Bradford of slacking his duties and worse. That sally raised such a partisan outcry that she felt obliged to issue a statement that she did not "hate" the Republican party ("I . . . could not hate the republican party, any more than I could hate an erring or deceased friend"). Bradford angrily countered that of all the groups with which he had to contend, the third-party Prohibitionists were "the most unreasonable, unjust, unfair and untruthful."[18]

As the saloon menace subsided, Rastall turned her attention to the drugstores. No progress was made, she said, by replacing open saloons with "open drug stores." Many formerly honorable druggists operated businesses that protective husbands and brothers had pronounced "unfit for ladies to enter." By 1887 she had mellowed enough to declare: "Kansas leads the States in the dignity with which she has clothed her womanhood. But the ultimate is not yet attained and nothing less than complete triumph will satisfy." Witnessing as well as contributing to the marked improvement in enforcement that the Martin-Bradford administration had produced, she had become an enthusiast by 1889. Responding to a California inquiry about the success of prohibition, she noted that only "a few conservatives," clinging stubbornly to outmoded ideas, were still opposing the law. Prohibition, she wrote, is "the greatest success on record. I do not believe anything else ever succeeded so well in so short a time."[19]

IRONICALLY, THE MOST CONSEQUENTIAL accomplishments of the WCTU occurred in the legislative halls, where the women were totally devoid of formal authority either as legislators or as electors. The remarkable list of legislation that was significantly influenced by them in the 1885, 1887, and 1889 sessions would have brought acclaim to a throng of veteran lobbyists, which they were not. Skillfully utilizing their chief weapon, the petition, the women participated fully in a series of social and political reforms which led the *New York Times* in 1889 to call Kansas "the great experimental ground of the Nation."

They played a role in the modification of the Benson Act, though clearly a secondary one to that of the KSTU. The section of the 1887 amendment that had the most direct impact on them required an applicant for a druggist's permit to acquire the signatures of twenty-five "reputable" local women in addition to twenty-five male electors. When a number of women refused to sign any permits whatsoever, President Rastall counseled prudence. Concerned that the most notorious druggists would end up with the permits, she reminded the sisterhood that they had petitioned for this provision. She urged them to sign petitions when they could be reasonably assured that the druggist would follow the law. Women in large numbers proceeded to sign petitions selectively, though there is scant evidence that the new law materially diminished the size of the drugstore loophole.[20]

The union incorporated concern for the use of tobacco, as well as alcohol, into its rapidly expanding program. White ribboners circulated tobacco-abstinence pledges and successfully lobbied the 1889 legislature for a law prohibiting the sale of tobacco to children under sixteen. ("There is no more common sight in our cities than to see little boys from six to ten years old with cigars in their mouths.") They had gained even more satisfaction two years earlier, when they had convinced the legislature to raise the age of sexual consent (the age of protection, they called it) for young females from the ridiculously low figure of ten to eighteen.[21]

Quietly and of a sudden, in 1889 the senate passed a bill that lowered the age of consent back down to twelve. Alarmed at the threatened loss of their hard-earned victory, Rastall sent out a clarion call to the local unions, asking for their immediate response in what had become a familiar and effective mode. Affording us an insight into their *modus operandi,* the corresponding secretary has told what happened next: "And they came, by telegraph, and mail, as quickly as our women could get pencil and paper in hands and bonnets on their heads, and get out to secure the thousands of names which came pouring into the legislature. The latter did not even take the Bill out of [the] committee room and our law was preserved for the time at least."[22] And such it remains to the present day.

Acting on a suggestion by Olive P. Bray of the Topeka chapter, Rastall wrote the membership in 1886 about her concern for the "poor needy" girls who lacked a proper influence "to arrest them in a course that must lead to degradation and worthlessness." The state had an orphans' home, a reformatory for boys, and a home for "fallen" girls, she said; but "what shall we do for the class . . . who are in danger of being led into paths of vice, and whose natural guardians are unworthy the trust given to them?" In the next mail the local unions received from their president legislative petitions to establish an industrial school for girls.[23]

The 1887 legislature did not act, but Fanny Rastall did. "We find ourselves," she told the membership in January of 1888, "pledged to open an industrial school for girls on or before February 1, 1888. . . . By doing so, it is hoped a double purpose will be secured—rescue for those in peril and a training to fit them for useful lives, as well as a demonstration of the fact that girls are not all angelic, but need such care as the state does afford its boys." She then made a plea for material support for the school at Beloit "to aid a helpless class which, if left unaided, will very soon become a hopeless one."[24]

The unions did not disappoint their intrepid president. In response to her "send everything" call, they sent money and books, furniture, and coal. A generous but pragmatic farmer donated an unruly cow, which neither he nor his burly sons had been able to manage. But the cow caught the spirit of the occasion and quickly became "subdued." The school opened promptly in February, as Rastall had promised, and by January 1889, twenty-five "unmanageable" girls between the ages of ten and fifteen, who had been referred by their relatives or by law officers, were calling it home.[25]

The WCTU flooded the 1889 legislature with petitions for the state to assume control of the home. The state's Equal Suffrage Association endorsed the WCTU project and helped to circulate petitions in its behalf. Though the union's treasurer, Sarah A. Thurston, spent nearly full time in the legislative halls, the issue remained in doubt until the closing hours, when the bill finally cleared both houses. The concrete action taken by the union had evidently spoken more eloquently than its entreaties alone. The bill made the Girls' Industrial School a state institution and authorized $25,000 for a new building. Later that year, during the state convention, the cornerstone was laid in a formal ceremony which included Frances Willard and Anna Gordon as the honored guests.[26]

Recognizing the critical importance of the education of children during their formative years, the national WCTU placed Scientific Temperance Instruction (STI) high on its list of priorities. Under the ardent leadership of the national superintendent of the STI department, Mary Hunt, the WCTU sought to weld the temperance reform firmly to the leading scientific and educational thought of the day. In this it achieved marked success; by the early 1880s it had gained the support of many leading educators and of the American Medical Association.

The cornerstone of the educational campaign was the absolute insistence that alcohol in any form and in any amount was a poison to the human system. Mary Hunt characterized her five-year search for appropriate authors and publishers of physiology and hygiene texts as an "almost superhuman effort to secure absolute scientific accuracy, not modified in favor of occasional or moderate use of alcohol." When moral suasion that was directed at teachers and school boards produced disappointing results, the STI campaign shifted to the political arena. In 1884, four northeastern states had compulsory temperance-education laws; by 1900 nearly every state in the nation had them.[27]

The first agitation in Kansas came in 1882, when the state WCTU convention urged women to use their school ballot to elect board members who would adopt textbooks that espoused temperance. (The 1861 legislature had given all women the right to vote in school-district elections, the first state in the nation to take such action.) That same convention appointed a blue-ribbon committee of Amanda Way, Drusilla Wilson, and Laura Fields to petition the legislature for a STI law. With Fanny Rastall as superintendent of the department from 1883 to 1885, not unexpectedly, things began to happen. Employing a full measure of letters, circulars, petitions, and speeches, she built a broad base of public support which included the endorsements of teachers, ministers, college presidents, the superintendent of public instruction, and both gubernatorial candidates. "With voice and pen" she "led the hosts, aided by . . . a rank and file of earnest workers."[28]

The 1885 legislature passed a temperance-education law that was based in part on a bill drafted by Mary Hunt, which she had sent to Rastall. It provided that, beginning in 1886, no certificate could be granted to teachers who had not passed an examination "in the elements of physiology and hygiene, with special reference to the effects of alcohol stimulants and narcotics [which included tobacco] upon the human system." It required the instruction of public-school pupils in all the grades, but disappointingly for the temperance workers, it did not provide specific penalties for noncompliance.[29]

Over the next several years, temperance instruction hardly received the same attention as reading, writing, and arithmetic. Teachers seemed sympathetic, but their preparation was meager and the available materials were fragmentary and uneven in quality. Enforcement, also uneven, was especially lax in the larger towns. The WCTU raised the consciousness of the teachers and improved their preparation by securing a place on the program at numerous county normal institutes. Heretofore at these training sessions, the union charged, teachers had been taught that one could use alcohol and tobacco with impunity and that the production of drunkards was mainly due to inadequate mothers. The most effective piece in the union's arsenal was a forty-page pamphlet, published in 1889, entitled "An Appeal to Kansas Teachers." Written by Laura M. Johns of Salina and subsidized by an affluent patron, the pamphlet went to every one of the state's 11,500 public-school teachers.[30]

The brilliant Laura Mitchell Johns had become a certified schoolteacher in her native Pennsylvania at the precocious age of fourteen. She had later married a schoolteacher in Illinois, and they had moved to Salina in 1883, when she was thirty-four. She quickly became a leading figure in politics, organizing and serving as the first president of the Kansas Women's Republican Association; in suffrage, as the eight-term (1887–95) president of the Kansas Equal Suffrage Association; and in temperance, as the state superintendent of the STI department of the WCTU.

Widely utilized by the teachers, the Johns pamphlet reminded its readers that though saloon keepers inveighed against drunkenness, they forgot to add that "it is wrong to drink." To teach temperance properly, one must impress on the students "the fact which science had indisputably established beyond question, that the use of alcoholic beverages *at all* is an abuse of the human system in exactly the proportion to the amount taken." "The children in our schools do not need to be *reformed*," Johns said, "but they do need to be *formed*. . . . To teach the danger of forming the awful, insidious, inexorable appetite, is the especial province of the teacher."[31]

In the 1890s a prestigious national study group, the Committee of Fifty, concluded that temperance instruction for children in the primary grades might be undesirable and that moderate drinking should not be universally condemned. Some teachers in the Northeast began to oppose the temperance-education laws as being a reflection on their professional integrity and as a threat to academic freedom. But in Kansas the State Teachers' Association wholeheartedly endorsed the education law in the 1890s and resolved in favor of "retaining, enforcing, and, if necessary, strengthening the present prohibitory law."[32]

For the first time, an 1897 law required statewide uniformity in textbooks. The State Textbook Commission in 1902 adopted a WCTU-approved physiology series. A year later the union excitedly reported "splendid results" with the new adoption. Well into the twentieth century the WCTU continued to pressure local school boards and county superintendents for better enforcement and to give STI, along with woman suffrage, its highest priority. Shortly after temperance education had become mandatory, a union member commented to her colleagues that it could not be expected "that any one here . . . to-day will live long enough

Laura Mitchell Johns (courtesy of the Kansas State Historical Society, Topeka).

to see the great and good results that will come . . . from the work.'' Though precise measurements of the efficacy of social education are impossible to obtain, ''great and good results'' surely followed. The educational seeds that were sown abundantly in the late nineteenth century produced flowers that bloomed profusely in the early twentieth: in Kansas, as the second "golden era" of temperance; in the nation, as the Eighteenth Amendment to the federal constitution.[33]

AGITATING FOR WOMAN SUFFRAGE provided WCTU members with their most profound political indoctrination, enabling them to make one of their most far-reaching contributions. Suffrage came somewhat uneasily to the national WCTU agenda, as an adjunct to its basic concern for protection of the home from harmful influence. The vote for women, it was said, would result in the election of temperance-inclined public officials and would reverse the growing saloon influence in politics. In Kansas the "timid" women and their male allies argued that woman's vote was essential for the full success of the prohibitory law. Although their rhetoric remained in the "home protection" mode throughout the nineteenth century, suffrage as a "natural right" became increasingly important to both state and national leaders. Endorsement by a solid middle-class organization such as the WCTU helped to defuse the frequent charge that the incipient reform was "radical."[34]

The Kansas union first formally supported woman suffrage in 1880, a year before Frances Willard persuaded the national WCTU convention to take a stand and four years before the formation of what became the principal Kansas suffrage organization, the Equal Suffrage Association (ESA). The Kansas suffrage movement had been hibernating since its crushing defeat in 1867. Save for the endorsement of the small Temperance party in 1874, the union's resolution in 1880 broke the prolonged silence at the state level, initiating a continuum of agitation which ultimately culminated in full state suffrage.

Several local suffrage organizations formed between 1879 and 1884 under the leadership of Anna C. Wait of Lincoln, a member of the Prohibition party. In 1884 the union welcomed the statewide organization (ESA) to the fray and cooperated intimately with it thereafter. The memberships soon overlapped so extensively that one union member, just returned from a state ESA meeting, exclaimed that "the familiar faces of so many white ribboners, almost made us feel that we were in a W.C.T.U. convention."[35]

The union reaffirmed its 1880 suffrage resolution throughout the decade. The 1882 blue-ribbon committee (Way, Wilson, Fields) was charged with petitioning the legislature not only for a STI law but also for the ballot for women. That convention also indignantly declared that the time was nigh when men would have to decide, as regards suffrage, whether "their wives, mothers, sisters and daughters shall be longer classed with lunatics, paupers, criminals and Chinese." Delegates at the 1884 state convention heard Frances Willard assert that "this reform [prohibition] can never be accomplished until woman has her vote." In 1886 the state union again called for the ballot and, employing very modern phraseology, demanded laws that "shall make no discrimination on account of sex."[36]

The union's support for suffrage during the early 1880s had consisted of general importunities only, nothing specific or operative. But with the emergence of the cities as the chief obstacle to prohibition enforcement and the formation of the ESA, municipal suffrage began to look both attractive and possible. Supported by the omnipresent petitions of both the WCTU and the ESA, plus the aggressive "fact and force" tactics of their leaders, Fanny Rastall and Laura Johns, the prospects for a municipal suffrage law for women in 1886 seemed bright. But the outlook for the bill, which had been introduced by Senator Lyman Beecher Kellogg, quickly dimmed behind the cloud of a "Third Party scare"—that is, charges of collusion between the suffragists and the Prohibitionists, who were still anathema to the dominant Republicans. But with renewed vigor (and additional petitions) the suffragists guided the bill to an easy victory in 1887. The Republicans overwhelmingly supported the measure; the Democrats overwhelmingly did not.[37]

Distraught at the suffragists' victory and its temperance implications, the Democrats saw a deep, dark triangular plot. They claimed that the Republicans, alarmed at continuing defections to the third-party Prohibitionists, had struck a devilish bargain with the WCTU and with the Methodist Church. If the church would encourage its wayward ministers to retrace their steps back from the Prohibition party, the Republicans would support the temperance-related bills (of 1885–87) and would allow the WCTU and its minions to call the legislative tune. The real purpose of the suffrage law, the Democrats said, had been less to further the interests of temperance than to further those of the Republican party. Eschewing a direct attack on the women, the Democrats claimed that "designing politicians and unscrupulous office hunters" had duped the sincere but gullible females. "Hypocrisy, deceit, immorality, and oppression still reign in high places," they said, "and hide their hideous faces under the mantle of religion, sincerity, good morals and human freedom."[38]

Passage of the bill delighted the women, of course, since it gave to them a right not enjoyed anywhere else in the thirty-eight states. The triumph of the white ribboners' tasted all the sweeter when they received the personal congratulations of their revered national leader, who had often referred to Kansas as the state of "First Things." "The Women of Kansas," she wrote to them, "live on the world's vanguard plot of ground; the freest, the most favored. We all wish we lived there, too."[39]

The suffragists held high hopes for the new law. The *Lawrence Journal* editorialized that "prohibition has come to stay in Kansas. The last stave in the whisky keg has been broken in by granting suffrage to women in the cities." In a circular letter to pastors of all the Kansas churches, Fanny Rastall rejoiced that God had given Kansas men "a large reinforcement in their conflict against evil. The home guards are to be sent out to aid the main army in every city in Kansas."[40]

The law, which permitted women to vote for municipal officials in cities of the first, second, and third classes, became effective with the April 1887 election. To increase interest among the potential voters and to instruct them in their new responsibilities, Rastall, for the WCTU, and two officers, for the ESA, coauthored and distributed fifty thousand copies of a leaflet addressed to the women of Kansas. The flyer gave specific instructions on registration and voting procedures and a sketch of the duties of the several city officers. It asked a series of questions that were calculated to put the new electors in the proper frame of mind, such as: "Do you not wish to have all dram shops, gambling dens and houses of prostitution closed in your city?" The WCTU also sponsored mass meetings before the election in order to stir up additional interest. At one of them an observer noted that it was "hard to tell whether it was a political meeting or a good, old Methodist love feast."[41]

Although only twenty-six thousand women, compared to sixty-six thousand men, voted in the election, virtually everyone, except a few disgruntled Democrats, pronounced the event a grand success. The sun did not gyrate in its orbit, nor did the earth tremble on its axis as the "timid" women exercised the franchise for the first time. The election actually proceeded in a more orderly fashion than usual, and not surprisingly, the men appeared better behaved than usual.

Franklin G. Adams, executive secretary of the Kansas State Historical Society, and William H. Carruth, a prominent professor at Kansas University, made a detailed study of the election. Adams later wrote to Frances Willard what she most wanted to hear: "In every instance," he said, "the women voted for home and fireside." Actually, the female voters tended to follow the voting preferences of their menfolk, which was overwhelmingly Republican, though they did favor temperance-inclined candidates to a somewhat greater extent, when presented with a clear choice. As the *Atchison Patriot* said, "The women generally voted the political sentiment of the head of the household, and the women of very few Democratic husbands or fathers were registered."[42]

The little city of Argonia (Sumner County), population four hundred, surprised itself and all the world by electing Susanna Madora Salter, a twenty-seven-year-old Quaker with four children, as the first woman mayor in the United States. By 1900 she had been joined by about twenty-five others in Kansas, at least half of whom headed all-female city councils. An officer in the local WCTU, Salter saw a great potentiality in the new law: "Woman's ballot as a temperance weapon," she said, "will be as powerful as dynamite is destructive."[43]

Municipal suffrage for women did improve the quality of the candidates for office, resulting in some local dry victories and an earlier retirement for the "bummer element." But suffrage did not fulfill Salter's prophecy, nor did it usher in the dry millennium. As an instrument of prohibition enforcement it was less consequential than, say, an injunction in the hands of a county attorney eager to rid his community of saloons. Extension of the franchise was, not a cause, but a result of the sharply accelerating dry momentum that began in 1885—though it supplied an additional push—nor was it sufficient to stem the wet tide that ushered in the new decade. The novelty of women voting passed quickly, as did the satisfaction that the suffragists derived from their original reform. Only five months after the 1887 election the WCTU unhesitatingly renewed its demand for full suffrage.[44]

The package of temperance-related legislation that was influenced by the WCTU in the 1885–89 period materially aided in sustaining the pronounced shift in public opinion in the dry direction. But events on a grand scale would soon transpire to turn the drys' sanguine optimism to black despair. Unforeseen circumstances would threaten to engulf the newly enfranchised women and to overwhelm the most conscientious of enforcement officials.

6

The Wet Nineties

The signs of the times are portentous.
—Kansas Woman's Christian Temperance Union

The Populist party was organized for the purpose of correcting certain economic evils. . . . I did not join the Populist party to hunt joints nor to fight resubmission.
—Governor John W. Leedy

It is the privilege of every adult person to judge what he shall take into his stomach.
—Democratic candidate David Overmyer

The one source of ridicule abroad and trouble at home, which, like the poor, is always with us, is our prohibitory law.
—Ed Howe

THE FIRST SERIOUS BREACH in the temperance dike during the 1890s came suddenly and from an unexpected source. In April 1890 the United States Supreme Court ruled, in an Illinois-Iowa case, that liquor which had been shipped into a prohibition state could be sold once within the state if retained in the "original package." This meant that Missouri liquor dealers could legally ship their product into Kansas and sell it to customers there through an agent. The decision represented a clean victory for the interstate-commerce clause of the United States Constitution over the police power of the states.[1]

Within days the prohibition situation in Kansas changed dramatically. In all the larger cities and in many of the smaller towns, "original package houses" or "Supreme Court saloons" sprang up like toadstools from the damp forest floor. Missouri wholesale dealers flooded Kansas, not only with the usual cases, kegs, and barrels, but also with individual bottles of beer and half-pints of whiskey wrapped loosely in "original," flimsy pasteboard cartons. Stout, mustached German saloon keepers tended their flourishing businesses "with an exultant and defiant mien." The unanticipated oases attracted large crowds of imbibers and

106

many of the simply curious, who gawked wide-eyedly at the huge liquor supplies and the novelty of open selling.[2]

Outraged, the temperance-inclined organized and fought back, fully determined to resist the "invasion by Missouri whiskey hellions." In some communities, church bells sounded the alarm that called the townspeople together for discussion and action. Furious citizens demanded that the dealers desist and called on the officers of the law to repel the invasion. In a throwback to the Woman's Crusade of 1874, ten members of the Lawrence WCTU visited a saloon and pressured the owner to close it. Images of the ancient territorial struggle abounded as the original-package ruling became the Dred Scott decision of temperance and the Missouri liquor dealers became the "border ruffians." "This state has been invaded by Missourians once before trying to . . . [fix] a hateful institution on it," said one county attorney, "and now [they are] invading it again for the same purpose."[3]

The temperance passion reached a grand crescendo on July 16, at a Topeka convention called by the KSTU and attended by three thousand "desperately in earnest" delegates. The meeting drew many prominent businessmen and leading politicians, as well as several hundred of the "best women." That evening on the Statehouse lawn, a mass assemblage of twelve thousand listened to rousing calls, by KSTU's President Jimmie Troutman and others, to resist the federally induced invasion and to petition Congress for redress. "Fighting Joe" Hudson, publisher of the *Topeka Capital*, lived up to his name as he read to the cheering throng a long list of defiant resolutions. "There wasn't power enough to bring Kansas into the union as a slave state," a speaker roared in conclusion, "and there is not power enough in the union to make Kansas a saloon state."[4]

The "monstrous decision" resulted in a great deal of legal activity and nearly led to a serious state and federal confrontation. When Governor Humphrey and Attorney General Kellogg urged local officers to curb the outbreak, numerous arrests followed. The saloonists were accused of keeping "nuisances," of selling from opened packages, or of permitting drinking on the premises. But no sooner were the arrests made than the lawyers for the accused obtained their release through habeas corpus proceedings in the federal district court. In order to stop this legal revolving door, the exasperated federal court enjoined county attorneys and other local officers from making further liquor-related arrests. The plucky governor then asked the attorney general to continue the good work in lieu of the neutered county attorneys. For several tension-filled days the two sides pawed the ground and glared angrily at one another.[5] A showdown was averted only by a new development in Washington.

With a great deal of pressure from Kansas and other dry-inclined states, Congress passed the Wilson Act in August, which divested liquor of its interstate properties upon its arrival in a state. The law nullified the open-package decision and forced the rapid closure of the saloons. The drys' joy was dampened in October, however, by a curious ruling by two federal district judges, one of whom, C. G. Foster, had long been an unabashed enemy of prohibition. They ruled that since the state prohibitory law had been enacted before the Wilson Law, it remained inoperative with respect to original packages until the state legislature reenacted it. The decision lit "the fires anew in the prohibition altars all over Kansas." As the case went forward on appeal, the open-package houses reopened, though on a more limited scale than before. In May 1891 the United States Supreme Court unanimously struck down the opinion of the federal judges, and open-package saloons became permanently enjoined.[6] But the prohibitionists had received a psychological body blow from which they would not fully recover for years.

THE MOST DISTRESSING CIRCUMSTANCE that befell the prohibitionists in the nineties did not arrive as suddenly as a supreme-court decision, but its roots were deeper, and its consequences were more widespread and lasting. During the amendment campaign the drys had confidently predicted that an era of prosperity would follow the passage of the amendment, as a natural consequence of the reduced consumption of alcohol. They then merrily rode the prosperity wagon that rumbled through most of the eighties and, of course, took credit for it as often as they could.

But by 1888 the boom had begun to fizzle out, and a year later it had totally collapsed. Overextension by too-eager farmers and other entrepreneurs, high interest and railroad rates, sharp declines in the prices of corn and wheat, and several years of bad weather for crops had all conspired to produce a major depression, which extended well into the new decade. Discontented, debt-ridden farmers coalesced around a third party, the People's party, or Populists, to issue a serious challenge to the dominant Republicans and to alter profoundly the temperance landscape, which had stabilized during the preceding decade.

The Populist party came into being as a response to pressing economic issues, and though it included many avid prohibitionists, it never took a formal stand on prohibition. In 1890 a Populist leader declared that "the issue this year is not whether a man shall be permitted to drink, but whether he shall have a Kansas home to go to, drunk or sober." Annie Diggs, a Populist leader who had been an official in the Prohibition party and was active in the WCTU, claimed that she was neither surprised nor disappointed that the national convention had soundly rejected a prohibition plank. "No person who is conversant with . . . the purpose of our political revolution," she said, "could . . . expect that any other than the industrial and economic issues would be made vital or prominent." But to the delight of the Republican press, John St. John sniffed in disgust that a "third whiskey party" had been born.[7]

Though it never included a prohibition plank in its platform, the Populist party wrestled fretfully with the question, and with the companion issue of woman suffrage, throughout its decade-long existence. These volatile social issues became major points of contention within the party and between it and its sometime allies, the Democrats. Populists came to the party in subequal numbers from Republican, Democratic, and Union-Labor ranks. They divided not very cleanly into two groups: "middle-of-the-road" ideologues, who were strong for prohibition and woman suffrage and were uninterested or hostile to fusion with the Democrats, and the more pragmatic fusionists, who were often antiprohibitionist and antisuffragist and were anxious to avoid these issues because they so offended the Democrats with their substantial German constituency. The ideologues failed to write prohibition into the party platform, but they did influence the 1890 convention to nominate a prohibitionist for governor and, in 1894, were successful, after a bitter convention battle, in gaining party endorsement of a woman-suffrage constitutional amendment.[8]

A THIRD DISCOURAGING CIRCUMSTANCE for the drys in 1890 related to events that had been transpiring on the national scene. Passage of the amendment in 1880 had lifted the national temperance movement from the doldrums and had sparked a renaissance which produced a second major wave of prohibition activity. Voters in Iowa (1882), Maine (1884), Rhode Island (1886), and North and South Dakota (1889) all adopted the "Kansas plan." If one included Vermont and New Hampshire, which still retained statutory prohibition, eight states embraced prohibition in the 1880s, the largest number since the initial wave of the 1850s. But in fourteen other statewide elections during the decade, culminating in a bitter contest in Nebraska in 1890, the constitutional proposition had been defeated, sometimes soundly. Twelve of these defeats came within a three-year period (1887–90) to plunge the rising hopes of the movement, at the beginning of the decade, into gloomy despair by its end.

The most devastating reversal occurred in Rhode Island. In 1886 that state had incorporated prohibition into its constitution, a welcome surprise to the drys, since the state included in its electorate a high percentage of Catholic voters. But just three years later it did what many in the movement had complacently believed to be virtually impossible: it had proceeded to vote prohibition out again. Iowa lost its amendment in a court ruling (1882), South Dakota followed Rhode Island in dropping the amendment (1896), and Vermont and New Hampshire repealed their laws (1903). The prohibition states had once again dwindled to three: Maine, North Dakota, and Kansas. The second national wave had dashed furiously but futilely against the rocks of public opinion.[9]

With adoption of the amendment, Kansas began to rival Maine as the crown jewel of the national movement and as the principal bane of the liquor interests. As the decade progressed, national attention focused approvingly on Kansas and the broad impact of its antiliquor amendment. But by 1890, the state's image had begun to suffer as a result of the recessions both in the Kansas economy and in the national prohibition movement. The eastern press shifted to a more caustic mode, with the question of how long the state could forestall repeal lurking just below the surface of the frequently derisive editorials.[10]

In a critique from a source closer to home, the *Omaha Herald* noted that the population of Kansas had shrunk by some fifty thousand in the late eighties and attributed the decrease to prohibition and the politicians who kept that policy in force. "The people will not stand it," the paper warned, "and if the politicians rule, the people will move on to a place where they do not." The Topeka attorney Charles S. Gleed, responding in a national magazine, *Public Opinion,* claimed that the loss could be readily accounted for by the 1889 rush to Oklahoma and by three years of drought in the western half of the state. He wryly added that it was the first known instance in human history in which a decrease in population had been ascribed to too much temperance. "Thousands of families" had come to Kansas because it was a prohibition state, he said, and "the world may depend on it that Kansas has never lost a citizen she cared to keep, because she has scourged the saloons out of the holy temple of her homes and institutions."[11]

The effect of the prohibitory policy on the size and composition of the state's population continued to be a matter of speculation for years. The wets claimed that the policy drove out the Germans and the more "liberal-minded" and discouraged them from immigrating. The drys countered that the enhanced attractiveness to the temperance-inclined more than compensated for such losses. The apparent impact of the policy on the state's religious composition can be seen in figure 6.1.

Following the dichotomy suggested by Paul Kleppner and Richard Jensen, the religious denominations were divided into two groups, based on their attitudes toward prohibition (see chap. 1). During the 1870s neither the evangelical-pietists nor the liturgicals had established a clear numerical superiority. But during the 1880s the evangelicals increased at a phenomenal rate, while the liturgicals remained almost constant. The major evangelical spurt came during the second half of the decade, a period during which the antiliquor policy became much more firmly established and much better enforced.

During the decade the state's population increased by 43 percent; the liturgicals gained 23 percent, and the evangelicals, 147 percent. The predominant evangelical denomination, the Methodists, gained 128 percent, while the principal liturgical group, the Roman Catholics, increased by 17 percent. The evangelical to liturgical ratio increased from 1.33 in 1880 to 2.68 in 1890. This profound shift in religious composition had a significant influence on the political response to prohibition and probably saved the amendment during the "dark nineties."

During the 1890s the harsh economic conditions overshadowed everything else, and the official closing of the frontier in 1890 reflected the fact that immigrants could no longer be as selective in their choice of future homes. More directly, the relaxed enforcement mode, which began in 1890 and continued into the twentieth century, markedly reduced the effectiveness of prohibition as a selective filter. Reflecting these circumstances, the ratio of the two religious

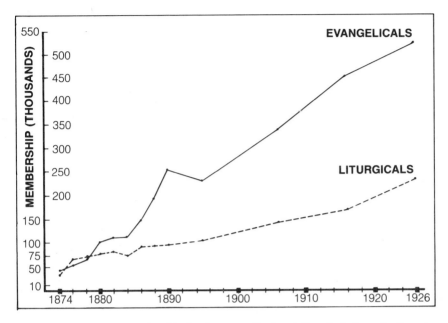

Fig. 6.1. Growth of membership in the evangelical and liturgical denominations in Kansas, 1874–1926.

groups stabilized at a relatively high value, not falling much below 2.0 during the twentieth century. By 1890, then, the state's characteristic religious profile had clearly been established and has been sustained thereafter, though the membership of both groups has increased severalfold.

In the nonprohibitory and competing state of Nebraska, a very different profile developed. In 1890 the evangelical to liturgical ratio was 1.35, one-half that of Kansas. In that year the liturgicals represented 27.2 percent of the total churched in Kansas, 40.8 percent in the United States, and 42.5 percent in Nebraska. During the twentieth century the Nebraska ratio has ranged from 1.10 to 0.61, less than one-half that of Kansas. Relative to the evangelicals, the liturgicals continued to be two to three times as numerous in Nebraska as in Kansas. Although a variety of factors determined the precise ratio at any given time, prohibition policy strongly suggests itself as the most salient cause of the differential development of the two groups in Kansas and the contrasting pattern in her sister state Nebraska.[12]

THE ECONOMIC UNREST and the original-package decision, coupled with the "foreign" agitation, encouraged the growth of resubmissionist sentiment in the state. Public opinion shifted substantially from that of early 1889, when the newly elected Governor Humphrey could confidently declare that resubmission was "as dead as slavery." During the summer of 1889 the *Kansas City* (Missouri) *Times* began sustained agitation for resubmission, claiming that a new election should be held forthwith, because the voters had gone to the polls in 1880 amid "camp meeting excitement." The Democratic paper said that Kansans should immediately throw off "the yoke of hypocrisy which their politicians have placed on their necks." Now on the defensive, the drys lamely countered that Missouri should be the one to resubmit the question in order to obtain the blessings of prohibition.[13]

Republican resubmissionists had been more or less active since 1882. They represented a group of men who, though firmly Republican in outlook, had been unable or unwilling to reconcile their political views with prohibition. Even the nomination in 1884 of the moderate John A. Martin had not placated them. They met at the same time and place as the Democratic Convention, but carefully nurtured their Republican proclivities by endorsing a platform similar to that of their erstwhile colleagues in all save the temperance plank. In return for their support of the state Democratic ticket, they were sometimes permitted to name the lieutenant governor, as in 1884 when the Democrats endorsed their nominee, Cyrus K. Holliday, as Glick's running mate.[14] As the radical, or St. John, wing of the party diminished in strength, some resubmissionists returned to the fold or, alternatively, joined the Democrats or Populists. With the renewed interest in resubmission in 1890, they all became more hopeful and more visible.

Much of the interest in resubmission centered in the Wichita area, where a resubmission club claimed eighteen hundred members in Sedgwick County, most of whom were Republican businessmen. The club asserted that prohibition had brought a "cloud of officials," with consequent costs that had become far too great for the suffering public to bear, and had put "many a blathering hypocrite into office . . . , but it won't do so hereafter."

The emergence of the Populist threat provided the resubmissionists with an additional weapon. In a letter to the chairman of the Republican National Committee, the president of the Kansas Resubmission Club wrote that prohibition had "no place in the policy of the [state] Republican party" and warned that a continuation of the policy would bring "disaster." The secretary of state put the matter more precisely: "I would rather have republican principles win at the polls without the endorsement of prohibition than to have the party defeated with it."[15]

The Republican resubmissionists published two lengthy pamphlets in 1890, entitled "Prosperity and How to Obtain It" and "Looking Forward: or Kansas Redeemed," in which they presented mostly financial arguments, trying to take full advantage of the prohibitionists' discomfiture at the miserable turn of economic events. The most provocative thoughts in the pamphlets came from the pen of federal Judge Cassius Gaius Foster, who ruled on the state law in the original-package cases.

True to both his Roman and judicial heritages of impartiality, Judge Foster admitted that prohibition had reduced consumption in Kansas "to a greater or less extent" and that the saloon had disappeared in some localities. But prohibition, he said, had discouraged the immigration of "hardy and industrious" people and had produced, instead, "an army of soft-handed nonproducers, who live by looking after the moral[s] and habits of their neighbors." He felt that having to sign the form at the corner drugstore in order to obtain a pint of whiskey "degraded" his "manhood": "Fie on a law that treats the citizen as a malefactor and unworthy of trust and confidence."[16]

Anxious to take advantage of the mounting public pressure and fearful that momentum on the volatile question might shift again before the 1891 legislative session, resubmissionists of every political hue agitated for a special session of the legislature. Group petitions and individual letters urged the governor to issue the call. The drys answered with their own much-more-numerous petitions, and on May 4, ministers across the state, except for Catholic and Episcopalian ones, devoted their sermons to resubmission and woman suffrage. The *Topeka Capital* added a conciliatory note, calling the resubmissionists "the greatest liars on earth."

In late May, just as the original-package saloons came into full bloom, the resubmissionists convened in Topeka to hold an audience with the governor. Humphrey endeared himself forever to the beleaguered prohibitionists when he refused to join the resubmissionists at their meeting in the house chambers.[17] Resubmissionist sentiment receded somewhat after that embarrassment, but the blood pressure of the drys elevated a few months later at the prospect of a severe scrambling of their comfortable political situation.

The 1890 election returns had brought a rude shock to the heretofore invincible Republicans: the Populists had captured 92 of the 125 House seats and had carried 5 of the 7 congressional districts. With Governor Humphrey at the head of the ticket, standing squarely "for sound Republican doctrine and for prohibition," the Republicans did manage to salvage all of the state offices, with one startling exception. The official who was most prominently linked in the public mind with the enforcement of prohibition, Attorney General Lyman Beecher Kellogg, had been defeated.

Hoping to end their party's endorsement of prohibition, the wet Republicans blamed the antiliquor policy for the crushing losses and offered Kellogg's defeat as exhibit number one. "Prohibition Kellogg," they charged, had made the liquor law "his specialty," as indeed he had. But an alternative explanation is not difficult to find. Kellogg had run slightly ahead of the rest of the Republican state ticket, and yet he was the only one to be defeated. Apparently without any prior planning, the Populists and the Democrats had fused on the attorney generalship, and only on that position.[18] Thus Kellogg became the first Republican, but hardly the last, to fall victim to the fusionist policy of the Populists and the Democrats during the nineties.

THE MAN WHO WON the attorney generalship and became the first statewide fusionist officeholder was John N. Ives, a Democrat from Sterling who had resided in the state for only a few years. He was something of a political unknown, though he was known as a staunch antiprohibitionist. He came to his new position with economic, not social, reform priorities. But as attorney general he inherited the unenviable task of responding to the liquor-related correspondence that flowed in from dismayed and angry citizens who were unwilling to accept anything less than bone-dry conditions in their communities.

The rumor mill had it that Ives would deliberately sabotage law enforcement in order to promote resubmissionist sentiment and repeal.[19] However, no compelling evidence has been found that this was his primary purpose. He frequently reminded his correspondents that the prohibitory law should be enforced because it was the law. But where his predecessor Kellogg had been prompt, cheerful, accommodating, and encouraging with his clientele, Ives was often dilatory, curt, obscure, and dissuasive with his. He struggled manfully with the eternal question, but at times—many times—it seemed about to get the best of him. Along with a series of governors and attorneys general who would hold office over the next fourteen years, he profoundly wished that the whole exasperating matter would just go quietly away.

Much of Ives's correspondence was with and about county attorneys. Citizens frequently complained that their county attorney was not doing his job and requested that an assistant attorney general be assigned to the county. Such requests were often accompanied by only the most sketchy and unintelligible evidence of liquor violations. One county attorney, who had been "turned in," acidly commented that if the petitioners had consulted him first, "they would have known more and guessed at less."[20]

Occasionally a nervous county attorney defended himself even before a complaint had reached Topeka, but the accused usually waited to respond to the attorney general's request for an explanation. To one official, Ives wrote that he had been presented statements, which, if true, showed "a shameful neglect of duty upon your part." To this he received a long, rambling reply, which began thus: "Now General, I presume your experience . . . has taught you, that it did not require a great deal of ability, any alarming degree of patriotism, nor any extraordinary love for the majesty of the law, in some individuals, especially four political enemies, to lay back in their most virtuous easy chairs and in pious tones that would do credit to a thoroughbred Pharasee of the B.C. period to roast . . . the County Attorneys of this state."[21]

The character of the frequently female "informers" was a common theme in the response of the county attorneys. Greeley County's attorney wrote that "two malcontents" had "worked the ladies up." "Mrs. Dr." Rachel Packson, a physician who was mayor of Kiowa, stirred things up enough in her town to be labeled as "very Crankey." She was overly fond, the county attorney said, of posing "as a martyr and saint and gain[ing] a cheap notoriety by her letters to and interviews by the newspapers.'' The assistant attorney general for Ellis County took the prize for hyperbole. He solemnly told the attorney general that a female complainer who belonged ''to the class that no one can please'' had been blackmailing the jointists by offering them ''protection'' from the WCTU in return for financial considerations![22]

One of Ives's most persistent ''pen pals'' was Ben S. Henderson, a prominent Populist who was appointed as assistant attorney general for Cowley County in 1891. A zealous prohibitionist, Henderson had ''graduated'' from the Keeley Institute—that is, he was a reformed drunkard. He had been assigned to the premier temperance county primarily to bring defiant Arkansas City to heel. When he took legal action against the popular county attorney for conspiring with violators of the liquor law, Henderson found himself in the vortex of hostilities and the subject of personal abuse. He wrote Ives that ''I now have upon my hands a war, the likes of which never was known in a community . . . claiming to be law abiding citizens.''[23]

Through their prolific correspondence, Ives grew fond of Henderson and began to share unguarded thoughts with him, personal views that he would have been loath to confide to a less understanding colleague. He asked Henderson to take firm action to stop the liquor selling at the old-soldiers reunion at Arkansas City. These annual reunions, which featured Republican fellowship and liquid refreshments in equal proportions, had become notorious for their open flouting of the liquor law. Ives's concern for enforcement, he told Henderson, would, of course, apply equally to any group but ''more especially . . . with reunions designed to strengthen the party [that] has passed as the great reform party, and [that is] responsible for the prohibitory enactments of this state.'' A few weeks later, in a particularly biased mood, Ives wrote: ''We, as executive officers, are not responsible for the statutes which have been placed upon our statute books by the representatives of a party [that] . . . openly boasts of being custodian of all that is good, pure and moral.''[24]

While Ives wanted to be of service to his constituents, he hardly was disposed to lead a temperance crusade. He felt especially hard-pressed when he received a well-formulated request for action that was based on substantial evidence. Such was the case when sixty-nine residents of Junction City asked for his help in ousting city officials for permitting flagrant liquor selling. The well-developed case deserved a succinct, clear-cut response. Instead, Ives gave them over three thousand words of legal gobbledegook, liberally sprinkled with quotes from the Declaration of Independence, the United States Constitution, and other equally impressive and totally irrelevant documents.[25]

As the months passed, Ives grew increasingly frustrated with his liquor-law responsibilities and more caustic in his responses to the public. To a county attorney he confided that he was getting ''very weary of the annoyance'' of letters complaining about lax officials. When the president of the Carbondale (Osage County) WCTU reported that they needed his help ''desperately,'' he testily responded three weeks later that he had been busy with more important matters and could not be expected to give "personal attention to complaints coming up from every hamlet."[26]

The WCTU proved to be his greatest nemesis, but it inadvertently prodded him into the most satisfying accomplishment of his administration. During the winter of 1891/92 the white ribboners deluged Ives with petitions demanding that he stop the sale of "hop tea" and malt. In a moment of sheer genius, Ives hit upon the final solution to his most vexing problem. He prepared a lengthy circular letter, addressed to the state president of the WCTU, but he had it distributed "to almost every village and hamlet in the State."

In the circular, Ives carefully but firmly explained that his official powers were much more limited than the average citizen could possibly imagine. Whatever evidence they had should be shared first with their county attorney, but they needed to understand that both he and the county attorneys had many other "very grave duties" to perform besides worrying about prohibition. The people read his unmistakable message loudly and clearly. In his formal report at the conclusion of his single term, the attorney general proudly proclaimed that as a result of his circular, "the communications upon that subject . . . have very materially decreased."[27] So also, we may be sure, had enforcement of the law.

THE ELECTION OF 1890 also led directly to the unseating of the veteran United States Senator John James Ingalls (1873–91). The unexpected flood of Populists into the Kansas House of Representatives sealed the fate of Ingalls, who they felt was insensitive to their economic concerns. Born in Massachusetts of a Congregational lineage, Ingalls grew up to become a "Christian agnostic," with perhaps a greater emphasis on the noun than on the adjective. An Atchison lawyer, he had been a major drafter of the Wyandotte Constitution and a creator of the state seal and motto.[28] Kansas produced no more conspicuous politician in the nineteenth century on either the state or the national scene.

Down through the decades, several Kansas politicians, whose views on temperance fell somewhere to the moist side of John St. John, struggled fretfully with their public position on prohibition. John J. Ingalls may be taken as a type specimen of the species for the nineteenth century. Ingalls always kept liquor in his home and even made his own wine, at least in the preprohibition period. Temperate in his own drinking habits, he often condemned drunkards, but never drinking. While public opinion was still crystallizing in the early 1880s, he cautiously ventured that perhaps the law was not working, and by 1883 he had been labeled in the press as an antiprohibitionist. His Senate record on national temperance legislation was consistently on the wet side. And his opposition to woman suffrage was as complete as for prohibition: "In politics the virtues of women would do more harm than their vices."[29]

With growing public support for the prohibitory law, which began to manifest itself by the middle eighties, Ingalls found himself in a position not unlike that of his fellow Atchisonian, Governor John A. Martin. They both held deep attachments for Kansas and for Republicanism but no affection at all for prohibition. They didn't ask for it, they didn't need it, they didn't want it; but there it was in all its pristine beauty, the hated official doctrine of their beloved state and party. Immersing himself in the mechanics of enforcement and the enthusiasm of the movement, Martin became a convert. In far-removed and worldly Washington, D.C., Ingalls remained recalcitrant. He began to bob and weave, hedge and trim, for his own political survival.

His trimming exercises were aided immeasurably by his extraordinary literary talents, the most impressive that any Kansas politician has ever possessed. Over a period of several years, beginning in the late eighties, Ingalls made a number of statements about prohibition in private letters, in state and national magazines, and in public speeches. In his most celebrated piece, written in 1889 for *Forum,* a national magazine, he made a lively defense of Kansas prohibition.

In the ten-page essay he declared that prohibition was "right in principle" and repeated approvingly many of the standard temperance arguments concerning its efficacy in reducing poverty and crime and in creating a salubrious environment for the young. The drink habit, he said, was "dying out," consumption having been reduced to only 10 to 25 percent of its former level. For those who were concerned about the liberty issue, he stated, somewhat cryptically, that the impacts of the law "practically cease with the closing of the saloons, leaving personal liberty unimpaired." And in a paragraph of pure Ingallsese he wrote: "Kansas has abolished the saloon. The open dram-shop traffic is as extinct as the sale of indulgences. A drunkard is a phenomenon. The barkeeper has joined the troubadour, the crusader, and the mound-builder. The brewery, the distillery, and the bonded warehouse are known only to the archaeologist."[30]

Two years later his tone and thrust had changed diametrically. The law was being widely ignored, he said, and for good reason. "This condition does not imply," he sarcastically noted, that "the advocates of prohibition who make no protest are canting hypocrites, snivelling Pecksniffs or unprincipled pretenders. . . . It shows the inefficacy of statutory morality; the superficial quality of virtue created by act of the legislature; the futility of attempting to compel communities to observe laws that reason rejects, or to refrain from innocent indulgence because there are some who cannot resist the temptation to excess."[31]

Ingalls's several pronouncements on temperance during this period left his readers and auditors, both friend and foe alike, puzzled and bewildered, which evidently was his purpose. A frustrated reporter for a national publication went to a prominent Republican, Daniel R. Anthony of Leavenworth, for some enlightenment on the senator's mercurial views. Another interviewed Ingalls, along with the rest of the Kansas congressional delegation, when the resubmissionist fever approached its zenith. He obtained clear-cut statements from all the others (they uniformly opposed resubmission), but the perplexed editor could only report that the senator "expresses himself after a somewhat Delphic fashion." One detractor described Ingalls's statements on prohibition as "ingeniously arranged in links like sausage, so that you can take a Prohibition link, or a license or local option link, just as you wish."[32]

It is a remarkable fact that John J. Ingalls remained senator for as long as he did in temperance-inclined Kansas and an ironic one that he was replaced by a devoutly dry Populist in a substitution that had almost nothing to do with temperance and almost everything to do with economics. As to Ingalls's "true" feelings, perhaps he summed it up best in a sarcastic remark that he made to the press a few months after his senatorial demise. "I am myself a prohibitionist in practice," the former senator said, "that is to say, I never take a drink except when I want it."[33]

THE ECONOMIC UPHEAVAL directly and indirectly produced a significant relaxation from the level of law enforcement that had been gained during the period 1886 to 1889. Concerned with the more immediate and pressing problem of economic survival, the people lapsed into apathy and eventually into silence on the liquor question. Seeking a winning formula to reassume its accustomed position of dominance, the Republican party retreated dramatically from its forthright espousal of prohibition during the 1880s. In 1892 it called for "the full, vigorous and manly enforcement" of all laws, specifically mentioning prohibition. But for sixteen years beginning in 1894, the state platform did not include a syllable of encouragement for prohibitionists. This retreat caused the Methodists to threaten to withdraw the support of the "Christian element" from the party unless it maintained its fidelity "to this supreme question."[34]

Laxity of enforcement during the 1890s permeated every governmental level from the Statehouse to the precinct. A series of governors and attorneys general and myriads of local officials gave less because the people expected and accepted less. By mid decade the forces of law and order were in headlong retreat. Even the common practice of assigning assistant attorneys general to the most troublesome counties had ceased.

Attorney General Fernanda B. Dawes (1895–97) lamented that his efforts to enforce the prohibition law had produced few tangible results in spite of the fact that "more time has been spent for its enforcement than for all the others combined." He appointed an assistant attorney general for Sedgwick County, and for six months "an incessant warfare was carried on." But in the end, enforcement lost because the officers failed to receive the "moral support of the people." Especially in the urban areas, the locals viewed the attorney general's appointees as "interlopers and meddlers." Dawes decided henceforth simply to work more closely with the county attorneys, since he didn't believe that "in a single instance" his appointments had resulted "in a particle of good being done."[35]

This elaborate joint in Junction City was operating on the "fine" system near the turn of the century (courtesy of the Kansas Collection, University of Kansas, from the Joseph J. Pennell Collection).

The practice of "fining" joints on a systematic basis for the benefit of the municipal treasury began to creep back in the larger cities, and even the middling-sized towns such as Winfield, Salina, Abilene, Junction City, Clay Center, and others began to imitate the manners of their big-city cousins. The rural countryside remained relatively dry, but in one form or another the saloon returned to over half of the counties of the state. A conservative estimate placed the number of joints at one thousand in 1897 (0.7 per thousand of population, compared to 1.2 per thousand in 1880). As its critics had claimed, prohibition in theory had brought local option and license in practice.[36]

The degree of visibility of the joint varied considerably with the time and the place. Of the four first-class cities in 1890, Topeka forced its jointists to run the most clandestine operations. This condition stemmed in no small part from the energy of the "crusading" Shawnee County attorney Charles Curtis (1885–89), who subsequently became vice-president of the United States (1929–33). The police caused something of a sensation in 1891, when they discovered in the downtown area what surely must have been one of the most humble liquor dispensaries in all of Christendom.

Fritz Durein, a prominent turn-of-the-century Topeka jointist, carefully hides his wares at his Hall of Fame Saloon (courtesy of the Kansas State Historical Society, Topeka).

The raiders found the joint hidden off an upstairs back room, tucked in amongst a barbershop, a tailor shop, a bakery, and a grocery. Masquerading as a closet and lit by a solitary gas jet, its sixteen square feet scarcely accommodated the proprietor and two customers. The raid interrupted the libations of the lone customer, who unfortunately turned out to be a city councilman. In the basement, which was honeycombed with a labyrinth of long dark hallways and small dank cellars, behind an "ironed and bolted" door, they found the liquor "warehouse," which served the puny upstairs joint.[37]

The opposite end of the visibility spectrum was represented by the brazen and seedy Klondike, not a single joint, but an entire hamlet of them, situated strategically three miles south of Leavenworth, hard by the National Old Soldiers' Home. During its heyday in the late 1890s the Klondike included some thirty rickety "dives, saloons and murderous dens," which specialized in prostitution, gambling, and mayhem. They preyed on three thousand disabled Civil War pensioners from the home, who were "too weak in body and mind to defend themselves either against temptation or violence." Despite a 1891 state law that made it illegal to sell to residents of the home, the veterans continued to flock to the joints, especially on pension day. Most spent their meager stipend all too freely, some had been attacked and robbed, and a few had been murdered. One disturbed citizen declared that "language is simply inadequate to convey the awful enormity of this diabolism of inebriety and debauchery."

The public, especially members of the KSTU and the WCTU, pressured Governor William E. Stanley (1899–1903) to do something about the Klondike. The numerous Leavenworth saloon keepers joined in the chorus, righteously claiming that they were "entitled to protection from these interlopers." But the governor continued to apply his patented "do nothing" policy until June of 1899, when the chief administrator of the home asked him for help. Responding with reluctance, Stanley hired two Leavenworth lawyers to prosecute the proprietors of the Klondike, and by the end of the year the area had nearly been closed down. The federal government helped with a directive that any pensioner who was found patronizing a joint within one mile of the home would be discharged. Some limited activity rekindled within a few months, but the Klondike never again regained its former glory.[38]

While some of the antiliquor activity deprived the working class of its friendly glass, other economic levels also were disadvantaged under the law. Social clubs organized primarily for drinking purposes and usually with a middle-class membership became relatively common during the 1880s. Actually, drinking clubs had been on the scene years before prohibition came to Kansas. In 1875 an illegal club in Hiawatha (Brown County) had generated a series of armed confrontations, a jailbreak, a posse of angry citizens, and extensive litigation before it was finally closed.

Clubs bought liquor wholesale, for consumption by their members on the premises. Numerous variants developed on the basic plan, probing for the weakest spots in the law, but the Kansas statute seemed to cover most every exigency. It classed as a misdemeanor the patronizing or maintenance of clubrooms in which liquor was kept for the purpose "of use, gift, barter or sale" or for "distribution or division" among the members. In 1899 the State Charter Board began to require social organizations that applied for charters to insert a clause that no liquor would be available at the meetings. This precaution was taken after the Free Thinkers' Club of Wichita, which had been chartered as a "literary" society, turned out to be "a plain everyday drinking" club. Among the several sources of "leakage" in the prohibitory system, drinking clubs contributed a persistent though relatively minor volume.[39]

Historically, the people of Kansas have tended to be democratic in their philosophy and unostentatious in their manners. Class distinctions have gone relatively unnoticed as the more affluent have generally maintained a low profile, eschewing conspicuous consumption, especially in the rural areas. In this egalitarian sea the Topeka Club appeared as a small island of elitism. Organized in 1889, it quickly became the home away from home for a number of the "most respectable people" in Topeka and for many of the most "distinguished men" across the state. "It affords a place of meeting," explained the *Topeka Capital*, "where gentlemen can come together to discuss the news of the day and the interests of the city." And to enjoy a friendly glass with their peers, it could be added.

All went well in the sedate quarters of the Republican gentlemen until 1893, when the Populist governor, Lorenzo D. Lewelling (1893–95), appointed a Democratic chief of police, Henry C. Lindsey. Lindsey closed the working-class joints and then cast his egalitarian eyes in the direction of "the upper ten," which included most prominently the Topeka Club. "The only difference between a club and a joint," the chief explained, "is that the club sells liquor by wholesale and the joint at retail. I am going to do my part toward closing them all."

He proceeded to confiscate a great deal of liquor at the Topeka Club and to arrest seven members on the premises. Among the latter was the star-crossed Joseph C. Wilson, who, as mayor ten years earlier, had signed the very ordinance under which the arrests were made. Perhaps his mother, the "mother" of Kansas prohibition who was now far removed in Indiana, never heard the news.

The arch defender of prohibition, the Republican *Topeka Capital*, thought that Chief Lindsey had not played the game fairly. "There is no more respectable institution of its kind in the country [than] the Topeka Club," it sputtered, "probably none so jealous of the observance of the spirit of the law." Seeing it all as a Populist plot, the paper accused Lindsey of "malice" in equating the Topeka Club with the repulsive "liquor holes" of Topeka. The seven defendants accused Lindsey of more than that, filing $10,000 damage suits against him and five other officials. Though the action was later dismissed, Lindsey's defense cost him $1,300. He seemed to feel that it was worth it, however.[40]

SPORADIC AND ISOLATED antiliquor violence, often the work of women, manifested itself throughout the decade, as the frustrated drys on occasion took the law into their own hands. The Kingman WCTU, "with songbook in one hand and axe in the other," raided several joints in 1890. In an 1891 protest against illegal drinking and gambling, women from Madison (Greenwood County) smashed the windows in the mayor's home and in the drugstore-saloon. Foreshadowing more celebrated occurrences to come, in 1894 a Salina woman, armed with an axe, demolished the furnishings in a saloon, which included a picture of "Venus at the Bath." At Woodbine in Dickinson County, angry citizens celebrated their Christmas in 1898 by dynamiting a recently established joint. At Wellington a mixed crowd of WCTU members and young men chose gentler methods by visiting all of the town's joints and praying for their deliverance. The mayor of Fort Scott received the most unkind cut of all when the Methodist Church publicly expelled him in 1899 because of his inefficiency in closing the saloons. The mayor's wife, whose sympathies are not known, was president of the local WCTU.[41]

The most important temperance victories of the 1890s, such as they were, occurred in the halls of the legislature. Dry anxieties about the predilections of the new political party reduced perceptibly when the 1891 resubmission bill drew only one-third of the house votes needed for passage. The legislature continued to receive lengthy petitions on the subject as each side sought to impress the lawmakers with the popularity of its position. The resubmissionists were aided by a number of short-lived, secret male organizations that sprang up, such as the Personal Liberty Association, the Army of Liberty, the Order of Sovereign Citizens, and the most publicized, the Order of the Mystic Brotherhood. The drys claimed that the acronym for the last one stood for "Order More Beer."[42]

The petition drives reached their peak in 1895, when each side produced nearly 40,000 signatures. Of the 36,517 who opposed resubmission, 13,887 were produced through the efforts of the WCTU. The resubmissionists came the closest to passing their bill in 1897, when the Populists controlled both houses of the legislature for the first and only time. The resubmissionists produced fifty-six votes in the house, twenty-eight short of the total needed for passage.[43] Whatever the problems of enforcement, Kansans continued to cling stubbornly to the principle of prohibition as the preferred mode of regulating alcohol.

Although the 1891 legislature soundly defeated resubmission, it caused concern among the drys when it sent to a 1892 referendum the question of calling an open-ended convention to revise the state's constitution. Many Kansans, including a substantial number of drys, had come to feel that the constitution was badly in need of modernization. Advocates argued that the state had grown from one hundred thousand to one and a half million since the constitution had been written and that because of the technological and social changes that had occurred, it no longer served the needs of society.

Many drys were wary, however; they saw the convention proposal as "a dose of resubmission sugar-coated." The WCTU, especially, worked diligently to defeat the convention proposal, assigning a local committee to nearly every voting precinct. The drys appeared to have had a close call when the proposal came within five hundred votes of receiving a majority of those voting on the question. However, the constitution required that such a proposition receive a majority of all those voting at the election, which it failed to do by forty-four thousand.[44]

The legislature gave the WCTU a major issue to work for when it submitted a woman-suffrage amendment to a vote of the electorate in 1894. For the year preceding the election, the union gave top priority to the work of its Department of Franchise. As local superintendents for this critical work, they tried to select "the best, brightest and most lovable women, and if possible, the women who are happy in their own home relations." The union worked hard for the amendment, and it set aside a day of prayer for its success. But despite its efforts and prayers and those of the ESA, the proposition lost by thirty-five thousand votes. An analysis showed that, among those who voted on the amendment, 14 percent of the Democrats, 38 percent of the Republicans, 54 percent of the Populists, and 88 percent of the Prohibitionists supported the proposition.[45]

INCONSTANCY AND EQUIVOCALNESS in the office of governor during the decade contributed to the slump in law enforcement. For the only time in Kansas history, five different men occupied the governor's chair in as many consecutive elections: Humphrey (1890), Lewelling (1892), Morrill (1894), Leedy (1896), and Stanley (1898). The struggle for dominance by the political parties is reflected in the alternation of the two Populists, Lewelling and Leedy, with the three Republicans. A leader of the KSTU observed: "The struggle for political power always impoverishes administrative strength. Revolution for offices is devolution of principles. Prohibition has felt the shock."[46]

Ambiguity from the ever-changing leadership combined with the ever-present ambivalence in the state's temperance sentiment to produce a climate of unsettledness. In many respects the dry community had more difficulty with its wavering friends than with its forthright foes. Never expecting much from the upstart Populists and their Democratic allies, the drys expressed only relief and gratitude when a resubmission bill failed to pass a fusionist-controlled legislature. The Republicans had formally separated themselves from the temperance question when they ceased to support prohibition in their platforms. But the drys continued to expect much more from Republican officeholders and to eject much more venom when they failed to get it.[47]

The case of the irresolute Governor Edmund N. Morrill (1895–97) illustrates the disappointment and frustration of the drys. Morrill brought an impeccable temperance reputation of long standing to his candidacy for the governorship. As a state senator, he had been among the faithful who had

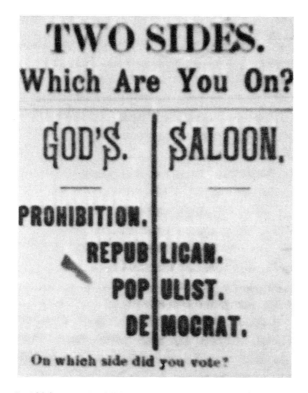

In 1896 a state Prohibition newspaper, *The Fulcrum,* ranks the political parties of Kansas in respect to the liquor question (courtesy of the Kansas State Historical Society, Topeka).

encouraged J. R. Detwiler when the young implement dealer came to Topeka in 1879 on his historic mission. Morrill was a teetotaler, an "exemplary" family man, a leader in the Congregational Church, an honest businessman, and a successful four-term congressman. With such sparkling credentials and with the disappointing Lewelling seeking reelection, the choice of the drys was easy and hopeful.[48]

But the bemused Morrill vacillated scandalously on the prohibition issue, as well as on other major questions. He encountered especial difficulty in trying to administer the metropolitan-police law and its associated patronage. And he didn't endear himself to the temperance community when he declared, not illogically, that "the law cannot be enforced where local public sentiment is against it." At the conclusion of his term the KSTU cried that "a more weak, truckling, subservient, cowardly administration never was elected."[49]

The Metropolitan Police Commission system became the bane not only of Morrill's existence but of every other governor's during the law's stormy tenure. The 1887 legislature had established the system at the behest of Governor Martin, as a response to the "open rebellion" in the largest towns. Since the locals could not control their own affairs, the theory had it, the central administration in Topeka would take charge in an aseptic and apolitical fashion.

The statute provided that the governor could, at his discretion, appoint a board of three police commissioners for each city of the first class to administer its police affairs. The commissioners had the authority to appoint and set policy for the entire police force, including a police judge, a police chief, and the police officers. The law established an apparatus that was totally outside the control of the city council and the mayor; it was responsible only to the commissioners and to the governor. Fines that were collected by the police went into the city treasury, but the city had the responsibility for paying police expenses and for taking care of any deficits that might accrue.[50]

One of the major problems of the system concerned the nature of the appointees to the boards. The law required that commissioners must have resided in the city for at least three years, a provision that compromised to a great extent the primary purpose of the statute. The governors were subjected to a great deal of pressure from all the political parties, since one of the three commissioners had to be of a different political persuasion. The system added several hundred appointments to the patronage that was firmly under the governor's control.

A second major problem concerned finance. Since the cities were responsible for the budget, most of them eventually succumbed to the "fine" system, which had first been installed in Topeka in 1881 by Mayor Wilson. The systematic handling of relatively large amounts of money in the quasi-legal fine system led to numerous opportunities for graft and corruption, which were all too often realized. The drys branded the fine-for-revenue system as "nothing less than nullification and treason."[51]

Although Governor Martin had called for the commissioner law, he made few appointments himself. Humphrey became the first governor to appoint commissioners to all of the first-class cities. His Topeka board was especially distinguished: it included P. I. Bonebrake (J. R. Detwiler's Sunday School teacher), Charles F. Spencer (a partner of James Troutman in launching the *Palladium* in 1879), and Dr. F. S. McCabe (a temperance leader). The capital city received the acclaim of outsiders as being the "cleanest and best policed city of its size in the world." But most of the other commissioners didn't function as effectively, those in Leavenworth, Atchison, and Wichita being particularly impotent.[52]

Wichita waged an especially strenuous fight, the outcome of which allegedly determined whether it was "greater than the state of Kansas." Joints commonly ran wide open, but on some occasions they were precipitately and mysteriously closed. Charges of corruption among officials became commonplace. In 1888 a grand jury indicted the county attorney and seven other officials for taking bribes from jointists. The police commissioners were charged with the same offense four years later, but an ouster suit had to be dropped when the Kansas Supreme Court ruled that only the governor had the power to remove them.[53]

On a December day in 1890, no less than fifty-two joints were closed by the Wichita commissioners, but most of these joints were soon back in business. In 1891 the saloons closed for two weeks but reopened just as suddenly after the two commissioners who had ordered the closings had been removed. Soon thereafter all the gambling houses except one were closed, and when board members attempted to move against it, they were removed. Eventually the city settled down to a system of $50 monthly "fines" per joint. When resubmissionist interest was near its height, the public learned, to its dismay, that some of the joints had not been paying regularly. This revelation caused one of the jointists to wail that "now they have advertised us, and I tell you this is a business which don't flourish under too much advertising. . . . Why couldn't they talk resubmission without saying so much about the joints running without paying anything."[54]

The experience of Atchison sheds additional light on the machinations that could occur under the metropolitan-police law. Balie P. Waggener, the general attorney for the Missouri Pacific Railway, told an 1891 investigating committee that he had been shocked at the state of affairs that he had found when he became mayor. A staunch Democrat, Waggener had flirted with the Prohibition party during the early eighties but had come to favor license and local option, though he firmly believed that the law should be enforced. He discovered that the chief of police, with the full knowledge of the police commission, collected an unknown sum of money each month from each of the forty-odd "tippling shops, gambling dens, . . . [and] houses of prostitution." Waggener called it a "fine"; the chief called it a "forfeit"; the contributors called it a "license."[55]

Waggener learned that neither the commissioners nor the police judge nor the city treasurer knew how much the chief collected. They did not require him to file reports or to give receipts to the donors. When the mayor began to evince an aggressive interest in these matters, an additional $1,245 suddenly appeared in the city treasury, which the chief had "forgotten" to deposit. And when Waggener began to talk to some disturbed jointists about the collections, two of them suddenly found themselves under arrest by order of the vengeful chief.[56]

Concerned about the recurrent rumors of corruption and suspicious that at least some of the commission appointments stemmed from a nullification impulse, the legislature called for a complete investigation of the system in 1891. Through extensive hearings and its own field work, the investigating committee found much evidence to confirm its worst fears. In all of the cities except Topeka the commissioners either condoned or actively participated in the "fining" of joints on a regular basis. And in all but Topeka the police departments ran on a self-sustaining basis from the fines, which averaged from $2,000 to $4,000 a month. Topeka collected only $7,000 per year in legitimate fines and suffered an $18,000 per annum departmental deficit, which the city had to make up.[57]

In its summary the discouraged committee stated that "the more vigorous the effort made to enforce prohibition in the cities, the more irresponsible and debased are the men who are engaged in the traffic, the more deceptive their devices, and secluded their places of business." The committee concluded that it had been a mistake to establish dual governments in the cities, and it recommended that the system be abolished. An increasing number of Kansans of every political and temperance hue came to share that view. A Populist legislature, concerned about "the notorious friendship existing between the whisky men and the police commissioners," finally repealed the law in 1898. No one—wet or dry—shed a tear.[58]

THE NIGHTMARE OF THE NINETIES spread gloom and despair throughout the temperance camp. Politically the drys had become orphans—despised by the Democrats, ignored by the Populists, forsaken by the Republicans, loved only by the feisty but impotent Prohibitionists. The liquor dealers openly crowed that "no political party in Kansas [is] big enough to undertake the job of enforcing the prohibitory law."[59]

Unable to shake either themselves or the public from their "too timid" sentiments, the drys fell to reminiscing about the halcyon days of 1886–89, when an aggressive and confident temperance community perceived the millennium as being only a few years away. In 1896 the newly appointed secretary of the KSTU, Thomas E. Stephens, after a quick survey of the scene of listlessness and stagnation, characterized the WCTU, the IOGT, the KSTU, and the preachers of Kansas as "only half awake." A member of the WCTU expressed the feelings of many when she uttered the deeply felt Jobian cry "How long, oh Lord?"[60]

While the movement was down, it was far from out. A good deal of fight remained; indeed some of the most zealous seemed almost to enjoy their downtrodden status. A white ribboner who seemed to relish the underdog role was the Reverend Eugenia Shultz St. John. When her husband, a cousin of Governor St. John's, had had permanently to give up his preaching duties in Illinois because of failing health, Eugenia jumped into the breach and rode the demanding circuit in his stead. A few years later she became an ordained minister in the Methodist Protestant Church and the first woman of her denomination to be elected to the General Conference.

The St. Johns came to Kansas in 1887 and soon became temperance leaders known for their innovative ideas. "I am glad we are going to be tested," she said. "We have got to do more than talk to win this battle. . . . We have got all the churches and the goody-goody people, but what of the rest, the boys on the street corner. . . . I, for one, am not going to make any more temperance speeches in the churches. For God's sake let us take the churches out into the streets."[61]

Paralleling the economic conditions and a function of them, temperance sentiment bottomed out from 1895 to 1897 and began a slow, modest ascent throughout the remainder of the decade. Led by their energetic secretary, Tom Stephens, the KSTU began to exhibit new vitality and confidence, though the effects of this renaissance on law enforcement would not be apparent for some time. The union decided to concentrate on renewing temperance sentiment and to stop "dabbling in politics." It was especially grateful that a strong antiliquor law remained on the books. "The institutions for the enforcement of this law are more complete," the union modestly proclaimed, "and its machinery, when put in operation, more effectual than any other known statute in the world."[62]

In 1898 the KSTU affiliated with the Anti-Saloon League of America, which was developing into the dominant temperance organization in the nation. Adamantly rejecting a complete takeover, the union clung tenaciously to its name, its funds, and, especially, its cherished autonomy. It began to publish a monthly newspaper, the *Kansas Issue,* with twenty thousand copies going to paid-up subscribers and three thousand going gratis to college students. The budget shot up from a paltry $600 in 1896 to a respectable $4,700 in 1899 and to a whopping $7,000 in 1900. Drawing over one thousand enthusiasts, the annual convention often resembled an old-fashioned Methodist prayer meeting, as a front row of venerable ministers liberally punctuated the platform utterances with their amens.[63]

In a development that would carry profound consequences for the twentieth century, the KSTU began to attract a more-practical-minded, civic-oriented type of individual. The role of religion, though it remained critical, threatened to become subordinated to civic and business concerns. Thus the "mental microbe" of "progressivism" had unmistakably infected the temperance body before the close of the century. The image of the joyless, reclusive crank, which had never been accurate or deserved, became even more difficult to sustain as the energetic and optimistic "go-getters" flocked to the ranks in numbers.

A wide range of opinion molders began to send a revitalized temperance message from the platform, the pulpit, and the press. Among the academics we find almost all the presidents of Kansas' colleges and universities and many of their leading faculty; among the nonpolitical state officeholders, Foster D. Coburn, the highly regarded secretary of the Board of Agriculture (1894–1914); among the clerics, the Congregationalist Charles M. Sheldon and the Methodist John T. McFarland, cerebral types known for their community involvement; among the women, the Quaker minister Mary Sibbitt, the WCTU organizer Minnie Johnson Grinstead, and the WCTU president and lawyer Ella Brown, representing a "young turk" element which was replacing the old guard; and among the journalists, Arthur Capper *(Topeka Mail and Breeze),* Harold Chase

(Topeka Capital), Edward W. Hoch *(Marion Record)*, and William A. White *(Emporia Gazette)*, young men of increasing influence determined to make their mark in both the moral and the material worlds.[64]

By the turn of the century the KSTU had established several direct services for its constituents. Expert legal advice on enforcement problems could be obtained from its Legal Advisory Committee, which boasted some of the state's top legal talent. If you wanted the names of all those in your county who held the federal liquor stamp, your curiosity could be satisfied by sending $2.50 ($1.00 for a town) to a Methodist minister in Leavenworth, who handled this work for the KSTU.

The union's most practical, but controversial, service consisted of furnishing experienced detectives to local communities to ferret out evidence against liquor sellers. For $15 a week and expenses, the temperance sleuth would produce the evidence and testify in court, if necessary. The union preferred that the detectives remain undercover, however, for if they testified, they lost their usefulness forever in that section of the state.

Many drys had ambivalent feelings about using these undercover agents, a practice that flew directly in the face of the rural Kansas ethos of "openness." Of more pragmatic concern, judges and juries did not always regard the evidence so obtained "as of the highest quality." Convictions depended heavily upon the sympathies of the prosecutors. "It is pretty nearly useless to try to push these matters successfully," the KSTU warned its potential patrons, "where the officers are on the other side."[65]

The KSTU exerted its greatest educational influence through the corps of lecturers that it supported in the field. It had maintained lecturers off and on since its inception, but this activity had become another victim of the doldrums of the nineties. With the renaissance in interest, the union began to sponsor several speakers on either a full-time or a part-time basis. It expected thereby to rekindle something of the "old time Francis Murphy enthusiasm." A revival of the gospel-temperance sentiment would lead, it hoped, to a renewal of interest in the battered prohibition statutes.[66]

The tour of Professor George R. Kirkpatrick of Winfield in 1899 may be taken as representative of the work at the turn of the century. A moderate but forceful speaker, the studious Kirkpatrick toured for over a year in what must have seemed an interminable series of one-night stands in small-to-moderate-sized railroad towns. He lived a lonely, suitcase existence, which would be all too familiar to a modern entertainer or to a dance band. He signed the standard KSTU contract, which called for a salary of $100 per month plus expenses. The salary would come from the freewill offerings and subscriptions that he obtained at his meetings; the remainder, if any, would go to the union. His "entertainment" (that is, his board and room) was frequently supplied gratis by local people sympathetic to the cause, who often were members of the WCTU.[67]

Kirkpatrick made weekly confidential reports to the union as he hopped from town to town. In these he systematically recorded the size of his crowd, and on a scale of zero (driest) to four, he rated the temperance conditions in the town. He often listed the number of joints and noted the names of the leading temperance workers and their politics. He added a few succinct remarks about each locale, leaving us a candid portrait of conditions at the end of the century:

White Cloud (Doniphan County): Sentiment good. Some boot-legging among the Iowa Indians nearby. . . . White Cloud illustrates that a few good citizens in a border town can defy repeated attempts to establish a saloon.

Everest (Brown County): Sentiment, low. Bohemian Catholic Population. . . . Everest is a very bad town. Urgent need of temperance organization.

Marysville (Marshall County): Sentiment, extremely low (German Catholic). No temperance organizations of any kind.

Beattie (Marshall County): Sentiment first rate. . . . Joints or saloons had been running for ten or fifteen years before the present feminine administration. Within three weeks after the ladies took their oath of office they ousted the wide open joint.

Cuba (Republic County): Sentiment, very low. The town is surrounded by Bohemians. Cuba is in a foul condition. People humiliated by surrounding foreign population who prefer beer to books.

Munden (Republic County): Sentiment, low. An unusual number of men in the audience.

Leonardville (Riley County): Sentiment fair. Sheriff was killed two years ago by a saloon-keeper. As a result a Law and Order League was immediately organized with the mayor as president. Is not now in existence.

Lyndon (Osage County): The town is "clubbed, ordered and lodged" to death. . . . People will not tolerate liquor selling; yet apparently considerable apathy.

Osawatomie (Miami County): Sentiment, very low. W.C.T.U. is practically dead. Newspapers against temperance. Editor of "Globe" is a drinker.

Yates Center (Woodson County): W.C.T.U. nearly dead. Drug Stores vicious, some boot-legging. Sentiment, good, but in constant danger of waning. Is kept in wholesome condition by a few brave, watchful, intelligent friends of sobriety.

Anthony (Harper County): Sentiment, indifference. Pastors "would like to be active" but are "fearful."

Girard (Crawford County): Sentiment low. Best people greatly discouraged. The churches at present are somewhat unamiable toward each other because of some misunderstandings in spring election.[68]

Not long after the Kirkpatrick tour the KSTU began to alter its speaker format in response to demands for modernization. A one-week program of specialized lectures (for children, youth, businessmen, town officials, etc.) at a single site replaced the one-night stands. The new programs incorporated state-of-the-art visual technology, such as the Edison kinetoscope for moving pictures and the McIntosh double stereoptican "of the highest grade" for slides. Illustrated topics included "Liquor and the Boy," "Do Women Get Drunk?" "Cigarette Smoking," and "A Large City by Night," as well as "The Life of George Washington" and "A Visit to Yellowstone National Park." A gospel singer often toured with the speaker, and an admission fee was charged, at least for some performances during the week. These changes were designed to broaden the temperance appeal, since the people whom they hoped to reach cared "more to be entertained than just to be instructed."[69]

One of the most effective and colorful lecturers of this period was Maj. Edgar T. Scott, who was originally from southern California. His wife toured with him, which was unusual; on some occasions she gave the evening lecture, or they shared it. She held afternoon teas for the ladies, "enthusing them, . . . insuring their aid and sympathy, consequently their male friends. Net result: good audiences and better offerings."[70]

After a 1902 meeting at Liberal in Seward County, Scott reported an attendance of fifty-two, which included only seven men, many of the latter being at a "shin-dig" of some sort. "The devil has full swing," he said; "every other man's breath smells of whiskey. All the people seem to care for so far as the church is concerned, is to have a minister to marry them, christen children, officiate at the burial, and then claim they have a minister." But he said he liked western Kansans because they gave more freely. "It takes" was his comment in regard to his offer of a 20-cent reduction on a $1.20 annual subscription (10 cents a month) with a cash payment of $1.00. At the conclusion of his sojourn in Liberal he boasted that in another week the town "would have been turned inside out, and right side up."[71]

At the little town of Cunningham (Kingman County), Scott reached his pinnacle of enthusiasm: "Apparently the community is revolutionized. One hundred dollars to fight a joint could be raised in an hour. . . . Was never more pleased with present manifestations of universal approval." And four days later: "The tide was high last night—a tidal wave. That is the time to quit. We always did like Sunday, you know, to close a series of meetings. Oh, but it was fine!"[72]

BY THE END OF THE DECADE the temperance community had experienced a revival sufficient to restore its self-respect, its enthusiasm, and its courage. Tenaciously, the enthusiasts clutched the cherished law and the revered amendment. And scientific temperance instruction did its quiet but inexorable work daily in the public schools. At best, however, the drys had only stemmed the liquor tide, which had been awash over Kansas since 1890. Joints seemed omnipresent in the larger towns, and the friendly drugstore beckoned to the more timid. Bootleggers and private clubs ministered to those who found the more public outlets inconvenient or embarrassing. In the middling-sized and larger towns at least, practice daily violated theory; King Alcohol ruled arrogantly and supremely. Onto this scene suddenly appeared an obscure old lady, who would almost literally bring revolution to Kansas and in the process would become one of the half dozen most famous women in all of American history.

7
Mrs. Nation

She was large for her age, had yellow hair, and a fair complexion. She was inclined to be a tom-boy, was very strong-willed and absolutely afraid of nothing. She dominated the school, and was distinctly a leader of both boys and girls. Frequently she led us younger children into mischief. I especially recall the martial spirit, and how she used to delight in assuming the roll [*sic*] of a conqueror.
—A primary-school classmate of Carry Nation

BY 1900 KANSAS had become a hybrid cauldron of frustration and hopefulness. The renaissance of the KSTU and the WCTU had raised expectations as well as morale. If joints could be closed by the city fathers on Sundays, holidays, election days, and when the WCTU came to town, why couldn't they be closed permanently as the law required? The milieu recalled the late 1870s, when the Murphy Movement had left the state quaking with emotion and searching for the igniting spark. "All felt that the state was a seething, surging volcano of suppressed emotion," an observer noted in 1899, and "that a mighty conflict was inevitable."[1]

The catalyst for the "mighty conflict" came from a most unlikely quarter. Isolated outbreaks of violence against saloons had been part of the Kansas scene since 1855. They often involved women, alone or in groups, and not infrequently the weapon of choice was a hatchet or an axe. But nothing approaching a continuous sequence had ever been sustained.

In 1900 Carry Nation was living in Medicine Lodge, a sunbaked little frontier town in southwestern Kansas. She had advanced to the proximate edge of old age after a lifetime of total obscurity spent laboring at the cookstove and the washboard. Like thousands upon thousands of other pious women, she held a fervent religion-anchored interest in temperance. A less likely candidate for leadership of a revolution and for international fame would have been difficult to find.

Her biographers have speculated at length, often derisively, about the origins of her intense religious convictions and her hatred of alcohol. Whatever the genesis and anatomy of her private religious experiences, she produced an absolutely unequaled impact upon the Kansas community. During her heyday, Kansans responded to her actions and to her supplications as to none other in their history. Inspired by a deep religious faith and fueled by an extraordinary energy, she translated her formidable personality and raw courage into a direct-action campaign that carried beyond her local neighborhood into the larger Kansas world. The time and the person had been joined to produce events that would rock the state and the nation.

Carry Amelia Moore was born in 1846 in Kentucky of English, Irish, and Scotch-Irish descent. Her father was a stockman and farmer of some means, whom she adored. ("If I ever had an angel on earth, it was my father.") Her mother, though "a very handsome woman," was mentally unstable and unavailable to her children much of the time. As a consequence, Carry was frequently mothered by Negro "mammies," and slave children became her most frequent playmates. She absorbed much of her spirituality, if not her theology, from these early childhood experiences.

During her childhood she suffered several bouts of serious illness, at times becoming virtually an invalid. But by her teens she had fully recovered to enjoy robust health throughout the remainder of her life. She underwent her first formal religious experience at the age of ten, when she was baptized into the Campbellite Church (Disciples of Christ). By the onset of puberty, most of her salient personality traits had become firmly established: intelligence, dominance, combativeness, drollness, generosity, an almost childlike candor, and a high-voltage energy which led to an insatiable fascination with the spiritual and moral values of humankind.[2]

When Carry was nine, her restless father moved the family to Cass County in western Missouri. There, at the age of nineteen, she met a young physician, Charles Gloyd, and they were married in 1867. Two years later the man "I loved more than my own life" was dead, a victim of alcoholism, which was evidently well advanced at the time they married. To support the family that she had inherited from Gloyd (their infant daughter and his elderly mother), Carry attended the teachers' college at Warrensburg for a year and then began to teach in a public grade school. Her four-year teaching career (1870–74) came to an abrupt end when a member of the school board alleged that he didn't care for the way in which she was teaching word pronunciation to her pupils. His niece became her successor.

Shortly thereafter she married the "very good looking" David Nation, a newspaperman-lawyer and sometime Christian Church minister, eighteen years her senior. They moved to Texas in 1876, where they nearly became destitute trying to make a living from a run-down cotton plantation that they had purchased. ("We were as helpless on the plantation as little children.") While David made desultory attempts to establish a law practice, his wife took over the management of a dilapidated local hotel. "Managing" the hotel included the backbreaking chores of cooking, washing, cleaning, and buying as she struggled to eke out a subsistence for the entire family.[3]

In 1890 the Nations moved to Medicine Lodge, where David found sufficient success as a lawyer to support them both and free his wife to pursue her developing civic, religious, and temperance interests. "Mother Nation" (a sobriquet that the town soon bestowed on her for her benevolences) organized a sewing circle which made clothes for the poor; every fall she made certain that no child failed to attend school because of a lack of proper clothing. She invited the town's needy to their home on Thanksgiving and Christmas, where they partook of a hearty festive board. Mother Nation's generous impulses comingled with a fierce determination to have her own way. "Whatever she believes in she believes with her whole soul, and nothing except superior force can stay her," a contemporary noted; "she has done much good [for the poor], but when she sets out to get contributions she cannot be shaken off."[4]

As the decade wore on, she turned her active mind and boundless energy increasingly to temperance concerns. During 1899, together with a few zealous WCTU cohorts, she managed to close the town's seven illegal liquor outlets through the nonviolent avenues of song, prayer, and oral confrontation. In the spring of 1900 she made her first out-of-town foray, traveling in her buggy to Kiowa, twenty miles distant, where she smashed three joints with rocks and brickbats. Such immoderate behavior evoked a town consensus that she was of "unsound mind" and should be kept at home "by her people."

Six months later she had screwed up her courage enough to attack and demolish the handsome bar of the Hotel Carey, Wichita's finest. A few days after her release from jail—following a three-week incarceration based on a spurious small-pox quarantine—she set to smashing again in Wichita and was promptly rearrested. Her next logical move should have been Topeka, the capital city. But she detoured instead to Enterprise, a small community in Dickinson County, flattered that she had received an invitation from the wife of the town's leading citizen, C. B. Hoffman, the "millionaire socialist." After a hectic forty-eight hours of smashing, wrestling, and hair pulling there, she entrained for Topeka.[5]

THE ENTRANCE OF CARRY NATION into the capital city, like that of Jesus into Jerusalem, created a moral crisis of multiple dimensions. For the long-suffering temperance workers, gathering for the annual convention of the KSTU, her arrival threatened to cause a split in the ranks of the faithful. No longer would pious resolutions, feverish denunciations, and a good heart suffice; one had to stand up and be counted. The harassed president of the state WCTU, Elizabeth

P. Hutchinson, guardedly announced that the WCTU had only a legal interest in Nation's crusade, but, she charitably added, "I do not believe Mrs. Nation to be insane." The president of the Topeka WCTU, Olive P. Bray, came more directly to the point. The local union, she said, "is not in accord with her methods." Bray's sister, temperance and suffrage leader Sarah A. Thurston, added succinctly: "I wouldn't do it."

The veteran prohibitionist and former lieutenant governor Jimmie Troutman found Nation's tactics "indefensible." The minister of the Atchison Christian Church said that she was a "disgrace" and was acting the fool. But many agreed with Bank Commissioner John Breidenthal, who said: "There comes a time with people when forbearance ceases to be a virtue and they take the law into their own hands," and with Secretary of Agriculture Foster D. Coburn, who noted that "people who persistently spit on the laws have mighty small claims on the law's protection."[6]

Nation's appearance in Topeka focused attention on the growing tension between the sexes on the temperance issue. Her hostess at Enterprise, Catherine A. Hoffman, concerned herself with this often-hidden issue. A cultured woman of "refined and handsome appearance," Hoffman told the KSTU convention that she had helped to smash a joint because "the men would not do it, [so] we women did it. . . . This conduct from us women means something. . . . I do not believe in war, I did not believe in violence. But I tell you, this is a revolution that is coming on us in this state. . . . We have begun to act now, and we have put an end to uncertainties. That is what Mrs. Nation signifies to-day—action, revolution."[7]

For the forty Topeka joints, Nation posed a clear and present threat to their livelihood. Topeka had not licensed its saloons nor enjoyed the monthly fiscal benefits derived therefrom since the Kansas Supreme Court had ordered the practice stopped in 1883. Since then, joints had become more or less numerous, depending upon the predilections of the particular city government in power. The latter, of course, was a function of the mercurial attitudes of the citizenry. The wets and the drys had struggled bitterly for dominance in the capital city, ever mindful of the symbolic significance to the state as a whole. A citizens' law-and-order group in the 1880s, the Committee of Fifty, had become the Committee of Two Hundred by the late 1890s, led by the Congregational minister Charles M. Sheldon. Currently, the drys pinned their hopes on Frank M. Stahl, the colorful, no-nonsense chief of police, who was given to using unorthodox methods of trapping an unsuspecting jointist.[8]

Paralleling the statewide trend of the nineties, Topeka's joints tended to operate with increasing openness and handsomeness during the decade. They came to maintain a much higher visibility than the secluded and puny operations that the police had uncovered in 1891. Still, they did not run as brazenly as in Leavenworth, Kansas City, or Wichita. They kept to the lower (northern) reaches of Kansas Avenue, largely out of sight of the female shoppers and office workers. They were always buffered by a front, or anteroom, occupied by a legitimate business frequented by male customers, typically a cigar store, a poolroom, a drugstore, or a restaurant. Often they could be found on the second floor of a building, which circumstance led to a wry observation by Senator John J. Ingalls: "In some cities, deferring to the majesty of the law, the saloons are banished . . . from the street floor to the second story, upon some occult theory that a nefarious transaction conducted fifteen feet above ground ceases to be offensive to the moral sense of mankind."[9]

The significance and impact of the crusader in Topeka differed in kind and in degree from what had occurred before. At Kiowa, Wichita, and Enterprise she had employed essentially hit-and-run tactics, smashing a joint or two and then leaving town or going to jail. Her action, though startling, had been cursory, superficial, ephemeral. Shortly after arriving in Topeka, she had decided to make it her home, and so it remained until 1905. Through a continuous presence in the capital city she planned to influence not only the immediate community but also the entire state and the nation. She had long since recognized that she could not single-handedly run the joints out of Kansas. By settling down in Topeka, she expected to establish a militant organization, composed principally of women, which would soon rid the state of the offending establishments.

WHEN MRS. NATION appeared on the Topeka streets in the early evening of 26 January 1901, the local citizens immediately recognized her. The chunky figure wore her now-familiar old but clean "uniform": a full-length shiny black dress, topped at the neck by a huge bow of white ribbon; black cotton stockings; square-toed, "pitifully thin and worn" shoes; and a fringed gray shawl. A black poke bonnet, tied firmly under the chin, covered a bun of gray hair coiled tightly at the crown of her head. On this occasion she also wore a veil, drawn tightly about the face, which hid from view her pleasant, motherly countenance and her bright, flashing eyes. But her determined stride and self-possessed manner affirmed the "iron purpose in her soul."[10]

She quickly became the hub for anastomosing streams of males, young and old, drawn toward her as iron filings to a magnet, looking for some unusual excitement to brighten a Saturday evening. Within the hour she found herself surrounded by a spirited crowd of two thousand, who hoped for a "hatcheta-tion," though she assured them that she had left her hatchet at home. "Incessant and boisterous yelling" so filled the air that she could not be heard a few feet away though she talked "at the top of her voice."[11]

She did manage to visit a few joints on lower Kansas Avenue to warn them to close their "murder shops" or else. Her most embarrassing moment came after a joint keeper's wife had whacked her on the head with a broom, knocking her bonnet off. When Nation stooped over to retrieve it, the incensed woman "smote her upon that portion of the anatomy which chanced to be uppermost." The crowd, which had initially been amiable enough, grew steadily more rowdy as the evening wore on and its size increased apace. When it had degenerated into "a wild, howling mob" which threatened lynching, her armed escorts guided her into the Columbian Building for safety. Soon thereafter they spirited her out a rear door into the night, while remnants of the mob milled restlessly in front, setting off yowls like so many frenzied coyotes at full moon.[12] Topeka had been introduced to its new resident, and vice versa.

A sketch of Carry Nation during her interview with Governor Stanley, drawn by Albert T. Reid, who later became a prominent illustrator (courtesy of the Kansas State Historical Society, Topeka).

On Monday next, Nation paid her respects to the state's chief executive, the Honorable William Eugene Stanley. The governor's prohibition-enforcement policy had been the height of simplicity: leave the thorny matter entirely in the hands of the local communities. For this posture his administration had been labeled "miserably weak" by the disappointed drys, who had expected so much from the former Methodist Sunday School superintendent and had received so little. Stanley typified the Kansas politician who could adroitly "carry a Sunday school on one shoulder and a joint on the other." Even before Nation made her appearance, he had no doubt about how he stood with her. While in the Wichita jail, she had declared that "Stanley, the head of prohibition, is only a synonymn for hypocrisy."[13]

She made an appointment with his secretary and returned shortly thereafter with an entourage, which included her husband, David; Annie Diggs, the widely respected Populist and suffrage leader, currently the state librarian; and enough reporters and legislators virtually to fill the room. Stanley lost control from the first moment, when she firmly commanded him to "sit around where the light strikes you, I can't see your face."

In her soft Kentucky accent and her unassuming, "perfectly natural" manner, she pleaded, she scolded, she threatened. To his every defense she gave a sharp, pithy, and logical reply. She said that she didn't smash on impulse but only as a last resort. "I've prayed and cried and laid down on the floor and wept. Something must be done." As her vigorous chastisement continued unabated, the rattled governor lost what little composure he had left. "You are a woman," he said; "but a woman must know a woman's place. They can't come in here and raise this kind of a disturbance." As the meeting wound down, he assured her once again that he was powerless to act and palmed her off on the attorney general, with an audible sigh of relief.[14]

In an editorial after the interview, the *Kansas City Star,* no friend of prohibition, wondered aloud how a public man with fiber enough to be elected governor could be so intimidated at the approach of "this avenging lady." To see the head of the commonwealth lose all presence of mind in such a public forum was a pitiful sight. "It would have been better—much better—had the fear which seized upon him as he contemplated the steady and resolute advance of his accuser caused him to flee and leave Mrs. Nation in possession of the field. The Governor is not to be censured for not having done the best thing that was possible under the circumstances, but the very worst." And where was Henry J. Allen, the governor's "urbane and tactful" private secretary, at the critical hour when his tormented employer needed him most?[15]

A great deal of speculation centered around the probable response of the KSTU convention to the crusader. The KSTU's secretary, Tom E. Stephens, had pithily announced that Nation was free to attend the meeting, since it was open to the public, but that she had not been tendered a special invitation either to attend or to speak. But wild horses could not have kept Carry away. Almost immediately after she entered the hall, she was loudly called for, and as she went forward to the platform, "the whole house [of one thousand] sprang to its feet and waved handkerchiefs and cheered." From that moment the usually staid meeting began to resemble an old-fashioned revival, as the members got the "power." Isolated pockets of conservative resistance melted before the onrushing tide of enthusiasm. The union's president saluted her for her courage, and the delegates passed resolutions praising her and scoring Stanley for his laxity in enforcement.

As long as she remained in the hall, Nation was "the orbit around which the convention revolved." She "charmed everyone by her good humor and wit combined with [a] fiery earnestness." One captivated woman came up the aisle with a bouquet of flowers and lovingly presented it to her. Messenger boys brought her telegrams and letters "by the dozen." The grateful delegates took up a collection of $117.50 for a gold medal to be inscribed "To the Bravest Woman in Kansas." With an irony that Nation must have enjoyed, the WCTU's president was appointed to chair the committee to design and purchase the medal. Shortly thereafter, the jointists presented a miniature golden broom to their heroine, the joint keeper's wife, who had applied the solid whack to the crusader's posterior on Saturday night.[16]

While the town and state waited expectantly for the next hatchet to fall, Nation reconnoitered the new territory and attempted to organize the women into an "army" of Home Defenders. She accepted as many of the dozens of speaking invitations as she could squeeze into the day and the night, and she planned some meetings of her own. Brimming to overflowing with the "inexhaustable subject," she told her venerating audiences that what Kansas needed most was agitation. "You agitate water," she said, "and it will run up hill." To the apprehensive women she tried to impart some of the exhilaration that could come from wrecking a joint: "I tell you, ladies, you don't know how much joy you will have until you begin to smash, smash, smash. It is wonderful."[17]

She reserved her most righteous scorn for those who suggested that a moral-suasion campaign to increase public support for prohibition might be more appropriate than her more direct method. "Moral suasion!" she cried. "If there's anything that's weak and worse than useless it's this moral suasion. I despise it. These hell traps of Kansas have fattened for twenty years on moral suasion."[18]

THE LIVING, BREATHING flesh-and-blood relationship between Mrs. Nation and the Kansas people has been buried for decades beneath gallons of printer's ink, immersed in equal parts of derision and disparagement. She has been called variously a crank, a freak, a lunatic, a bizarre clown, a sinister bigot, a demented creature, the Hitler of morals, and the Joe McCarthy of personal conduct. From these vitriolic depths has emerged a one-dimensional cardboard doll with a wild-eyed look, which produces, upon squeezing, an instant hatchetation.

What has remained submerged has been her wit, her warmth, her joyfulness, and her intelligence—the vibrant humanity that so impressed her contemporaries. Her regard for and sensitivity to blacks, Jews, and Catholics, for example, far exceeded that of the average WASP of the period. Her sans-hatchet personality was powerful, unforgettable, unique. Very few human beings, of whatever walk or station or education, ever bested her in a one-on-one parley. Governor Stanley was not the sole beneficiary of her "charming unconventionality," as the jointists of Topeka were soon to discover.[19]

On January 31, Nation decided to pay a social call on the jointists of lower Kansas Avenue, leaving her weapons safely at home. Forewarned of her impending visit, the owners feverishly barricaded their businesses and them-selves behind mounds of furniture and every other conceivable bulky object. They peeked nervously through the cracks in the ramparts, awaiting the imminent arrival of the grey-haired grandmother. When she appeared on the scene with five hundred men and boys at her heels and saw the ridiculous configurations, she gave a hearty laugh and called to the anxious men: "Aren't you going to let your mother in, boys? She wants to talk to you."[20]

With a face "full of amusement and kindliness" and in a "soft deep" voice, she told them that she loved them and would help them if they were ever in trouble. Her voice, her manner, and her obvious sincerity began to weave their magic spell on the hidden jointists. They peered out from their lairs like apprehensive prairie dogs from their burrows, and soon the barricades began to come down. The Pied Piper of Hamelin could not have charmed them from behind their ramparts more skillfully or more quickly.[21]

A reporter for the hard-nosed *Kansas City Star* tells us what happened next:

> Astonishing as it may seem, incredible as it may appear, these saloon men were strongly moved by the talk Mrs. Nation gave them. She meant what she said—they understood that. They knew she was not resentful and did not despise them just as they understood how resolved she was to make them close their joints.
>
> It was a curious scene to observe. It was interesting to see the countenances of the saloon men. They showed little bravado. Those who had been blustering about what they would do if the saloon wrecker came around became as meek as lambs and looked very much ashamed of themselves. Mrs. Nation enjoyed their discom-fiture. Her eyes were laughing all the time.[22]

Gaining recruits in the agitated capital city for her upcoming war proved to be easy for the chief recruiter. Within a few days the Topeka Brigade, Kansas Division, of General Carry's Home Defenders' Army numbered several hundred—mostly, but not exclusively, women. A mass meeting for last-minute inspiration and final instructions was held on the evening of February 2 in the Topeka Auditorium. Some of the women had had difficulty obtaining hatchets, but the general assured them that "pokers will do as well." Most of the men left the meeting early, but the enthralled women stayed on. "It's always the women who have to stand in the breach," the leader said scornfully as the men drifted out. "There is only one place worse than a saloon, and that's a church full of hypocrites."[23]

On February 4, Nation and a detail of her female followers attempted to rush a joint, but they were repulsed by a large crowd, many of whom had been hired by the jointists for the purpose. The pushing-and-shoving exercise resembled a rugby match, with several hundred players on each side. The general and three of her followers were arrested but were soon released. The next dawn, in the bitter cold of a blizzard, they had better luck. They completely demolished one of Topeka's finest, the Senate Saloon.

This incident featured two shots, fired in the air by the guard, and the usual smashed furnishings; but the list of disabled items also included slot machines and a heavy cash register, which Nation held aloft before ceremoniously hurling it to the ground. She received an "ugly wound" in the melee, but she took no sick leave. At the jail she implored her keepers for help: "Oh men, don't be mice. Stand up for us, for God's sake!" The Senate Saloon reopened within hours to a rush business in booze and beer and souvenirs of broken glass and splintered wood. The next day the *State Journal* carried a front-page sketch of the revelers at the Senate bar, including a fourteen-year-old boy.[24]

The continuing presence of one of the world's greatest agitators inevitably produced an atmosphere of mounting tension. The situation passed beyond that of good-humored concern about smashing into something much more serious and ugly, bordering on insurrection and revolution. The pent-up passions of the drys could no longer be denied. An anonymous "prominent Topekan" warned: "The people mean business. The situation in Topeka at present is desperate. The feeling of anger against the jointists is most intense. It only needs a spark to kindle this feeling into riotous flame."

The attack on the Senate Saloon increased the intensity still further. Within twenty-four hours, many men "who count in the business and social life of Topeka" rallied to the radical temperance standard. Fearing for "the peace of the city," on February 6, Police Chief Frank Stahl ordered that all the joints be closed. On February 7, seventy of the "best" professional and businessmen called a mass meeting of male citizens for Sunday February 10.[25]

THE COMING OF CARRY NATION to the Kansas scene cast into bold relief the longstanding differences between the two factions within the "law and order" community, but paradoxically it also narrowed those differences. Both factions profoundly wanted all the joints in the state closed tight and stricter enforcement of the prohibition law. But they differed about what tactics they deemed appropriate to obtain those ends.

The radicals, much the smaller numerically but considerably more vocal, often Prohibitionist in politics, wanted to take direct action against the joints at once. Their aggressive position had been strengthened immeasurably by the advent of Mrs. Nation. The more conservative minded, who dominated the KSTU and the WCTU, usually Republican or Populist politically, wanted only to step up the pressure on law-enforcement officers to do their duty. They felt uneasy in sponsoring lawlessness in the name of the law. But as a concession to the headstrong radicals, they were inclined to put a short-term "or else" on their proposed injunction to the law officers. Some even envisioned the forces of a "citizen soldiery, drilled and officered," which would sweep the jointists from the state and bring the millennium to Kansas. Indeed, the core of such a unit, which included some one thousand male citizens, had already begun to drill in the capital city.[26]

The leadership that emerged among the temperance forces at this distressed hour represented the broad spectrum of public opinion, except for antiprohibition, whose partisans grimly maintained a stony silence. The leading spokesperson for the most radical position was Dr. Evilela Harding, a forty-five-year-old native of Ohio who was one of the few trained female physicians in Kansas. Simple, unpretentious, with a strong will and a "good natured" face, she devoted much of her life in Kansas to social, political, educational, and philanthropic causes. An outspoken suffragist, she became successively a Populist, a Democrat, and a Socialist. As a Democrat in 1916, she became the first woman in Kansas to run for the congressional nomination of a major party. Her home in Topeka had become a bustling nerve center for the Home Defenders. She was the principal aide-de-camp for General Carry, though the combative physician did not hesitate in the least to disagree with her leader over tactics.[27]

Only slightly to the right of Dr. Harding was the tempestuous Reverend Frank W. Emerson, pastor of the First Christian Church and editor of the *Kansas Endeavorer.* Active in the Prohibition party, Emerson accepted its nomination for governor in 1902, polling 6,065 votes. Though a man of the cloth and of peace, Emerson had a reputation for masculine pugnaciousness which made him uneasy about an aggressive feminine presence in temperance matters. "The world needs men," he said. "Men to work and watch and pray, yes, and men to fight—to fight against the wrongs and abuse inherited from another age, that have fastened themselves like festering, cankerous sores upon the body politic and social."[28]

The Reverend John Thomas McFarland, pastor of the First Methodist Church, played the role of the citizen-philosopher during the emergency. He bridged the ideological gap between the two factions and, respected by both, acted as a liaison between them. The fifty-year-old native of Indiana had served as president of Iowa Wesleyan University and had come to Topeka in 1899 from a pastorate at the New York Avenue Church, Brooklyn, New York. Within a few years he became the "biggest man" in the Methodist Church in Kansas.[29]

A temperance leader since his arrival in Topeka, the "intellectually massive" McFarland delighted in the discomfiture that was being felt by the jointists at the hands of Mrs. Nation. He saw that she had placed them in their most difficult position in years and had aroused public enmity to unprecedented heights. Still he thought that mob action was not the answer, most especially when it was led by a woman. Like his colleague Emerson, McFarland felt that the men should take the lead. If all legal remedies should fail, then "let the men of the city, from the highest to the humblest . . . step out into the light and sweep the unendurable nuisance from our streets." Exactly how such an august assemblage would differ from a Nation-led "mob," except in gender, remains unclear.[30]

The renowned Reverend Charles M. Sheldon, minister of the Central Congregational Church, was a leading representative of the "conservative" temperance faction. Educated in the best eastern schools, the forty-four-year-old native of New York had been called to the Topeka church in 1889. He had soon become a prominent social gospeler and a leader of the temperance forces in their perennial effort to sweep the joints from Topeka. No Kansan of the day was held in wider or deeper respect.[31]

In his autobiography, published in 1925, and in a series of articles in the *Christian Herald,* published in 1930, Sheldon declared his deep admiration for Mrs. Nation and her campaign of violence. But on Sunday February 10, at the hour of decision, Sheldon, along with the majority of his fellow ministers, preached caution. He did not approve of having citizens take the law into their own hands, he told his congregation, for even if all the joints in Topeka were smashed, the relief would only be temporary. It was the far better part of wisdom to insist that law officers do their duty, and to elect ones that would.[32] The vast majority of Topekans, and Kansans, would have agreed. But revolutions always begin with a minority.

The mass meeting of Sunday February 10 was one of the most remarkable in Kansas history. Nearly three thousand aroused citizens trouped to the auditorium, with a "conviction and determination that showed itself on every face." The all-male meeting had been called three days earlier, immediately after the leaders of the conservative faction had learned that Nation would be on a one-week lecture tour in Iowa and Illinois beginning on February 8. The written agenda featured the confrontation of the joints; the unwritten addendum called for recapturing the initiative from the women. Open joints in the capital city brought embarrassment enough to the temperance enthusiasts, but having women take the lead in doing something about them was intolerable. Though only men were present, the spirit of Mrs. Nation "seemed to pervade the entire audience."[33]

The audience heard stirring speeches from Stahl, Troutman, Emerson, and McFarland. The last of these exclaimed reassuringly that the "Anglo-Saxon vigor which has gone from Run[n]ymeade to John Brown is still present." In its chief business, the meeting organized itself into a "committee of public order" and issued an ultimatum. They gave the jointists until noon Monday to close their doors and until Friday to remove their fixtures from the premises. The group had not assembled to debate the finer points of jurisprudence: when one poor soul dissented on a resolution, the crowd angrily cried, "Put him out!" After the last irate resolution had been passed, the assemblage rose, lustily sang "America," and happily filed out, content that they had at long last found a solution to the joint problem. The cerebral McFarland said that the meeting represented "the public speaking in the imperative mood."[34] Evidently even the conservatives had had enough.

Returning from her out-of-state speaking tour on February 14, Nation faced a bevy of irate women. The Home Defenders were upset that they had been given no representation on the Committee of Five, to whom the mass meeting had delegated its authority. Nation herself was disturbed that the men had permitted the jointists to retain their bar equipment, which could then subsequently be used for a "hellish purpose." Although the beleaguered joints, with few exceptions, had closed up tight and the drugstores had adopted a much more cautious policy as a result of the ultimatum, the women decided to act.[35]

A crowd of five hundred women and men gathered stealthily at the east steps of the dark and massive Statehouse before dawn on Sunday February 17. Everyone had wrapped a white handkerchief around his or her neck, a mark of the Home Defenders. The group quietly assembled on the lawn in military fashion: "Company C, we meet at the southwest corner. . . ." The day before, Nation had issued a democratic call for "all men and women of any color or clime to be of us." Many members of the all-male Law Enforcement Army accompanied the women, but Commander McFarland, who was conspicuously absent, later insisted that his group took no "official" part in the proceedings. After several Washburn students belatedly arrived carrying a seven-foot, cement-headed battering ram, General Nation gave her well-armed troops a few brief words of encouragement and then ordered them toward lower Kansas Avenue.[36]

What followed made February 17 forever after a red-letter day in the annals of organized violence in Kansas. Before the hectic day had done, a prominent joint, a barn in which bar fixtures were stored, and a cold-storage warehouse, thought to hold beer, had been smashed. The police station bulged with first-time visitors; General Nation herself was arrested no less than four times.

Between smash number one and smash number two, the crowd straggled back to the Statehouse to plan its next move. A "warm argument" broke out between the exhilarated, Nation-filled women, who wanted to proceed posthaste to the next joint, and the disquieted, apprehensive men, who argued that having made their violent point, they should disband and go home. The philosophical dispute came to center in the personages of Dr. Evilela Harding and the Reverend Frank Emerson.

The two assistant generals stood nose to nose and screamed somewhat uncomplimentary epithets at one another. When she called him a coward, his face turned "white with wrath." But he couldn't stop her or the other women, who were learning firsthand what Nation meant when she called smashing "wonderful." The women marched off joyously to their newly discovered work, with the overruled men "plodding sullenly" in the rear.[37] The Harding-Emerson confrontation furnishes a second symbol illuminating the evolving public relationship between men and women, contrasting sharply with that of Mrs. Greever pleading with her husband in 1879.

In the last outbreak of this type in Topeka, a week later, an all-male band of fifty to seventy-five raiders, armed and masked, smashed a liquor warehouse in North Topeka. One man suffered a severe gunshot wound in the foray, which was led by a local physician and the revolver-toting Reverend Emerson. "That preacher was like a tiger cat," admired the police officer who arrested him, "the fiercest man in the crowd."[38] Evidently, Dr. Harding's accusation had struck home more profoundly than she could have imagined.

THE REACTIONS to the controversial acts encouraged and perpetuated by Mrs. Nation were as varied as the human imagination and as profound as the human spirit. The Kansas countryside reacted explosively in a series of extralegal acts against illegal institutions that has gone unduplicated to this day. During the month of February, which framed the violent activity, over one hundred saloons in at least fifty towns felt the wrath of the crusaders, both male and female.

At Anthony (Harper County) a group of fourteen WCTU women from the town's "best families" wrecked three joints and a drugstore with their hatchets. Fifteen "prominent" women, led by the wife of a Methodist minister and the wife of a bank cashier, duplicated the feat at Perry (Jefferson County). When twenty masked women broke into the Missouri Pacific depot at Goff (Nemaha County) and destroyed the liquor therein, Balie P. Waggener, the general attorney for the company and a former member of the Prohibition party, decided, in his mature wisdom, that things had gone too far. He advised the company to instruct its agents to deal with the temperance crusaders as "common burglars" and to prosecute "to the fullest extent of the law."

The most violent events occurred at Winfield, where the uprising featured an ultimatum to the jointists by a mass meeting of two thousand; two menacing cannons, drawn into the town square; a desecration of one church; and an attack on three hundred women and children who had sought sanctuary in another. When the ultimatum went unheeded, a group of one hundred and fifty, which included ten "determined, resolute" women and numerous businessmen, ministers, and college students, marched double file to one of the most offensive joints. In twenty minutes of mayhem, during which both attackers and defenders were seriously injured, they destroyed all semblance of a saloon "except the smell." The gratified crusaders then marched in an orderly fashion back to a church, where the Christian Church minister rendered "one of the finest prayers ever delivered in Winfield."[39]

As a result of the direct action taken by the aroused populace, the legal process began to make itself more visible in the station house, the courthouse, and the Statehouse. The rejuvenated KSTU demanded "the immediate, the absolute, the uncompromising enforcement of the prohibitory law." Jointists were arrested and enjoined from operating a nuisance; many closed their doors before either the law or an irate temperance mob could work its will. Often a warning was sufficient, and even the rumor of a prospective visit by Nation could work wonders. At Emporia, only minutes after a prankster had signed her name on the hotel register, all the town's joints closed.[40]

The 1901 legislature reacted by passing the first significant temperance legislation since 1887. It had been anticipated that a strong bid for resubmission would be made at the session. But the legislators had been duly impressed by the outpouring of temperance sentiment which they had heard about from their hometowns and had witnessed directly in the capital city. In addition, they had an opportunity to hear from Nation herself when she visited the Statehouse early in February.

She made informal remarks (she was incapable of making any other kind) to each body, at its invitation, receiving a somewhat warmer welcome in the rural-dominated house. In the senate she pleaded for help in putting down the liquor traffic. "If you don't do it," she said, "then the women of this state will do it." To the house she said, "You refused me the vote and I had to use a rock."[41]

The legislature responded to her, both directly and indirectly, by burying efforts in behalf of resubmission and constitutional-convention bills, passing instead the Hurrel Act, which could more appropriately have been called the Nation Act. Drafted by the KSTU and lobbied by the WCTU, the act tightened the injunction and the search-and-seizure provisions of the liquor law. It made the presence of bar fixtures or a federal liquor stamp prima facie evidence that a public nuisance was being maintained. A companion bill gave the county attorney virtually "inquisitorial" powers to subpoena witnesses who had any knowledge of liquor-law infractions and to require them to testify under penalty of a misdemeanor if they refused to cooperate.[42]

At both the state and the national levels, the WCTU had considerable difficulty in adjusting to the unorthodoxies of its former county president. Early in February the national office cautiously declared that it had "no unkind words for Mrs. Nation." On her eastern tour, Nation spoke in Willard Hall, Evanston, Illinois, the national headquarters. She no longer had much use for the WCTU, she said; it usually wouldn't help and was far too slow when it did. But the next day the president, smiling through clenched teeth, announced that henceforth their national publication would print only favorable items about Nation.[43]

The state organization could not escape the teeth of the dilemma so readily. As Nation moved to the front pages on a daily basis, state headquarters began to be bombarded with inquiries, from members and nonmembers alike, about the official posture of the organization. Some of the "most earnest" women pressed the leadership hard to take a more aggressive stance. The latter reaffirmed its permissive position, pointing out that individuals and local unions could act as they deemed advisable as long as they did not fly in the face of state or national policy. "If they saw fit to raid," President Hutchinson said, "there was none to say them nay." She stressed that the KSTU and WCTU, through their educational efforts over the years, had developed the climate that permitted such an explosive response. "Mrs. Nation . . . threw the bomb, but the combustible material igniting here and there over the state was but an outraged and long suffering people that had borne defiance of law . . . so long that 'patience had ceased to be a virtue.' "[44]

Three years later, Nation proposed to deed some Topeka property to the WCTU to be used as a "Prohibition College" for "healthy Christian girls." She met with the WCTU's Executive Committee, most of whom had never seen her before. A "deep impression" was made on the curious members, who were relieved to discover for themselves that the "masculine and unworthy" press image was untrue. Later that year she made a presentation before the state convention to explain her proposal. Though grateful for her "unselfish and generous" offer, the convention rejected it because she insisted that the governing board be composed only of women who were members of the Prohibition party.

After the vote, she rose to say, more sadly than bitterly, that she thought the union had made a mistake. To relieve the tension the convention rose in a body and sang "Some Glad Day." No lasting animosity resulted, for in her will she bequeathed the rights to her autobiography to the Kansas WCTU. After she had been safely secured in her grave, WCTU esteem for her earthly activities rose measurably and rapidly. In 1918 it dedicated a drinking fountain to her memory at the union station plaza in Wichita.[45]

Newspaper reaction to Nation varied from admiring endorsement through mild rebuke to sputtering hatred. Although the national Prohibition party vacillated on the wisdom of her actions, the organ of the state Prohibition party, the *Fulcrum,* found the "pleasant faced old lady" full of conversation "as sensible as any person you will find." It strongly supported her methods, finding it ironic that her activities had resulted in a "strange sensitiveness" to law and order in quarters that had heretofore remained indifferent to the illegal joint. The paper published many letters from lively correspondents who pointed out the limited options available to women as the common victims of alcohol abusers. "She can't vote it out," one said, "but she can spill it out." Some correspondents, however, did not support women uncritically. A Topeka woman thought that men should come to the aid of the long-suffering women, but, she admitted, there were "impure women enough . . . in Topeka, to dam up the Kaw river in its widest place."[46]

The *Topeka Capital,* which had become virtually the official organ of the "conservative" temperance forces, took a strong anticrusade position. It called for an end to the "sporadic anarchy" that blazed across the state and for increased pressure on officers of the law, rather than for violence. Nation, it said, was "a ridiculous person," a feeling that had become mutual.[47] The *Topeka State Journal* saw much merit in the outbreaks. The people had become increasingly frustrated during the nineties, it said, as they watched "the jug, the tin cup and the 'bootlegger' " give way to "French plate mirrors, mint juleps and lavish fixtures." Above all, Kansas had no reason to apologize for the uprising to the smirking eastern cities that had been derisively asking of late "What's the Matter with Kansas?"[48]

The *Wichita Beacon* applauded her without flatly endorsing her methods. But the *Wichita Eagle* had become her implacable foe from the time of the smashing of the Carey bar. After that incident, it defiantly proclaimed that the "Medicine Lodge woman" would not run Wichita. Among the many slings and arrows that the crusader had to suffer during her eventful career, it remained for the *Eagle* to give, in a word, the unkindest cut of all. Nation, the paper declared, was "unkissable."[49]

Down in Emporia, young Will White gave his wide audience the benefit of his several views on temperance in the pages of the *Emporia Gazette* and in such widely read national magazines as the *Saturday Evening Post*. White had just begun his formal temperance career as a member of the Executive Committee of the KSTU and would later become a vice-president. Bursting with fictional plots at this stage in his writing career, he also contributed to the *Kansas Issue,* the official organ of the KSTU, short morality pieces about fast-living young men who had fallen victim to Demon Rum.[50]

On 28 January 1901, White told his *Gazette* readers that "Carrie Nation is wrong—dead wrong. . . . She is crazy as a bedbug. There is no doubt about that. And she won't stop the sale of beer by her foolish crusade. . . . She has, by her unwomanly conduct, forfeited every claim she may have had to respect as a woman." Just two weeks later they received his more enduring opinion: "She is all right. She is not crazy. She is doing a good, sensible work, and is doing it effectively. . . . She is a brave, fat old heroine, and the *Gazette* hereby apologizes that it didn't discover her worth sooner. . . . Drive the jointists from Kansas. They have no rights that a white man is bound to respect. Hurrah for Carrie Nation! She's all right!"[51]

From among the innumerable personal views of the crusade, two have been selected as forceful examples of the polar positions, each of which was held by many. A Wisconsin man wrote to a Topeka friend: "The woman is clearly . . . looking for cheap advertisement and the money there is in it. Her sympathizers . . . can never convince *me* that *any lady* would do what she has done . . . she is unsexed, and of all things on gods green footstool which are hateful to man, an unsexed woman ought to be most hateful." A woman writing to *Our Messenger,* the WCTU publication, took the opposite position: "What if a few people do get killed[?] . . . I'm tired of this sentimental gush about 'stopping before it comes to bloodshcd.' . . . I for one, hope a thousand more of them will be smashed in Kansas before she stops.''[52]

The state's Nation fever subsided as rapidly as it had developed; near normalcy had returned everywhere by early March. The intensive period had lasted less than two months, only fifty-two days (including seven days of smashing) having elapsed between the Carey Hotel and the Topeka uprising of February 17. Thereafter her outbursts in Kansas included chiefly two minor incidents in Topeka, in which she acted alone, in the winter of 1902/3, and a last fling with three old friends in Wichita in 1904. Although she traveled extensivcly during this period, Topeka remained her home until 1905. At that time she moved to Oklahoma Territory, where she helped to bring thc new state into the union with a dry constitution. She took an extensive European trip in 1908/9 and lived briefly in Washington, D.C., before she settled in a rural area of northern Arkansas in 1909. After an illness of five months, she died on 9 June 1911, during her sixty-fifth year, in a Leavenworth hospital.[53]

THE SIGNIFICANCE of the Nation crusade to Kansas history has been grossly distorted by her biographers. Thousands of Kansans, including many of the most intelligent and best educated, flocked with enthusiasm to her messianic standard. How could this "crazy old woman" have commanded such power over events, yet have been utterly innocent of authority of any sort? The answer, of course, is that her perception was their perception; her concern, their concern; her moral agenda, their moral agenda. She had struck a responsive chord deep in the Kansas psyche, a chord that vibrated all the way back to the direct-action days of the territorial period. As a revealing reflection of the Kansas mind of the period, her crusade amounted to much more than the destruction of a few joints.

The predominant image of the demented freak, which has so endeared itself to the popular media, has come mainly from three sources. Nation herself contributed significantly to the image in her increasingly bizarre behavior outside of Kansas after the middle of 1901. She began to act the caricature of herself in appearances at carnivals and flea circuses, on the vaudeville and burlesque circuits, and as a truly "freak" attraction at New York's Coney Island. Who could be expected to take such demeaning behavior or its eccentric perpetrator seriously or respectfully? And it made a world of difference in the quality of the ensuing publicity whether she had smashed an illegal joint in her home state, which had had a prohibition law for twenty years, or a perfectly legal saloon in Kansas City, St. Louis, or Chicago.[54]

The contemporary eastern press made a major contribution to the popular image. Thirsting for new western objects of ridicule, after the demise of Populism, and inherently hostile to prohibition, it found an easy target in Nation as a prohibitionist, a woman, and a Kansan. Pouncing derisively upon her often-inflated words and actions, it denounced her as the "irresponsible victim of her own violent fanaticism." The most significant source for the modern view has

Carry Nation with a group of supporters in Rochester, New York, 1901 (courtesy of the Kansas State Historical Society, Topeka).

been the product of journalists, biographers, and historians writing principally about her in relation to national prohibition. This derisive outpouring has perpetuated the attitude that was institutionalized by the press. A long-overdue revision has recently appeared in the more-balanced scholarly treatments of temperance as a serious reform.[55]

In many respects, Nation was far too candid with the world—shared far too much of her inner spiritual life in person and in her autobiography—for her own good and that of her enduring reputation. Early in her public career she worried that full disclosure of her God-directedness might bring charges of insanity, and she was right. The issue continued to plague and worry her throughout the remainder of her life.

When her short-lived newspaper, the *Smasher's Mail,* folded, she declared that at least "the public could see by my editorials that I was not insane." After a tour of several Ivy League colleges in 1902, she wrote perceptively that "the great controversy between Yale and Harvard now, is, which shall excel in brute force, and foot-ball seems to be the test. Colleges were founded for the purpose of educating the young, on moral, intellectual, and spiritual lines. . . . It used to be conceded, that the mind made the man, now the forces of the mule and ox are preferred."[56] If that be insanity, we need much more of it.

Just as her most important successes stemmed from her steel-willed determination and dominant personality, so, too, did her most conspicuous failures. With temperance sentiment fanned into a white heat, she had an

The Freethought Ideal.

SUPPLEMENT.

VOL. VII.   OTTAWA, KANSAS, MARCH 1, E. M., 301—1901.   NO. 16.

War Between Rum and Religion.

The Bible the Saloon Keeper's Shield & Shelter.

"Lay on McDuff, and damned be him who first cries 'Hold enough.' "—Shakespeare.

"This army of the Home Defenders declares its intent in its name.   We are the fathers and mothers who, as God's host, have come to the help of the Lord against the mighty and we are here to withstand all the 'fiery darts of the wicked' with the shield of faith.   We demand defense and will have it. No whisky, no tobacco or profanity shall defile our hearthstones.   No man or woman who uses any of these defilements shall have or need ask to serve us.   We will be your brother to help you to cleanse yourself from the filthiness of the flesh, but you need our assistance.   We cannot use you in our business until you clean up.   We are going to place before the people men and women who must be examples of virtue and strength, who shall serve us to reward good and punish evil.   'Happy is that people whose God is the Lord, yea, happy is that people in such a case.   Kansas shall be free and we will set her on a hill that her light may go to every dark corner of the earth. 'Come with us and we will do the good, for the Lord hath spoken good concerning such a people."—Carrie Nation."

This 1901 cartoon in the Ottawa newspaper of the Kansas Freethought Association ridicules the Biblical claims of the Nation crusaders (courtesy of the Kansas State Historical Society, Topeka).

unparalleled opportunity to establish an organization that could maintain a continuing political presence in the state. She recognized this need herself, as did some of her lieutenants, by encouraging Kansas women to organize and by recruiting the Home Defenders in Topeka. But she was too much the loner and the individualist, too taken by her own God-inspired course of action, to make the painful compromises and adjustments necessary to perfect and manage an effective organization. Administratively she was no Frances Willard.

An excellent example of her inability to work with others in a quasi-democratic setting occurred shortly after the smashing had ended. The temperance forces were making a determined effort to elect J. W. F. Hughes as mayor of Topeka against an acknowledged wet. Three weeks before the election, Nation abruptly announced that she planned to launch a write-in campaign for Frank Emerson, a wholly impractical suggestion that could only have split the temperance vote. She strode imperiously into a meeting of a dozen of her most devoted disciples and, with her eyes "snapping," announced that she didn't want anyone "to come to this meeting and talk for Hughes. . . . We don't want dissenters here; we want workers." Glaring at her intimate associates "over and under her glasses," she began quoting rapidly from the Bible, much as the less holy might, under similar circumstances, use profanity. When only one of the disciples showed any sympathy to her proposal, she branded them all "a pack of traitors and hypocrites" and stomped angrily from the room.[57]

One of the least-commented-upon aspects of her influence may have been one of the most far-reaching. Nation had an especially profound effect upon the women of the state. At a time when women were rarely seen in a public advocacy role, she stomped fearlessly up and down the commonwealth, demanding a new social order in temperance affairs and a greater sensitivity to the plight of women as victims of male alcohol abusers. Whatever their individual temperance views, Kansas women could not help but experience a vicarious thrill in seeing the old lady so befuddle and discomfit the authorities. Cries from her detractors that she was illegal or insane or both could not erase the delectable image of her tweaking the nose of the distraught governor, before God Almighty and a roomful of pitiless newspaper reporters.

Nation's views on the role of women in society can best be described as protofeminist. Although the first item on her agenda was alcohol, she conveyed a basic, almost primitive, instinct for the rights and dignity of women. She did not directly attack the sexual mores of the day, though she felt their sting, as few women did. She was constantly reminded that she had passed beyond the pale so far as "lady like" behavior was concerned. "Unsexed" and "unkissable" were only two of the many cruel epithets that she had to absorb. When Governor Stanley did manage to get a word in during the famous interview, he appeared less upset at what she had been saying than at the fact that it was a woman who had been saying it.

Throughout her public career she remained sensitive to women's issues. One evening in Ottawa she declined to see a reporter, pleading exhaustion; but when she learned that the reporter was a young woman, she quickly changed her mind and granted her a cheerful and lengthy interview. Nation often linked her violence against saloons to her lack of authority in matters political, as when she told the Kansas house that she had resorted to rocks only after "you refused me the vote." She established a home in Kansas City, Kansas, for the female victims of male alcohol abusers. On the board of her proposed Prohibition College she would have permitted only women. As time passed, she placed a greater emphasis on suffrage and less on violence. The masthead of her 1905 Oklahoma paper, *The Hatchet,* carried the motto "Your ballot is your hatchet." A few years earlier she had been telling Kansas women just the reverse.[58]

The impact of Nation on prohibition enforcement was heatedly debated by her contemporaries within the temperance movement. Her rough-and-tumble Populist manner proved to be at least as critical as the legality of her methods in determining the individual reaction. Those who felt comfortable with her boisterous Washingtonian style tended to find her behavior and its results more than acceptable. "The Kansas band wagon's again leading the national procession," enthused a KSTU lecturer, "this time with Mother Nation in the driver's seat, wielding her beerstained hatchet for a whip, while the wheels are crushing the life out of the whisky rebellion against the constitution of Kansas." But drys who identified with the more prim and proper "Lyman Beecher" tradition found her conduct repugnant. A Topeka Brahmin curtly stated that "the law was adopted without her or her methods; it has been retained and improved without her or her methods; . . . and its future will not be perceptibly affected by her or her methods."[59]

As the temperance tide receded in the spring, the joints began cautiously to reestablish themselves. By the end of 1901, little outward manifestation of the crusade could be seen. Another five years of relaxed enforcement passed before the authorities moved systematically against illegal selling. At about the same time a distinct movement, which culminated in national prohibition, could be discerned. Some of her biographers have claimed that she was the "chief architect" of that movement, but that surely reaches too far.[60]

How much of the delayed reaction in Kansas can be attributed to her efforts is not easy to assess. She gave a tremendous morale boost to the movement at a time when it desperately needed it. She helped to thwart resubmissionist efforts and certainly influenced the 1901 legislature to enact more-stringent enforcement provisions. Thus she assured the survival of the law during one of its darkest hours, until the subsequent day when enforcement would become more popular, and therefore more effective.

It would be a serious mistake, however, to judge her influence solely from a count of the joints that she wrecked or from the impact of the legislation that she influenced. For thousands of Kansans, and subsequently millions of Americans, she became an all-pervasive and eternal symbol of opposition to the liquor traffic and of protection for the home. By molding herself into an almost-perfect temperance instrument, she became a legendary standard against which future sentiment and action could be measured. In her monomania, her fearlessness, and her God-driven determination, she became the fleshly embodiment of the geometric theorem that the shortest distance between two points is the straight line.

Nation played a powerful role as an educator of both the Kansas and the national publics. She brought the harsh glare of adverse publicity to bear on the outlawed joint and the discredited saloon, both of which would be fighting a losing battle for their lives within a few years. Sometimes her discreditors became unwitting allies in her antisaloon campaign. Even the august and hostile *New York Times* gave her crusade an inadvertent boost. After expounding at length about the pitiful spectacle that the crazy old woman had made of herself, the *Times* contemptuously charged that she didn't have "the slightest conception of the magnitude of the liquor evil in large cities."[61]

Annie Diggs, who became a Nation convert, once said that Nation was a throwback not only to the Puritan days but also to the Biblical ages. She makes one feel, Diggs said, that "an old Hebraic personage has stepped into our own lax and nerveless time." William Allen White placed her in a long line of Kansans, beginning with John Brown (which would have pleased her immensely), who had taken "a very short and absolutely direct cut from [their] ideals to the realization of them." Like the Puritans of yore, who strove to make their community the object of universal emulation, Mrs. Nation attempted to set Kansas on a hill "that her light may go to every dark corner of the earth."[62] She deserves an honored place in the pantheon of Kansas saints for her dauntless courage, her artless integrity, and the insight that her crusade brought to concerns of the human heart.

8

A Glorious Victory

If these church people once get organized they are going to knock hell out of things.

—Anonymous

Constitutional prohibition has done more than any other one thing to make Kansas the garden spot, morally, of the universe.

—Charles M. Sheldon

Kansas has helped to solve for the world the greatest civic problem of the age.

—Lillian May Mitchner

IN THE WAKE of the Nation phenomenon the state returned to a period of quiet unease, with law enforcement largely where it had been in 1900, but tending toward increasing laxity. Drugstore-joints, as well as joints that made no pretense of being drugstores, became more numerous and more brazen than ever. With Carry Nation devoting her time and attention to matters in the East, the momentum shifted back to the wets. Isolated outbursts by the most zealous of the drys shattered the surface calm, the last feeble eruptions of a dying volcano.

In 1902, Blanche Boies, a thirty-five-year-old Topeka nurse who was a Nation protégé, gave vent to her pent-up emotions by horsewhipping Topeka's Mayor Albert Parker in his office. After delivering "a blistering tongue lashing" to the mayor for his laxity in law enforcement, the attractive former farm girl from Jackson County turned to the more corporal and indelible form of punishment. Parker blamed the attack of the "slight little woman" on the recent "inflammatory" sermons of the Reverends Sheldon and McFarland, toward the latter of whom he had difficulty in maintaining even a "grim cordiality." Boies's initiative represented the only successful portion of an ambitious plan of the Home Defenders, which called for numerous women simultaneously to horsewhip the governor, the attorney general, the district judge, and half a dozen local officials.[1]

156

A year later, Boies smashed the glass fronts of four Topeka joints and two drugstores with a short-handled ax. "I was just marking them so the police could find them," she impishly explained on her way to jail. In a prepared statement, she scored McFarland and Sheldon for "weak-kneed leadership" and taunted Kansas men for not insisting on more rigorous enforcement of the law. "Smashing joints and rawhiding perjured officials may not be very dignified," she said, "but they are last resorts, and so we have no apologies to offer."[2]

In 1904 Boies struck once again, this time destroying a picture entitled "Custer's Last Fight," which had hung in a Statehouse room of the Kansas State Historical Society since 1895. The cheap reproduction had been presented by Adolphus Busch, the beer baron, to Governor Morrill, who donated it to the society. Boies and others of like mind had been offended, because the picture carried the name of the brewery (Anheuser-Busch) in large block letters across its lower margin. The last word in this saga, however, went to the opposition. In 1905 a person or persons unknown ripped beyond repair a framed photograph of Carry Nation, which hung in a room of the historical society. A note left at the scene explained the motive: "Goasts sometimes do funny things. General Custer's done this." The new copy of "Custer's Last Fight" seemed to nod approvingly from the opposite wall.[3]

Another zealot who began an eventful career at about this time was Myra Warren McHenry of Wichita. Recently divorced from her lawyer husband after twenty-eight years of a marriage that produced seven children, she launched her civic activities in 1900. Her first public notice came when she fought the application of a Howard (Elk County) druggist for a liquor permit. She went on to a colorful career that included the donning of men's clothes to avoid the sheriff, frequent extemporaneous speaking on the streets of Wichita, and the raiding of numerous joints and liquor warehouses. Her aggressive tactics and "stinging tongue" made the ninety-pound crusader a major nuisance around the Sedgwick County Courthouse and the Statehouse. In the latter she once claimed to have located a "joint" behind a locked door on the third floor. By 1910 her sundry activities had resulted in no less than thirty-three arrests, the most remarkable of which charged her with disturbing the peace at a KSTU convention.

Eccentric is perhaps the kindest characterization that can be offered for McHenry's manifold activities. Yet she seemed to have generated a surprising amount of political clout, always receiving the wary attention of the nervous politicians. She published a newspaper, the *Searchlight*, and became one of Kansas' most prolific pamphleteers. One of her pamphlets, published in 1909, flayed John Marshall, a rising star in the temperance firmament, for liquor-related misdeeds as an attorney back in Elk County at the turn of the century. The title of the tract, "John Marshall a Dangerous Man and Should Be Exposed.—What I Know about Him," would have been enough to shake the most confident of young office seekers. But Marshall's reputation as an honest and astute lawyer remained unscathed, enabling him to subsequently serve sixteen years on the Kansas Supreme Court bench (1915-31).[4]

Not all of the violent outbursts came from women. In July 1905 a male "crank" dynamited three joints in Iola (Allen County) in a single night. The next day the venerable former congressman (1884-94) Edward H. Funston, father of the Philippine War hero Fred Funston, loudly announced that if the local authorities had done their sworn duty, there would have been no joints to blow up. Whereupon Funston suddenly found himself under arrest for "inflammatory talk" and for disturbing the peace. The latter charge stemmed from his vigorous resistance to the arresting officers. The burly policemen finally managed to strap the furious old man in his own buggy before ignominiously leading him off to jail.[5]

AS THE NEW CENTURY unfolded, temperance prospects seemed to diminish in inverse proportion. In 1901 the Kansas Supreme Court held that a private citizen could not abate a nuisance without due process and, in 1903, that a brewery had the right of recovery for the "wrongful destruction of its property." The annual conventions of the KSTU and the WCTU created interest but no effective agenda. Slumping to less than two thousand members by 1901, the Good Templars could discover no formula by which to reverse the long-term trend. They would play no significant role in twentieth-century temperance affairs. Contrary to the common national pattern, the state Prohibition party and the state temperance union established an amiable working relationship. But leaders of the small political party diminished what little influence it did possess with debilitating personality clashes and internecine warfare.[6]

For the two major political parties, prohibition had become virtually a nonissue. The Republicans had not mentioned the question in their platforms since 1892. By 1902 the shrill antiprohibition invective of the nineteenth-century Democratic platforms had become muted. The Republican state chairman, acknowledging that both parties were badly divided on the question of liquor control, announced that the Republicans had no intention of declaring for resubmission in 1902. If the Democrats do, he said, "we will whip them bad." By 1904 neither party mentioned the temperance issue in any form in its platform.[7]

Liquor sentiment and conditions in Topeka, the state's flagship city, may be taken as representative of the first half dozen years of the twentieth century. In May 1902 the wets held a Sunday-afternoon resubmission rally that was attended by fifteen hundred persons; that same evening a dry rally attracted twenty-five hundred. The 60:40 ratio approximated the sentiment in the city and, arguably, across the state.

The popular secretary of the State Board of Agriculture, Foster D. Coburn, chaired the temperance meeting; suffragist leader Lucy B. Johnston, *Topeka Capital* editor Harold Chase, banker Joab Mulvane, several professors from

Washburn College, and virtually every Protestant minister in the city graced the platform. The "liberal" wets heard the 1894 Democratic gubernatorial candidate, David Overmyer, declare that "the ministers of certain Protestant churches have undertaken to rule this city; [but] they'll never do it." G. C. Clemens, another featured speaker, told the crowd: "We don't propose to have a few preachers and women and womanly men . . . run this city."[8]

The accommodating attitude of Gasper Christopher Clemens toward the prohibitory law, over the course of his multifaceted career, is illuminating. Variously described as "Topeka's Mark Twain," the "Topeka anarchist," an "erratic genius," and the "sociable socialist," Clemens developed a reputation as a brilliant lawyer as well as a droll writer and conversationalist. In 1880/81 he published an irreverent paper, the *Whim-Wham*, which often took aim at the prohibitionists, especially Governor St. John. But during the amendment campaign he stepped forward at a critical hour to help the drys counter the spurious legal argument of Charles Robinson that constitutional prohibition meant unregulated liquor. Three years later he served as an attorney for the state in two of the more important cases in prohibition history, the ouster suits against Mayor Wilson and the city of Topeka for the de facto licensing of saloons.[9]

By 1900 he had developed as a specialty the defense of jointists and others who had been accused of violating the liquor law. He also contributed a cogent statement of the liberal position: "Your prohibitionist constantly overlooks [the fact] that he is fighting the other half of the community—fighting scores of men who never touch intoxicating liquors, but who rebel against being forced by law to be provincials and against having their thriving and cultured city converted into a village; against having an entire population put into straight-jackets because there may be a dozen lunatics in the crowd."[10]

Clemens's biographers claim that "it was for him a deeply rooted personal fight" and that his "intense opposition to prohibition indicated that [he] had evaded the puritanical streak all too common among radicals of his era." Perhaps so. Nevertheless, in 1905, when the temperance-inclined of Shawnee County went searching for a strong candidate to nominate for assistant attorney general to clean out the joints, the name of the fifty-six-year-old radical surfaced as a serious possibility. His response to the question of his interest adds another dimension to his mercurial character. "I am in the law business," Clemens said. "I can put the lid on in Topeka and keep it on, [and] no prohibition attorney can do this. I would not think of accepting an Assistant Attorney Generalship for the fee allowed by law. It would require a good, substantial fee before I would consider the position."[11]

The "shameful debauchery" into which Topeka had settled drew a steady outpouring of anguished crys from the drys. "The situation," said the KSTU, "is a disgrace to the state. . . . Liquor selling, gambling and prostitution are carried on with impunity and with the full knowledge of the officials." The superintendent of the Anti-Saloon League of America stiffly admitted on a visit to Topeka that he was "somewhat discouraged with the outlook." J. K. Codding, the chief legal counsel for the KSTU, accurately placed Shawnee County among the five wettest counties in the state. "I will tell you," he said, "that our greatest obstacle to law enforcement is the question which is asked by all other counties and cities of the state, 'Why don't you clean up Topeka?' "[12]

The reality seemed to fully justify the lamentations. The "bold and shameless" joints no longer felt constrained to limit their activities to the environs of lower Kansas Avenue. They invaded the "uptown district" (between Sixth and Tenth streets), placing upstairs rooms there in great demand. Eschewing their typical dingy quarters, the prosperous jointists installed fancy cherry-wood bars, handsome mirrors, and upholstered furniture. Their elaborate "free" lunches infuriated the restaurant owners, even those of the liberal persuasion. In a statement that infuriated the drys, the mayor suggested that the "decent" places should be licensed and the "indecent" ones suppressed.[13]

In 1906 a committee of the City Council made an inventory of the illegal liquor establishments. Among the eighty-one outlets they identified thirty-one upstairs "resorts" and ten of the ground-floor variety; nineteen drugstores, with or without permits; twelve private homes that doubled as joints; seven restaurants; and two "disorderly" houses. But by 1908 the city was accurately described, with some discount for the hyperbole, as so tightly "lidded" that "not even the crack of doom could start a leak in it large enough to let through a drop of booze."[14] What had happened to cause this remarkable shift in the rigor of enforcement in Topeka and throughout Kansas?

THE RENAISSANCE of temperance sentiment that enveloped both Kansas and the nation in the late 1890s did not produce merely a new suit tailored in the old style. The revival developed on a rising base of confidence and prosperity, differing subtly, yet profoundly, from the older tradition. Religion still served as the nuclear core of inspiration, but temperance now wore less emotional, more prosaic clothes. The older evangelicals had been characterized as "men and women . . . made up of nothing but nerves, tied together by bands of faith in God." But in the nascent movement, the saloon question was discussed "as a purely practical matter to the consideration of which mere feeling is wholly foreign."[15] The progressive era had been born.

Progressivism held the center of the state and the national stages from early in the century to the entry of the United States into World War I. The leaders of progressivism tended to have been reared in middle-class, evangelical Protestant homes, in an atmosphere of strict morality but diffuse theology. Rejecting a ministerial career as too intellectually confining, they often opted for law, journalism, politics, or social work. Robert Crunden has depicted progressivism as a "climate of creativity" in which reform-minded individuals, respectful of science, worked for a spiritual, social, and political reformation "to fulfill God's plan for democracy in the New World."

If the inspiration emanated from the Christian religion, the *modus operandi* came from the pragmatic world of business. Progressives prized reason, discipline, competency, and organizational efficiency above all else. In their civil religion, "go-getting" and "do-gooding" became inseparably fused. They believed in the reform of the individual and the reform of society for the good of the individual. And they urged that the government intervene directly to effect these ends. If prohibition had not existed at the beginning of the twentieth century, the progressives would surely have invented it.[16]

With its reform tradition and its generous supply of evangelical Protestants, Kansas, not surprisingly, furnished a fertile soil for progressive reforms. Commencing in 1904, Kansans elected progressives to the governorship in nine successive elections. During this interval, reform legislation brought significant changes in the areas of taxes, banking, public health, public utilities, civil service, child labor, and workmen's compensation, among others.

The activity from 1905 through 1911 was especially intense and unmatched in the legislative history of the state. As a contemporary political scientist noted, "It would be hard to find a state with more progressive measures than Kansas." The quintessential Kansas progressive, Governor Walter R. Stubbs (1909–13), described the movement's philosophy succinctly in 1912: "The people know now that government, properly conducted in the interest of the governed, is as much a business proposition as the building of a railroad or the managing of any other commercial enterprise."[17]

By 1905, when the first progressive governor took his oath, the predominant temperance tone had shifted from pietistic to civic righteousness. The vigorous scion of the young political reform had been firmly grafted to the emaciated temperance stock. Harmfulness, rather than sinfulness, now dominated the antiliquor rhetoric. The individual would enjoy enhanced savings and improved health; business would profit from a more disciplined work force and greater productivity; and society would benefit from a more responsible citizenry and a reduction in antisocial behavior—every component and the whole would gain from increased sobriety and, ultimately, total abstinence.

The first progressive governor, Edward W. Hoch (1905–9), came into office with sterling temperance credentials. A devout Methodist, he had uncompromisingly championed prohibition for twenty-five years as the editor of the small-town *Marion Record*. But prohibition as a salient issue was as nonexistent in the 1904 campaign as it had been in the St. John election of 1878, which subsequently produced such large results.[18]

For the first few months the new governor did next to nothing to stem the liquor tide. He seemed to be unable to decide on an effective course of action, contenting himself instead with writing benign letters to local authorities and issuing shopworn platitudes to the drys. "I would rather have the confidence and prayers of one good woman," he told the WCTU, "than the support of all the law breakers in . . . Kansas." Many temperance people suspected that another

Morrill or Stanley had been elected to the chair—a good-hearted, pious sort, long on promise and short on performance.[19]

At least thirty-eight newspapers across the state began to mount vigorous enforcement campaigns, however. The publisher of the *Iola Register*, Congressman Charles Scott (1901–11), said that Kansas had become the national "standing joke" to allow "this thing to go on in the face of the statute made and provided." The "standing joke" became even more amusing to the nation in August, when the governor's daughter christened the battleship *Kansas*, not with the traditional champagne, but with water from the "John Brown Spring" in Miami County. "The world may laugh at Kansas," the drys countered in defense, "but that will not hurt the State any."[20]

The increasing number of people fed up with the lax urban enforcement began to express their feelings more forcefully. The Wyandotte County WCTU asked the governor to call out the militia to enforce the law. A Leavenworth physician wrote: "We have been living in a state of absolute anarchy here so long that the people scarely know or realize that any other condition is possible." But a state senator from Leavenworth bristled at the rumor that military force might be employed: "The governor may call out the militia and make as hard a fight for prohibition as he likes, but the joints of Leavenworth County, like Tennyson's brook, will run on forever. . . . Leavenworth County will always have all the liquor it wants."[21]

Hoch and Attorney General C. C. Coleman held a lengthy conference in September, after which the first signs of a coherent administrative plan began to appear. Coleman appointed assistant attorneys general for a few of the more difficult counties, most notably Shawnee and Wyandotte. The Shawnee appointee began with a good deal of bravado: "Topeka is going to be decent. . . . It is going to be clean, respectable and law abiding." For six months he witnessed a series of futile raids on jointists, who had been tipped to the impending visit, and frustrating acquittals by juries that had been presented ample evidence for conviction. Finally, in disgust, he resigned in open court. The Wyandotte appointee made some initial progress and then bogged down. Coleman abruptly replaced him on 8 June 1906.[22] Hoch had struck out in his first two major efforts.

The new Wyandotte appointee, Charles W. Trickett, a forty-five-year-old Kansas City lawyer, was philosophically inclined toward license rather than prohibition. But the hard-nosed go-getter nonetheless firmly believed in enforcement of the law. He beheld the state's largest city, with its ninety thousand souls and its 256 open saloons. For years, Missouri breweries had owned or held mortgages on choice lots on the Kansas side on which they had built saloons. The final ignominy had come when a reform-minded governor of Missouri had closed the saloons tight on Sundays on the Missouri side, causing all the serious drinkers to flock across the state line, where they could partake of their libations unmolested. In Wyandotte County, prohibition Kansas could not even close its saloons on Sunday.[23]

For two weeks, Trickett worked in the traditional manner—obtaining search-and-seizure warrants, injunctions, contempt citations, and writs of abatement, the last of which directed the sheriff to destroy liquor stocks and the associated paraphernalia. But the full employment of the well-developed Kansas law made barely a ripple on the surface of the Kansas City liquor sea. At one saloon in one day, Trickett jailed six bartenders in seriatim. But the defiant brewery paid the fines, kept the jailed employees on salary, and taunted that it would recruit a new man for every incumbent that Trickett had arrested.

Trickett was outraged that a court of equity stood impotent before the world to enforce its orders. In his despair he reflected back to the great flood of 1903, when a federal judge had ordered United States marshals to take possession of a Kansas River railroad bridge. That mandate had prevented desperate citizens from blowing up the obstruction that was impounding the floodwater and thus threatening their homes. Inspired by that example of determination, Trickett went before a sympathetic municipal judge, William G. Holt, and obtained additional writs of abatement, this time to padlock the offending establishments.

More than sixty buildings were "decorated" with padlocks in three days. When one unconvinced jointist removed the padlock and reopened for business, Holt sentenced him to eighteen months in jail and imposed a $1,500 fine for his trouble. And then, *mirabile dictu,* the saloonists themselves began to padlock their buildings to prevent the loss of their valuable fixtures. Within a few days, dozens of wagons clogged the streets, hauling the fixtures over the state line to the east. With an estimated average of three loads per saloon, the transfer wagons made over five hundred trips to Missouri. In less than thirty days, Trickett closed Kansas City's saloons, and they stayed closed. No new law had been utilized, only the determined and imaginative use of the old. "July 4th, 1906," Trickett said, "was the first day since [Wyandotte] County was settled that the inhabitants lived, moved and had their being without an open saloon."[24]

At about the time of Trickett's triumph, Attorney General Coleman scored several significant victories in the state supreme court. The practice of the de facto licensing of saloons for revenue had continued to be widespread in cities of the first and second classes. In a 1905 survey, the *Topeka Capital* found 480 "licensed" saloons in fifteen counties. Acting on Coleman's writs, the high court ousted the city of Kansas City from such practice and ousted from office the Wyandotte County attorney and Kansas City's mayor, W. W. Rose.

Rose resigned three days before the ouster order and then mounted a vigorous campaign for reelection at the special election held a month later. When Rose won the election, Coleman instituted contempt proceedings, on the theory that the ouster covered the mayor's entire two-year term, which had commenced in April 1905. In July 1906 the high court found Rose in contempt and ordered him to pay a $1,000 fine plus costs. Rose resigned again, as did the chief and other police officers. The next election, held in December, did not include Rose as a candidate, but he ran again at his first legal opportunity in April 1907. He was defeated in that effort, partly because of a large vote by women.[25]

The Kansas City successes of Trickett and Coleman initiated a series of legal victories for the state that paralleled the rising tide of public resentment at the open flouting of the law. Ouster suits in the Kansas Supreme Court quickly brought to heel the cities and officials of Leavenworth, Wichita, Hutchinson, Junction City, Coffeyville, and Pittsburg. But for a time, the well-established licensing practice lingered on in a few of the more defiant localities. For example, after the Pittsburg ouster order, thirteen "public-spirited" saloonists organized a "lodge" which made monthly contributions to the salaries of the police judge and other key public officials. The Kansas Supreme Court found them in contempt and levied fines of from $500 to $1,000 per man.

The ouster suits proceeded amid a growing climate of inevitability as Atchison, Fort Scott, Parsons, Iola, and other prior offenders "voluntarily" gave up the licensing practice. The drys scored a number of municipal victories in the spring elections of 1907, including those in Kansas City, Wichita, Salina, Junction City, and Arkansas City. By the end of 1910 the attorney general could report that "there are no open saloons in the state and apparently no community where the local officers are not assisting in an honest endeavor to enforce the law."[26] With the exception of Leavenworth, Crawford, and Cherokee counties, the statement appeared to be a reasonably accurate description of reality.

Fred Schuyler Jackson (1907–11) succeeded Coleman as attorney general. "Fighting Fred" brought to liquor-law enforcement the old-time zeal that Kansas had last seen in the days of Lyman Beecher Kellogg. The new attorney general worked closely with the KSTU, claiming that its help equaled that of two assistants in his office. Not surprisingly, the KSTU found Jackson "a good, straight, clean, brave, kind, honest man." The old, outmoded method of fighting the joints, the union said, was "to pass resolutions, issue proclamations, . . . have a public meeting, kick up a storm . . . and as soon as the storm blew over, . . . business would resume." But taciturn Fred Jackson, it said, just kept on "prosecuting, arresting, searching and seizing, and filing injunctions, and the longer he fights the harder he fights."[27]

Out-of-state distilleries and wineries simply supplied their product, legally or illegally, to their Kansas customers. The breweries did that and more—much more, as Trickett discovered in Kansas City. Soon after taking office, Jackson accelerated the demise of the joints by moving directly against the brewers. In a surprise action he filed writs with the state supreme court, prohibiting the brewers from doing business in Kansas. He sought restraints against fifteen companies, including such giants as Pabst, Blatz, Schlitz, Goetz, Miller, Lemp, and Anheuser-Busch. The court granted the ouster requests, appointed receivers for the companies' property, and issued restraining orders to prohibit the removal of said property, which was valued at over $500,000.

The receivers directed that all of the seized liquor be destroyed and that the confiscated real estate be sold. All but two of the companies "confessed judgment as prayed for," paid their court costs, and left the state. Two St. Louis companies, Anheuser-Busch and Lemp, took legal issue with the "outrageous" appointment of the receivers, but they lost their case before the Kansas Supreme Court.[28] The breweries did not again become a significant factor in the Kansas equation until the 1930s.

AS THE JOINT PROBLEM diminished in magnitude between 1906 and 1908, the drys turned their attention increasingly to what Fred Jackson described as the "greatest evil" of the prohibitory law: the drugstore. The drugstore law of 1885, with its provision for self-diagnosis and prescription, had become a major source of embarrassment to the champions of enforcement. KSTU's Secretary Stephens wryly summarized the problem thus: "Drug stores multiply as if Kansans lived on drugs, and . . . [the druggists'] monthly reports disclose an absurd confidence on the part of the people in the medical efficacy of liquor." He also identified the major obstacle to obtaining the full cooperation of the druggists in law enforcement: "It is not pleasant and it is not profitable to tell a customer that he is a perjurer."[29]

Some druggists no longer bothered to ask customers to fill out the required statement, as Charles Sheldon learned firsthand in an exploratory trip down Kansas Avenue in Topeka. He and a friend bought drugstore liquor "as freely as we might have bought toothbrushes or hair oil until we had a big basket full." Though explicitly forbidden to do so by the law, some drugstores allowed their steady patrons to drink on the premises. In such drugstore-joints, one could usually find thirsty males gossiping about current events and lounging against the water hydrant or the prescription case, while "taking their medicine."[30]

Monthly sales in the drugstores continued to serve as a thermometer of the "heat" being applied on the joints. In Topeka, sales reached a record 8,000 a month in 1904, during a short-term "reign of terror" led by Police Chief Frank Stahl. Under the more relaxed conditions of 1906, sales averaged less than 3,000 a month. But as the joints came under intense pressure during the dry renaissance of 1907, sales shot up from 3,200 in December 1906 to 4,300 in January 1907, 11,400 in March, and over 20,000 in May. At an average of one pint per sale, this last figure translates into 30,000 gallons per year. (The average yearly in-state production of liquor for the 1901–9 period, all of which theoretically went to the drugstores, was 13,561 gallons of distilled spirits and 645,389 gallons of beer. This production was augmented by shipments from out of state.)

As the Topeka sales soared, the city's sanitary officer complained of the newspapers, discarded as beer-bottle wrappings, which choked the alleys behind the Kansas Avenue drugstores. The infirm had developed the unsightly habit of carrying their nostrum into the nearest alley and proceeding to alleviate their pain on the spot. The petulant official suggested that the culprits be made to eat the paper and wash it down with their own medicine.[31]

Several localities took legal action to curb the drugstore abuses, such as imposing a midnight curfew or requiring a physician's prescription. More importantly, probate judges became more circumspect in issuing, and in renewing, permits. By the close of 1908, sixty-five counties, mostly rural, had no outstanding permits at all. In the other forty counties a total of 309 permits had been issued. Six urban counties, led by Shawnee, Wyandotte, and Sedgwick, accounted for over one half (160) of the total.[32]

But the public continued its clamor for elimination of the "festering sore." William Allen White asked rhetorically why the state prosecuted the "lowly" jointists and permitted the "rich" druggists to go scot-free. Attorney General Jackson recommended, and Governor Stubbs supported, a bill in the 1909 legislature that would have replaced the probate judges with the State Board of Health as the responsible group for administering the druggists' permits. But the legislators, hard-pressed by the agitated public, reached beyond the politicians' recommendation to produce the final solution to the drugstore problem. In one quick stroke they eliminated all in-state sales for the three excepted purposes.[33] Henceforth, drugstores ceased to be an outlet for legal or illegal liquor in the state.

With the tightening of prohibition enforcement and the strengthening of the progressives' hold, the national perception of Kansas began to change. The state started to shed its image as the natural habitat of emotional cranks and unbalanced freaks, which had prevailed since 1890. The national press reported that the wild-eyed reformer would have a difficult time there now: "Its name is no longer a brand of misfortune; no curse of fleeing multitudes reverberates across its solitudes." The emerging image projected a rational, no-nonsense agricultural and business-based society, efficiently and effectively run by those of the progressive faith. That projection owed a great deal to the "biggest press bureau on earth," namely, the State Board of Agriculture, headed by Foster D. Coburn, said to be "the most useful person in Kansas."[34]

At the close of his second term, Governor Hoch lauded prohibition as being of great benefit to the state morally, educationally, and financially. "The business world is now a great temperance society," he said. Businessmen from all walks had endorsed the prohibitory idea, "not from sentimental, but from cold commercial considerations." With the first glimmerings of the third and final national prohibitory wave appearing on the horizon, Kansans had solid reasons for believing that they represented the vanguard of the promising future, rather than the joke of the discouraging past. "We confidently expect the Kansas idea to become universal," Governor Hoch said.[35]

THE TOTAL PROHIBITION of in-state liquor sales went into effect in May 1909. Law-enforcement officials used the occasion to tighten up their jurisdictions on all fronts. The Topeka police chief visited the drugstores and the clubs a few days before the law became effective. The liquor vendors gave him a begrudging, if surly, acknowledgment. He then paid his respects to the "swell club" of the state, the Topeka Club. "We have been around seeing the other fellows," the chief told the members, "and they have treated us all right." "There are no fellows here," he was corrected. "This is a club of gentlemen."[36] And thus was the battle joined.

As in the 1890s, the one hundred and fifty members of the Topeka Club included many of the leading business and professional men of the state, with a particular emphasis on federal judges, United States district attorneys, railroad attorneys, and physicians. The club had employed a locker system since before the Chief Lindsay incident of 1893. Under this arrangement, members kept liquor in small lockers for their personal use. The club itself did not buy, own, or sell liquor, though it did provide setups and its attendants did pour drinks when instructed to do so by the members. The "overwhelming majority" of the members, it was said, favored prohibition. But they sputtered in anger at the thought that their cherished rendezvous had, once again, been equated with a common joint, or even a middle-class brotherhood such as the Elks Club. With a fine display of arrogance, the leadership announced that while the club had not been chartered as an "educational institution," it had been compelled "once upon a time [1893] to teach certain officious officials [Chief Lindsay] a lesson," and it hoped it would not "again be forced to continue a course of instruction."[37]

The club's membership included Governor W. R. Stubbs, a progressive Republican who was not on the best of terms with many of the conservative members. In early July, Stubbs announced that in his opinion the locker system was outside the law and that if the honorable club did not drop it, he would drop them. It didn't, and two weeks later he did. The outspoken governor declared that the members were "swells" and that the club was "a rich man's saloon." For this politically sound stance he received the plaudits of leading progressives such as William Allen White, who publicly reproached the "wealthy, aristocratic social organization of excellent gentlemen." In late July, Attorney General Jackson filed a writ in the state supreme court to "oust, enjoin and prohibit" the locker-system practice.[38]

The supreme court cited the clubroom law, which prohibited the maintenance of places in which liquors are "received and kept for the purpose of use . . . as a beverage." The Topeka Club, the court said, was such a place, and it clearly was violating the law. The popular decision furnished useful ammunition for those who had maintained that the prohibitory law was enforced, by and large, in an egalitarian manner.

The several estimates of the number of "excellent gentlemen" who drank provides an interesting sidelight to the case. In the initial skirmish the club's flustered steward had admitted that all eighty-seven lockers held liquor. Upon more sober reflection, the estimate shrank to about thirty-five. In the supreme court's brief the magic number was further reduced to fifteen.[39] If the case had been appealed to the United States Supreme Court, . . .

DURING THE STUBBS ADMINISTRATIONS (1909–13), enforcement of the prohibitory law received a very high priority. The legislature helped with laws that enhanced the "inquisitorial" powers of the attorney general and of the county attorneys, detailed the procedures for removing "unfaithful" public officers, banned drinking on passenger trains, and pronounced that second liquor offenders were guilty of a felony and would be subject to one year in the State Penitentiary. As trouble spots, Leavenworth, Wichita, and Hutchinson commanded attention. But no locality exceeded the counties of Crawford and Cherokee in the frequency or flagrancy of liquor-law violations.[40]

Farmers of old American stock initially settled the southeast corner of the state. But the discovery of mineable coal, zinc, and lead wrought an economic revolution and created a sharp cultural fault line separating the region from the rest of the state. Italians, Sicilians, Poles, Slavs, and Austrians emigrated directly from the Old World in such numbers that the region became known as the Little Balkans. Typically Roman Catholic in religion, the new arrivals came from the working class, which had tended to be less enthusiastic about liquor regulation than the middle class, and from European cultures that drank liquor in copious amounts and with an unassuming manner. At first the immigrants didn't understand the Kansas law, and after they got an inkling, they didn't want to. The dominant Anglo-Saxon culture accepted the challenge and struggled mightily to "Americanize" the "foriners."

Encouraged by the statewide level of compliance, Governor Stubbs and Attorney General John Shaw Dawson (1911–15) brought intense pressure on the area to conform to the general pattern during 1911/12. They held inquisitions, hired private investigators, and appointed assistant attorneys general, utilizing fully a contingency fund that had recently been increased from $4,000 to $10,000. Stubbs threatened to send the militia; Dawson threatened deportation. They closed the joints in the larger towns of Pittsburg, Girard, and Columbus and obtained numerous injunctions and prosecutions, but far fewer convictions. In Cherokee County they ousted a half dozen justices of the peace, two constables, the county attorney, and the sheriff. By the close of 1912, Dawson reported that he had been "tolerably successful" in Crawford but could not say as much in Cherokee.

Investigators frequently received death threats, sometimes from the "Black Hand," a mafia type of organization. Even if the Black Hand were a fiction, an official said, "the whole Italian race is an organization and they shield each other from the officers . . . in every possible way." An alarmed citizen claimed that there was "more general disregard for law and decency in Cherokee County than any place its size within civilization."[41]

Reversing the usual rural/urban disparity, liquor activity centered in the countryside, rather than in the towns. Officials found it easier to rid the middle-class-dominated towns of their joints than to clean out the mining camps that dotted the area. Composed of dilapidated shacks and makeshift hovels, the grim camps often shocked the uninitiated with their pitiful sights and rancid smells. The WCTU supported a "foreign missionary" in the area who visited the sick, held classes for the children, and distributed food and clothing to the poorest families.

Although a plethora of "beer signs and beer calendars" hung on the walls, the homes contained no "magazines, papers or books." Empty beer bottles and kegs accumulated behind the shacks "like hay stacks." A local observer noted that "a man with all his nerves gone except the olfactory could very soon locate numerous saloon[s] from their stench." The heartbreak of alcohol abuse reared its ugly head, as the poignant words of a miner's wife written to the governor illustrate: "I am one off the ladys and I got six children. Write away after my mans got his pay he goes to the saloon [.] he dont come back before hes got every penny gone and after he comes back home and he hits me and I after ran away with my children and sleep on the ground. I hope you remember what I tell you now."[42]

When the increased pressure closed most of the established joints, the "foriners" quickly adjusted to the changed circumstances. "Kitchen joints" sprang up as a source of libation and income for many of the unemployed. The even-more-modest "portable joint," consisting of a tub of ice and a couple of dozen bottles of beer, could be moved swiftly from cellar to cellar when danger lurked. Given the location of the camps, close to the Missouri border, the supply line was short, quick, and easy. "There are more teams on the roads hauling it out [here] and gathering up the empty kegs and boxes," a citizen said, "than there are meat, bread, tea and huxter wagons all put together."[43]

A difficult situation for the drys became almost intolerable as cries of "politics," "graft," and "corruption" filled the air. The wets accused Stubbs of "grandstanding" to promote his campaign for election to the United States Senate in 1912. Internecine warfare broke out among assistant attorneys general, county attorneys, sheriffs, justices of the peace, and other authorities. Each intimated that the others had been accepting bribes from the law violators to minimize enforcement. It was said that a surtax of $1.00 per barrel of beer went to local officers and "a few fixers" on a monthly basis.[44] It became nearly impossible even for the most discerning to determine who deserved to wear a white hat. The most cynical said that no one did.

District Judge Edward E. Sapp of Cherokee County added a large log to this fire during the summer of 1911 when he charged that enforcement in the area had been a sham for years. The people believed, he said, that enforcement had been primarily "a fee-grabbing proposition." In many instances, local judges had indefinitely continued liquor cases after extracting court costs from the defendants, a strictly illegal procedure. Confiscated liquor was often sold to the thirsty by the authorities before they got back to the courthouse from the evening's raid. Legally attached bar fixtures, the property of the court, decorated the homes of many Columbus drys. A modified abatement system had been developed, Sapp said, one that would not have been approved by C. W. Trickett: While padlocks graced the front doors of the joints, the back doors stood wide open "for the purpose of transacting business."[45] In all, Crawford-Cherokee demonstrated graphically the monumental difficulties of law enforcement when a majority of the local community, unconvinced morally of the rectitude of the law, offers almost total resistance to it.

Unfortunately, squabbles among enforcement officers did not remain confined to the lower echelons. A major-league controversy broke out in 1911 between Stubbs, the governor, and Dawson, the attorney general. A wealthy Lawrence contractor, the red-headed and energetic Stubbs gave Kansas one of its most honest, efficient, and noteworthy administrations. He came by his temperance proclivities naturally, as a Quaker and as a progressive reformer. But he could be brash, tactless, and blindly obstinate, too often carrying his virtues and strengths across that nebulous boundary into vice and weakness. A native of Scotland, Dawson had joined a temperance organization as a boy and had immigrated to Hill City (Graham County) as a young man. A "massive" man with a booming voice, the attorney general had the reputation of being genial, well read, intelligent, and principled. "A faithful ally," his friends said, "but a dangerous foe."[46]

The two men had enjoyed an amicable relationship during Stubbs's first term, when Dawson had served as the governor's private secretary. But after Dawson's election in 1910, the governor had difficulty remembering that the attorney general was not still a member of his personal staff. During the early months of the new relationship, Stubbs ordered Dawson ("You are hereby directed . . .") to look into this liquor violation and that, often giving detailed instructions for proceeding. A full-blooded prohibitionist, Dawson responded promptly and politely at first, but he grew increasingly irritated at being treated like a house servant. He also chafed at the daily, minute, and confidential reports on liquor violations that the governor was receiving in a never-ending stream from private investigators, whom he paid and directed. The imperious Stubbs shared as much, or as little, of these reports as pleased him. Dawson grew to feel that Stubbs always held superior information and that he monitored Dawson closely, especially in wet areas such as Crawford-Cherokee, just to see if Dawson would make the correct moves.

As relations between the two men degenerated, the salutations on Dawson's letters changed from "My dear governor" to "Your excellency." "We are living in Kansas under a constitution," Dawson told the press, "not in Russia under a czar." The *Topeka State Journal* opined that the two were trying to settle a "personal matter" through the prohibitory law, "a long suffering beast of

This cartoon in *The Kansas Issue* portrays the Stubbs-Dawson dispute (courtesy of the Kansas State Historical Society, Topeka).

burden in Kansas.'' The liquor vendors down in Crawford-Cherokee looked on in amazement, the more skeptical being convinced that the public row was a ''sham battle'' to entrap them.[47]

When Stubbs commanded Dawson to subpoena Jay House, a muckraking Topeka newspaperman, to obtain information on liquor violations, Dawson flatly refused to do so, declaring that he had constitutionally endorsed discretion in carrying out the functions of his office. After the exchange of several recriminatory letters, all of which were fully published in the press, the governor unprecedentally filed in the Kansas Supreme Court an action to require the attorney general to carry out his orders.[48]

The high court seemed embarrassed at being asked to resolve the dispute between the state's two principal officials, both of whom were highly respected. In a split decision, the majority held that the governor's ''supreme executive power'' was no mere ''verbal adornment.'' The power ''to name the witness to be subpoened and examined'' fell fully within the governor's constitutional authority. Stubbs won the battle, and Dawson complied with his directive, but everyone, save perhaps Stubbs, felt it had been a Pyrrhic victory.[49]

THE FORTUNES OF THE WCTU followed the same path as that of the general temperance sentiment. As the ''mental microbe'' of progressivism spread in the body politic, it also infected the women, though to a lesser extent than the male-controlled KSTU. The religious impulse dominated the thought and activities of the women, as it had in the nineteenth century. At their meetings they continued to hold lengthy devotionals, to refer to their deceased members as ''promoted comrades,'' and in closing, to clasp hands, sing the doxology, and render the benediction in unison. As always, the ''sweet face'' of Frances Willard looked down approvingly on the gatherings.[50]

In the dark days before the renaissance the WCTU had gained a reputation as an organization that ''never quits under fire, never retreats, but is always ready for action.'' In 1910 John Marshall of the KSTU reflected that ''our law would have been dead quite a long while ago if it hadn't been for the [WCTU]. There have been times when the women had all the fighting to do.'' While the WCTU and the KSTU shared similar goals, they had employed different tactics from the beginning. ''I look upon our work as the mothers work of educating,'' a WCTU leader wrote to a KSTU official, ''your work as the sons to enforce [the] law.'' And withal, the women maintained, almost fiercely, their precious independence. ''I believe we should stand with them, not back of them, nor for them,'' the WCTU's President Elizabeth Hutchinson said of the KSTU.[51]

The organization grew hardly at all in the wet 1890s, maintaining approximately the same size at the beginning of the decade (2,500 members in 150 chapters) as at its end. But by 1906 it had nearly doubled, to 4,600, and by 1911 it had doubled once again, to almost 10,000 members in 500 chapters. During this span a great turnover occurred in the active membership: for example, only six members who had attended the 1892 state convention were present at the 1908 meeting. To encourage the return of ''lost'' members, the leadership thought it important to ''keep sweet and patient and use tact, permeated with prayer.''[52]

Ever since the bright and busy days of Fanny Rastall the WCTU had been a force in the political and social affairs of the state. On the political front the white ribboners had worked and voted for dry candidates in numerous municipal elections, forming a solid opposition to Mayor Rose in Kansas City, for example. They aided materially in pushing to successful conclusions the Anticigarette Law (1909) and the White Slave Act (1913). At their behest the 1915 legislature decreed September 28 as Frances Willard Day in the public schools. On this day each year a special program extolled the benefits of prohibition, in addition to the regular temperance lessons, which continued to exert ''a great influence.'' By 1914, Kansas had become such a focus of national attention on the prohibition question that the state president received five minutes on the national convention's program, while the other state presidents had to do with one minute each.[53]

Union members exhibited a protracted interest in eugenics, though in a 1905 debate on the proposition that heredity had a greater influence on character than environment, the negative position prevailed. They circulated among the public hundreds of "mercy" petitions, which opposed cruelty to animals. Members worked to suppress patent medicines and to encourage physicians to stop prescribing intoxicating liquor. After the 1909 law eliminated the medical exemption, Dr. Charles F. Menninger assured them that the change gave "greater efficiency" to his growing practice. In 1916 they deplored the military build-up both in Europe and in America and resolved that "our country shall fit itself for leadership in the disarmament of nations."[54]

The WCTU also frowned upon a number of growing social customs of the day, stances that jar and dismay the modern Kansan. These anxieties generated the union's enduring reputation as the natural home of the crabbed, joyless bluenose puritan. The membership opposed divorce, the use of tobacco, Sunday entertainment, and pool halls, "those Schools of vice and idleness." They resolved against "unseemly pictures" in public places and literature that produced "impure thoughts." Vulgar and suggestive popular songs brought their condemnation, as did the "modern ultra-fashionable dress" of women.[55]

The Reverend Mary ("Mollie") Ferguson Sibbitt of Wichita, a leader who headed the state union's war work in 1917/18, typified the more conservative wing of the organization as regards social mores. In 1917 she said that she was "a Quaker by training, but a Methodist by ancestry," and that in recent years "her Methodist blood had gotten the better of her Quaker brains." She hoped that in the future, not only alcohol and "coffin nails" would be legally proscribed, but also "chewing gum, playing cards and face powder."[56]

During this period the state organization came under the skillful guidance of Lillian May Early Mitchner, who assumed the presidency in 1909 and did not relinquish it for twenty-nine years. Born in Iowa in 1862, she married businessman Charles Mitchner in Indiana in 1882, and they settled in Newton shortly thereafter. She headed the Industrial School for Girls at Beloit for four years (1915–19) and had become so popular as a state figure by mid decade that she had to issue a denial that she intended to become a candidate for the United States Senate.

Topeka Capital columnist Zula Bennington Greene ("Peggy of the Flint Hills") described Mitchner as "a woman of strong personality, with charm and good looks and energy and humor thrown in, a born leader." Despite these impressive assets, Mitchner refused to enter the public arena until after she had raised a son and four foster children. With such a "Home Comes First" personal credo, stressing the "organized motherhood" image of the WCTU came easily. Her aggressive tactics, especially in the legislative halls, quickly

Lillian May Early Mitchner (courtesy of the Kansas State Historical Society, Topeka).

dispelled any lingering wet hopes that the union would assume a more passive role in public affairs. "Lillian Mitchner can make the best chocolate pie you ever tasted," an experienced adversary said, "and I wish to Heaven she would stay at home and make pies."

Forceful, quick-witted, and doggedly determined, Mitchner led the union during its most influential years. With her stress on sharply focused goals and administrative efficiency, she fitted the Fanny Rastall mold much more closely than that of, say, Drusilla Wilson. An indefatigable worker, Mitchner visited local unions almost continuously and, as the campaigns for state and national prohibition warmed up, came into great demand as a regional and national speaker. In 1914, for example, armed with "Fifty Facts" on Kansas prohibition, she traveled over six thousand miles in eleven weeks while speaking in several western states.[57]

An incident at the 1917 state convention yields a third symbol of the evolving public relationship between women and men in Kansas society. Attorney General Sard Brewster (1915–19), a dedicated prosecutor of the prohibitory law, spoke to the delegates about the close cooperation between his office and the WCTU. "While Mrs. Mitchner is not always satisfied with the manner in which I conduct my office," he said, "I try to be satisfied with the manner in which she conducts hers." When he turned to ask Mitchner how much time he had left, she told the audience not to worry, "when his time is up, I will stop him." To which Brewster ruefully replied, "She has the advantage over me, I don't know how to stop her."[58]

The WCTU made essential contributions to the most important victory of the era for women: full state suffrage. After the second defeat in 1894, enthusiasm for suffrage declined markedly, though not as completely as after the 1867 loss. Shortly after the turn of the century the union noted that it was "difficult to find a White Ribboner that is not ready for her full enfranchisement." In 1911 the superintendent of the Franchise Department, Sena Hartzell Wallace, told the members that "woman suffrage has at last become fashionable; make it more so by bringing every pressure to bear, always in a womanly, dignified way."[59]

Though the old "home protection" rhetoric could still be heard, the leaders now claimed suffrage as a natural right. Margaret Hill McCarter, a staunch prohibitionist and a prominent authoress, said she was a suffragist "because it is my inherent right to have the ballot." Minnie Johnson Grinstead, a WCTU organizer and ESA president of the "Big Seventh" district in western Kansas, held similar views: "I am indeed anxious that the third time is the charm and that we win what is ours, but withheld from us."[60]

The WCTU played its most critical role in getting the suffrage amendment before the voters. Its 1910 convention resolved to make suffrage "the leading work of the year." The number of different kinds of petitions that were carried that year reveals its priorities: 10 against Sunday baseball, 9 against pool halls, 8 for federal liquor legislation, 2 against the white-slave traffic, and 101 for suffrage. WCTU-sponsored petitions, which bore twenty-nine thousand names, and "hundreds" of letters and telegrams flooded the 1911 legislature. Mitchner and Wallace, for the union, and the leaders of the ESA lobbied the legislature for weeks, though with a considerable disparity in their respective political clouts. In early 1911 the WCTU had ten thousand members, while the ESA could boast of no more than a thousand or so. Every effort by both organizations was needed as the resolution passed the senate with only twenty-seven votes, the bare minimum.[61]

The WCTU rejected the ESA's overtures in 1912 to fuse the two organizations for the campaign, but it readily complied with the ESA's dictum that suffrage speakers should inject no other doctrines (such as prohibition) into their presentations. "The suffrage oar is the one the unions are pulling on," *Our Messenger* reported in August. The statistics of WCTU participation in the campaign are impressive: 509 suffrage essays by school pupils; 1,294 lectures provided; 1,728 columns furnished to the press; 215,435 copies of articles printed; 1,043,600 pages of literature distributed.[62]

Some historians have maintained that since the liquor interests strenuously opposed suffrage for fear that it would lead to prohibition, perhaps WCTU support was more a hindrance than a help. But in Kansas, with prohibition already firmly planted in the constitution by male voters, that argument loses most of its force. The continuous effort by the WCTU over the years made it a much more potent force in selling its viewpoint than was the sporadic organization of the opposition.

The manager of the ESA's campaign, Lucy B. Johnston, did not equivocate in her evaluation of the temperance role in bringing the victory. She cited members of the WCTU as "faithful allies" and stated that the "one thing [that] entered more largely than any other" in the victory was the fact that "Kansas has been a prohibition state for 32 years." Aside from the work of 1894 and 1911/12, a review of WCTU support for suffrage from 1880 forward can leave no doubt that it helped materially in gaining "respectability" for the amendment, especially among the critical mass of conservative middle-class voters.[63]

The suffrage amendment carried by sixteen thousand votes, almost exactly the same percentage of victory as that carried by prohibition in 1880. Kansas became the seventh state to endorse woman suffrage and the only one at the time to have written both suffrage and prohibition into its organic law. Six years later, the WCTU organizer whose first public activity had been as a white ribboner, forty-nine-year-old Minnie Johnson Grinstead of Liberal, "a pleasant looking woman of stout build," became the first of her sex to be elected to the Kansas Legislature.[64]

In 1916, near the zenith of temperance success in the state, President Mitchner noted that while men specialized in business, women concentrated on motherhood and homemaking. The WCTU, she said, is "almost entirely made up of housekeepers and women grown old under the cares of the home." Perhaps more defensively than the times required, she summed up the reaction to her organization over the years:

> Concerning us and our organization, some have smiled, and some have sneered, and some have cursed, and some have hated, and some have feared. Smiled at our seeming impotence, sneered at our apparent helplessness, cursed our persistence, and, because of all for which we stand, hated our organization and feared our

success. But no coward heart beats beneath the ribbon white, and we have gone on unaffrighted and undismayed.[65]

IN 1912, KANSAS elected its second Democratic governor and, for the first time in history, a Democratic majority to both houses of the legislature. But these startling events produced no threat to the firmly entrenched prohibition policy. After over twenty years of more-than-firm opposition to prohibition, the Democrats in 1906, prodded by their younger members, scorched the Republicans for their hypocritical liquor policies but warmly endorsed the enforcement of the prohibitory law. The Democrats subsequently claimed, with considerable justification, that the tightening of enforcement derived to a significant extent from the unprecedented bipartisan support.[66]

Governor George H. Hodges (1913–15), a Disciple of Christ and a progressive reformer, had been one of the leaders insisting on a dry plank in the Democratic platform. His attitude toward prohibition contrasted sharply with that of his Democratic predecessor, G. W. Glick, thirty years earlier. "The Democratic Party is the prohibition party of this state," Hodges said. He pledged that his administration would close the few remaining joints and would drive the bootleggers from the state. He prided himself on an effective but low-key administration of the law ("without brass bands [and] without display"), no doubt a welcome relief to the public after the big noise of the Stubbs-Dawson term.[67]

The continuing opposition by the liquor interests to the prohibition laws, Hodges was fond of pointing out, was "the strongest argument for their effectiveness." To the perennial grumblers about violations of the liquor laws, Hodges's office gave a very "progressive" response: "Quit complaining and get the evidence." When a Lebo (Coffey County) man wrote that he had met a traveling salesman who claimed to have found an open saloon in Kansas City, the governor's secretary declared that the salesman was "probably not only a foreflusher but a liar as well." If the informer would be good enough to forward specific information, the governor and the attorney general would "have it closed before night."[68]

The state held a referendum of sorts on resubmission in 1914. All five parties fielding gubernatorial candidates (Democrats, Republicans, Progressives, Socialists, and Prohibitionists) adopted planks declaring for the fact of state prohibition and for the hope of national prohibition. "No political party dares to declare against it," the governor's office said. But a popular and respected Democrat and former mayor of Topeka, Jules B. Billard, who ran as an Independent, made resubmission the major thrust of his campaign. Billard received only 47,000 (9 percent) of the 528,000 votes cast in the election. He did not attract all of the wet votes, however, since he was given little chance to win. His vote represented from one-third to one-half of the total antiprohibitionist

A campaign billboard in Independence for the reelection of Governor Hodges in 1914 (courtesy of the Kansas State Historical Society, Topeka).

sentiment of the period (20 to 25 percent), according to the most reliable estimates.[69]

As the nation began to debate the question of constitutional prohibition, the state continued to be nudged into the spotlight. "All eyes seem to be on Kansas," Governor Hoch had said in 1908. In the period from 1906 through the early 1920s the state attracted more positive attention than it had enjoyed since the territorial period or would receive thereafter. The old mirthful image of a Kansas, known chiefly for its grasshoppers, cyclones, droughts, mortgages, and cranks, was undergoing a profound metamorphosis in its own and in the national eye. The state could be found in the van of the two leading political and social movements of the day: progressivism and prohibition. Kansans largely shed their diffident, apologetic, and defensive attitude and adopted a more confident, buoyant, and aggressive stance. As Mrs. George Hodges said in 1914: "The very name of Kansas signifies energy and progress."[70] And no one laughed, or at least not so many.

As state after state held referendums on the prohibition question, conditions in Kansas, real and imagined, became a central feature of the campaigns. Prohibition in Maine, the only state that could challenge Kansas on historic grounds, had fallen on hard times, leaving Kansas as the unquestioned model prohibition state. As the debate intensified, the wets and drys hurled data on every conceivable social and economic parameter at one another with reckless abandon: on population growth, retail business, farmland values, livestock sales, home ownership, bank deposits, and rates of death, disease, divorce, literacy, pauperism, crime, and insanity.

A knowledgeable former Kansan in a referendum state became a prized possession for the combatants. In California a forty-seven-page booklet entitled simply "Kansas" was a central feature of the wet campaign. In Washington, dry groups formed Sunflower Clubs, dedicated to tell "the truth" about Kansas prohibition. Their exaggerated claims led a Seattle newspaper to remark that apparently the question of liquor control in Washington was going to turn on how many crazy people there were in Kansas.[71]

Out-of-state drys wailed that Kansas prohibition was lied about enough "to make Ananias weep with envy." The leader of the wet forces in Congress, Senator James Reed of Missouri, declared that there were "more drunkards to the square acre in Kansas than in any place I ever was." The self-styled Kansas expert said that he had "always thought the worst combination on earth was a Kansan and a quart of Bourbon. . . . If there ever was a place on the earth where they [needed] to regulate the habits of the people it was in Kansas." Kansas baiting by wets across the nation reached such heights that the 1915 legislature felt constrained to respond to the "false and defamatory" statements. In a lengthy formal resolution, it labeled the wet charges "libelous" and declared its undying "allegiance" to prohibition.[72]

WITH THE NEAR EXTINCTION of the joint and the total extinction of the drugstore-joint, temperance advocates turned with quickened interest to the importation of liquor from outside the state. Importation had long concerned the prohibitionists, having been marked for elimination along with the manufacture and sale by the Temperance party in 1874 and in the original Good Templar formulation of 1878. The latter dropped the prohibition on shipments, probably due to its unpopularity and to the potential conflict with the interstate-commerce clause of the federal constitution.

Until 1885 Kansans could order liquor in any amount directly from a foreign (out-of-state) vendor, could place an order with a drummer (a traveling salesman representing the vendor), or could order liquor C.O.D. The Kansas price did not differ significantly from that in Missouri, the shipping costs being offset by the absence of a middleman. The legal theory that made such sales possible held that when the wet goods passed from the vendor to the common carrier (in, say, Kansas City, Missouri), the sale was consummated at that time and place, and the carrier became merely an agent of the buyer. In 1885 an amendment to the law made it illegal for a drummer to take orders in Kansas, and in 1890 the attorney general opined that C.O.D. shipments were outside the law, since in this transaction the carrier served as an agent of the seller, and the sale occurred in Kansas.[73]

In 1902 the state supreme court found the antidrummer section repugnant to the United States Constitution and also held that in C.O.D. orders the express agent "makes no sale and is guilty of no offense under the law." But in 1907 the United States Supreme Court ruled, in a South Dakota case, that order taking within a dry state could be prohibited by state law, and three years later a federal law went into effect which banned all C.O.D. shipments of liquor.[74] Thus, by 1910, Kansans could only obtain legal liquor through prepaid mail orders to foreign vendors.

Empty beer cases and kegs awaiting return shipment at the Dwight (Morris County) depot in 1911 (courtesy of the Kansas State Historical Society, Topeka).

As in all other facets of the liquor law, numerous schemes evolved to evade the importation provisions. When the 1909 law put the druggists out of the liquor business, the Missouri wholesalers pestered them for lists of their former "patients," offering a 20 percent commission on all sales thereby effected. The suppliers sometimes shipped to the names so obtained even without an order, on the expectation that the known liquor consumer would accept the serendipitous shipment rather than reject it. On occasion they addressed the package to a fictitious name or merely to a letter of the alphabet. Obviously the shipper required the services of a "cooperative" depot agent to effect such sales. When the agent "made a market" locally, he received a commission for his trouble. Though illegal, such sales usually went undetected even by the most conscientious of public officials.[75]

Policing "interstate" sales became an especially onerous task in the eastern border counties of Atchison, Leavenworth, Wyandotte, Crawford, and Cherokee. In Leavenworth, beer wagons peddled their wares "like milk" on the streets; if queried, the buyer would claim that he had ordered by phone. In Kansas City, apprehended drivers produced back-dated orders to cover the sales in question. In the Crawford-Cherokee area, wholesalers, who had recently been driven across the state line, required all orders taken in Kansas to be written on postcards, to give some semblance of compliance with the interstate law. But by 1916 Attorney General Brewster had successfully brought a series of ouster suits which enjoined the Missouri breweries from sending their wagons into the border counties to peddle their goods illegally.[76]

A good deal of the imported liquor did not go directly to the consumer; rather, it went to the ubiquitous and legendary bootlegger. When liquor for "personal use" arrived frequently and in cases and barrels, it usually ended up in the consignee's pockets, rather than in his stomach. Some states limited the amount of liquor that could be shipped at any one time. But such sentiment, though it existed in Kansas, never cystallized into law. Bootleggers also profited from the federal policy of allowing them to back-pay their retail liquor stamp ($25) upon apprehension, thereby avoiding prosecution. Governor Stubbs led his fellow governors in pressuring the government to change that policy, and in 1910, Stubbs received assurances from President William Howard Taft and from Attorney General George W. Wickersham that henceforth, stampless bootleggers would be prosecuted. But two years later, county attorneys reported that the time-honored procedures were still being followed.[77]

But the impecunious bootlegger lived a precarious existence, far down the social scale, despised by the holy and by his customers alike. In an opinion that was heartily shared by the "respectable" stratum of society, Governor Stubbs declared that liquor selling attracted only the "lowest class" of people, the "waifs, wrecks and driftwood" of society. Frank Stahl, who became the KSTU's secretary in 1908, characterized the bootlegger as "a poltroon, a double-dealer, a pariah and a sneak . . . you find him in the cellar, the attic, the shed, the alley." The well-known journalist and mayor of Topeka from 1915 to 1919, Jay House, an outspoken foe of prohibition, characterized bootleggers of the period as "shiftless, inefficient, improvident, inconsequential gentlemen—white and black—who barely kept a fire in the kitchen stove."[78]

By mid decade the bootlegger faced mounting adversity, especially in the more rural areas. In 1914 there were 437 convictions of bootleggers statewide; in 1915, 561. County attorneys maneuvered to confront defendants with a "female jury" as often as possible. In Anderson County, no bootlegger had dared ask for a jury in five years. The Ellsworth County attorney developed a novel solution, of doubtful legality, to the problem. When he had insufficient evidence to convict, but felt "morally certain" that a party was guilty, he filed a charge in district court and held the defendant in jail. In sixty to ninety days, when the judge called the case, the county attorney would move to dismiss the case. "And that," he proudly stated, "I consider equivalent to a conviction."[79]

The devices and shifts of the bootlegger have become part of the folklore of the state. He delivered his goods in everything from an inside coat pocket to a covered wagon to a bright, shiny automobile. Frequently the contact man merely served as an "errand boy" for the supplier. The errand boy, often an impoverished type with a large family, usually was the one who came a cropper of the law, while the more prosperous and respectable supplier went free, thanks to the blind loyalty of his employee. Sometimes the contact merely feigned the role of the errand boy, promising only to help "find" a bottle. He then took the liquor from his own supply and in court swore that he didn't know "the stranger" from whom he had made the purchase.[80]

In central and western Kansas, "hobo" bootleggers supplied the small-town and rural markets. They rode jauntily into town, with liquor stuffed into their sooty leather grips, sold a few bottles, and caught the next train out. Or they might consign shipments to real or fictitious names at several towns along the route. They hopped off the freight, claimed their package from the depot agent, and sold while the freight switched cars in the yard. To curb this practice the conscientious Trego County attorney advised the sheriff to "destroy at once" any liquor consigned to a "non-resident." In all these transactions, of course, thirsty male citizens dutifully and courageously did their part by "hanging around" the depot, each no doubt with a wheat straw in his mouth and a stealthy look in his eye.[81]

Although liquor-law violations centered in the cities throughout Kansas history, the denizens of the less densely populated areas frequently voiced their concerns in vivid language. The small-town wet, a largely ignored variety of *Homo sapiens kansensis,* made a significant contribution to the ongoing dialogue. A Cowley County man, who was well known for his "picturesque effusions," longed for the good old days "when a man was a man and could drink like one, something that these measley cranks now [1915] so much in evidence in this state will never understand." In a more philosophical vein a Rossville (Shawnee County) man proclaimed that "$2/3$ of the people in the state uses liquor and at the same time want prohibition [.] these people looks to me like hipocrats [.] something they say is wrong and at the same time do it."[82]

The loudest and most persistent voices came from dry mouths. State officials received a constant stream of urgent letters from the distressed in the more sparsely settled counties. These epistles often conveyed a good deal more about the community social life than even the most fervent dry politician cared to hear. An Osborne County informant furnished a minutely detailed picture of the iniquity that raged daily in Covert[!], a village of 225: "Louis Bailey drunk December 16 . . . where he gets his liquor is unknown, as he does not touch it unless tempted severely. . . . Harry Sandy cursing at Hoar's store. . . . Last

February or March a gang of these fellows among whom were _____,
gathered at Harry Sandy's house and played cards all night, of which a flash light
picture was taken."[83]

The voluble informant who did not want to get "personally" involved
represented one of the most frustrating problems for state officials:

> Now there is a place out here in Pratt County . . . where it seems that whiskey runs
> like water. Now the leading man of that place is a Metodist Preacher [.] But it seems
> as though the liquor element . . . are so well organized that it is impossible to catch
> them. But I have been thinking that if we could get a right good detective out in to
> this part of the county that we possible could clean some of that up. Now of course I
> wouldn't want my name mentioned in this as I am in business here . . . and I don't
> want to get mixed up over there if I possible can help it as I don't exactly know
> anything.[84]

THE MOUNTING CONCERN about liquor shipments resulted in 1913 in the
passage of an unusual state law. The Mahin Law required every liquor consignee
to sign a statement for the common carrier (usually a railroad), declaring that he
was in fact the consignee, that he was over twenty-one years of age, and that the
liquor was intended for his own use. Most importantly, the law required that
within thirty days the carrier must file with the county clerk the consignee's
name and address and the kind and amount of liquor that had been delivered.[85]

The legislators expected the Mahin Law to produce useful information for
the authorities in their war against the bootleggers. In this respect it helped
hardly at all, since the thirty-day period enabled the nimble bootleggers to
dispose of their goods before the record could become available. Soon the
authorities called for daily reporting by the carriers, a recommendation that
never became law.[86] But the existing law made it possible to obtain what was
ordinarily impossible in dry territory: namely, a reliable estimate of the total
liquor consumption in the population.

Under prohibition the public obtained legal or illegal liquor in five modes:
(1) at fixed-address outlets (saloons, joints, "blind tigers," clubs); (2) at
drugstores; (3) from stills (or other local production devices); (4) from
bootleggers; (5) from direct importation. By 1913 the drugstores had been
eliminated as a source, and the fixed-address establishments had virtually been
eliminated. In the entire period from 1881 to 1920, only twenty stills were
confiscated in Kansas, though thousands were seized annually across the
nation.[87] Determination of the amount of imported liquor, then, should reliably
estimate total consumption from the only two viable modes of the day:
importation by the public and by bootleggers.

The *Topeka State Journal* used the Shawnee County clerk's records to
report the importation of about seventy-five thousand quarts for the month of
June 1913. The sheriff estimated that about 25 percent of the total went to
bootleggers. Based on records from seventeen counties for the first two months

under the Mahin Law, the *State Journal* estimated statewide consumption for 1913 to be the equivalent of 3.5 million gallons, or about 3 gallons per capita of the drinking-age population, aged fifteen or over. It continued these reports, always in quarts, sporadically over the next few years, setting off derisive howls from the wets about the monumental quantity of liquor that was being shipped into the nation's banner prohibition state.

Late in 1913 Governor Hodges made a study of importation into an urban county (Wyandotte), a rural county (Johnson), and an intermediate county (Marion). Based on this data, his office projected a statewide consumption rate for 1913 of 5.4 gallons. These figures became widely broadcast over the nation during the next three years, although they were treated as something of a hot potato by both sides.[88]

Governor Arthur Capper (1915–19) and the state Board of Administration commissioned Dr. Frank W. Blackmar to make a systematic study of the 1914 shipment records of all 105 counties. A well-regarded social scientist and dean of the Graduate School at Kansas University, Blackmar received an appointment as an assistant attorney general to facilitate his access to the county records. After several months' study he reported in early 1917 that in 1914, Kansas had imported 4.5 million gallons of liquor. He added approximately 15 percent for unrecorded liquor brought in by private vehicles or pedestrians in the border counties. (In 1914 the state registered 50,000 motorized vehicles; in 1985, 2.1 million.) He then estimated total importation at no more than 4.4 gallons per capita of the drinking-age population, or 14 percent of the national average of 32.2 gallons.

Dividing the state, like Gaul, into three parts, Blackmar found the highest importation rates in the eastern region (5.4 gallons), intermediate rates in the central region (3.5 gallons), and the lowest rates in the west (1.8 gallons). Values for the most densely populated counties varied from 9 to 10 gallons for Shawnee, Sedgwick, and Leavenworth to 3 to 6 gallons in Reno, Wyandotte, and Atchison. About 90 percent of the imported gallonage was beer (the national consumption figure was 92 percent). He found consumption greatest among the foreign-born. Whereas the United States population spent 1.66 times as much for liquor as for meat, in Kansas the quotient was 0.20. Based on his data, Blackmar estimated that Kansans had saved almost $29 million on liquor in 1914, compared to the national average.[89]

Additional systematic illumination on consumption came from the reports of the county attorneys in response to a 1915 call from Governor Capper for an overview of conditions in their counties. A number of disinterested citizens in the communities, also asked by Capper to respond, confirmed the officials' judgments. Overall, the county attorneys reported strict law enforcement, with a few lingering trouble spots in the largest cities. "The chief obstacle," said one, "is the reluctance of those who buy liquor to testify to the truth when they are put on the witness stand."

The number of liquor prosecutions per county per annum ranged from over two hundred in Shawnee County to zero in a few of the far-western counties, with a median of about ten. Stevens County reported only two liquor prosecutions in the county's history, while Grant County (named in honor of the liquor-loving Ulysses S. Grant) declared that it had never had a prosecution. The conviction percentage ranged from around 35 percent (Cherokee, Montgomery, Wyandotte) to at or near 100 percent (Anderson, Barton, Rawlins). The interior counties reported that bootleggers often were blacks, Mexicans, or migrant laborers or that they represented the "I.W.W. influx" or the "criminal swarm" from Kansas City. Defendants often left the jurisdiction before their cases came to trial. Some respondents deplored the fact that the "better element" shipped in so much liquor, thus serving as a bad example for the rest of the community.[90]

In three western counties the county attorneys remarked on the volume of legal importations in recent years. Since the amount imported into this area is known for 1914, a rare opportunity is afforded to "calibrate" statements on consumption made by trained observers in a prohibition state. In two instances the county attorneys reported that "a great deal" had been shipped in; in the other, that the county had received a "heavy shipment" over the past two years. At this time, these counties averaged less than two gallons per capita of imported liquor, about 5 percent of the average national consumption.[91]

THE RIGHT TO IMPORT LIQUOR into a dry state had always depended upon the strong, protective arm of the federal government, which enforced the interstate-commerce clause of the Constitution. The Wilson Act of 1890, which had put the "original package" saloons out of business, declared that liquor lost its interstate character "upon arrival" in a state. But in 1898 the United States Supreme Court interpreted "upon arrival" to mean at the point of delivery to the consignee, rather than at the state line. A state, therefore, could not prevent shipments that originated from beyond its bounds; the legal right to import remained unimpaired.[92]

As the national temperance movement regained its momentum early in the new century, a federal law permitting state jurisdiction to attach to liquor at the state line became a top priority. With the full support of the Anti-Saloon League, Senator Charles Curtis of Topeka and Congressman James Miller of Council Grove introduced a bill in Congress in 1910 to this end. The Curtis-Miller bill failed, but a renewed effort three years later did not. With encouragement from the KSTU, the Kansas WCTU, and the Kansas Legislature, among many others, Congress passed the Webb-Kenyon Act in early 1913, making it possible for states to regulate or to prohibit entirely liquor importation if they chose to do so.[93]

Congress passed the bill over the veto of President Taft, who had been persuaded that it was unconstitutional. Its constitutionality remained under a thick cloud for the next few years, which discouraged states from taking action.

But in January 1917, just as the Kansas Legislature was convening, the high court ruled that the act was valid. Since the drys could obtain most any legislation they wanted by merely asking for it, a significant change in the Kansas law appeared certain and imminent. But the final form that it took came as a surprise to many.[94]

Over the decades the temperance community had centered its attack on what it deemed to be the sordid, seamy, and shameful threats to the home: the saloon, the drugstore, and the bootlegger. A responsible citizen, enjoying a quiet glass in his own home, represented a distant and untouchable point on the respectability spectrum. Wets often chided drys that if they were really serious about prohibition, they would push for antidrinking legislation. The drys tended to stammer, equivocate, and steer the conversation to the weather. In 1910, for instance, the Anti-Saloon League urged the passage of the Curtis-Miller bill in order to curb the bootlegger and the "speakeasy proprietor." Prohibition of the use of liquor, they warned, would be a "very drastic" measure.[95]

Therefore, when a "bone-dry" bill received early and serious legislative attention, even some of the more zealous drys felt that such a law might be going too far. But the state's temperance sentiment ran at flood tide, as the "Kansas idea" became adopted by state after state and as submission of a national prohibitory amendment loomed on the immediate horizon. Liquor houses in Kansas City, Missouri, attempting to salvage what they could from a bad situation, wrote lachrymose letters to their customers, urging them to "fortify themselves against the impending drouth."[96]

The general counsel for the Anti-Saloon League of America, Wayne Wheeler, testifying before a state senate committee, urged the legislators to produce "a model bone dry law." The WCTU forwarded one thousand individual petitions, but it took no stand on the controversial proposal that communion wine be exempted. The common carriers declined to fight the bill, consoling themselves that "the business in Kansas is not so big and profitable as in the old days." Rumors of a $15,000 slush fund generated by Kansas City liquor interests, to be distributed by a "Topeka politician" to bottle up the bill in committee, only seemed to hurry it along. In late February the bill passed, making it unlawful for any person "to keep or have in his possession, for personal use or otherwise," any intoxicating liquors. Communion wine constituted the sole exception.[97] In prohibiting possession, temperance sentiment had produced the ultimate in antiliquor legislation.

At precisely 10:28 A.M. on February 23, Governor Arthur Capper signed "the most drastic anti-liquor enactment written in this nation." Unprecedentedly, he signed the bill, not in his office, but in Representatives Hall, before an appreciative and jovial crowd of legislators and temperance leaders. "No act in my term as governor has given me greater pleasure than the signing of this bill," he said. One legislator broke into a chorus of "Nobody Knows How Dry I

Governor Capper signs the ''bone-dry'' bill in Representatives Hall in 1917 (courtesy of the Kansas State Historical Society, Topeka).

Am,'' and the others good-naturedly joined in. The pen used in signing the landmark legislation, and much of the credit for its passage, went to the WCTU. ''Perhaps no other person in Kansas,'' said the KSTU, ''deserves more credit in

. . . securing the passage of the Bone Dry Bill . . . than Mrs. Lillian Mitchner. . . . We . . . congratulate Mrs. Mitchner and the entire organization she represents in the glorious victory in the . . . legislature."[98]

The temperance movement paused a moment to bask in the warm satisfaction wrought by the "glorious victory." A long and rocky road had led from the dark days of feeble public sentiment and lax law enforcement, when Kansas prohibition seemed little more than a grim joke, to the new era that C. W. Trickett had initiated when he had padlocked the Kansas City joints. The progressive-fed renaissance in the temperance ranks (1897–1901) had been followed by renewed interest among the public (1901–6), which had led directly to the great improvement in enforcement of the law (1906 et seq.).

In June 1917, Topeka hosted a three-day convention to heighten state sentiment for national prohibition. Symbolizing the dominant spirit of the day, one historic session, chaired by Governor Capper, consisted of temperance presentations by the previous four governors of the state (Bailey, Hoch, Stubbs, and Hodges).[99] The prohibitionists looked confidently to the future as the nation moved ever closer to adopting the Kansas idea. All seemed serene across the dry and tranquil prairies—unless they had gone too fast and too far.

9
The Federal Era

A short sighted nation was somewhat annoyed by the noise and confusion that proceeded from the general direction of Kansas. Annoyed, and mildly amused. For the nation was too busy about trifles to realize that Kansas was in labor, and that the ridiculous offspring she would soon bring forth would live to betray a continent.
—Newspaperman Charles B. Driscoll

Not to enforce [national] prohibition thoroughly and effectively would reflect upon our form of government, and would bring into disrepute the reputation of the American people as law-abiding citizens.
—Commissioner of Internal Revenue, 1919

NATIONAL PROHIBITION had been the ultimate goal of temperance leaders for many decades before it became a reality. When the second prohibitory pulse faded at the end of the 1880s, any hope of federal prohibition in the near future went with it. In the first decade of the new century, interest in state temperance legislation rekindled across the nation. After 1889, Oklahoma became the first state to adopt prohibition, when it came into the union in 1907 with a dry constitution, a significant development in which former Kansans played no small role. Centering in the South initially, the third wave increased the number of states in the prohibitory column from three to twenty-seven by the time Congress submitted the Eighteenth Amendment for ratification in 1917. By 1919, thirty-three states had either statutory or constitutional prohibition.[1]

In 1880 Kansas Senator Preston B. Plumb (1877–91) had become the first to introduce in Congress a constitutional amendment that would have banned all intoxicating liquors. Such a proposal had no chance of passage for the next three decades, as the drys focused their attention on an interstate-commerce law. Soon after the Webb-Kenyon bill passed in 1913, the leaders announced their plans to push for a constitutional amendment. In 1914 the House gave a small majority to an amendment resolution, but the measure died because it lacked the necessary two-thirds. A more temperance-inclined Congress, elected in 1916, produced the requisite majority and submitted the resolution to the states as the Eighteenth Amendment in December 1917. Thirteen months later it had been ratified by three-fourths of the states and ultimately received the endorsement of all but two.[2]

Societal stresses and tensions, such as wars and economic depressions, tend to reduce markedly the priority that the public places on social reforms. The conjunction of the Eighteenth Amendment and World War I seems to have been a major exception. Some writers have claimed that the drys "put one over" while the nation was focusing on the war effort and "the boys" were making the world safe for democracy. But a strong and organized temperance impulse had been manifest in the nation since early in the nineteenth century; the powerful third wave of national sentiment had commenced more than ten years before the declaration of war. By 1917, 50 percent of the states, 60 percent of the population, and 80 percent of the counties were living under prohibition. After the election of 1916 the dry lobbyist *par excellence,* Wayne Wheeler, declared that the new Congress would unquestionably submit the amendment. At the time of the Armistice on 11 November 1918, almost a year after submission, only fourteen of the necessary thirty-six states had ratified the amendment. Thirty-two proceeded to do so after the conclusion of hostilities.[3]

As veteran opportunists, the drys took full advantage of the wartime situation. They mounted a "bread not beer" campaign and at every turn encouraged the war-generated enmity against the brewing industry, dominated as it was by those of German ancestry. But the war simply came along at about the time when the campaign for national prohibition peaked. It bears essentially the same relationship to passage of the Eighteenth Amendment that the Great Depression does to its repeal. Each served as a relevant milieu for the debate, and each hastened the passage of the proposed amendment. But in neither case was the specific climate necessary or sufficient to produce the end result.[4]

Most Kansans, of course, were delighted that the nation had adopted the "Kansas idea." In 1918 Governor Capper said that "no people received the action of Congress in passing the . . . amendment with a greater degree of satisfaction and gratitude than did the citizens of Kansas." Early in the year the governor received numerous petitions urging him to call a special legislative session to ratify the amendment. Principally for monetary reasons, the economy-minded Capper refused to do so. His office assured the anxious citizenry that the 1919 regular session was as certain to adopt the amendment as it was "to pass a law appropriating money to pay its own members." On 14 January 1919, Kansas became one of the six states to ratify the amendment unanimously. Two days later, Nebraska became the thirty-sixth state to endorse the amendment.[5]

Kansans had good reason to feel a strong sense of accomplishment at the triumph. As the model prohibition state, she had been weighed, measured, pinched, and poked by friend and foe alike. And given the outcome, she had manifestly passed the test to the nation's satisfaction. More directly, her twentieth-century congressional delegations, both Democrats and Republicans, had always furnished solid support, and often leadership, for dry measures. Several of her most prominent citizens, including the venerable John P. St. John, former Governor George Hodges, Charles Sheldon, and Lillian Mitchner, had made extensive national tours for the cause.[6]

Chancellor Frank Strong of Kansas University led the petition drive for national prohibition among Kansas college students; at one memorable mass meeting, he persuaded fifteen hundred students to endorse prohibition unanimously. When the Senate took up the debate in the summer of 1917, Senator Charles Curtis received a petition containing the names of thirty thousand citizens. In December, as the House considered the measure, a train load of Kansas businessmen went to Washington as "flesh and blood petitions" for the reform.

Still, Kansas was not as fully involved as she might have been. Some easterners and dissatisfied Kansans carped that the state had done only "a little dab" and had in fact straggled at the "tail end of the procession." Such criticism stemmed largely from the unusual and stressful relationship that had developed between the KSTU and the principal force behind the drive to national prohibition, the Anti-Saloon League of America (ASL).[7]

THE ANTI-SALOON LEAGUE had originated in 1893 in a Congregational church at Oberlin, Ohio, in the heart of the "New England belt." It developed as a nondenominational, nonpartisan single-issue organization whose bête noir, as the name suggests, was the organized liquor traffic. Evangelical Protestant denominations selected members of its board, and in exchange, the churches allowed the league to solicit funds from their congregations on a regular basis. Although organizationally separate from the denominations, the league drew its support and personnel almost exclusively from the involved churches. From 1893 to 1913, 60 percent of the league's leadership came from the ranks of the clergy itself. The prototype of the successful political pressure group, the league liked to call itself "the church in action against the saloon."

The league's genius came, not in florid exhortation, but in focusing in an intense, laserlike beam the influence of those who had already been converted. It gained its ends by skillfully utilizing the "balance of power" concept in elections and by pushing for only that legislation which a realistically assessed public sentiment would support. A product of the progressive era, it prided itself on being "as thoroughly organized and as scientifically managed as any institution in America." It became a respected power on the national scene in 1905, when it helped to defeat for reelection a popular Republican governor in Ohio, a Republican state, because of his unacceptable views on liquor control. Initially it concentrated on local option, then urged statewide prohibition, and then, in 1913, set national prohibition as its goal. Its nonpartisan political approach incurred the bitter opposition of the Prohibition party, which held, as a primary article of faith, that prohibition laws could not be effectively enforced unless they were administered by officials who wholeheartedly embraced the principle.[8]

By 1905 the ASL had an organization in virtually every state, except Kansas. The KSTU had developed a rather nebulous "affiliate" relationship with the national organization in the late 1890s and had become an "auxiliary" in 1908. The younger and more progressive-minded KSTU members wanted to see the ASL take charge and to see the KSTU slip silently into the night. Others, especially the veteran members, opposed such a change "vigorously."

Along with the WCTU, the KSTU had led the state temperance fight since the late 1870s. Its letterhead proclaimed its scope and purpose: "Kansas is its field, the moral well-being of Kansas, its aim, the elevation of humanity, through the example of Kansas, the wider result of its labors." Although they occupied the same "ecological niche," the ASL and the KSTU differed markedly in their temper, style, and priorities.

The KSTU held open, often rambunctious, meetings which featured the candid exchange of views among its members in a quasi-democratic setting. It gave its top priority to Kansas law enforcement, prized its close cooperation with the WCTU, and contributed little financially or otherwise to the drive for national prohibition. Since 1908 the organization had been led by Frank ("Old Alfalfa") Stahl, the lanky, plain-spoken former Topeka chief of police, who had become a legend in his own time. The league represented a much more centralized, disciplined, and bloodless organization, with a more distant style in both the geographical and temperamental senses. Its first priority was national prohibition, with little direct concern for state enforcement or the WCTU.[9]

After a series of frustrating annual KSTU conventions, characterized as raucous scenes of "strife and bickering," the proponents of change took a new tack. They abruptly organized a branch of the ASL at Lawrence in December 1916, behind the back of the KSTU, as it were. The twenty-two-member Board of Trustees included three former governors (Hoch, Stubbs, Hodges), the incumbent governor (Capper), a future governor (Henry Allen), William Allen White, and K.U.'s Chancellor Frank Strong—all leading progressives. Recognizing that the state could not support two competing temperance organizations, the KSTU champions withdrew from the field, though not without a final blast at the victors.[10]

That the venerable organization would be discarded on the eve of the national victory proved especially difficult for the older members to accept. The ASL, they charged, had "found fault and harassed [Kansas] for years." The ASL organizational meeting had been as much "a violation of a solemn agreement as . . . when the Germans invaded Belgium." "Not much will be said," the ousted superintendent, Frank Stahl, remarked, "but there will be heart-aches, and tears will drop unbidden from the eyes of many a man and woman who has been in the fight when it cost something to stand for the right.'' The ASL responded by tactfully wishing Stahl well ''in his declining years.''[11] But before the ''Roaring Twenties'' had run their course, many who had worked for the ''modernization'' of the KSTU would fervently wish that they still had honest old Frank Stahl at the helm.

THE EIGHTEENTH AMENDMENT prohibited the manufacture, sale, and transportation of intoxicating liquors in the United States of America. It gave Congress and the several states ''concurrent power'' to enforce the law. In practice, enforcement was left largely, or exclusively, to the federal government, especially in states that had a predominantly wet sentiment. The United States Supreme Court held that the amendment was not the source of state prohibitory power and that it did not ''displace or cut down'' state laws that were consistent with it. An act that violated both federal and state laws could be prosecuted in both jurisdictions, though in practice it rarely was.[12]

The National Prohibition Act, popularly known as the Volstead Act, went into effect on 17 January 1920, one year after the ratification of the amendment. The Kansas and federal laws differed in a number of important respects. The state ''bone-dry'' law prohibited the possession as well as the manufacture and sale, while the Volstead Act banned only the manufacture and sale. Kansas proscribed ''intoxicating liquor,'' but fixed no specific alcoholic content; the federal law defined intoxicating beverages as those that contained more than 0.5 percent of alcohol by volume. Physicians could not prescribe intoxicating liquors for any purpose in Kansas, though they could under the federal law. In common with several other states, Kansas had somewhat tougher search-and-seizure laws than did the similar provisions of the Volstead Act.[13]

During the first few years of prohibition, the maximum penalty for first offenses in Kansas (a $500 fine and six months in jail) compared closely to the federal sanction. In response to the increasing frequency and flagrancy of violations, Congress in 1929 passed the Jones ''five and ten'' Act, which provided penalties for first offenders of up to five years in prison and $10,000 in fines. Kansas did not toughen its first-offender statute, but it did deal harshly with the persistent violator. The 1927 legislature provided that any third felonious conviction would bring confinement to the offender ''during his life.'' Because a second liquor infraction had automatically been considered a felony since 1911, the 1927 law meant that the fourth conviction for, say, possession would bring life imprisonment. No record of such a conviction has been found, however.[14]

During the twenties the Kansas Supreme Court handed down a series of important decisions in liquor-related cases, most of which supported the dry side of the litigation. In an opinion upholding the validity of the bone-dry act, Justice John S. Dawson, the former attorney general, set forth the court's evolving social philosophy while acknowledging the impact of the WCTU's educational project: "The times change. Men change, and their opinions change; their notions of right and wrong change. The United States . . . [has] come a long, long way since the Washingtonian society was organized in 1840 to combat intemperance. A whole generation of Americans has been born and educated, and has grown to maturity . . . , since instruction in the evil effects of intoxicants upon the human system became compulsory in our public schools."[15]

In response to the rapid obsolescence of the horse and wagon, the 1919 legislature assigned liquor-transporting automobiles to the same category as saloons or joints, that is, it declared them to be "common nuisances." As such, they became subject to forfeiture by a juryless court, the proceeds derived therefrom to go to support the local public schools. In a decision that was subsequently affirmed by the United States Supreme Court, the Kansas court declared that the state's power to forfeit property extended even to the automobile of an "innocent" owner, that is, to one who had unwittingly trusted his car to the wrongdoer.[16]

The state's high court ruled that the Allen County district court had not erred when it had allowed a jury to smell the malodorous contents of a whiskey jar in a bootlegging case. The jury got its turn after watching the "violent convulsions" of two defense witnesses as they attempted to demonstrate that the liquid in question was not potable. In this case the defendant had been found guilty of selling, but had been exonerated of a possession charge—a combination that seemed to defy elementary logic. "The verdict of guilty is perfectly consistent with itself," the high court said. "If there be logical inconsistency between the verdict of guilty and the verdict of not guilty, there is no legal inconsistency between them."[17]

In one of its most far-reaching and controversial decisions, the Kansas Supreme Court conferred upon the attorney general a great deal more authority than many of the state's "best lawyers" thought appropriate. A Shawnee County man had gone to Attorney General William A. Smith (1927–30) to report a still that was running in the man's neighborhood. When arrested, the operator implicated the informer, who was also arrested. The district court judge overruled Smith's motion to dismiss the case and convicted the informer. The high court said that the case should have been dismissed upon the attorney general's motion. As the "central law-enforcement head," the attorney general was "empowered to make any disposition of the state's litigation which he deems for its best interest," it said, including the dismissal of any case, whether he had brought the action or not.[18]

Although the professional class had helped to lead the movement for a drier and more progressive Kansas, some of its members could be found among the bootleggers' most dependable customers. They took special interest in two decisions of the Kansas Supreme Court which specifically related drinking to professional fitness. In 1923 a Hutchinson dentist was convicted of public drunkenness and, nine days later, of driving while intoxicated. The State Board of Dental Examiners found him guilty of "dishonorable conduct" and revoked his license. On appeal, the high court agreed that the behavior of the defendant involved "moral delinquency" and held that those who do what is forbidden and penalized by the law do not possess "the character and fitness" required for the profession. In a sweeping philosophical conclusion, it declared that "whatever is forbidden by law must . . . be considered as immoral."[19]

Kansas law provides that a lawyer must be disbarred upon conviction of a felony or a misdemeanor that entails "moral turpitude." In 1926 the Kansas Supreme Court ordered the disbarment of an Elk County attorney who had been convicted on a misdemeanor charge of possessing liquor. A "jug" containing "a small quantity" of intoxicants had been found by the sheriff on the defendant's back porch. In lone dissent, Justice Dawson, a confirmed prohibitionist, lectured the court on the distinction between *malum in se* (an "evil in itself," such as murder, rape, arson) and *malum prohibitum* (an "evil prohibited," such as breaches of police or traffic regulations). Dawson said that he would have had no difficulty following his colleagues if the defendant had violated the prohibitory law for personal gain. However, he could not agree that "having had a bottle of liquor on his kitchen shelf this man has been guilty of moral turpitude and should be deprived of his license to practice law."[20]

WHILE MUCH OF THE NATION experienced prohibition as a new phenomenon, Kansas had lived under a dry constitution for almost forty years when the Eighteenth Amendment went into effect. In some respects the decade of the twenties would prove to be relatively calm on the liquor front. No saloons, drugstore-joints, or even legal shipments served as liquor conduits. Notably absent also were organized efforts to effect repeal, bitter contentions over prohibition between the political parties, and intensive legislative struggles over liquor-related bills. The national controversy of the preceding decade had served only to unite the state more solidly around the "Kansas idea." With the imminent arrival of a dozen full-time federal prohibition agents to reinforce the state officials, the prospects for even-more-effective enforcement seemed bright. Never did a people look forward with more confidence to the political realization of their social ideals than did Kansans at the dawn of the era of national prohibition.

The enthusiasts predicted that the moist island, previously surrounded by a sea of wet neighbors, would become transformed into a twentieth-century version of the Great American Desert. Actually, state consumption had fallen sharply before the Volstead Act went into effect. Passage of the bone-dry act in 1917 ushered in the driest period in state history. With legal importation banished and with local production yet to be firmly established on a broad scale, consumption reached its nadir over the next several years. In addition to the state law, federal wartime prohibitory measures, which began to go into effect in

1917, made illegal liquor increasingly more difficult and more expensive to obtain. With whiskey costing $1.25 to $1.50 a quart in Kansas City, Missouri, the bootleg price in Topeka went from $2.00 in June of 1917 to $4.50 in August to $6.00 in November. By 1920, quality "corn whisky" brought $20 a quart and "bonded whisky" brought $35 in Wichita.[21] Annual consumption during this period probably dropped to 50 percent or less of the five million gallons estimated by Blackmar from the county clerks' records for 1914.

Sharing the fate of Kansas' other fixed-address liquor outlets in the second decade of the century, Fritz Durein's Hall of Fame Saloon in Topeka was abandoned. A pop stand was erected on the sidewalk in front of the building (courtesy of the Kansas State Historical Society, Topeka).

While most Kansans observed the law during this period, not many could reach the moral heights achieved by a Franklin County man concerned about the composition of the medicine that his doctor had prescribed for external use in his ears. The solution smelled of alcohol, he wrote the governor in 1919, and if its use would violate the state constitution, he would destroy it at once. With a well-bitten lip, the governor responded that he appreciated "the delicacy of your scruples," but thought it would be constitutionally sound to use the medicine as directed.[22]

Only an occasional outburst interrupted the pre-Volstead calm. In the volatile southeast corner, hundreds of "foreigners" in the mining camps petitioned the governor in 1917 to either exempt them from the bone-dry law or to furnish drinkable water. Later that year a group of irate farmers burned some of the Missouri "line houses," which served as liquor outlets just across the state line from Crawford County. An even larger concentration of liquor-dispensing establishments, replete with prostitutes, gamblers, and other criminals, had collected directly across the Missouri River from Leavenworth, as a direct result of the dry conditions in Kansas.

Ironically known as Drydale, the thirty-odd wooden shacks constituted the Missouri equivalent of Leavenworth's erstwhile Klondike. The Leavenworth Chamber of Commerce joined individual citizens in petitioning the federal government to do something about Drydale after the War Department threatened to stop sending new recruits to Fort Leavenworth because of the "moral climate" of the area. But during the summer of 1917 the department itself dealt Drydale a fatal blow by ordering a five-mile dry zone around Fort Leavenworth.[23]

In one of the most celebrated cases of the day, the egalitarian nature of state enforcement came under its most severe test since the Topeka Club incident of 1909. In 1919 the sheriff arrested a wealthy and influential Wichita man, J. M. "Jack" Hussey, when the cases labeled "olive oil" found in his high-powered Packard turned out to contain 120 quarts of sparkling burgundy wine. Dismissal of the case resulted in outraged cries from the press and public, among which Myra McHenry's was one of the most shrill. Whereupon Attorney General Richard J. Hopkins (1919–23) induced the Sedgwick County attorney to prosecute Hussey, who was well known for his reform and church activities.

After Hussey received a sentence of $300 and ninety days in jail, his "close neighbor" and prominent dry leader, Governor Henry J. Allen (1919–23), paroled him. A thirty-seven-foot-long petition from Rotary Clubs, the Chamber of Commerce, and other leading civic groups of Wichita encouraged Allen to do so. The governor's office defended the action to the disquieted public by asserting that first offenders, even bootleggers, often received paroles. If a poor man deserved to receive the same justice in court as a rich man, then "a rich man should have the same considerations as a poor man."[24]

THE COMMERCIAL PRODUCTION of liquor within Kansas had been virtually eliminated during the first prohibitory decade. Since consumers and bootleggers could legally import quality goods in unlimited quantities from Kansas City, Missouri, until 1917, demand for a home-grown product of doubtful potability remained low. But not long after the Volstead Act became effective, the commercial and home production of liquor became widespread, as it did in the nation as a whole. For the first few years the volume was not great enough to alarm the proponents of law enforcement. Not until 1923 did the legislature specifically outlaw the production of "mash, wort or wash" and the possession of "any still, boiler or other vessel or apparatus" that could be used in the production of distilled or fermented beverages.[25]

The home production of wine and beer during national prohibition has assumed legendary proportions in the collective memory. In many families a few fumbling experimental efforts have become fixed forever among their most cherished traditions. Wines were made principally from grapes but also from various fruits, dandelions, elderberries, potatoes, and even wheat. By the latter part of the Volstead era, national wine production or, more accurately, sales of the materials of production had increased significantly over the 1911–15 period, the last interval unaffected by prohibitory measures. Prohibition wine continued to account, however, for no more than 10 percent of the total consumption of absolute alcohol, as its alcoholic content averaged only about one-half of the 18 percent in preprohibition wine.

Many men tried to make home-brew but soon gave it up as too "troublesome and messy." Hugh F. Fox, secretary of the U.S. Brewers Association and one of the wets' leading spokesmen, declared that it was impossible to produce "a light, palatable and wholesome brew" without highly specialized and costly apparatus. Based primarily on the sale of hops, the most reliable studies estimate that during the early 1920s, national beer consumption fell to about 10 percent of its 1911–15 average but increased to about 25 percent by 1930.[26]

Some brewers produced a "near beer"—that is, a beverage that was identical to beer except that its alcoholic content had been reduced to the legal limit. Kansans soon learned to "needle" near beer (fifteen cents) with a one-ounce vial of alcohol (twenty-five cents), "thumbing" the mixture vigorously to produce a palatable 8 percent beer. A near beer brewed in St. Joseph, Missouri, became especially popular with the needlers, because it mixed well with alcohol, and the brewery conveniently left an extra space in the neck of the bottle to accommodate the "needle."[27]

The commercial production of moonshine—that is, hard liquor with an alcohol content of 40 percent or more—represented the most serious rent in the national prohibition cloth. Compared to beer, moonshine was about as easy to make, was less bulky to transport, and netted far greater profits per unit of time, energy, and capital. The operations uncovered in the early twenties tended to be small, isolated experimental ventures, often producing a product so strong that it would "make a jackrabbit spit in a bulldog's face."

But by the close of the decade, with the widespread use of corn sugar and other technical refinements, the best moonshine approached pre-Volstead liquor in quality. With enhanced quality and production came an increased concentration of the industry in a relatively small number of liquor "rings," organizations that were controlled by mobsters such as Al Capone. During the early 1920s, the national consumption of spirits dropped to about 50 percent of its 1911–15 value, but by 1930 it had recovered to its preprohibition value.[28]

The production of moonshine in Kansas followed the national pattern with respect to the quality and quantity of the liquor produced and the size of the organizations that produced it. In the early Volstead years, stills typically operated with capacities of less than one hundred gallons; confiscated whiskey and mash were often valued at only a few hundred dollars. But that output had evidently not been enough to satisfy the market, at least not that fraction which sought a high-quality product and was willing to pay for it.

In 1922, federal officers uncovered a "big whiskey ring," with over thirty employees, which had been importing "Canadian Club" into Wichita from Canada and Mexico via airplanes and "high powered" motor cars. With the liquor going for $15 a quart, the ringleader reputedly had cleared $250,000. (In some instances the labels and stamps on such allegedly esoteric liquor were faked and the bottles were filled in Kansas City, Missouri.) By the late twenties, liquor hauls involved alcohol and whiskey stills that had a capacity of several hundred gallons and contained equipment and liquor valued at thousands of dollars. In a 1929 raid in Crawford County, for example, federal officers seized stills with capacities of up to 600 gallons, 127,000 gallons of mash, and equipment and liquor valued at $75,000.[29]

Crawford and Cherokee counties continued their historic reputation as forming one of the wettest areas in Kansas. Stills, operating in abandoned mines, barns, and shacks or in edifices built especially for the purpose, dotted the landscape. The region's unemployed miners developed a reputation for producing a high-quality corn-sugar product, carefully blended and aged, which went for $4 to $10 a quart under labels such as Deep Shaft, Corona Rye, Cherokee Red, and Camp 42. The distillers' reputation enabled them to establish markets not only in Kansas and the adjacent sections of Missouri and Oklahoma but also in Kansas City, Missouri, and other urban centers to the east.

In such an environment, bootlegging became as commonplace as moonshining. One observer estimated that the number of outlets in Crawford County in 1930 was upwards of four hundred. Frontenac, which had a population of twenty-one hundred, reportedly had ninety-four, which, if true, would have meant that one of every five families was selling liquor. And some of the region's bootleggers, such as "Pretty Mary" of Frontenac, achieved more than local fame by supplying their wares to prominent folks in and about the Statehouse.[30]

Crawford-Cherokee kept its reputation untarnished for electing the most easily corrupted public officials in Kansas. In 1925 the state successfully brought ouster proceedings against A. H. Carl, the county attorney of Crawford County, on charges of official misconduct. After only a few months in office, Carl had compiled an enviable record of duplicity and corruption. He collected his $25 conviction fee as county attorney on cases that had never come to trial and on injunctions that had never been filed; he encouraged constables to leave behind part of the liquor discovered on raids so that additional arrests could be made the following day; he arrested the state's star witness against one of his minions who had been charged with accepting bribes; he turned over commitment papers to the convicted, leaving it to "their own good time and pleasure" when, if ever, they would present themselves for incarceration. Carl's most memorable maneuver consisted of collecting his attorney's fee, a few days before he assumed office, from a client charged with a liquor violation and then claiming his conviction fee as prosecuting attorney when the case came to trial.[31]

AMERICANS WHO WERE DESPERATE for liquor turned to a wide variety of surrogates for relief, many of which could cause serious illness or even death. The novel situation called for novel solutions. Anything and everything that contained alcohol might be utilized if the need were sufficiently urgent: radiator alcohol, rubbing alcohol, wood alcohol, canned heat, cologne, hair tonic, bay rum, paregoric, extracts, tinctures, and essences. During the early years of Volsteadism a rumor circulated that buttermilk contained alcohol in sufficient quantity to make it an illegal beverage under the law. That unfounded rumor led to this bit of epic poetry:

> If the "wets" had a cow that gave such milk,
> They'd dress her in the finest silk,
> They'd feed her on the choicest hay,
> And milk her forty times a day.[32]

The United States Pharmacopeia listed the formula for a compound known as "Jamaica ginger" as containing 90 percent alcohol and 10 percent extract of ginger. In pre-Volstead Kansas the use, as a beverage, of this medical tincture, which was often prescribed for colic and diarrhea, had become so common that the Kansas Supreme Court had declared it to be an intoxicating liquor. In the twenties it became one of the more popular high-alcoholic drinks in the nation.

During the spring of 1930 an outbreak of a toxic paralysis caused by "bad" Jamaica ginger spread across the country. A total of fifteen thousand cases were reported, of which Kansas had one thousand and Wichita had half of those. Called "multiple peripheral neuritis" by physicians and "jake-leg" by the man on the street, the condition could result in the loss of motor control of the arms and legs for weeks, months, or years or, as in several hundred instances, in death. The malaise hit the lower income level the hardest, adding a significant number of the impoverished to the already hard-pressed relief rolls of Wichita. Not everyone could afford the $3 to $8 for a quart of "hooch," but the fifty cents needed for a two-ounce vial of Jamaica ginger was within the economic reach of all. The alcohol in the tainted Jamaica ginger came from a ring operating in Brooklyn, New York. The ring had imperfectly "stripped" denatured alcohol from legally produced preparations such as perfumes, hair tonics, and after shave lotions. Isolated sites in the South and the West had the misfortune to be the recipients of the deadly concoction. The nearly one hundred federal indictments that were handed down in Kansas included a number of druggists who covertly sold the beverage at the soda fountain, where it could be mixed with a soft drink. Among the culprits was a white-haired little old lady who ran a drugstore on the courthouse square in Phillipsburg. She looked more like the president of the local WCTU than an indictee for "conspiring" to violate the Constitution of the United States in consort with a sordid group of New York hoods.[33]

The Wichita area had challenged the mining district for the laurels as the wettest spot in Kansas long before the "jake-leg" tragedy. With respect to the absolute magnitude of liquor production and consumption and the corruption of public officials, Sedgwick County was peerless. Once, after the authorities had proclaimed the city to be bone dry, the *Wichita Eagle* ran a picture of fourteen bottles that had been ordered by telephone from as many different bootleggers over a period of two days. Numerous roadhouses, the Kansas version of night clubs, flourished in rural Sedgwick County. There one could gamble, dance, and buy liquor by the drink or "red" whiskey by the pint, quart, or gallon. An especially notorious roadhouse, the "elaborately furnished" Green Gables, known as the "Monte Carlo of Kansas," served as headquarters for many who made their living in some phase of the liquor, gambling, or prostitution businesses.[34]

A never-ending stream of avaricious county and city officials—sheriffs, county attorneys, justices of the peace, mayors, police chiefs, patrolmen, election commissioners, dogcatchers—came under suspicion, indictment, or arrest. In 1927, former Governor Henry J. Allen, publisher of the *Wichita Beacon,* personally directed an investigation into the allegations that protection was being offered to the liquor interests by those in the public trust. As a United States senator in 1929, Allen testified as a hostile witness at the trial of a former city commissioner and grand kleagle of the Kansas Ku Klux Klan, who had been accused of shaking down the area's bootleggers.[35]

Though the public had become largely inured to the frequent reports from Sedgwick County of liquor violations, it gasped at the magnitude and the drama of the liquor bust of 12 May 1930, the largest ever in Kansas. Late that evening, some forty-five federal agents and a small contingent of highly trusted local officials simultaneously descended upon a number of sites in western Sedgwick and adjacent Reno counties. They seized six giant stills, with five-hundred-gallon capacities; seven distribution depots; "tons" of sugar; six thousand gallons of quality sugar whiskey valued at $60,000 wholesale; and a denatured-alcohol "stripping" plant camouflaged as a dry-cleaning establishment. In all, they broke up a half-million-dollar liquor organization. Among the fifty-nine indictees were the ringleader, Marcus Gorges, a Wichita businessman, and Everett C. Minner, the Ford County attorney.[36]

The grand catch became possible only because the federal officials had been able to plant agents within Gorges's organization. John B. Madden, the new assistant prohibition administrator for the Nebraska-Kansas-Oklahoma district, and Gorges, the bootlegger king, each had a problem. A former marshal of Dodge City and a former sheriff of Ford County, Madden could not stop the flow of liquor into the pool halls, roadhouses, hotels, and homes of Sedgwick and Reno counties. He could easily apprehend the small-time operators, but the "big boys" continued to function with impunity. The sporty, debonair Gorges, who lived in an "exclusive neighborhood," had become known as the "Al Capone of Kansas." He boasted that he had the "fix" in all along the line and would "have the world by the tail" if he could only add the "dangerous" Madden to his payroll.

In late 1929, Madden had paid a social call on his boyhood chum, Everett Minner, in Dodge City. The county attorney shocked Madden by suggesting that Gorges would be pleased to pay Madden a monthly stipend for services rendered. Recovering his composure, Madden went along with the scheme, receiving, through Minner, payments of $1,000 in February, April, and May. Minner received a 20 percent "commission" from Gorges for his role in the bribery scheme. To produce evidence that was as clean as possible, Madden had himself searched by two trusted Dodge City friends, including the newspaper editor Jess C. Denious, immediately before and after visiting Minner's office for the payoffs. Madden never dealt directly with "Al Capone."

Madden planted an experienced federal agent, Brice Armstrong, alias "Tommy Jones," in the Gorges organization as his contact. Armstrong gathered detailed information on the operation and on its competitors, pretending to use the knowledge gained to protect the former and raid the latter. A short, freckled "strutting peacock" of a man, Armstrong ingratiated himself so thoroughly with Gorges and his lieutenants that they soon came to rely heavily on him for technical and strategic advice. The chief deputy in the organization bragged to Armstrong, in his rich Irish brogue, that he had "more officers on me pay-roll than any other rum-runner in all holy Kansas." When the jake-leg scare hit in the spring, the bottom dropped out of the local liquor market, and Gorges considered moving the entire operation to Oklahoma. Anxious to move before Gorges did, Madden ordered his agents to close the trap in mid May.

In June the federal grand jury at Topeka returned indictments against those involved in the Gorges and Jamaica ginger cases and against four Leavenworth policemen who were charged with accepting bribes. Gorges received a sentence of two years in the Federal Penitentiary and a $10,000 fine. His first trial ended in a hung jury, but in the second trial, Minner received the same sentence as Gorges.[37]

THE EVIDENCE THAT KANSANS frequently broke the liquor laws is plentiful, ubiquitous, and persistent. But so also are the data that during the Volstead era the state maintained its position as one of the driest commonwealths in the Union. In the immediate pre-Volstead period, Kansans had received some national attention that reflected positively on their prohibition policy when Gen. Leonard Wood, the commanding officer at Fort Riley, announced in late 1917 that Kansas recruits were outperforming their peers from other states. ''These Kansas boys were brought up in a clean atmosphere—they started right,'' Wood told Governor Capper. ''You can tell the Kansas people for me that they have got the finest, the cleanest, the healthiest and the most vigorous soldiers in point of endurance, we have ever seen. The official records show this.''[38]

When the detractors of prohibition publicized the availability of liquor in the larger towns, they often hedged their statements in the interests of accuracy. For example, in one of the most vitriolic attacks of the period, entitled ''Holy Hypocritical Kansas,'' the eastern author claimed only that a stranger could obtain liquor in any town ''over 5,000 population . . . within twenty minutes.'' And not all the cities had a reputation for being dripping wet. In the early 1930s a distinguished French scientist and alcohol expert from the Sorbonne University said that ''for a city its size, Topeka is the driest town I have seen in this country.''[39]

In 1926 a committee of the National Federation of Settlements sent questionnaires to numerous social workers concerning the impact of prohibition on their neighborhoods. The director of the survey concluded that there had been a number of positive economic and social consequences of the reform. She noted that from the study's inception, people had been asking ''How are things in Kansas?'' Welfare workers in Topeka, Wichita, and Emporia partially answered the question by reporting ''90 percent'' enforcement, relatively little impact of federal prohibition, and few families on the public dole due to excessive drinking by the wage earner.[40]

In 1930 the national superintendent of the Anti-Saloon League pronounced the enforcement situation in Kansas ''the best in the nation.'' A few states, such as New York and Wisconsin, had repealed their state enforcement laws, placing the entire burden on the central government. Assistant United States Attorney General Mabel Walker Willebrandt, who had charge of prosecutions under the Volstead Act, asked in 1929 if ''the dry state of Kansas, which in good faith enforces the Constitution of the United States concurrently with the Federal Government,'' did not have ''the legal right to expect the state of New York, or

Wisconsin . . . to bear a proportionate share of the responsibility [and expense]?"[41]

Kansas college students reflected the general temperance attitudes of the state. In 1929 the student governing association of Kansas State Agricultural College voted to suspend two students who had been arrested for drinking in their off-campus room. Kansas University's chancellor, E. H. Lindley, said that only "a few silly ones" among the four thousand students still thought it "smart to take a drink." The legendary basketball coach Forrest C. ("Phog") Allen remarked enthusiastically that prohibition had produced "the best crop of girls and boys this old world ever saw." The most systematic study of the temperance attitudes of American college students (all seniors) was reported in 1932. The responses of the Kansas students with respect to national prohibition (60 percent favored unmodified prohibition) and their own drinking habits (75 percent said they did not drink at all) were among the driest in the nation.[42]

Prohibition sentiment among the general public, an excellent barometer of enforcement, remained high throughout the period. The *Literary Digest* conducted polls on the Eighteenth Amendment in 1922, 1930, and 1932. The polling technique tended to favor the wets, as an occasional state referendum demonstrated. Nevertheless, the polls proved to be accurate in identifying national trends and the relative sentiment among the several states. In all three polls, Kansas led all the states in dry sentiment. It registered a 58.2 percent vote for enforcement of national prohibition (as opposed to modification or repeal) in 1922, 57.7 percent in 1930, and 50.2 percent in 1932. The average figures for the nation were 38.6, 30.5, and 26.5 percent, respectively. In 1932, only Kansas and North Carolina had a predominantly dry sentiment.[43]

Two years after prohibition became the law of the land, the Prohibition Bureau ranked the forty-eight states from wettest to driest on impressionistic grounds. Kansas ranked forty-seventh. Nine years later a much-more-detailed report came from a blue-ribbon committee appointed by President Herbert Hoover in 1929. Officially designated as the National Commission on Law Observance and Enforcement, but popularly known as the Wickersham Commission, the eleven-member commission included a former attorney general as chairman, a former secretary of war, the dean of the Harvard Law School, the president of Radcliffe College, and several prominent jurists. After "exhaustively and painstakingly" investigating the problem for eighteen months, they issued a 3,330-page report in six volumes in 1931.[44]

Those sections of the report dealing specifically with Kansas gave it relatively high marks for enforcement, one of the few states to be so commended. The "complete cooperation" among state and federal courts and enforcement agencies drew praise, as did the work of the federal district officers, who were "wholeheartedly enforcing the law and obtaining excellent results." One investigator struck a more hyperbolic note when he claimed that "there is probably no such complete agreement upon any subject in Kansas as upon that of prohibition.'' The United States district attorney for Maryland, Amos W. W. Woodcock, who was later appointed as prohibition commissioner, served as a roving investigator for the commission, visiting and comparing selected areas of the country. In an eleven-page analysis he made point-by-point comparisons between dry Kansas and wet Wisconsin, to the entire detriment of the latter. He declared that Kansas and Maine were "the dry spots" of the nation.[45]

The report of the Wickersham Commission summarized the familiar problems of the most troublesome spots: the cities of Wichita, Hutchinson, Kansas City, Leavenworth, and Topeka and Crawford and Cherokee counties. On a specially prepared map the investigators located the chief arteries of liquor shipments within the state and assigned a score to each county according to the prevailing enforcement conditions. Four counties received "bad" marks (Crawford, Cherokee, Sedgwick, Reno), and one received a mark of "fair" (historically dry McPherson, where a recent oil strike had attracted "a great transient and floating class of people"). The five problem counties contained 16 percent of the state's population. The remaining one hundred counties received "fairly normal" scores.[46]

TABLE 9.1
THE MEAN ANNUAL AMOUNTS OF SIX FEDERAL CATEGORIES
OF PROHIBITION ENFORCEMENT IN KANSAS

Fiscal Years	No. of Stills Seized	Mash Seized (in gals.)	Liquor Seized (in gals.)	No. of Autos Seized	Property Seized ($)	No. of Persons Arrested
1921–24	247	22,027	2,526	18.3	13,373	288.0
1925–28	213	61,435	9,644	19.3	8,708	366.8
1929–33	956	84,806	7,576	35.2	57,538	577.0

Sources: Annual reports of the United States Commissioner of Internal Revenue and of the United States Bureau of Prohibition.
Note: Seizures of stills and mash indicate production activity; the other four categories include both production and distribution. For the entire period, the category of liquor seized includes a mean annual value of 4,080 gallons of spirits (61 percent), 1,131 gallons of wine (17 percent), 973 gallons of cider (15 percent), and 475 gallons of beer (7 percent).

Federal enforcement data for Kansas, on a mean annual basis, are presented for six categories in table 9.1. The data are arranged in three temporal groupings over the Volstead period. As shown in the table, the latest period (1929–33) has considerably higher values for all six factors than does the earliest period (1921–24), with the middle period (1925–28) generally being closer to the first period. These data support the impressionistic conclusion that liquor violations increased significantly during the late twenties in Kansas, as they did in the nation.

Table 9.2 compares the same six categories in Kansas with those of the four neighboring states, three "dry" states commended in the Wickersham report (Maine, North Dakota, Virginia), a "notoriously wet" state (New York), and the mean of the forty-eight states. The data are presented on a mean annual basis over fiscal years 1921 through 1933 and are adjusted for population size to a Kansas base. All the amounts in Kansas are lower than those in Nebraska, Oklahoma, Missouri, Colorado, Virginia, and New York; lower than those in North Dakota in five of six measures; and lower than Maine in four of six. The Kansas amounts range from 6 to 38 percent of the national means, with an average of approximately 20 percent.[47]

TABLE 9.2

MEAN ANNUAL

FEDERAL ENFORCEMENT OF PROHIBITION IN KANSAS

IN COMPARISON WITH SELECTED OTHER STATES, 1921-33

State	No. of Stills Seized	Mash Seized (in gals.)	Liquor Seized (in gals.)	No. of Autos Seized	Property Seized ($)	No. of Persons Arrested
Kansas	509	61,321	6,658	25.7	28,924	423.4
Nebraska	1,909	144,816	16,513	73.3	52,058	1,176.9
Oklahoma	2,501	150,605	11,908	84.9	66,650	1,263.1
Missouri	1,542	438,609	88,755	56.1	63,855	1,065.8
Colorado	1,107	105,147	16,503	155.3	86,749	1,423.2
Maine	42	331	9,054	72.4	98,137	448.6
North Dakota	918	35,154	9,607	40.1	41,914	1,150.4
Virginia	7,439	975,394	78,560	85.9	361,206	1,106.3
New York	532	165,326	236,200	141.9	386,115	1,762.8
National mean	2,328	316,617	106,240	109.4	257,896	1,110.5
Kansas as percentage of national mean	22	19	6	23	11	38

Sources: Annual reports of the United States Commissioner of Internal Revenue and of the United States Bureau of Prohibition.
Note: The values for other states have been adjusted to the Kansas population base.

The "Number of Persons Arrested" column in tables 9.1 and 9.2 includes not only those arrested by federal officers but also those apprehended by state officers aided by or on information supplied by federal officers. For the nation the ratio of these federal:state arrests averaged about 5:1, but for Kansas the ratio was about 1:3. The disparity reflects the relative aggressiveness of state enforcement, the close cooperation between the two agencies in Kansas, and Federal Judge John C. Pollock's reluctance to handle prohibition cases in his court. These data, taken together with the other cogent lines of evidence, cumulatively suggest that during the Volstead era, Kansas remained one of the driest, if not the driest, state in the nation.[48]

THE TEMPERANCE ORGANIZATIONS continued to make significant contributions to the relatively dry climate. They had been elated, of course, that the nation had given all the states the chance to realize the "material, moral and spiritual blessings" that prohibition brings. WCTU's President Lillian Mitchner said in 1920: "The time we have all been looking forward to so eagerly has brought us a wonderful victory over King Alcohol; surely our hearts should be full of gratitude and praise to our Heavenly Father for a Saloonless Nation and a Stainless Flag."[49]

The WCTU expressed its "unalloyed gratification" that the first woman elected to the legislature, Minnie Johnson Grinstead, was "one of our own white ribboners." Grinstead reciprocated by serving as a fountainhead of "inside" information on bills of interest to the WCTU and by sharing her "lone woman" experience in detailed reports to the sisterhood. The union wholeheartedly supported Miss Lorraine ("Lizzie") Wooster—the prim and proper state superintendent of public instruction (1919–23) and the first woman to be elected to a statewide office—in her "uncompromising" attitude toward the use of tobacco by teachers in the public schools. Despite the traditional forms of pressure from the union and from others, the 1927 legislature repealed the anticigarette law, which had been in effect, though not rigorously enforced, since 1909. The fight against repeal was led by Stella Haines, one of the first women to serve in the legislature and the daughter of a WCTU district president.[50]

The WCTU worked against bills that would have permitted Sunday movies and weakened child-labor laws; lobbied for a bill that permitted censorship of movies (talkies); and supported an income-tax amendment that earmarked the derived revenues for the state colleges. The ongoing evolution of social mores evoked its maternal concern, as the members lamented the "unheard of laxity in parental control." This had led, they believed, to the widely publicized breakdown in moral standards among the period's "flaming youth," who were running rampant with their bobbed hair, hip flasks, and suggestive dances. As pressure mounted for the modification or repeal of the Eighteenth Amendment during the early 1930s, the state WCTU concerned itself increasingly with saving the national law. Along with the ASL, the WCTU lashed out at the more blatant claims of the wets. For example, in 1931, Mitchner attacked the "unsupported assertions" that there was now "far more drinking than before prohibition."[51]

The Anti-Saloon League of Kansas filled the reform niche that had been vacated by the KSTU. Each of some twenty evangelical Protestant bodies selected two representatives for the Board of Trustees, of which over half typically were ministers. Fifteen "trustees at large," mislabeled as "represen-

Minnie Johnson Grinstead (courtesy of the Kansas State Historical
Society, Topeka).

tative men of the state,'' included former governors in profusion and other
prominent political, academic, and business figures. The ten-member ''headquarters committee'' appointed the trustees at large and generally conducted the
league's business. Its membership always included the current governor, to
ensure a political connection at the highest level. The league continued the
pattern of broad-based public and religious support established by the KSTU,
with about 85 percent of its funds being funneled through the cooperating
churches. In its peak budget year of 1922, some fifteen thousand individuals
contributed over $52,000, an average of about 30 cents a month or $3.50 a year,
per person.[52]

The league celebrated the ratification of the Eighteenth Amendment as the
dawning of a new Age of Enlightenment. The 1919 trustees meeting was nothing

if not a "triumphal gathering." The state superintendent, W. J. Herwig, declared that national prohibition was "perhaps the most important event in the history of our nation." Perpetuating the familiar nineteenth-century metaphor, he confidently predicted that it would bring "a new emancipation by which millions of slaves to the habit of strong drink shall be made free."[53]

With the nation now subdued, the temperance movement looked for more distant pastures to conquer. The 1920 board meeting of the league authorized the superintendent to launch an educational campaign "on Prohibition and Americanization" among "a certain foreign element" in Kansas City and in the Crawford-Cherokee area. It hoped to employ the new recruits in their European homelands to help bring about worldwide prohibition. To that end, the board kicked off a $20,000 fund-raising campaign to defray the costs of distributing literature on Kansas prohibition to a global audience. Kansas had to keep her interest high, Superintendent Herwig said, to maintain "her rightful place as the leader in the world Prohibition crusade."[54]

Although world conquest was not without its allurements, a problem that was much closer to home raised its ugly head. A temperance victory tends to carry the seeds of its own destruction, namely, a solid advance results in a significant decrease in interest, support, and enthusiasm. A success-generated slump occurred after the passage of the Eighteenth Amendment, just as it had after the adoption of the state's prohibitory amendment.[55]

To pump up morale among the faithful and to build up support among the general public, the ASL organized a number of drives, pledges, and groups during the twenties. It frequently led campaigns for funds and for the stricter enforcement of the law. It combined the pledge of allegiance to the flag with the pledge for total abstinence, declaring that drinking was "an insult to the flag." But its most pronounced organizational success in most of the counties of the state came with the development of "civic leagues."[56]

The civic leagues served as organized nemeses to the bootlegger and helped to teach the citizen how "to take hold of the problem of law enforcement" at the local level. They steadfastly disavowed any interest in "smelling out" liquor in the home. The blueprint called for a group in each county of from one hundred to three hundred persons, to be drawn from every interested religious and civic organization. As usual, the leadership came from the "opinion setters" among the business and professional classes. For example, in Clay Center (Clay County) the Steering Committee included the mayor, two bank cashiers, the owner of the local electric company, the manager of the J. C. Penney store, a grocer, and the Methodist, Christian, and Baptist ministers.[57]

For the first few years after the dissolution of the KSTU, the league gave its first consideration to national prohibition, just as the KSTU partisans had feared. But when the Volstead Act became effective, the league shifted its top priority to state law enforcement. To lead the enforcement campaign the Kansas league inherited, in late 1920, the superintendent of the Wyoming league, Fred L.

Crabbe. A red-headed, personable "go-getter," Crabbe seemed to be exactly what the Kansas situation required. Even his detractors admitted that he could "conduct a money-raising campaign in a church, or raid a bootlegger's joint, with equal grace and gusto."[58]

In the course of the next few years, Fred Crabbe developed several bad habits, all of which flowed from a central defect of his character: he was dishonest. By far his greatest sin consisted of collecting funds from citizens to conduct local liquor "clean up" campaigns and then personally pocketing the money. His next greatest transgression involved collecting political funds in the name of Attorney General Hopkins and his successor, C. B. Griffith (1923–27), and commingling these monies indistinguishably with league revenues. When these notorious practices came to light in 1925, the Headquarters Committee demanded restitution and resignation. Crabbe restored $4,500 that the league felt "morally bound" to repay and resigned forthwith.

The league's embarrassment reached even greater heights when the acting superintendent proclaimed loudly that the Headquarters Committee had attempted to whitewash the whole affair. The organization continued to scrape egg from its face as it replaced the acting superintendent with yet another. Two inveterate and politically conservative foes of the league, William G. Clugston of the *Kansas City Journal Post* and A. L. ("Dutch") Shultz of the *Topeka State Journal,* had a field day with the damaging revelations. They claimed that Crabbe had been made a scapegoat and that the real culprits were Hopkins, Griffith, and the league's unofficial policy of showing favoritism toward liberal Republicans. The most damaging evidence against Hopkins consisted of his having received from the league a total of $1,200 in expense money over four years for his work as a state and national officer. While Griffith was an assistant attorney general (1921–23), the league paid him a total of $3,700 for law-enforcement work. Though a very questionable practice, such multiple employments in the attorney general's office continued to be countenanced by the public for a number of years thereafter.[59]

The league scrambled hard to regain its unruffled composure and to restore its public respect. The new state superintendent, the Reverend Joseph A. McClellan, reassured the national superintendent, F. Scott McBride, that though it was "an awful experience . . . the folks will come back to our support." McBride said that it should be made very clear to the Kansas constituency that "we do not approve of either the financial or political method of Supt. Crabbe." Stung by the Clugston-Shultz charges of bias toward liberal Republicans, McBride added that "our policy [is] to be absolutely non-partisan and as well non-factional."

The obfuscating sand thrown by Clugston and Shultz kept the affair alive long after it otherwise would have died a natural death. Without question the scandal cost the league some public support, especially among the KSTU partisans who still viewed it as an "Eastern organization" and an "interloper."[60] A mortal blow it was not, but somehow the league never seemed to regain fully its old snap and zeal as the battle for the hearts and minds of the electorate warmed up. And from that time to the present day, an ordained minister of an evangelical Protestant denomination has headed the state's dry forces.

THE ORGANIZED NATIONAL MOVEMENT for the modification or repeal of the Eighteenth Amendment began even before the amendment had been ratified. The Association Against the Prohibition Amendment (AAPA) was formed in 1918, attracting mostly conservatives worried about federal infringement on local and state rights. At its reorganization in 1928, it came under the domination of Pierre du Pont and other men of wealth and influence. They were concerned about the threat to the stability of society represented by the increasing frequency of Volstead violations and about the loss of liquor revenues which had to be recouped through income taxes. In 1932 a former Democratic congressman from Kansas (1915-19), Jouett Shouse, who had regularly supported dry measures during his terms in the House, became president of the AAPA. Most "unkansan" in his appearance and demeanor, the "courtly" Bourbon from Kentucky dressed like a fashion plate, wore spats, and carried a walking stick. The drys suggested that he should drop the "h" in his name.[61]

Initially the AAPA maintained a low profile, working primarily for the modification of the Volstead Act so as to permit light wines and beer. Some frustrated wets urged nullification, a strategy that the elitest law-and-order-minded AAPA could not endorse. Though the law grew increasingly unpopular, especially in the urban centers along the eastern seaboard, the prospects for repeal seemed dim to partisans on either side. A fervent wet, the famed defense attorney Clarence Darrow, said as late as 1931 that there was no hope that two-thirds of the Senate would ever vote for resubmission. A leading dry congressman proclaimed that "there is as much chance of repealing the Eighteenth Amendment as there is for a hummingbird to fly to the Planet Mars with the Washington Monument tied to its tail."[62]

But the AAPA took as its own the nonpartisan, single-issue pressure tactics that the ASL had perfected. In a well-financed campaign it presented to the public, in a multiplicity of forms, its three principal tenets: The nation was drinking as much or more under prohibition as it had before, was seized with an unprecedented "crime wave," and had lost sorely needed revenues from liquor. Though only the last was demonstrably true, the influence of the organization grew rapidly during the late twenties. In 1929 it had gained an invaluable ally in the Women's Organization for National Prohibition Reform, which was organized by a group of fashionable women from New York society's "smartest set." The provoked temperance women promised to "outlive them, out-fight them, out-love them, out-talk them, out-pray them and out-vote them." But by 1933 the organization had branches in every state save Kansas and five others, and its membership had grown to one million strong.[63]

In 1929 the AAPA-led wets launched a major propaganda offensive in the leading national magazines and big-city dailies. Sensing that after nearly a decade of trial, prohibition had become a disappointment to many moderates, the wets pushed their campaign with renewed vigor. The drys had won the 1928 presidential election when Herbert Hoover defeated the New York wet Al Smith. But by mid 1929 they had lost that mystical ingredient which fuels all successful reform movements: momentum. And after the autumn of 1929 they had to debate the question against the backdrop of the Great Depression. Both sides unblushingly mangled the truth, ushering in what Herbert Asbury has called the era of the "Big Lie." "The drys lied to make prohibition look good," he said; "the wets lied to make it look bad; the government officials lied to make themselves look good . . . ; and the politicians lied through force of habit."[64]

After a brief visit to Kansas in the spring of 1930, a reporter for *Collier's* magazine condemns both state and federal prohibition (courtesy of the Kansas State Historical Society, Topeka).

As during the prewar period, Kansas found herself thrust bodily into the national limelight, scrutinized for an intense year or so even more painstakingly than before. After brief whirlwind visits, roving journalists published sensationalized stories about the abject failure of prohibition. Declaring that the state afforded "a study in applied hypocrisy," the *Chicago Tribune* published a series of articles devoted exclusively to Kansas prohibition, by an "Inspector X." He found that politics, the church vote, and the liquor question were "welded together" with "strange ethical results." Kansas was the "birthplace of the dual personality politician who votes dry and campaigns in the churches with dry speeches, but keeps a private bottle in his locker." He found Topeka the "dryest of its size in the country," but in Wichita he claimed he saw more drunks in two nights than "in a four months tour of Europe or in a trip . . . through 36 states."[65]

Another national correspondent admitted that Kansas had been "comparatively dry" before 1920, but he approvingly quoted a Hutchinson man who claimed that there was ten times as much drinking as ten years ago. "Kansas politics are dominated by a triumvirate—the W.C.T.U., the Anti-saloon League and the Methodist church," he said. "It would be the sheerest folly for any aspirant to public office to pit himself against these powerful and arbitrary organizations."[66]

Some of the most acrimonious pieces came from Kansans and former Kansans. Charles B. Driscoll, a former editor of the *Wichita Eagle,* blamed Kansas for national prohibition. In H. L. Mencken's *American Mercury,* Driscoll reminisced about those "precursive years" when "you met Kansans everywhere, tirelessly . . . preaching Prohibition. They went into the far fields . . . for silly-looking Prohibition party candidates . . . , taking defeat with the same angelic smile with which an idiot takes castor oil." Frank Doster, the former Populist chief justice of the Kansas Supreme Court (1897–1903), wrote that only a few backward plains states, such as Kansas and the Dakotas, continued to embrace puritanism. "Its only the jackass politicians running for office before yokelry very nearly as ignorant as themselves who any longer affect regards for the old-time Puritan as a model of civic and religious virtue."[67]

Jay House, the former Topeka mayor who had moved on to the "bigtime" in Philadelphia in 1919, continued to cause trouble for friend and foe alike. In his Philadelphia column he reported that the fast social life of Topeka caused him to spend several days in recuperation after a visit to Kansas. "They drink too hard and too often out there for me," he said. The capital city averaged four drinking parties to the block per night, House claimed, many of which were plain "debauches." On his 1928 Christmas visit, alcohol flowed freely at thirteen of the fourteen house parties he had attended.[68]

Governor Clyde Reed (1929–31), the most impulsive chief executive since Walter Stubbs, was under attack for allegedly using a special $40,000 enforcement fund to cover himself with "personal glorification." Anxious to show his "true" prohibition colors, Reed saw in Jay House no more good citizenship than Stubbs had seen eighteen years earlier in the Dawson dispute. Reed risked ridicule by ordering Attorney General Smith to make a full investigation of

Jay House (courtesy of the Kansas State Historical Society, Topeka).

House's "Christmas-party" allegations. Smith and the Shawnee County attorney interrogated at length six of House's more prominent hosts, all of whom solemnly denied having served liquor at their parties. Two later admitted that they had "lied like gentlemen." At that point, everyone seemed to be satisfied, but the incident yielded one other strange spectacle.[69]

One of those who had been questioned was Arthur J. Carruth, the managing editor of the *Topeka State Journal* and one of the most respected figures in Kansas journalism. Two days after the Star Chamber proceedings, the *Kansas City Star* editorially accused Carruth of displaying a flippant attitude toward drinking and of colluding with House in an attempt "to ridicule and discredit"

Kansas prohibition. Carruth wrote a long, agonizing response to the rival *Star,* flatly denying the charges. He feared that the public would be led to believe that he and his paper didn't take Kansas prohibition seriously. The gravest charge that could be made against a Kansas newspaperman, after irresponsibility to the public, he said, was the assertion that he is "guilty of attempting to discredit prohibition."[70]

The most publicized piece came from Walter W. Liggett, a reporter for the magazine *Plain Talk,* who wrote stories with a decidedly wet slant about each of a half dozen places of special national interest. His 1930 article on Kansas began by declaring that "Bleeding Kansas" had become "Boozing Kansas." After covering the usual wet spots, he said that he had found liquor and girls relatively easy to procure even in Topeka, especially in the "sordid speakeasies" of the colored section. He claimed that several of the "snoopers" whom Reed and Smith had hired from the special enforcement fund were bootleggers who continued to practice their trade while on the public payroll. Attorney General Smith called the charges "false, libelous and untrue" and called the reporter "a damned liar."[71]

Even more disturbing to the public peace and tranquility, Liggett repeated his charges before the Judiciary Committee of the United States House of Representatives as the Wickersham Commission collected evidence in the state. He alleged that annual liquor consumption in Kansas came to 25 million gallons, a total that included 5 million gallons of distilled spirits, or 3.7 gallons per capita of the drinking-age population. Blackmar's figure for spirits for 1914 was about 450,000 gallons, less than 10 percent of Liggett's figure. (In the entire postrepeal period, the greatest consumption of spirits has been 3,294,000 gallons in 1979, 1.8 gallons per capita of the drinking-age population.) The pure-alcohol equivalent of Liggett's estimate is 2.65 gallons, a value slightly in excess of the 1911–15 national average.[72]

The most reliable estimates of national alcohol consumption during prohibition are based on sources of liquor production and alcohol-related death rates. Consumption, as measured by gallons of absolute alcohol per capita of the drinking-age population, dropped from its 1911–15 value of 2.56 to 1.40 (55 percent) in 1918/19, due to state prohibition and federal wartime restrictions. Relative to the 1911–15 benchmark, the best estimates of alcohol consumption for the early 1920s range from 20 to 33 percent and for the middle and latter twenties, from 50 to 60 percent. During the immediate postrepeal period, consumption increased from 38 percent (1934) to 47 percent (1935) to 60 percent (1936–41) of the 1911–15 value.

Based on Blackmar's survey of the county clerks, Kansas' consumption for 1914 was 14 percent of the national average, or 0.35 gallons of absolute alcohol per capita of the drinking-age population. Due to the bone-dry law, the decrease in state consumption during the period 1917–19 must have at least kept pace with the sharp drop at the national level. With the advent of national prohibition,

Kansas traded importation for local production. Assuming the 14 percent state-national relationship, the 1914 state figure of 0.35 gallons dropped to 0.07–0.12 gallons in the early twenties and increased to 0.18–0.22 gallons by 1930. Under an upper-limit assumption of a 30 percent relationship, the values become 0.15–0.26 gallons for the early twenties and 0.38–0.46 gallons by 1930. On the latter assumption, state consumption began to exceed that of 1914 sometime during the mid twenties.[73]

"Hit and run" journalists had portrayed Kansas prohibition as an abject failure, though the only systematic study of the period had found quite otherwise. But by 1931/32 the national media campaign had convinced most "moderate" Americans that prohibition as a public policy was a mistake that needed to be corrected. Although Kansans themselves firmly held to their traditional antiliquor position, the imminent repudiation by the nation would carry profound consequences both for the state's policy and for the state's image.

10

The Depression Years

Hypocrisy has become the settled policy of Kansas in regard to prohibition. The law is repudiated in private life, but loudly endorsed in public.
—Journalist Ernest A. Dewey

The prohibition philosophy is not that it will make others good, but that it will make life in a complex civilization safer and simpler and more profitable.
—William Allen White

AS THE GREAT DEPRESSION deepened and the nation moved inexorably toward repeal, a Kansas governor found himself in serious difficulty with the temperance public for the first time since Ed Hoch's sincerity was questioned back in 1905. During his first months in office, Democratic Governor Harry H. Woodring (1931–33) gave vent to prohibition declarations that could have issued from a nineteenth-century zealot. His 1931 legislative message set the tone. In it he declared: "[Kansas] always will oppose with the utmost vigor and with every weapon at her command any attempt to weaken the prohibitory principle. I believe in this principle insistently and energetically and under my administration will leave nothing undone which [would] strengthen and make efficient the enforcement machinery. . . . Triumph over the forces of lawlessness, so far as prohibition is concerned, will come eventually in the nation as it came in Kansas."[1]

Woodring's problems arose soon after he endorsed Franklin Delano Roosevelt for president. Roosevelt had "trimmed" a good deal on the liquor question during his public career, even maintaining an official, albeit strained, neutrality on repeal during the months before the 1932 Democratic National Convention. But he had been closely identified with the wet Al Smith and, as such, was anathema to Kansas drys. Woodring acknowledged that Roosevelt's position might not be "strictly in accord with the Kansas idea" but insisted that

Governor Woodring (second from left) campaigns in Kansas City in September 1932 with the national Democratic nominees, Franklin Delano Roosevelt and John Nance Garner (far left) (courtesy of the Kansas State Historical Society, Topeka).

prohibition was "of less importance at this time than the question of enabling the men who want work to provide for their families."[2]

In the spring of 1932 both the ASL and the WCTU exerted intense pressure on Woodring to work for a dry plank at the Democratic National Convention (which he half-heartedly agreed to do) and to reconsider his presidential choice (which he adamantly refused to do). Often "hostile and unforgiving" toward those with whom he differed, the governor lashed back at his tormenters. He publicly broke with the ASL by labeling it an "auxiliary" of the Republican party and a practitioner of "cheap politics." The rupture proved to be ill advised both for the governor and for the organization. For Woodring it became a contributing factor in his narrow defeat that fall; for the ASL it marked the end of a nearly thirty-year honeymoon with the state's top elected officials.

During this stressful period the word *prohibition* disappeared abruptly from the governor's vocabulary, to be replaced by its nonsynonym "temperance." He showed great impatience with those who questioned his unwavering devotion to principle. "I always have been, am now, and always shall be," he repeatedly said, "for temperance and law enforcement." *Prohibition* didn't reenter his vocabulary until 1946, when it returned in a very different context.[3]

In late February 1933, a few days before Franklin Roosevelt took his first oath of office, Congress submitted to the states the Twenty-first Amendment, which repealed the Eighteenth. The Kansas delegation continued its dry tradition by voting solidly against the resolution, which provided for ratification of the amendment by popularly elected delegates at state conventions, rather than by state legislatures, to eliminate the possibility of a small number of dry legislators blocking its adoption.[4]

The wets in the Kansas Legislature were elated at the prospect of a public vote on the issue. At a temperance conference, the dry leaders concluded that there was "no doubt as to Kansas voting dry." They reasoned that an early Kansas vote might have a salutary effect on other less firm states, and they petitioned the governor to set up the necessary convention machinery. The stage seemed to be set for an early public expression on the question.[5]

A bill providing for the election of convention delegates by congressional district at the 1934 general election promptly passed the state senate unanimously. But a week later the house drys defeated the measure 64 to 54. The drys lamely explained that while they did not oppose submission, they did object to the specific form of representation in the senate bill. Evidently there had been second thoughts, since both sides had agreed on the bill before it had passed the senate.[6]

The infuriated wets vowed to "go after" the sixty-four representatives who had voted against the bill. The wets claimed that these legislators were of the "wet drinking, dry-voting" type who feared the ASL and the WCTU more than death or taxes. Beset by pressing economic problems, Governor Alfred M. Landon (1933–37) received numerous petitions calling for a special session to submit national repeal to the people, but the drys continued to oppose such a session. By June the wets were blasting Landon for declaring against repeal, for allowing "Czarina" Mitchner to kill the convention bill, and for insisting that legislators promise to pay their own expenses before he would call a special session.[7]

The more salubrious climate for repeal forced the drys into a defensive posture they hadn't known for twenty-five years and propelled the wets into levels of activity they hadn't experienced since the 1890s. Woodring's break with the ASL encouraged the heretofore-intimidated wets to espouse their cause more openly and more forcefully. The Anti-Prohibition Society of Kansas organized at Salina in August 1932, with the mayor of Hays as its president. The following May it began publishing the *Kansas Repealist* at Hays (Ellis County), a Catholic stronghold and self-proclaimed "center" of the wet movement. Though short-lived, the magazine served as a release for the pent-up frustrations of the dedicated wets, much as similar publications had functioned for the drys over the years.[8]

In their new vehicle the wets matched the drys mile for mile in shrillness and righteousness. The editor said that he had worked in the nation's largest cities from New York to San Francisco but had seen "more drinking in Kansas than anywhere else." Bill Clugston assured the readership that the Kansas ASL was "the most corrupt, intolerant, unintelligent organization ever put together under the cloak of a holy cause" and that its "blood sister," the WCTU, was "little better." Jay House, now a reporter for the *New York Post*, hadn't forgotten his old Kansas friends. As mayor of Topeka from 1915 to 1919, he had admitted becoming "as fanatical as the most zealous Dry" in enforcing prohibition. But in 1933 he described prohibition as a "tyrannical, grotesque and preposterous thing." Kansas prohibitionists, he said, "are the most merciless crew that ever scuttled human freedom. In no other state was the relentless fanaticism of the Kansas drys ever matched."[9]

Though national prohibition served as its chief target, the *Repealist* did not entirely neglect the state law. Among the reasons it advanced for elimination of the bone-dry law, driving bad liquor from the market had a high priority. The available quality, it said, ranged from the "more aged of the deep-shaft vintages and the Reno County sandhill red liquor . . . to some of the vilest liquid junk that ever gave an honest man the D.T.'s."[10]

In state after state voting on the Twenty-first Amendment, the wets swept to victory with their core argument that the issue resolved itself into an economic, not a moral, question. Kansas became one of only five states that failed to establish a convention to vote on repeal. The thirty-sixth state ratified on December 5, only nine months after Congress had submitted the question. In his formal repeal proclamation, President Roosevelt called for temperance in drinking habits and the elimination of the illicit (untaxed) liquor traffic. He also warned against the return of the ancient social pariah: "I ask especially that no State shall by law or otherwise authorize the return of the saloon in its old form or in some modern guise."[11]

Though it scarcely came as a surprise, the loss of national prohibition had a profound effect on Kansas drys. Repeal meant the loss of federal prohibition agents and a return of the beleaguered dry island, struggling to survive amid wet neighbors. But of greater consequence, repeal meant the loss of the principle of prohibition as a national ideal. The Kansas idea had auditioned on the national stage and had failed, or, more precisely, had been rejected. The bright and hopeful flame that had been kindled by the Eighteenth Amendment had been snuffed out, leaving only the bitter ashes of sorrowfulness and disillusionment. "When the 18th Amendment was adopted, everybody thought we had reached the promised land," Lillian Mitchner said. "But like the Children of Israel, we seem now to face a journey through the 'wilderness,' where there are yet 'idols' and 'golden calves' to be destroyed."[12]

The change in national status, with its associated loss of confidence and self-esteem, had an impact on more than the militantly dry segment of the population. The image problems of the entire state became essentially the problems of the drys writ large. With the loss of the Eighteenth Amendment, all

Kansans became vulnerable to charges, often clothed in mirthful terms, of being "backward," "unprogressive," "unsophisticated," even "antediluvian." With the cruel climatic conditions of the 1930s, which brought record heat, drought, dust storms, and grasshoppers to the plains, the Kansas image regressed fully to that of the 1890s, when her name had been a generic term for misfortune and a bitter curse on the lips of fleeing multitudes. Once again, diffident Kansans found themselves on the defensive, forever apologizing for their state's climate, misfortunes, lack of culture, and, most especially, her peculiar and puritanical social customs, writ into law. How the citizens of 1915 would have hooted at that!

CONGRESS, SOON AFTER SENDING the Twenty-first Amendment to the states, increased the legal limit of alcohol in beverages from 0.5 to 4 percent by volume, or 3.2 percent by weight. When this amendment to the Volstead Act went into effect on April 7, Jacob Ruppert, president of the U.S. Brewers Association, issued a solemn warning against intemperance. But the long-denied beer drinkers joyously celebrated the occasion in the most fitting fashion, most especially at the historic sites of production. Milwaukee marked the occasion in a "jubilant mood"; St. Louis welcomed beer back amid "a carnival spirit." Two cases from a prominent St. Louis brewer arrived at the White House gates shortly after midnight, with the greeting "Here's to you—President Roosevelt."[13]

The legalization of 3.2 beer by Congress did not make it one whit more legal in Kansas than it had been, though many would-be sellers and buyers thought otherwise. Conscientious state and local officials enforced the law in the time-honored Kansas fashion. The first conviction for selling came in late April in a police court in Wichita; similar convictions followed in Topeka and Salina. Attorney General Roland Boynton (1930–35) failed in his attempt to stop the government from issuing federal tax stamps to Kansans to sell 3.2 beer, reviving the ancient battle between dry states and a wet central authority. The drys fared better in federal court, where Judge Hopkins ruled in May and Judge Pollock reluctantly confirmed in June that the federal government could not restrain state officials from enforcing the state law.[14]

But despite the restraints of state law and the pronouncements of federal judges, a full-scale "open beer rebellion" broke out in Wichita during the last week of June. About one hundred "substantial" businessmen, mostly owners of groceries and restaurants, established a common "defense fund" and proceeded to sell 3.2 beer openly. Initially it sold for thirty-five cents a bottle, twenty cents over the price in Missouri, but that quickly dropped to twenty cents as the beer became more available. To the local officials, Attorney General Boynton sent lists of those who held federal beer stamps and plaintively asked what plans the officials had made to control the situation. But Judge Pollock encouraged the revolt with his gratuitous remark that "people do what they want to do." During the first week the Wichita police made twenty-two perfunctory arrests, the violators being released after paying a $25 fine and costs. By early July, upwards of one thousand dealers were selling beer openly across the state, the most widespread total defiance of authority in the history of the prohibitory law.[15]

Onto this rebellious scene the Kansas Supreme Court dropped a legal bombshell on 13 July 1933. The Reno County district judge had enjoined two men from selling 3.2 beer at a sandwich stand in Hutchinson. The judge had denied the defendants' offer to prove that the beverage in question was not, in fact, intoxicating. The Kansas Supreme Court held that though the malt beverage commonly known as beer was "presumed" to be intoxicating, "this presumption may be met by evidence . . . that it is not intoxicating as a matter of fact." The district judge had erred in denying the defense a chance to offer its proof, however flimsy that might have been.[16] Presumably the court would have rendered the same decision even if the liquid at issue had been two-hundred-proof alcohol.

In 1914 the state supreme court had modified the threefold taxonomy of alcohol-containing liquids that it had established in 1881 (see above, p. 65). The court entirely eliminated the second category, which had included those items deemed to be outside the law (toilet articles, culinary items, and medicines whose formulae were given in the U.S. dispensatory). It reassigned these items to the last category, where their intoxicating nature became a question of fact for a jury.

The beer decision in effect moved beer from the first to the (new) second category. It explicitly did not legalize 3.2 beer, though the court recognized that the decision might readily be misinterpreted. The decision came at a time when the country was awash with 3.2 beer, including the neighboring states in all four directions, and Kansas itself was in open revolt on the issue. The high court's sensitivity to the nullification atmosphere can be deduced from the fact that only seventeen days had elapsed between the decision of the Reno County court and the opinion of the Kansas Supreme Court.[17]

Governor Landon called the situation "intolerable"; the public called for a special session to eliminate the "beer chaos." Rolie Boynton predicted that the decision would make it "very difficult to get a conviction"; several months later he said that the ruling had made it "impossible" to enforce the law. In an editorial entitled "The Shame of Kansas," the *New York Times* took the occasion to sneer at the state's historic effort to limit alcohol consumption. For fifty years, it mocked, Kansas had been "the citadel of virtue and the capital of prohibition. The names of John P. St. John and Carry Nation are among the priceless treasures of mankind."[18]

Although no one was fully satisfied with the situation, beer selling flourished over the state in its new quasi-legal status. By the end of summer, both judges and juries were dismissing beer defendants with regularity. Subsequently, a 3.2 case became a rarity. The price of twenty-five cents for a twelve-ounce bottle brought a lively trade even at the nadir of the depression. In early August the *Emporia Gazette* reported that "night life . . . last evening was a dizzy whirl, what with half a dozen stores selling 3.2 beer." By August, over fifteen hundred federal beer stamps had been sold, and many towns had begun to license "cereal malt beverages." Some WCTU members threatened to take up their rusty hatchets to stop the trade, but the volume continued to grow. By mid 1935 at least sixty six towns were regulating beer, and fifty-five hundred Kansans held federal beer stamps. Many of the retailers reportedly sold hard liquor as a covert sideline.[19]

Beer represented no minor leak in the prohibition dike. Ninety percent of the alcoholic beverages that were consumed and 60 percent of the absolute alcohol came from that source during the "normal" years before the war. The widespread public approval of beer dealt another profound blow to the drys, who had fully expected that after more than fifty years of prohibition, Kansans' appetite for intoxicating liquor would have largely disappeared. The widespread acceptance and usage, with legal impunity if not full legal sanction, signified a marked shift in community sentiment from the pre-Volstead days. A large proportion of the population had come to accept or at least tolerate a low-alcohol malt beverage as "nonintoxicating," that is, as neither sinful nor harmful. The national prohibitory experience and the ever-persistent forces of secularity and modernity had produced during the twenties that which would have been unthinkable a decade earlier.

GOVERNOR LANDON called "the most important special session" ever held in Kansas for 30 October 1933. It considered especially the Finney bond scandal, unemployment relief measures, the beer question, and a prohibition referendum. The WCTU inundated the legislature with "thousands and thousands" of antibeer signatures, ninety-two hundred coming from Reno County alone, Lillian Mitchner's home territory. A house bill that would have legalized 3.2 beer lost narrowly, 58 to 63, after the representatives had defeated an amendment, 41 to 57, that defined intoxicating liquor as any beverage that included more than 0.5 percent alcohol. Democrats tended to give proportionally more support to the wet side of the questions than the Republicans did, but the votes were not highly partisan.[20]

Since any possibility that the state could get organized in time to vote on the Eighteenth Amendment had vanished by late spring, attention shifted to the state's constitution. Landon had told the WCTU in September that the "majority has a right to rule" in a representative government. He would not oppose the submission of the amendment, he said, "in the firm belief that it will be reaffirmed and not repealed." The WCTU itself did not oppose submission, instead cautiously announcing that it and the other organized drys "rather welcomed it."[21]

With such unusual concurrence the legislature caught the democratic virus and promptly passed a resolution submitting the question to the electorate at the general election in November 1934. The proposal would have repealed the prohibitory amendment to the Kansas Constitution and would have substituted the following: "The legislature may license and regulate the manufacture, sale, possession and transportation of all liquor having any alcoholic content, and may impose special taxes on all malt, vinous and spirituous liquors, and may provide for the prohibition of such liquors in certain areas."

Some critics thought the substitute was overly wordy; Attorney General Boynton believed the verbiage to be unnecessary since the legislature would hold the specified powers once the amendment had been repealed. Some drys worried that the substitute might make future statewide statutory prohibition impossible, since it provided only for prohibition in "certain areas." Still others noted with satisfaction that the substitute did not provide safeguards against that most insufferable of human institutions: the saloon.[22] After fifty-three years the wets had finally carried the resubmission battle, but the drys had won a significant verbal skirmish.

The repeal campaign lacked the fireworks that the subject usually engenders in Kansas, being overshadowed by the stresses of the depression and the state bond scandal. Though crestfallen and on the defensive, the drys still commanded a substantial majority of public opinion. The wets drew comfort from the repeal of the national amendment and the near-universal selling of beer. Both sides seemed to understand that the drys would win the referendum.

The drys united in the Prohibition Emergency Committee, headed by Dr. John R. Golden, a Disciples of Christ minister and a veteran temperance lobbyist. Although the Eighteenth Amendment had been repealed, the drys said, the deleterious effects of alcohol had not. Repeal would bring more crime, poverty, drunks, and suffering. The drys felt that the younger generation, especially, was vulnerable. Campaigning on the slogan "Keep Kansas Dry for Kansas Youth," they declared: "We must have a Wall of Total Abstinence built so high that the children . . . may be protected from the flood of liquor which surrounds us on every side."[23]

The wets were not as well organized or as militant as the drys, but they did attract support from statewide service organizations such as the American Legion. The wets argued that prohibition had become a discredited doctrine nationally and that in Kansas it had resulted in lax enforcement of the law and in the corruption of public officials. As on the national scene, the wets stressed the increased revenues that repeal would bring and insisted that the liquor issue was "not a question of right or wrong."[24]

For the first time since early in the century the two major political parties differed perceptibly on the liquor question. Both parties had stood foursquare for state prohibition in 1932, despite the fact that the national Republican party had adopted a "moist" position by advocating the resubmission of the Eighteenth

Amendment, and the national Democratic party had gone drippingly wet by endorsing repeal. In 1934, Kansas Republicans affirmed their "traditional stand" in support of prohibition, while the Democrats, badly divided on the question, fell mute on the issue for the first time since 1904.

In 1932, candidate Alf Landon had taunted the Democrats about supporting both Kansas prohibition and national repeal, as Clyde Reed had done in 1928 when Al Smith was running for president. In 1934, Governor Landon gave "very vocal" support to the drys, while the Democratic candidate for governor, Omar Ketchum, "skillfully sidestepped" the issue on every occasion. The position of the Democrats—that the referendum was nonpolitical and nonpartisan—virtually eliminated any chance the wets had for victory.[25]

John Golden "outgeneraled" the opposition by keeping the public's attention centered on the abuses that the saloon and hard liquor would bring, thus diverting it from the much more ticklish question of legalizing beer. The alcoholic content of beer was best left to the legislature, he said, a position that was shared by many moderates, both wet and dry. But the "indecent" conditions that were spawned in and around the beer taverns had raised the specter of the old-time saloon. Thus many who had favored the legalization of beer cast their ballots against the saloon and repeal. The drys won the election by 89,000, with 56 percent of the vote, 436,688 to 347,644.[26]

Eighty-nine of the 105 counties (85 percent) voted to retain prohibition, compared to 53 of 80 (66 percent) that voted for the amendment in 1880 (see app. A). The driest counties included (in percentage dry) Jewell (80), Kiowa (78), Smith (74), Linn (72), and Coffey (71), all of which had low population densities and relatively high proportions of Republicans and evangelical Protestants. The wettest counties included Ellis (27), Leavenworth (29), Wyandotte (36), Ellsworth (36), and Sedgwick (40). Repeal strength centered in the Missouri River counties, the mining area, the metropolitan centers, and a cluster of counties that had large German Catholic populations in the west-central region.

The correlation coefficient between the 1880 and 1934 elections was +0.42, statistical testimony of the persistence of the basic nineteenth-century voting pattern. Although ethnic integrity as such had diminished substantially over the years, the areas that had opposed prohibition historically on religious and/or ethnic grounds continued to express strong wet sentiment, an indication that for them the temperance educational effort had failed. The correlation coefficients between the percentage of dry votes and the percentages of Republican, rural, and evangelical votes were 0.30, 0.35, and 0.57 respectively (see app. B).[27] Support for prohibition was greater both in absolute numbers and in proportion than it had been in 1880. But dry strength unquestionably had diminished markedly from its high-water mark during the period 1910–25, when it probably reached 80 percent, and even from its level during the late twenties, when it still commanded 65 to 70 percent of the electorate.

THE SAGE OF EMPORIA and the voice of all Kansas, William Allen White, made frequent and lengthy pronouncements on the prohibition question over the years to a wide and appreciative public. What Mr. White said not only advertised the Kansas position to the nation, as he saw it, but also helped to clarify for Kansans themselves what they felt and thought. As an earnest young man holding a KSTU officership at the turn of the century, his "rabid" views had been indistinguishable from those of thousands of other idealistic young Kansans, bitten by the twin reform bugs of temperance and progressivism. But as his talents and contacts led to the enlargement of his reputation on a wider stage, he became the unquestioned interpreter for the nation of prohibition and other social issues of moment in Kansas.

White sometimes held that prohibition was basically an economic, not a moral, question and chided the East for not recognizing this elementary "fact." But at other times he argued on moral grounds that the liberty to drink had to be circumscribed by society in order to protect the potential victims of alcohol abusers. Although he practiced and preached a strict moral code, he was too good-humored and too accepting of the frailties of others to fit the mold of the bluenose crank.

In one celebrated instance he seemed to show intolerance, but that incident has been widely misinterpreted. White resigned in 1922 from an editorial position on the New York–based humor magazine *Judge,* ostensibly over its policy of advocating light wines and beer. His friends later claimed that he took this action as a matter of principle. But the magazine itself seems to have initiated the divorce proceedings because of the logistical difficulties posed by the distance (apparently cultural as well as geographical) between Emporia and New York City.[28]

Like most Kansans, White confidently expected the nation to warmly embrace the Eighteenth Amendment, once it had given the reform a fair trial. But unlike most Kansans, the well-traveled *Gazette* editor soon saw firsthand the nullification attitudes of the East. In a 1922 article in *Collier's* entitled "A Dry West Warns the Thirsty East," he noted the growing disparity in attitude between the two sections of the country and uncompromisingly declared that if "absolute prohibition" could not be maintained, "partial prohibition" would also fail. Again in 1928 he warned of the spreading "whiskey rebellion" from its eastern epicenter, ending his *Collier's* article with a somewhat belligerent question: "Do the unquestioned economic benefits of prohibition to the lower economic nine tenths of society offset the unquestioned evil that comes from the more or less openly treasonable attitude of the upper tenth of society?"[29]

As the state and national mood shifted in the wet direction, White tended to follow, rather than lead, the procession. Declaring that he wanted above all else to be "fair," he called for a referendum on the Eighteenth Amendment in May 1932, a position that had been widely adopted by Republicans by that date. Later that summer, as the Republican National Convention endorsed a resubmission plank, he "debated" the issue on national radio with the president of Columbia University. "We relied too much upon enforcement," he said. "We abandoned our campaign of education. We met the bootlegger with force instead of meeting his patrons with reason."[30]

As the popularity of 3.2 beer in Kansas became increasingly evident during the summer of 1933, White declared, not very convincingly, that it had become a nonissue. "Beer makes little difference to this town, or to any other for that matter," he said. Should a jury declare 3.2 beer legal in Emporia, not many would buy the "pale watery fluid," and it would never become "a steady year-around seller." As the resubmission resolution glided noiselessly through the 1933 special session, White took the occasion to opine that all sorts of "social diversions," such as the automobile, movies, radios, parks, and libraries, had developed in the twentieth century as competitors to the saloon, should it return. "It is folly for the dead hand of yesterday's experience to impose a civic and social morality upon this generation. . . . Sooner or later we Kansans must come to a vote."[31]

Evidence that White continued to adjust his attitude to parallel that of the general public can be adduced from the quality of the support that he gave to prohibition in the 1934 referendum. An occasional lukewarm editorial supported the dry position, but nothing resembling the red-blooded, two-fisted, tub-thumpers of which he had become the acknowledged master. He took the occasion of Frances Willard Day (September 28) to blast the temperance programs in the schools as "not just bad" but "terrible." Prohibitionists, he said, "are barking up the right tree but their barks are out of date."

Although serious drinkers had long since discovered that anyone who couldn't get drunk on 3.2 beer "just ain't trying," White continued to laugh at the "innocuous" brew. The beverage, he said, was "the goofy-goof of booze, a thin 3.2 hogwash. Not one man in 10 could hold enough without sideboards to get sufficiently squizzed to wink at his wife in a mirror." More than any other public figure, he promoted the "hope" that if prohibition did stay in the constitution, 3.2 beer would stay in the taverns. Many moderates took his "word" for that when they went to the polls in November.[32]

Only three days after the referendum had produced the solid dry victory, White dropped a bombshell among his temperance colleagues. He suggested that they should avoid an "arrogant, bigoted" attitude and pointed out that a large minority, composed chiefly of voters under forty, were especially unhappy with the "bone dry" provisions of the law. He proposed a six-point plan which included the legalization of 3.2 beer, as well as home-made beer, wine, and cider, and the right to possess and transport up to one quart of hard liquor or one gallon of wine.[33]

For his trouble, Mr. White brought down upon his cherubic countenance the full wrath of the uncompromising drys. Local chapters of the WCTU denounced the plan as "sopping wet," declaring that it was impossible "to be neutral between right and wrong." They scolded him as a "church member" for using his influence "to send men to hell." The broadcasting of his plan, they said, had been "as a crown of dandelion seed blown by the wind, . . . never [to] be gathered up again. . . . We censure you as a traitor to the dry cause."[34]

A BILL DEFINING the alcoholic content of intoxicating liquor became the focal point of a monumental struggle in the 1935 legislature. Fresh from their convincing triumph at the polls, the drys championed the Fossey bill, which set the limit of legal beverages at 0.5 percent, the same as that of the unamended Volstead Act. The Prohibition Emergency Committee, which continued to be the "clearing-house" agent for the organized drys, inundated the house and senate with petitions containing 100,000 names. The temperance-inclined house passed the Fossey bill in early February, by a vote of 75 to 43.

But the senate proved to be a more difficult nut for the temperance forces to crack. The Fossey bill remained bottled up in committee for several weeks while the dry leaders in and out of the legislature squirmed and cried foul. The seventy-three-year-old Lillian Mitchner had to be removed bodily from the legislative floor by the sergeant at arms after she had delivered several "outspoken" remarks about certain members of the body. Democratic Senator Charles E. Miller attempted to put the noncommittal Governor Landon on the spot by introducing a resolution that demanded that Landon recommend a specific alcoholic content for liquor. The resolution failed on a highly partisan vote. In early March the senate passed the Fossey bill, but only after amending it to remove the possession clause of the bone-dry law. The house adamantly refused to compromise on the amendment through three conference committees. At that juncture, disgusted and exhausted, everyone gave up and went home. The status quo for beer remained.[35]

While they polished their weapons in preparation for the 1937 legislative battle, the drys received encouragement from two unexpected sources. After visiting all eight states that remained nominally dry, a reporter for *American Magazine* wrote that "there is only one real Noah's ark of prohibition afloat in the flood today. That is the state of Kansas." An editorialist on the Kansas University student newspaper noted that Kansans were often accused of being "the biggest hypocrites in the world." But, he said, "in spite of the more or less flowing of liquor in the larger cities . . . , Kansas is trying to be dry. If we are hypocritical because those of us who do not drink, who are far in the majority, will not give in to the minority who like their hard drinks at home, then we are guilty of the charge." He closed on a prescient note: "If Kansas goes wet it will be a new generation that makes it wet."[36]

As the 1937 legislative season approached, each side girded for a fight to the finish. Everyone wanted to see an end to the "jury option" arrangement, which combined the worst features of both wet and dry solutions: widespread beer selling, but without accompanying state revenues. Agitating for 3.2 beer,

White called the situation "a disgrace to the state."[37] Although the drys continued to battle ferociously, time and luck had become the ineluctable companions of the wets.

The drys in the house again introduced a 0.5 percent bill, which seemed certain to pass. In the ensuing debate a few wets manifested a maudlin concern for the "great evil" of spiking that was inherent in near-beer (0.5 percent). Taking the bait, the extreme drys supported an amendment that would have excluded all alcohol from beverages (0.0 percent). A digusted dry of the moderate persuasion moaned that the amended bill would become "a laughing stock" all over the state. A combination of extreme drys and cynical wets (who really wanted 3.2 beer) passed the measure in mid February. The extreme form of the house bill made it relatively easy for the wets in the senate to convince their colleagues to adopt a 3.2 amendment. After the first conference committee had failed to reach agreement, a repeat of the 1935 deadlock seemed certain.[38]

But the public, alarmed at reports that the unregulated beer joints "ran wild" over the state, demanded a solution. Searching frantically for an imaginative and face-saving proposal to offer the beleaguered drys, the wets suggested that a bill for "strict regulation" of the beer traffic be prepared as a companion measure. Many members of the house who had voted dry for years quickly agreed to accept 3.2 beer if the "proper regulations" could be written. Sitting as a Committee of the Whole, the house set to work, "gleefully" writing a regulatory law. Both houses accepted both bills on March 25, and Kansas had fully legalized 3.2 beer. For the first time since 1879 the legislature had passed a major piece of nonprohibitory liquor legislation.[39]

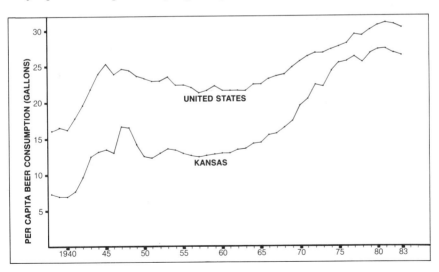

Fig. 10.1. Annual per capita (drinking-age population) consumption of beer in the United States and in Kansas, 1938–83.

Because beer had been widely sold since 1933, consumption did not surge during the first years after state approval, as it later would with spirits and wine. In the first four years, consumption averaged 44 percent of the national amount. From 1940 to 1980, per capita beer consumption in the Kansas drinking-age population rose from 7.0 gallons to 12.6 (1950), 13.0 (1960), 19.6 (1970), and 27.4, an increase over the forty-year interval of 291 percent (see fig. 10.1). Nationwide, consumption increased from 16.1 gallons in 1940 to 30.8 in 1980, a growth of 91 percent.[40] The legal consumption of beer in Kansas included only 3.2 until a later date, when the legalization of spirits and wine brought also the sale of "strong" beer, with an alcoholic content greater than 4 percent by volume.

11
Repeal

The wisecracks that "Kansans stagger to the polls and vote dry" and that "in Kansas the wets have their liquor, the drys have prohibition and everybody is happy" make Kansas and Kansas people appear hypocritical. Our people should either adjust their habits to their voting, or else vote in accordance with their habits.
—Attorney General Edward Arn

Personally, I am an extreme "dry," who holds that no man has the right to use anything that either limits his own usefulness or makes him a nuisance or a menace to society. However, I recognize that a great many people do not share my views, and that public policy and public performance cannot be much in advance of public opinion. . . .
—Topeka accountant Willard Greene

IN THE WAKE of the beer struggle, the liquor question lay relatively dormant, or at least as dormant as is possible in Kansas. The wets remained unorganized except in the liquor industry itself. They savored their beer victory and looked forward to the modification of the bone-dry law and to the resubmission of the constitutional question at a future date. The drys underwent several significant changes, both in organization and in leadership.

In 1937 the United Dry Forces (UDF) replaced the old federation—the Prohibition Emergency Committee—as the umbrella organization. A year later the UDF assumed a more restricted role as the successor to the ASL, which at the national level had fallen on difficult times. Dr. Ross E. Farley, a Methodist minister who had been the ASL's superintendent of the intermountain states, became general secretary. In 1943 the Committee of 100,000 organized in Hutchinson under the leadership of Frank U. Russell, a seventy-year-old lawyer from LaCrosse (Rush County). This organization attracted the "uncompromising drys," many of whom supported Prohibition-party candidates. By 1945 it claimed thirty-one thousand members, and a year later, a "mailing list" of sixty

231

thousand. By the early 1940s, then, Kansas had four statewide dry organizations, including the Prohibition party and the WCTU.[1]

In 1938, seventy-six-year-old Lillian Mitchner retired as president of the WCTU, after holding the office for twenty-nine years. Mitchner had repeatedly stressed that "the business of the W.C.T.U. is education, it never was organized to enforce [the] law." She had done much of her "educating" in the legislative halls and over the years had become a major power in state politics—venerated, respected, feared, and hated. Not unreasonably, the *Hutchinson News* claimed that she had had "a greater and longer influence on the history of Kansas than any individual of her time." The most pragmatic respect for her and her organization came from the opposition. "Whenever I see Lillian Mitchner," a veteran wet legislator said, "I think of the thousands of women that she represents."[2]

During the quiescent period that preceded and encompassed World War II, alcohol-related proposals did not disappear entirely from the legislative hopper, though none received lengthy consideration. The wets introduced bills to permit possession (1941) and to authorize state-owned package liquor stores (1939, 1941, 1945). The drys sponsored bills providing for county and municipal option on beer (1939, 1941) and limiting alcohol in beverages to 0.5 percent (1941, 1943, 1945). In 1941 the WCTU resolved to "re-double" its efforts to gain passage of the 0.5 percent bill, and in 1943 it urged the membership to work for repeal of 3.2 beer "by every righteous effort." As a haunting echo from the past, the 0.0 percent bill popped up in the 1943 session, introduced by a representative who was a Methodist minister. The leadership of the UDF and of the WCTU utilized the wartime milieu to urge as "patriotic" measures the cessation of liquor production and the diversion of alcohol to essential war materials such as rubber.[3]

IN ADDITION TO REPEALING the Eighteenth Amendment, the Twenty-first Amendment prohibited the importation of intoxicating liquor into any state "in violation of the laws thereof." Congress did not pass an enforcement act until mid 1936, which law provided penalties of up to $1,000 in fines and one year in prison for importation into states that banned liquor containing more than 4 percent alcohol by volume. Prior to this act, agents of the Alcohol Tax Unit of the Internal Revenue Bureau could concern themselves only with the evasion of federal taxes by moonshiners. The United States Supreme Court held in 1939 that under the Twenty-first Amendment, "the right of a state to prohibit or regulate the importation of intoxicating liquor is not limited by the commerce clause." To conform with federal requirements the legislature in 1935 and in 1939 provided a strict regulatory system for the transportation of liquor through the state and for the importation of alcohol into the state for sacramental, medical, scientific, and manufacturing purposes.[4]

Although the legal ducks seemed to be in line, Kansas received almost no help from the federal government in its ongoing struggle to suppress the importation of hard liquor. Attorney General Clarence V. Beck (1935–39) made several trips to Washington, only to be stalled on this pretext or that. In 1940 a federal judge in the western district of Missouri held that the government had no responsibility for importation into Kansas, since its law did not ban all liquor over 4 percent by volume. A few months later, Federal Judge Richard J. Hopkins of the District of Kansas, a loyal and abiding ally of the drys, ruled otherwise, dismissing as frivolous the contention that Kansas was ineligible for federal assistance because 3.2 percent by weight came to an iota more than 4.0 percent by volume. With the advent of World War II the by-now feeble expectations of federal aid disappeared entirely.[5]

As "the boys" began streaming home after the surrender of Japan in September 1945, federal officials suddenly wielded a potent mace, which had heretofore been made only of papier-mâché. In early November, agents of the Alcohol Tax Unit, under the direction of District Attorney Randolph Carpenter, made simultaneous raids at fourteen sites in seven of the wettest towns in Kansas. They seized 966 cases (11,592 fifths) of whiskey, valued at $100,000 retail. About 50 percent of the haul came from Wichita, the remainder from Topeka, Leavenworth, and Victoria (Ellis County) and from Russell, Lucas, and Dorrance (Russell County). Since the owners had not been caught in the act of transporting, no arrests could be made, but all the liquor was confiscated.[6]

The raids forcefully demonstrated to the public, which "buzzed" with excitement, that bootlegging had become big business in the state. That the raids were intended not only as enforcement exercises but also for didactic purposes immediately became evident. In the wake of the action, District Attorney Carpenter, a man with a political mote in his eye, rendered a short sermon on moral philosophy for the public's edification: "Let it be clearly understood that this is no liquor crusade . . . however, it is noteworthy that the violation of the liquor laws in this state leads to the violation of many other laws. The citizens should face the issue squarely—either support the enforcement of the laws or amend the constitution and repeal them."[7]

The belated federal action brought a great deal of discomfiture to the drys and essentially kicked off a continuous campaign by the wets for repeal of the amendment. Among the several big-city dailies to agree with Carpenter's assessment, the *Kansas City Times* noted that big-time bootleggers had been getting bolder in recent years, while infractions of the law had become increasingly accepted as "a natural condition." The influential paper concluded that "the liquor situation in Kansas is a disgrace to the state."[8]

Another group embarrassed by the federal words and actions was the host of state and local enforcement officials who, Carpenter had hinted, had been less than diligent in the performance of their duties. A scarcely submerged but all-important fact colored the interaction of federal and state officials: the former were Democrats; the latter, Republicans. Governor Andrew F. Schoeppel (1943–47), who had been under constant attack by the drys for lax enforcement, responded churlishly to Carpenter's strictures. Somewhat illogically, Schoeppel questioned the "good faith" of the federal authorities because the state had previously "besieged" the government for help, but to no avail. As his predecessors had done since 1881, he also upbraided the federals for continuing to sell retail liquor stamps in Kansas. (The stamps generated $19,917 in revenue in fiscal 1945. At $27.50 per stamp per year, this was equivalent to 724.25 full-time bootleggers.)[9]

A week after the federal raids a trial that had profound implications for the state's liquor-control policy opened in federal court in Wichita. The former superintendent of the state highway patrol, Will Zurbucken, faced charges of filing a false income-tax return for 1940. The prosecution alleged that he had not declared income of $5,950 (on which he owed $495) and that said income had derived from bootleggers in return for "protection."

One rumrunner testified that he had paid Zurbucken 50 cents a case on 2,400 cases of liquor (5,760 gallons); another swore that he had paid 25 cents a case on 6,800 cases (16,320 gallons). In return, the bootleggers had received "letters of introduction," to be used when and as necessary. The police chief of Dodge City, they said, had served as the go-between. The bribes had gone to a Topeka post-office box in the name of "Will K. Miller." The liquor had gone to Ford, Kingman, and Reno counties.

The defense offered character testimony by Lieutenant Governor Jess C. Denious (one of John Madden's two trusted friends in Dodge City in 1930) and Dr. Karl Menninger, the internationally famous psychiatrist, who was an "honorary colonel" in the highway patrol. Defense attorney Ed Rooney played on the jury's prejudices against outsiders by noting the "horde of federal employees . . . so thick in Wichita there isn't eating room for them." In an attempt to defuse the "protection" charge, Rooney established that years before Zurbucken had taken charge, the highway patrol had had instructions not to stop any car "for the sole purpose of searching for liquor."

But Zurbucken's best defense seemed to be the judge's instructions to the jury. Guy T. Helvering, a long-term power in state Democratic circles and a former federal commissioner of internal revenue, instructed the jury to treat character references as important evidence, to use great caution in accepting the word of known law violators, to forego judgment regarding Zurbucken's failure to testify, and to hold no prejudice toward bootleggers as the alleged source of Zurbucken's funds. Despite the compelling evidence to the contrary, the jury found Zurbucken not guilty after a week-long trial. Although the accused was exonerated, the trial raised many haunting questions in the public mind about the fidelity of enforcement officials to the liquor laws.[10] Prohibition was, once again, fully on the defensive.

THE POSTWAR MILIEU differed markedly from that of the years immediately preceding the hostilities. Most everything conspired to nudge the populace in the wet direction. The repudiation of prohibition by the nation continued to cast a shadow over contemporary attitudes. The small band of prohibition states had dwindled to a precious few; to friend and foe alike, the beleaguered survivors increasingly appeared anachronistic. In 1936, eight states were still banning spiritous liquor, but all except Alabama and Kansas had authorized beer. A year later, only five states were prohibiting spirits, and all had approved beer. By 1940, only Oklahoma, Mississippi, and Kansas retained a statewide prohibition on hard liquor. The magic number of three, which had been attained at the nadirs of the first (circa 1875) and the second (circa 1905) waves of national temperance, had been reached once again.[11]

The attitudes of many Kansans toward liquor consumption had shifted significantly in the "liberal" direction. Those who accepted Laura Johns's nineteenth-century dictum that alcohol in any amount or frequency "abused" the human system continued to diminish. Nowhere was this more true than among the younger members of the business and professional communities. But the greatest pressure for change came from the returning servicemen—two hundred thousand youngish males who had "seen Paree."

Most veterans had traveled extensively in the United States, some over much of the world. All had observed intensities of drinking, controlled and uncontrolled, that few had ever witnessed in staid old Kansas. Many had squirmed in discomfort as "foreigners," at home and abroad, smiled patronizingly or laughed raucously at Kansas and her "antiquated" system of liquor control. Some had made a mental note to try to change the situation at their earliest opportunity. The recurrent stories of large-scale bootlegging and its associated racketeering dismayed those who supported the law and would fight to retain it. But at least two of every three veterans, former GIs who would soon dominate the political scene, did not want the prohibitory law enforced, indeed did not want the law at all.[12]

The first politician to capitalize on the changed social landscape had been an old and enthusiastic "friend" of prohibition in the early 1930s. After his 1932 defeat for reelection, Governor Harry H. Woodring had been appointed assistant secretary of war and had been elevated to the full secretaryship in 1936. In 1940 President Roosevelt had reluctantly removed Woodring as a result of policy differences. By the mid 1940s his longing "for the days of glory and excitement" had led to rebuffed attempts to land the French ambassadorship and his old position as secretary of war. As early as January 1945 he confided to friends that he might seek the Democratic gubernatorial nomination. At the beginning of 1946, his biographer tells us, Woodring "began to search for an issue on which to build his campaign. That search did not last long, because he quickly found his cause—prohibition."[13]

Woodring exploded his "political dynamite" in a statement to his fellow Democrats as they gathered in Topeka for their 1946 Washington Day dinner. The erstwhile champion of prohibition now marched to a very different drummer. Noting that "a tremendous demand" for change had developed in recent months, he called on the Democrats to "denounce" constitutional prohibition and to put an end to the "hypocrisy of . . . drinking wet and voting dry. . . . It all sums up to making dishonest bootlegger wet Kansas an honest taxable wet Kansas! Let's take the millions from the bootleggers and give it to the taxpayers of Kansas!"[14] For the first time since 1914, when Jules Billard ran for governor on a wet platform, a major politician had come out foursquare for repeal.

The Democratic State Committee received Woodring's proposal so enthusiastically that they requested the governor to call a special legislative session to submit the question to the voters. A number of wets, including the Young Democrats, circulated petitions to that effect during the spring, but Governor Schoeppel held firm to his view that the regular 1947 session would be soon enough to deal with the question.[15]

Woodring denied having any political ambitions for himself, but no one took that disavowal very seriously. His dramatic statement had given him a running start for the gubernatorial nomination, but the "small, bald, old maidish" aspirant also had his liabilities. A fiscal conservative, as Kansas Democratic governors have tended to be, he was known to "despise" the New Deal and had even tried to organize a third party in 1944 to block the fourth-term movement for President Roosevelt. But despite the coolness of some members of his party, he won the August primary handily, with repeal of prohibition as his central theme.[16]

The dominant Republicans, of course, had also been reading the political tea leaves. By spring, party leaders were letting it be known that they were "leaning strongly" toward a resubmission plank. The party drys pinned their hopes on the influence of the eighty-one-year-old Senator Arthur Capper, who as governor in 1917 had signed the bone-dry law. "I am what is known as a dry both in principle and practice," Senator Capper said, promising a fight to keep the party in the dry column. But those who favored resubmission received considerable encouragement from a midsummer Gallup poll, which showed that the drys held only a narrow 49 to 46 percent lead on the question of repeal.[17] Such a division on such an emotional issue dictated political discretion—that is, submission of the question—as the far-better part of political valor.

Given the intensity building on the repeal question, the public read with uncommon interest the platforms that the party councils produced in August. After their awkward silence in the 1934 repeal campaign, the Democrats had reverted to their traditional twentieth-century position in 1936 and 1938 by warmly endorsing prohibition. But they had fallen silent, once again, on the question in 1940, 1942, and 1944. After Woodring's smashing victory in the primary, they wrote into their 1946 platform precisely those positions that he had been advocating: the repeal of constitutional prohibition; county local option; the establishment of state-owned liquor stores; and a ban on "saloons" and "speak-easies."[18]

In 1936 the Republicans had congratulated themselves on their wisdom in opposing repeal two years earlier and had continued to support prohibition, though with markedly decreasing fervor. By 1940 their advocacy had become diluted to merely the "fair and impartial enforcement of all laws"; in 1944 they had fallen silent on the question. Despite strong pressure from the Capper-led drys, the resubmissionist forces readily carried the day in 1946: "This question . . . presents a moral issue that should be determined by the citizens of Kansas on a non-partisan basis. . . . Therefore, we recommend that the 1947 Legislature should submit a constitutional amendment."[19]

The Republicans nominated for governor the fifty-three-year-old soft-spoken Frank Carlson, a farmer-stockman from Concordia. He had served in the legislature from 1929 to 1931, as campaign manager for Landon in 1932, and was just completing his sixth term in Congress (1935–47). Employing his patented "low-keyed" campaign style, Carlson earnestly advocated the people's right to vote on prohibition, but he doggedly refused to say anything else of substance on the subject. On the other hand, Woodring talked repeal at every opportunity and at every crossroads. He called on all "honest drys" to vote for the Prohibition party's candidate, David C. White, a recommendation that would have simultaneously boosted the Democrats and castrated the voters. Woodring claimed that Kansas would gain $16 million per year in liquor taxes, a doubtful proposition since wet Missouri, for example, with twice the population, realized less than $5 million. (In the first decade after repeal, revenue from spirits and wine averaged about $2.5 million per year.)

Even without Woodring's advice, the organized drys did not present a completely unified front. The UDF supported Carlson indirectly by attacking only Woodring, while the more militant Committee of 100,000 kept pressuring Carlson to back off from his resubmissionist stand. Carlson defeated Woodring by fifty-five thousand votes, with the Prohibition party's candidate receiving 2 percent of the total. But the drys had little reason to rejoice as Woodring and his prize issue ran fifty thousand votes ahead of his party's state ticket.[20]

Anxious to have the legislative mind concentrating on his impressive package of postwar economic proposals, Governor Carlson urged the Republican-dominated 1947 session (only 19 of the 165 legislators were Democrats) to dispose of the resubmission issue as quickly as possible. The House Judiciary Committee immediately began to work on a concurrent resolution. A few days later, Alf Landon, the elder statesman of the state Republican party, strode unannounced into a committee meeting and "raised hell" about its preliminary draft, which led off with a sentence about "prohibiting forever" the "open saloon." After listening to Landon's argument that the sentence would be highly misleading in that position, the committee moved it to the last position. Whether in first or last position, the "open saloon" provision has continued to be a controversial issue to the present day. In 1947 it remained undefined, serving principally as an expedient bone that was tossed to the drys by the wets.[21]

Although legislative action came as no surprise, the drys seemed to have been caught off balance by the early start. They quickly made their views known, though not in the great volume for which they had become noted in the past. The house debated the resolution on January 22 and passed it with two votes to spare the next day. Five days later it easily passed the senate.[22]

Several of those voting aye indicated that they would support prohibition and fight the wets "until Hell freezes over." But, as they nervously explained to their constituents, the people should be given the chance to vote, especially the veterans and the 350,000 who had reached voting age since 1934. One negative-voting legislator gave a most candid reason for his action: "I believe in letting the people rule when times are normal. At present this is not the case. . . . Therefore, I vote no."[23]

The proposed amendment to article 15, section 10, of the Kansas Constitution, upon which the electorate would pass judgment in November 1948, read:

> The legislature may provide for the prohibition of intoxicating liquors in certain areas. Subject to the foregoing, the legislature may regulate, license and tax the manufacture and sale of intoxicating liquors, and may regulate the possession and transportation of intoxicating liquors. The open saloon shall be and is hereby forever prohibited.[24]

The legislature gave brief consideration to a bill that would have permitted the transportation and possession of an unlimited amount of hard liquor, thereby eliminating the principal feature of the bone-dry law. Though it could have been taken up as a compromise measure, hardly anyone seemed interested. The fence straddlers found the constitutional resolution more attractive, just as their counterparts had in 1879, because it sent the controversial issue directly to the people. The dedicated wets preferred resubmission, while the unbending drys seemed no closer to compromise on the bone-dry provision than they had been during the 1935 deadlock. Everyone was determined to march to Armageddon on the constitutional question. The bill died quietly in committee.[25]

THE STRINGENCY AND FREQUENCY of law enforcement during the period 1945 to 1948 became the major setting for the drive for repeal. Slowly but inexorably, liquor-law violations had increased from the mid 1930s. When thousands of young males, the prime drinking group, returned from the war, the incidence and extent of violations took a quantum jump.

Because of the new and unsettling conditions, the citizenry stepped up their appeals to the chief executive. The wets often reminded Governor Schoeppel that "we are the laughing stock of the nation." Sometimes they waxed more philosophical: "The human animal cannot be kept from getting what he wants to eat or drink. . . . Prohibition was a noble experiment, and an ignoble failure, and the most casual observer of life and human psychology should have known that it would turn out that way."[26]

But the drys continued to voice their concerns more frequently and poignantly, as had been true throughout state history. A few blamed FDR for not having kept the federal promise "to help dry states [keep] dry." The public problem affected the personal lives of some: "I am not the only one losing sleep and getting gray hairs over this curse." A monitor of the affairs of several small towns reported that they had become either "loaded with whiskey sellers" or "just lousy with bootleggers." One correspondent urged that the law be strictly enforced, "even if you are obliged to call the militia to help. . . . Be a man of courage, a hero in the strife for better law and order."[27]

The dominant tone of the dry pleas derived from deep-seated religious beliefs. One woman wrote that "true greatness is not measured in money but deep convictions of right and righteousness." Another said that repealing prohibition "is repealing God's Laws of Righteousness and we will all suffer for that." One man declared that "the Methodist church is right. 'Liquor selling cannot be legalized without sin.' Let . . . your Christian conscience, guide you."[28]

Prodded into action by the agitated electorate and the federal raids, Governor Schoeppel bestirred himself in early 1946, though not with the pure motivation that his supporters claimed. In November 1945 he had said privately that he favored the enforcement of the prohibitory law "as long as it is on our books." A month later he wrote regarding prohibition to a close friend in Wichita, the vice-president of Boeing Aircraft, that "the way to have good riddance of a bad law is to enforce it."[29]

Schoeppel announced to the public in January 1946 that "you're going to see a lot of [enforcement] activity—and for obvious reasons." The "reasons" evidently weren't quite so "obvious" as the public was led to believe. He appointed special investigators and assistant attorneys general to prosecute violators, and he directed the highway patrol to charge drivers with possession and to confiscate any liquor that they discovered while making routine traffic arrests. After fourteen months of this policy, the highway patrol reported that only 325 cases of liquor had been confiscated and only 46 persons had been arrested. The amounts that were seized per arrest varied from 2 to 639 pints. The wets added another weapon to their growing arsenal when they learned that the former had received a sentence of sixty days; the latter, only thirty.[30]

The rigor of enforcement, though not its underlying philosophy, changed abruptly as a result of the 1946 election. Edward Ferdinand Arn, a prominent Wichita lawyer, had readily captured the attorney generalship. A Congregationalist and a recently discharged navy lieutenant, Arn represented the van of the politically active former servicemen who would increasingly influence

Kansas politics. During the campaign, both Carlson and Arn had solemnly promised that they would strictly enforce the prohibitory law.[31] Those ringing declarations had created no special stir, since Kansans had heard little else since 1906 from their candidates for public office, high or low. And since 1945 a disturbing tendency to expect Uncle Sam to shoulder the major responsibility for enforcement had crept into the collective psyche.

But the newly elected attorney general soon demonstrated that he meant what he said. He cajoled the 1947 legislature into increasing his full-time field staff from one to three, and he shepherded through the session a renewal of the lapsed 1901 law, which made possession of a federal liquor stamp prima facie evidence that a public nuisance was being maintained. This law aided enforcement materially and reduced the tribute paid to the government by stamp holders from $17,543 in fiscal 1946 to $7,808 in 1947 and to $4,550 in 1948.[32] On a full-time-equivalency basis, the reduction meant a decrease in stamp-holding bootleggers from 638 in 1946 to 165 in 1948.

Arn conducted raids in such traditionally wet counties as Sedgwick, Leavenworth, Wyandotte, and Russell and even in some nontraditional ones such as Jefferson. He went after local officials known to be lax on enforcement, obtaining the resignations of the sheriff and county attorney in Russell County, for example, despite the fact that it was a booming oil center with especially difficult liquor problems. He stepped up the confiscation of liquor-bearing automobiles along the Nebraska and Colorado borders, and toward the end of 1947, rumors floated that the next Arn shoe to drop would be the systematic checking of cars headed home from Kansans' prime liquor depot, Kansas City, Missouri.[33]

Those rumors received a decided boost from the "Haas Affair," which represented the culmination of Arn's "reign of terror." Three days before Christmas a twenty-eight-year-old former major of infantry, Melvin Haas, had gone to Kansas City, Missouri, on business. While there, he did what thousands of other Kansans had done and were doing: he purchased liquor to take back home, in this instance two bottles for himself and seven for friends for Christmas. On his return to Topeka, the highway patrol stopped him in the mistaken belief that his automobile fit the description of one that they were looking for. The judge fined Haas $200, issued a sixty-day suspended jail sentence, and confiscated his prize Lincoln Zephyr coupe. The incident upset a significant fraction of the populace, most especially liquor-drinking males under forty. A public subscription raised $1,500 for a new sports car for Haas, and a group in Wichita formed the "It Could Happen to Me" Club.[34]

Immediately after the Haas incident and just two days before New Year's Eve, Arn made it clear that his liquor policy included pedagogical and political as well as enforcement elements. He announced that there had been other unpublicized Haas-type cases, and he intimated that he might even go after that holiest of holies, the "one-bottle" man. He advised the citizenry against bringing liquor into the state via car, train, or plane and reminded them that liquor in the home was as illegal as in the family car on the highway. "It is absurd," he said, "for the public to blame any law enforcement officer for arresting any citizen . . . for having liquor in his possession. . . . That's the law and if the citizens are unhappy about this type of law they can blame only the law itself." The opportunity to change the law would come in 1948, "pursuant to the 1946 Republican platform." If it is a "bad law," "Professor" Arn told his students, "it should be changed and the people . . . will have that opportunity when they vote on the referendum."[35]

In January, Arn told a more circumscribed group of students, those in the Washburn Law School, that the most difficult law to enforce was the prohibitory law, which "a large percentage of the people do not want enforced, and which a large number of the people desire to violate." He admitted that his regime had been credited with "a fair degree" of enforcement, but he did not want the public to believe that prohibition was, or could be, a success. With only "meager facilities" at his command, he said, "we are only scratching the surface. Some of the largest, most flagrant, open and notorious violators are kept on the run—but I do not doubt but that with some shopping around, a bottle of liquor could be bought by a stranger in almost any county in Kansas."[36] Arn's threats to step up enforcement against the "one-bottle" man did not materialize, but they did force many a prudent citizen to proceed with greater circumspection. As the months passed, the haunting memories of the "Haas affair" reminded the voting public of life under a vigorously enforced bone-dry law.

In his "educational" policy, Arn had the full support of the governor. The taciturn Carlson shared with the public a good deal fewer of his thoughts about prohibition than did his attorney general. But an occasional slip nearly gave him away, as when he wrote to Agnes D. Hays, a former president of the WCTU, that the 1947 federal stamp law would be helpful "in forcing [sic] the prohibitory law." Throughout 1947 both Arn and Carlson received the heartfelt plaudits of the committed drys. They "congratulated" Arn for doing a "bang-up" job of enforcement and flattered Carlson as "one of the best Christian Gentlemen" ever to walk the earth.

But in the spring of 1948 the major journalistic voice of the drys, Arthur Capper's *Topeka Capital,* began to question whether Arn and Carlson were making a "fundamentally sincere attempt" to end the liquor traffic. The praise stopped abruptly, and the criticism began, as the drys came to the full realization that the administration's policy of alternately enforcing the law with aggressive action and then denying the efficacy of the effort played perfectly into the hands of the repealists. Drys of all persuasions spent much of 1948 begging the master trimmer, Carlson, to come out of the closet and endorse prohibition. In May the militant Committee of 100,000 called for Arn's resignation for his allegedly hypocritical enforcement of the liquor laws.[37]

The federal government continued to play a significant role in state affairs. After eight months of inactivity following the sensational raids of November 1945, federal officials declared that they had become so disgusted at the continuing spectacle of Kansas juries exonerating bootleggers, roadhouse operators, and public officials charged with evading federal income taxes that they might not stage any more raids in the state at all. But two months later, agents of the Alcohol Tax Unit raided eleven sites at six widely scattered localities. They struck simultaneously in Sedgwick, Leavenworth, Wyandotte, Reno, Crawford, and Russell counties, netting less than a thousand cases of liquor, compared to the nearly twelve thousand of the 1945 raids.[38]

Three weeks later, in October 1946, a federal grand jury in Topeka indicted the mayor and police chief of Leavenworth, accusing them of protecting a local liquor ring for $500 a month each. It also indicted seven Wichitans in connection with a $2 million bootleg operation, which had been importing about twenty thousand gallons of liquor from Chicago per year for two and one-half years. In mid 1946, Federal District Attorney Randolph Carpenter announced that during the past year the Bureau of Internal Revenue had received $5 million in back taxes and penalties from bootleggers and racketeers headquartered in Sedgwick County, the state's unquestioned center of "sin and iniquity." The government's biggest catches included Robert L. Carnahan and Max Cohen, Wichita "oil operators," who allegedly obtained most of their substantial incomes by furnishing "protection," under duress if necessary, to the operators of liquor and gambling establishments in Sedgwick County.[39]

District Attorney Randolph Carpenter resigned in 1948 to run for governor against Frank Carlson. Carpenter's successor, Lester Luther, continued the "educational" policy of the federal office. A month before the election, Luther expounded at length on the "intolerable" liquor situation, one of the more telling statements for repeal made during the entire campaign. "I am now reluctantly compelled to admit," he said, "that the prohibitory law cannot be enforced and that prohibition in Kansas is a complete and dismal failure." He worried about professional drys coming in from the East and pouring out "confusing" social statistics on the unsuspecting electorate. "The plain unvarnished truth," the federal official said, "is that liquor can be obtained in Kansas as easily and as cheaply as in any state in the Union."[40]

The question of the price and the amount of hard liquor in the state is subject to some verification. After national repeal the Kansas demand was met almost exclusively by liquor produced out of state. From 1945 to 1948, whiskey prices in neighboring states ranged from $3.50 to $7.00 a fifth. Kansas bootleg prices varied with the quality, the amount purchased, and the stringency of local enforcement. Generally, a fifth sold for $6 to $12, but it could bring as little as $4 or as much as $18. In 1946 a fifth of Old Granddad cost $15 from the "Soup Man" at the Meadow Acres ballroom in Topeka. Consumers constantly complained about the "stiff" cost of liquor in Kansas and the "unholy prices" that it commanded. Even the more affluent, such as a prominent Wichita businessman, carped that "the prices charged are all out of reason."[41]

Americans consumed just under two gallons of distilled spirits per annum per capita of the drinking-age population from 1945 to 1948, up from about one gallon in 1935/36. Had Kansans consumed at the national average, they would have drunk over two and one-half million gallons per year at a cost of over $100 million (at $8 per fifth). The wets variously estimated the state's annual prerepeal bill for hard liquor at from $30 to 60 million. In their most detailed calculations, published in their major campaign piece, they estimated consumption at 50 percent of the national average, at an annual cost of $48 million.[42]

Extrapolation from surveys of American drinking practices suggests that in the late 1940s, 40 to 50 percent of the drinking-age population in Kansas were total abstainers and another 10 to 20 percent were functionally so. Scattered contemporary evidence supports these estimates. The *Ottawa Herald,* a wet newspaper that clamored for repeal, estimated that 40 to 70 percent of the adult population took a drink "on occasion." A poll in Medicine Lodge disclosed that only 31 percent drank distilled spirits. Liquor was commonly not served at business, political, or professional banquets, and some social events had traditionally been remarkably dry. For example, several hundred of the state's most prominent civic leaders had gathered annually for a three-day fish fry and jollification on the Neosho River in Coffey County with nothing more stimulating than "soda pop and creek water."[43]

Health data closely related to the use of alcohol also suggest relatively low consumption in Kansas. Mortality rates from cirrhosis of the liver, a disease that is closely associated with alcoholism, fluctuated in the range of 4.0 to 7.5 per 100,000 from 1914, when Kansas was admitted to the United States death registration area, through the late 1940s. The state rates varied from 50 to 90 percent of the U.S. average, predominantly in the lower half of that range. Kansas death rates from alcoholism averaged 35 percent of the U.S. average from 1914 through the late twenties. Chronic alcoholism in the United States was estimated by E. M. Jellinek, the father of the modern disease concept of alcoholism, for 1930 and 1944. In the former year the Kansas rate was 70 percent of the U.S. average; in the latter, 54 percent. Between 1940 and 1948 the national rate of alcoholism increased by 31 percent, while the Kansas rate declined by 7 percent.

In the first calendar year of legalized distilled spirits the state taxed 1,959,042 gallons. This represented 1.40 gallons per capita of the drinking-age population, or 81 percent of the national average, at a cost of approximately $49 million. The state percentage of the national average had dropped to 70 in the mid 1950s and to 64 by 1960. Beer consumption, which had been averaging about 55 percent of the national figure, jumped sharply, to 68 percent in 1947/48, and declined just as sharply with repeal, an indication that the veterans' demand for alcohol was not being met by the bootleg traffic in spirits (see fig.

10.1). (A similar though less pronounced jump also occurred in Oklahoma and Mississippi.) During the 1945–48 period, the consumption of spirits probably varied between one-third and one-half of the national average, or from 0.8 to 1.3 million gallons per annum, the highest per capita rate since early in the twentieth century.[44]

TO SPEARHEAD THE DRIVE for repeal a group of prominent Wichita businessmen, headed by E. C. Moriarty, an oilman and a former mayor, organized the Kansas Legal Control Council (KLCC) in January 1948. It represented the wets' first attempt to organize since 1934. They announced that they would be strictly "non-partisan and nonfactional" and thereafter, steadfastly refused to endorse political parties or candidates. Memberships were available to "outstanding and influential men in all walks of life," who were asked to sign a pledge card that began thus: "Believing that prohibition has failed, . . ."

The organization immediately attracted the allegiance of two prominent clergymen—an Episcopalian minister and the Catholic Bishop Mark K. Carroll of the large Wichita diocese. Carroll said that prohibitionists erred "in putting the stamp upon liquor itself as an evil, when it is abuse of liquor that is evil." But he went on to criticize Missouri laws which permitted liquor by the drink.[45]

As executive secretary the KLCC employed a thirty-two-year-old army veteran, Leo W. Mulloy of Wichita. "Handsome, popular, and a brilliant speaker," Mulloy had graduated from Washburn Law School before becoming a public-relations man at Boeing Aircraft. He directed the repeal campaign with energy, intelligence, and imagination, personally making more than two hundred speeches for the cause.[46]

The KLCC offered cash prizes for the best two-hundred-word essays advocating repeal, a strategy that it adopted from the WCTU, which had utilized essay contests, sans cash prizes, for decades. The council distributed widely a sixteen-page pamphlet, "Dry Rot," which was replete with statistics "proving" that dry Kansas exceeded wet Nebraska in alcoholism, crime, juvenile delinquency, and other social ills. Memories of the "big lie" era wafted up from the historical miasma as the drys answered in kind with a brochure that was chock-full of refutational data. In addition to the liquor-industry organizations the repealists picked up the endorsements of the Hotel Mens Association, the Chamber of Commerce, and almost all of the large-circulation newspapers, and the sympathy of some groups that remained officially neutral, such as the state Federation of Labor.[47]

The repealists kept their central theme plain, simple, and unadorned, in the best Kansas tradition. They refined Woodring's and Arn's contentions that the state should bring into concordance her voting and drinking habits so as to eliminate hypocrisy. Liquor in quantity was here to stay, they argued. The basic issue, therefore, was simply the question of who should benefit from the liquor traffic: the general public, through taxes (and profits, if the state were to own liquor stores), or the disreputable bootleggers, through their ill-gotten gains and unconscionable rackets. The repealists were willing to leave the details of revenue distribution to the legislature, but they suggested roads, teachers, veterans, and the elderly as deserving beneficiaries. "Prohibition has never succeeded at any time, any place," Mulloy said. "There is and always will be liquor traffic in Kansas. Our desire is to control that traffic."[48]

To deliver effectively the KLCC's unitary message, Mulloy unfolded a strategy which hit the drys squarely at their point of greatest strength—namely, in the heretofore sacrosanct areas of morality and religion. Striving to convince the moderates that respectable people could support repeal, Mulloy coined the felicitous slogan "Vote Yes for Decency." A month before the election he blanketed the state with a huge newspaper ad that listed the names of ten thousand citizens for repeal, about 10 percent of whom were women. "Leading the march toward prohibition repeal," Mulloy said, "are 10,000 of the state's outstanding and sincere Christians who believe that prohibition has been a complete failure." They believed that true temperance, he said, could be effected through "education, not by an unenforceable and widely disrespected prohibition law."[49]

The repealist strategy caused the drys to boil with indignation at their opponent's effrontery in assuming the mantle of "Christian respectability" and in equating prohibition with intemperance. A KLCC radio spot especially upset the WCTU. A woman who identified herself as a "Kansas mother" had no qualms about invading the WCTU's turf: "I want my children taught that Christianity is temperance, true temperance. I want my children taught as future citizens to be Christian and temperate in all things." The message was subtle but inescapable: "Christian temperance" demanded the discarding of prohibition.[50]

Under Mulloy's skillful guidance the campaign for repeal rolled smoothly to election day. Two blunders did occur, which caused some consternation in the wet camp. On a hot July day in Hutchinson the "otherwise affable" Mulloy castigated his dry counterparts in a manner that brought more harm than help to his cause, because most of the recipients of his attention were men of the cloth. The professional prohibitionist, Mulloy said, "has had 80 years to perfect his rubbish. . . . [He] has the ethics of a Goebbels. He is a congenital but thoughtful liar, a persuasive propagandist, and the proud benefactor of a vicious Kansas criminal class."[51]

In September the KLCC hatched a plan that encouraged tavern owners to pass out free beer the day after election to all those who had voted for repeal. Taverns that signed up the most voters would receive one of thirty cash prizes donated by the KLCC, ranging from $10 to $250. Shortly after the contest information went out, it was withdrawn, and identical literature was substituted from the "Kansas Distributors." A few days after that, the whole ill-begotten scheme folded. The drys were quick to capitalize on the persisting public association between the old-time saloon and corrupt politics. After all, even the proposed "wet" amendment promised immunity from the evils of the saloon "forever." A brochure pointedly entitled "Would You Sell Your Vote for a Few Cents Worth of Beer?" helped keep the issue alive during the closing days of the campaign.[52]

The KLCC coordinated the wet campaign, but other repealists lent their voices to the effort. Writer Kenneth S. Davis, an assistant to Kansas State College's President Milton S. Eisenhower, wrote a deeply felt prorepeal article for the local newspaper, which the KLCC reprinted and distributed widely. Davis called prohibition "a phoney issue," which had taken up the valuable time of both the legislature and the citizenry for decades, time that might better have been spent on improving the roads and the schools. The drys called Davis's tone "derogatory" and said that his piece was full of "unnecessary sarcasm."

In a spring survey the publisher of the *Iola Register,* Angelo Scott, found that though many newspapers intended to support repeal, only 10 percent would accept liquor ads if repeal carried. "The Kansas conscience with regard to liquor," Scott said, "is undoubtedly the most prickly one in the nation." But in the fall, along with several other middling-sized newspapers, the *Register* discarded its dry policy, which went back to 1867. "The whiskey is here anyway and in veritable floods," Scott said; "enforcement is utterly impossible."[53]

Down in Emporia, the Athens of Kansas, William L. ("Young Bill") White attempted to knit into a common fabric the prohibitory past, which his father had at times championed, and the more refractory present. "The prohibitionists of yesteryear who fought to put these present laws on our statute books were neither bigots nor fools," he said, referring specifically to Stubbs, Capper, Allen, Scott, and White. "It was an experiment well worth trying. But . . . we still have the problem, and we still have in Kansas our old-time will to make this a better world. . . . If we are to be worthy of the idealism of [these] men . . . , we should also be worthy of their intelligence by recognizing that this particular experiment has failed, and end this sad and obscene mockery of all they hoped for by bravely tackling the old problem in a better way."[54]

FOR THE PERPETUALLY ORGANIZED DRYS the campaign only meant an increase in the intensity of their ongoing year-round activities. Because of ill health, Dr. Ross E. Farley, the general secretary of UDF since 1938, resigned on 1 May 1948, to be replaced by the sixty-year-old Dr. Coral D. Walker of Lawrence. The change in leadership meant the substitution of a Christian for a Methodist minister. The UDF kept its affiliation with the ASL, which by 1948 had become the Temperance League of America. The membership of both the UDF and the WCTU continued to age, though the latter had been trying for years to recruit young members. The WCTU had many women "whose days of activity are past," President Mable Gilbert said in 1947, "but whose desire for a Dry Kansas is as strong as ever."[55]

The UDF published several brochures and, along with the Committee of 100,000, kept in touch with its membership through a monthly newsletter. The UDF also organized rallies in many towns, large and small, and canvassed every block in some of the larger cities, such as Topeka. As a result of its imprecations, ministers continued to keep the issue before their congregations. The WCTU used the money raised through a "Save Prohibition Fund" to spread its word via radio, film, newspaper, and airplane. It had printed five thousand copies of a pamphlet entitled "The Black Book of Repeal," which summarized its antirepeal arguments.

The drys organized the Kansas Christian Youth Council, which placed red-and-white pasteboard "Prohibition Keys" on doorknobs, with this inscription: "You hold the key! Don't betray the youth of Kansas. Keep Kansas dry for Kansas youth." The dry position received the endorsement of several rural organizations, including the Grange and the Farm Bureau, and Protestant denominations that had four thousand individual congregations. But only a few of the leading newspapers, most notably the *Topeka Capital*, ardently supported prohibition.[56]

A parade of the Temperance Tornado in Horton (Brown County) in August 1948 (courtesy of the Kansas Collection, University of Kansas).

The most flamboyant antirepeal activity took place in late summer. To emphasize the critical importance that the referendum had for Kansas youth, Willard Mayberry, an Elkhart (Morton County) publisher-rancher and a former private secretary to Governor Landon, organized a modern wagon train, which he called the Temperance Tornado. It consisted of twenty-five vehicles and floats, a sixty-piece band, and some one hundred high-school and college-age young people, mostly from southwest Kansas. With the highway patrol as their escort, the caravan camped in parks and in church- and schoolyards across the state. The 1,500-mile twelve-day swing through central and eastern Kansas kicked off in mid August in Dodge City before an enthusiastic crowd of five thousand.

The tornado's chief attractions were Mayberry, a "witty, foghorned-voiced . . . Knife-and-Fork circuit lecturer," and Glen Cunningham, the world-class miler, who proudly declared that "the greatest record I have is that I have never tasted liquor." The colorful caravan played to only small to moderate-sized crowds, about equally divided between the committed and the curious. The tornado, the wet *Topeka State Journal* said, turned out to be "a mild summer breeze." Though he received a special invitation to a caravan rally on the Statehouse lawn, Governor Carlson tearfully sent his regrets, pleading "previous engagements" out of the city.[57]

Like a politician or a criminal with a record, the drys had to explain and defend the past. And since the mid 1940s, even they had to admit that the past left much to be desired. In defense of the longstanding public policy, they marshaled the traditional temperance arguments (economic, sociopolitical, medical, and moral-religious) and tried to counterattack the wet position. They called attention to the findings of the prominent Wichita industrialist W. C. Coleman, who maintained that because of prohibition, Kansas employers enjoyed a more productive work force and the state a higher level of "good citizenship." And they attempted to turn the "hypocrisy" issue by attacking the "smug hypocrisy" of the leading citizens who had called for repeal in the name of "decency."

Although they knew that liquor flowed freely in the state, the drys held that the rest of the nation consumed much more. Arthur Capper labeled as "poppycock" the wet theory that repeal would bring reduced consumption. "We are firmly convinced," a group of educators said, "that . . . no method of State or Local control . . . will reduce the consumption of liquor per capita, lower than it is under our present law."

Despite the reassurance in the proposed amendment the drys feared the return of the saloon, later if not sooner. The *Topeka Capital* said that it supported prohibition because it believed that repeal would be "an opening wedge toward restoring the open saloon." Senator Capper touched all the bases with nearly the same words that Governor Robinson had employed almost one hundred years before (see p. 54): "Whiskey is a health wrecker; a business wrecker; a home wrecker; a human wrecker."[58]

Indeed, much of the dry rhetoric of the late 1940s could have come from nineteenth-century prohibitionists. The latter-day adversaries of liquor peppered their language with phrases such as "evil forces," "evils of the traffic," "the liquor influence," "the curse of liquor," "the forces of darkness," and the succinct statement that said it all: "I hate liquor." Manifesting a deep pride in their state's historic stand for morality, the drys often referred to "our fair state," "a clean state," "dear old Kansas," "Kansas, a good place in which to live." One woman cried, "Surely Kansas will not join the nations that forget God!"[59]

While the prohibitionists employed a range of arguments as befitted the occasion, the religious ones exceeded all others in importance. Secular considerations had rivaled the religious as prime motivators during the progressive and early Volstead eras. But with national repeal, religion returned to its nineteenth-century position as the undisputed fountainhead of inspiration and action for the antiliquor movement. Though they often spoke of the secular consequences of alcohol abuse, the two leading temperance organizations, the UDF and the WCTU, were manifestly quasi-religious organizations which stressed the spiritual above all else.

A petition from a Topeka Presbyterian church, urging Governor Carlson to oppose repeal, put the classic position of evangelical Protestantism that was shared by many in the late 1940s:

> Whereas licensing the sale of liquor is a sin against God . . . and . . . against our fellowmen and especially against youth, selling them for pieces of silver, the . . . blood, unworthy money to be put into the treasury . . . and Whereas it is the duty of the Christian Church to fulfil its prophetic function to rebuke sin in high places . . . we charge you in the name of the Lord Jesus Christ . . . to use your utmost power to prevent . . . repeal.[60]

Tension between Protestants and Catholics on the liquor question, which always lurked just below the surface, emerged into the full light of day at the highest clerical level just ten days before the election. As the head of the Wichita Diocese, which included sixty-seven thousand communicants in fifty-two counties, Bishop Mark K. Carroll represented a major voice of Kansas Catholicism. In a Sunday homily devoted exclusively to the question of repeal, Bishop Carroll declared prohibition to be "unscriptural," "destructive of morality," "fatal to liberty," and "unpopular with the majority of citizens."

The basic issue, Carroll said, was not the efficiency of workers, the number of bootleggers, or the revenue to be won. "Prohibition is primarily a religious issue to be decided on the ethics of the question itself." His sermon received a hearty second from the Reverend Alfred Carney, head of the parish in Hays. Carney confirmed that "voluntary abstinence or moderation in drinking has always been the view of the Catholic church, not police enforced methods to prevent entirely the drinking of alcoholic beverages."[61]

It happened that the internationally renowned Methodist evangelist E. Stanley Jones was giving a series of sermons in Wichita when Bishop Carroll made his statement. Jones said that as an outsider, he had intended not to speak on the issue, but Carroll's remarks had melted his resolve. Jones took particular exception to the bishop's remark that you couldn't make a man virtuous "by legislation and authoritarian methods." "That is a strange and incongruous argument," Jones said, "from the lips of a man who represents . . . the most authoritarian [religion] the world has ever seen—which tells those under it what they can do and cannot do with reward of heaven for obedience and a penalty of hell for disobedience. . . . Logically Bishop Carroll . . . should abandon the imperious demands on his flock or he should abandon his argument. He cannot hold both."[62]

THE POLITICAL PARTIES made their declarations of principle in late August. The Prohibition party (which polled 17,035 votes) called for a 0.5 percent law and condemned those parties that refused to take a stand on the "moral question" of prohibition. The Socialist party (which polled 2,491 votes) affirmed what it chose to call its "traditional stand" for state-owned liquor stores, selling at cost. With Frank Carlson running for reelection, the Republicans surprised no one by affirming their 1946 nonpartisan position that the question was "a moral, not a political," one. They also made the politically safe declaration for "the absolute prohibition of any and every type of saloon." Like Woodring in 1946, the Democrats' gubernatorial candidate, Randolph Carpenter, fervently espoused repeal. Nevertheless the party leaders saw much wisdom in the nonpartisan approach, especially since the election seemed too close to call. They announced that the issue had become so important that "it transcends ordinary politics; and, therefore, it is not a proper subject for inclusion in a party platform."[63]

With the Democratic candidate openly calling for repeal and with the drys in their most precarious position since 1880, the pressure on Governor Frank Carlson to endorse prohibition mounted steadily as the campaign progressed. His political enemies claimed that he was only a puppet of the Landon "machine," which Alf was directing from "a castle on west Sixth Street." They referred to the governor as "Alfrank Carldon" and suggested that Landon had persuaded the personally dry Baptist Sunday-School teacher to endorse resubmission in 1946.

Carlson appeared to be headed for an easy victory (he won with a plurality of 126,000) and could have made a candid statement on the issue with little political risk to himself. In late 1947 he indicated privately that he would be "voting and working" for prohibition in the upcoming election. But as the campaign warmed up, he reiterated ad nauseam only that his administration had made an energetic effort to enforce the law, that he personally was "a total abstainer," and that he had been raised "in a good Christian home and grew to respect and uphold the laws of our lord." Formal questionnaires on the issue from organizations went into the files unanswered. To the most pointed inquiries his secretary responded that he was out of town.

In a last-minute desperation effort the drys' generalissimo, the Reverend Walker, attempted to save Carlson from Dante's hell and his own cause from

Dwight D. Eisenhower and Frank Carlson share a quiet moment of prayer (courtesy of the Kansas State Historical Society, Topeka).

oblivion. "Thousands of Kansans . . . are looking to you for moral leadership in this very crucial hour," Walker wrote on October 30. "I sincerely believe that the right word from you today will go far in determining the future of Kansas for the next fifty years." Carlson did not answer the fervent plea until a week after the election.

Reading the lines, as well as between them, in Carlson's correspondence, one can conclude that by early 1948 he had opted for repeal but had chosen to stay in the closet—probably to avoid facing the scornful wrath of the zealous drys. A clue to his attitude comes from his enforcement experience. A week after the election he wrote that "those of us who were trying in every way possible to enforce the liquor laws [including Arn, presumably] . . . were convinced that too many people were opposed to them to carry out a good enforcement program."[64]

Because prohibition had been a part of the Kansas Constitution for three generations, the more cynically inclined wets believed that it would remain there into the indefinite, and hypocritical, future. In the spring the drys bubbled with confidence, the most optimistic even proclaiming that the wet cause seemed to be virtually "hopeless." By early fall, more neutral observers predicted a dry victory, but a close vote. In early October a researcher at the Municipal University of Wichita published the results of a "scientific" poll of five thousand voters. He found the greatest dry strength among women, Republi-

Coming To An Oasis

This cartoon depicts the repeal of prohibition in 1948 (courtesy of the Kansas Collection, University of Kansas).

cans, those over fifty, and rural residents who did not live in a town larger than 2,500. Over-fifty farm women, for example, preferred prohibition by nearly 9 to 1. Wets were strongest among World War II veterans, Democrats, those aged twenty-one to thirty-five, and urban residents. Men of all ages and men and women from thirty-six to fifty were divided evenly in their opinions.[65] Among the subgroups the correlation is high between their voting preferences and their presumed drinking behaviors.

"Nearly every" evangelical Protestant minister preached on the temperance theme on October 10, and the Kansas Council of Churches called a day of prayer for prohibition for Sunday October 31. But public sentiment continued to swing toward repeal, so that by election eve some "experts" predicted a wet victory of up to forty thousand on the "overshadowing" question. Under favorable Kansas skies on 2 November, 780,604 voted on retention of the prohibition policy, sixty-eight years to the day after their forefathers had adopted it. The total vote was 3,728 less than the record vote on the amendment in 1934. The repealists won by the surprising margin of nearly 64,000 votes, 422,294 (54 percent) to 358,310 (46 percent).[66]

Four-sevenths of the counties voted dry (60), but no county that polled over 16,000 total votes did so (see app. A). All sixteen of the counties that voted wet in 1934 did so in 1948; they were joined by twenty-nine others. So general had been the shift in sentiment since 1934 that only two counties (Cherokee and Doniphan) recorded a drier vote in 1948. The wettest counties (in percentage of dry votes) included Ellis (18), Leavenworth (25), Ellsworth (27), Barton (28), and Russell (28). Large wet majorities were registered in the state's four most-populous counties: Sedgwick (20,466), Wyandotte (20,029), Shawnee (11,742), and Johnson (5,251). In the period between 1934 and 1948, these urban counties had gained a total of 173,445 in population, while the remainder of the state had lost 136,568. Including Leavenworth County (6,257), the five counties accounted for 63,745 of the 63,984 wet majority. The proposition broke even in the remaining one hundred counties. The driest counties included Jewell (72), Smith (68), Kiowa (68), Comanche (66), and Linn (65)—all of which were predominantly rural, Republican, and evangelical.

The correlation of the 1948 vote with the 1934 vote, by county, was very high—0.88. Although the average sentiment had shifted significantly, the influential factors had remained largely the same, or had even intensified. The correlation coefficients between the percentage of dry votes and the percentages of Republican votes, rural votes, and evangelical votes are 0.52, 0.41, and 0.69 respectively—all greater than their 1934 counterparts. The correlation of the dry vote with median income was -0.38: that is, the counties that voted dry tended to have below-average incomes and, by inference, a lower socioeconomic position. However, this variable added only 2 percent to the total explained variance. Seventy-two percent of the total variance is explained by the identified factors. The results of the multiple regression analysis are presented in Appendix B.[67]

12
In Conclusion

We may admit that [prohibition] has reduced to a greater or less extent the quantity
of liquors consumed in the State. . . . When this has been said, substantially all has
been said for prohibition in Kansas.

—Federal Judge G. C. Foster

Kansas was once known around the world for [her] high moral principles—but not
now. May we help her to again come into her own?

—Mrs. J. J. Ballinger, Winfield WCTU

THOUGH ONLY A MODEST AMOUNT has been written in recent decades about
the impact of prohibition on Kansas, nearly all of it has been of a highly critical,
even denunciatory, nature. From the mid twenties to the mid forties the most
persistent critic was William G. Clugston, political reporter for the *Kansas City
Journal Post* and a historian of the Kansas political and social scene. Clugston
held that political leaders ("Overlords") had fastened on prohibition as "the
right moral issue with which to keep the minds of the people occupied."
Politicians used prohibition, he claimed, "to perpetuate the old leadership in
power, and to keep the people's attention diverted from economic issues."
Clugston also pursued an important corollary of his theory, namely, that
prohibitionists never really wanted to dry up the state and thus lose their
nefarious control over the people. If that had occurred, Clugston said,
"prohibition as a safe moral issue with which to keep the people's emotions
under halter would have become as dead as the moral issue of slavery."[1]

Since the late 1940s this conspiratorial thesis has been extended and refined
by Kenneth S. Davis, a well-known author of both fictional and historical works.
In the late forties, Davis charged that prohibition was "designed to distract the
attention of voters from Kansas' deplorable tax structure, her need for highway
improvement, her need for better educational facilities." More recently he has
depicted prohibition as a "beclouding" issue, "militating against decisiveness

254

by the electorate on other matters of partisan dispute.'' Many other Kansans, including such outstanding figures as Milton S. Eisenhower, a former president of Kansas State University, and Dr. Karl A. Menninger, the eminent psychiatrist, have embraced most or all of the Clugston-Davis theory.[2]

It would, of course, be silly to suggest that no false-hearted politician or political party ever "used" the liquor issue by cynically attempting to manipulate the people in the name of prohibition, or of repeal. But a close reading of the record leads to the inescapable conclusion that in general, the people led the politicians, not vice versa. Senator John Ingalls and Attorney General John Ives were not the only discomfited elected officials who wanted prohibition to disappear as a public issue. But in the main, the politicians and the political parties cheerfully followed the broad public mood, insofar as they were able to divine it. The behaviors of the major political figures from John St. John to Frank Carlson serve as litmus indicators of contemporary public opinion. The officials acted as agents of the electorate, rarely as first causes. It was not primarily because of the manipulation of politicians that prohibition was written into the Kansas Constitution, sustained there for sixty-eight years, and then repealed.

Four Kansas governors, each of whom had had to deal with momentous liquor-related issues, meet in Topeka in 1949: *left to right* Landon, Capper, Woodring, and Carlson (courtesy of the Kansas State Historical Society, Topeka).

Another surviving political myth has it that the Republicans "always" supported prohibition and that the Democrats vigorously opposed it except during the Volstead era. Such allegedly steadfast support "always . . . helped Republicans at the expense of Democrats at the polls." The Republicans did not endorse prohibition in two of the three statewide referendums; they fell into stoney silence on the issue for extended periods during the 1890s, 1900s, and 1940s; and they strongly urged resubmission in 1946. It is true that they almost never adopted a wetter platform than the contemporary Democratic document.

When the constituency for their ardent nineteenth-century antiprohibition stance threatened to disappear, the Democrats reversed themselves and warmly endorsed prohibition in 1906. They did not repudiate that position until forty years later, when Harry Woodring identified for them a new repeal constituency. The party took no stand at all on the issue in any of the three state referendums. Becoming increasingly wary of the emotional sociocultural issue, the two parties have not offered the public an unequivocal wet/dry choice in their platforms since the early 1890s.[3]

The rigor of law enforcement, which waxed and waned over the decades, was also a function of public sentiment. Due to a variety of internal and external factors, the state situation shifted markedly in the periods 1885–87, 1889/90, 1900/1901, 1906–08, 1917–19, 1929–33, and 1945/46. No disjunction could long persist between the predominant sentiment of a community and the enforcement rigor delivered by its elected officials. At the local level the people almost invariably got the kind of enforcement that they asked for or would tolerate. It is not surprising to find relatively clean records in the counties that had the strongest temperance sentiment and to find the most flagrant examples of infidelities by officials in the wettest areas. Following a marked shift in the dry direction in 1909, the Wichita police chief cogently remarked that public sentiment was "of colossal magnitude, far-reaching and all-powerful. . . . It is the power behind the throne."[4]

IN THE LONG and eventful annals of Kansas prohibition, no word appears with more frequency or poignancy than *hypocrisy*. Excepting only their affection for the redeemed sinner, Kansans seem to love nothing more than to hurl charges of hypocrisy at one another. Over the entire course of geological time, no people has emerged which can so unerringly discern, at a distance of five hundred yards and with the unaided eye, the difference, say, between sham hypocrisy and hypocritical sham. If the written record is to be credited, the world has not witnessed such colossal displays of raw, undiluted deception since the "public lies and private convictions" of the Roman senators nearly two thousand years ago, exposed so brilliantly by Edward Gibbon in *The History of the Decline and Fall of the Roman Empire*.[5]

Hypocrisy is the practice of pretending to be what one is not or of proclaiming beliefs that one does not in fact have. A host of evocative connotations surround the word: snivel, snuffle, oiliness, phariseeism, pecksniffery, mealy-mouthedness. Generations of Kansans have been consigned to a historical purgatory because of their "hypocritical" views on prohibition. The virus of hypocrisy was evidently no respecter of persons or station; it infected them all: male and female, young and old, urban and rural, rich and poor, Democrats and Republicans (even Progressives and Socialists), in all walks of life and at all educational levels—and for year after deceitful year, decade after duplicitous decade.

The hypocritical posture has been most frequently framed by journalists and historians in the form of the aphorism attributed to William Allen White: "Kansans will vote dry so long as they can stagger to the polls." As early as 1947, E. M. Jellinek noted the inverse relationship among states between dry voting percentages on the Twenty-first Amendment and alcoholism rates and concluded that "Dry votes in general do not mean Wet drinking, but are to be accepted as evidence of Dry sentiment."[6] But the public has persisted in its belief that "dry voting" masked widespread "wet drinking."

In the three prohibitory referendums, only 35 percent (1880), 39 percent (1934), and 30 percent (1948) of the eligible electorate did in fact vote dry. The remainder voted wet or did not vote. Surveys of American drinking practices in the early post-Volstead years have identified over one-half of the general adult population as abstainers or very infrequent drinkers. For example, a 1961 survey of Iowa, a somewhat wetter state than Kansas, found that 41 percent abstained and another 25 percent averaged less than 5 ounces of alcohol (10 drinks) a year. (In recent decades the wettest one-half of the population has had a per capita consumption of over fifty times that of the driest one-half.)[7]

It is reasonable to postulate, therefore, that during the prohibitory period a large fraction of the adult Kansas population drank little or nothing at all. Using the mean from the 1914 data from the county clerks, for example, and assuming the standard log-normal pattern of consumption, at least 50 percent of the adult population is estimated as abstaining and another 10–20 percent as consuming less than 0.05 gallons of absolute alcohol per year. The available data simply do not support, much less demand, the "vote dry/drink wet" charge. Rather, they are compatible with the assumption that the great majority of those who voted dry drank little or nothing and, conversely, that those who drank in moderate or greater quantities generally voted wet.[8]

The hypocrisy issue is firmly joined to the core question of the effectiveness of prohibition, as measured by the per capita consumption of alcohol. The literature groans with scoffing comments regarding effectiveness, often delivered with a certitude that is untouched by the agonies of ambivalence. Such statements, at both the national and the state levels, have been rivaled in frequency only by those assuring that the earth is flat.

For example, one of William Allen White's biographers exclaims in wonderment that White "actually believed that Kansas was dry because it had a prohibition law." Woodring's biographer has written that in 1946 Woodring only pointed out "what every Kansan already knew, that prohibition was not prohibiting a thing." In the late 1930s, Karl Menninger discussed the collective psyche of Kansans, especially their penchant to be apologetic for their antiliquor laws. "I know, as everyone else knows," he said, "that there are relatively few total abstainers," but "to keep up appearances" the law proscribed liquor selling to the amusement of "our less hypocritical neighbors."[9]

In addition to the question of actual consumption, the problem of perceived consumption must also be addressed. Like an eclipse of the sun, consumption in large populations cannot be directly observed by the individual. Four logical possibilities suggest themselves: prohibition significantly reduced consumption, or it did not; the public perceived the reality, or it did not. Charges of hypocrisy can only be fairly leveled at those who lived in a community in which there was in fact no reduction but who proclaimed a reduction and knew their declaration to be false. Since the evidence for a sustained and significant reduction is overwhelming, the case for rampant hypocrisy again loses its force and validity. As Samuel Johnson observed in 1758, "It is not uncommon to charge the difference between promise and performance, between profession and reality, upon deep design and studied deceit; but the truth is, that there is very little hypocrisy in the world."[10]

Before turning to the state's history of consumption, two a priori arguments need to be considered. *Homo sapiens* is a gregarious, social species which cannot maintain its orderly communities unless most of their members follow the prescribed rules most of the time. It is still news when the law is broken, not when it is obeyed. Almost all laws have some impact in the desired direction; rarely does a well-publicized law produce an effect that is opposite to its intention. A case in point is the 55-mph speed law enacted in 1973. Although many drivers, perhaps most, violate the law by driving above the limit, the average speed of motorists has indeed been influenced by the law as measured by the sharply reduced number of highway fatalities. In 1984 there were in the city of Topeka (population 118,000) 2,500 moving traffic violations per month (30,000 per year), nearly one-half of which were for speeding.[11] Yet the traffic laws remain, and remain efficacious.

The second proposition concerns economic behavior and product marketing. Human beings respond in a wide variety of ways (consciously and even subliminally) to the powerful marketing message. The more visible, accessible, and desirable a product, the more will it be purchased. Alcoholic beverages are not supernatural substances, known to defy the laws of gravity or thermodynamics—or merchandising. It would be singularly remarkable if the relentless prohibitory pressures that drove liquor into a position of reduced product visibility, decreased economic accessibility, and lowered social respectability did not have a significant impact on its sales volume as well.

Too often the evaluators of prohibition have subsumed a model in which the demand for alcohol by the general public is as inelastic as that of the advanced addict. The most recently published general history of Kansas, for example, declares that despite the best efforts of state and national officials during the Volstead era, "there was no way to stop people with a thirst from trying to quench it!" Governor George Hodges described the market for alcoholic beverages in a more realistic manner in a letter written in 1914 after he had been defeated for reelection: "As a matter of fact, our state is not totally dry, but when a man has to go around the corner, up a back alley, go through three or four swinging doors, give seven or eight cabalistic knocks before he can buy a drink, you know the law is pretty well enforced and when a man is forced to do all that to appease his appetite, unless he is unusually thirsty, he will not go to all that trouble."[12]

The apparent annual per capita consumption, expressed in gallons of absolute alcohol among the drinking-age population of Kansas and the United States for the period from 1880 to 1980, is presented in figure 12.1.[13] Firm figures derived from tax revenues during nonprohibitory periods are distinguished from estimates, which are based on a variety of quantitative and qualitative sources during the prohibition years. The absolute values for prohibition Kansas, especially during the nineteenth century, are offered only as rough approximations for future refinement; more confidence can be placed in the relative values throughout the prohibitory interval.

Consumption in Kansas decreased sharply, except in the cities, during the period 1881–83 and again during the 1885–89 Martin-Bradford period. In this phase, drugstores replaced saloons as the major outlet, a substitution that resulted in the consumption of considerably less alcohol. Sales rose sharply in 1890 and continued at that level until about 1906, a wet period that was interrupted briefly by the Nation crusade in 1901. Enforcement tightened perceptibly from 1906 to 1908, and consumption took another abrupt drop when all drugstore sales were banned in 1909. The Blackmar survey and other contemporary data yield a benchmark figure of about 0.35 gallons of absolute alcohol (4.4 gallons of beverage) for the 1913–16 period, 14 percent of the national average. With the advent of the bone-dry law (1917), national wartime measures (1917–19), and the Volstead Act (1920), consumption reached its historic low in the period 1917–22.

Then began a steady increase that continued throughout the 1920s and accelerated in 1933 with the widespread sale of 3.2 beer. In the first years after full legalization in 1937, the consumption of beer averaged 44 percent of the national norm and was on the increase. Overall consumption increased markedly during the war years and received a sharp post-bellum boost from the returning veterans. With full legalization of all three types of beverages, Kansas' consumption of absolute alcohol in the 1950s averaged 63 percent of the national norm. Consumption throughout the nation has continued to increase, but in the

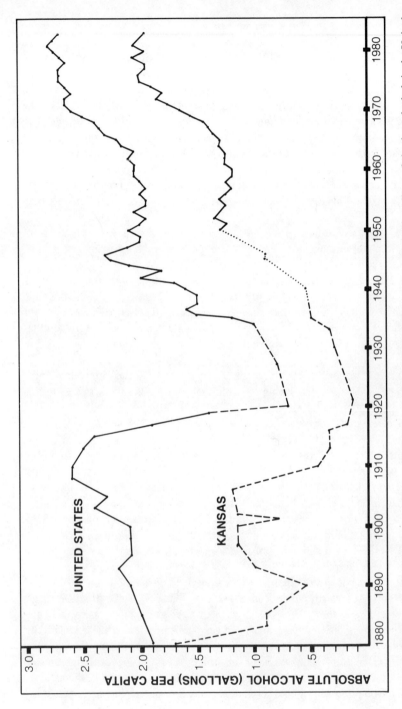

Fig. 12.1. Apparent annual per capita (drinking-age population) consumption of alcohol, in the United States and in Kansas, 1880–1983. Amounts based on tax receipts during nonprohibitory periods are shown by unbroken lines. Estimates based on tax receipts for beer and on circumstantial evidence for spirits and wine are shown by dotted lines. Estimates based only on circumstantial

state, it has increased at a more rapid rate, so that from 1974 to 1983, Kansas' consumption has averaged about 73 percent of the national amount. In recent years about 60 percent of the total absolute alcohol consumed in Kansas has been derived from beer, 34 percent from spirits, and 6 percent from wine. These figures compare with national ones of approximately 50, 37, and 13 percent respectively.

In figure 12.2, the per capita consumption by the Kansas drinking-age population is plotted as a percentage of the national average (mean) for each of the three types of beverages over the interval of their legal availability. The graph exhibits two striking features. In recent years, each of the beverage types has maintained a very different level in comparison to the national norm: about 90 percent for beer, about 65 percent for spirits, and about 35 percent for wine. The difference between the levels of spirits and wine is the Kansas manifestation of the general cultural tendency of midwesterners and southerners to prefer spirits and beer to wine. The second notable feature of figure 12.2 relates to the chronological profile of the three beverage types. Spirits and wine declined unevenly but persistently from their legalization in 1949 through the mid 1960s and have increased moderately (spirits) or not at all (wine) in the past twenty years. Beer, however, has moved steadily upwards since its legalization, from 42 to 90 percent of the national average.

It is tempting to relate the behavior of the types of beverages to their prohibition heritage and contemporary state law. The consumption of beer has been moving toward the national average from the prohibitory period in a regulatory atmosphere that is typical for the nation as a whole. Per capita consumption of spirits and wine in the state has increased significantly in an absolute sense from the 1950s to the 1980s (spirits from 1.32 to 1.58 gallons; wine from 0.54 to 1.00 gallons). But under regulatory restrictions that are decidedly more stringent than average, neither beverage type has increased in a sustained manner relative to the national norm. The end of the fifteen-year decline in the relative amounts of spirits and wine coincides with the Private Club Act of 1965, more precisely for the former than for the latter.

Health indicators that are closely related to the use of alcohol have remained relatively low in the postprohibition era, reflecting the state's relative consumption of absolute alcohol in the 60–70 percent range. The state's annual mortality rate from cirrhosis of the liver has averaged 63 percent of the national mean since 1950. A 1970 study that estimated the alcoholism rate among the states ranked Kansas forty-first. A 1974 composite state death rate from cirrhosis, alcoholism, and alcoholic psychosis was 51 percent of the national mean for women (ranking Kansas forty-sixth) and 71 percent for men (forty-first rank). The state ranked fortieth on an aggregate score of seven alcohol-related mortality rates for 1975–77 and forty-second on a composite index of alcohol-related problems, generated by factor analysis. In 1978, Kansas ranked forty-

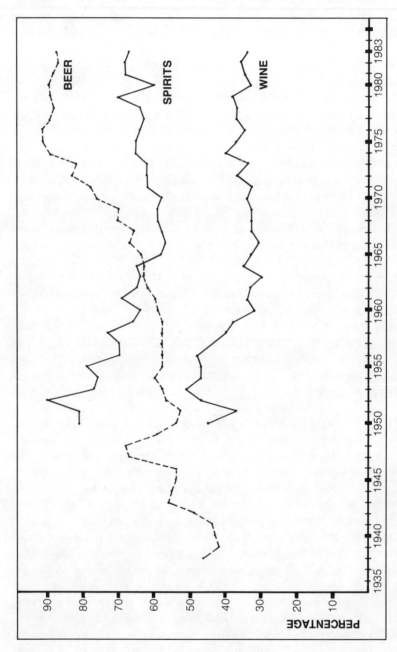

Fig. 12.2. Annual per capita (drinking-age population) consumption of beer, wine, and spirits in Kansas, as a percentage of the national average,1938–83. See fig. 12.1 for sources and calculation procedures.

eighth in the percentage of deaths attributed to alcohol-related causes among all deaths.[14]

The impact of the prohibitory laws on the case load of the Kansas Supreme Court is shown in figure 12.3. The number of liquor-related cases that the court has decided is shown for the century beginning with 1870. A record forty-two cases were decided in 1905/6 and again in 1925/26. The three major peaks of activity can be correlated with the original Benson Act and its amendments (1882–94), the litigation generated by the Nation crusade and the subsequent renaissance in enforcement (1902–16), and cases developed in Kansas during the Volstead period (1924–32). The smaller increases in 1950 et seq. and in 1966 stem from the Liquor Control Act of 1949 and the Private Club Act of 1965.

OVER THE COURSE of the state's history, the reasons proffered by the temperance-inclined for the reduction or elimination of alcohol consumption fall into four broad categories: religious (or morality), scientific (or health), sociocivic (or good order), and economic (or prosperity). The arguments advanced by Charles Robinson in 1856 for strict regulation (morals, health, good order, and prosperity), by J. R. Detwiler in 1880 for prohibition (right, reasonable, just, and profitable), and by Arthur Capper in 1948 in opposition to liquor (human wrecker, health wrecker, home wrecker, and business wrecker)— all sound essentially the same notes.

"Sinfulness" gave way to "harmfulness" as the primary rationale for the movement at the beginning of the progressive era. However, religion remained as the spiritual and organizational core of the ongoing reform. From the days of the KSTU to the contemporary "Kansans for Life at Its Best!" the state temperance movement has revolved around the evangelical churches and the secular organizations that they support. Its arguments are presented in secular clothes, but the temperance movement marches to the beat of a religious drummer.

Quantitative evidence for the close association of religion and the temperance vote is also compelling. The statistical correlation between the percentage of dry votes and the percentage of evangelicals is greater than for any other identified variable: 0.51 (1880), 0.57 (1934), 0.69 (1948) (see app. B). The increase in the correlation from the nineteenth century can be attributed more to the increasing precision of the religious-census data than to a real change in the strength of the association. The proportion of the total population that is affiliated with a church is unremarkable in Kansas (about 50 percent in recent decades). The correlation of the 1948 dry vote with the percentage churched is relatively low and negative (-0.27).

In 1970 the state narrowly rejected a proposal to remove the constitutional ban on the "open saloon" and to legalize the public sale of liquor by the drink. The correlations of the 1970 vote with that of 1934 (0.75) and 1948 (0.72) indicate that the public's pattern of response to the underlying issues has

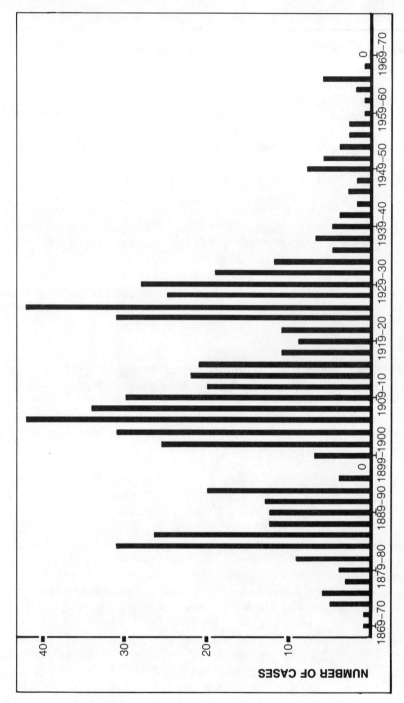

Fig. 12.3. Liquor-related cases before the Kansas Supreme Court, 1870–1970. Each bar represents the total number of cases for the biennium ending in the designated year. Data were derived from *Kansas Reports*, 1870–1970.

remained largely unchanged. Correlations were calculated for the percentage of dry votes and the percentage of Republicans (0.50), the percentage of rural (0.57), the percentage of evangelicals (0.52), and the percentage of churched (0.34). Relative to the two prohibition votes, the 1970 liquor-by-the-drink vote showed about the same level of importance of political affinity, an increased importance of population density, a decreased importance of denominational affinity, but a sharp increase in the positive association between dry voting and church affiliation.[15]

An oft-repeated adage that is closely linked to the question of liquor regulation claims that "you can't legislate morality." In a fundamental sense, of course, all legislation merely represents codified morality, since it necessarily entails questions of "right" and "wrong." But in the popular and more restricted sense, "moral issues" (or "sin issues") tend to be ones that are closely associated with personal behavior, such as drinking and reproduction. Evangelicals tend to support strong legislation to prohibit or regulate the former, while liturgicals urge equally harsh measures to control the latter. The twin issues of liquor control and abortion (birth) control have forged a clear consensus in the state and in the nation, at least among the churched, that some aspects of "morality" are proper subjects for legislative action.

A wide variety of one-dimensional theories has been advanced by students of the American temperance movement to explain its successes and failures over part or all of its 175-year course: disorderliness, industrialization, urbanization, modernization, neorepublicanism, status preservation, sexual hostility, rural backwardness, social control by an elite, the efficiency of the ASL, progressivism, and religious dedication. The last two have been found to be most useful in helping to understand the Kansas phenomena. John C. Burnham has cautioned about the dangers of drawing sweeping conclusions from "radically" different evidence derived from different periods and sections of the nation.[16] More work at the state and local levels must be completed before the diverse national phenomena can be successfully "reduced" to one or a few explanatory factors and before anything approaching a "unified" concept can be offered with confidence.

Organized public concern in America with the use of alcohol has been coextensive with broad public recognition of its potential abusiveness, that is, continuously since the veil of ignorance began to lift from the "good creature of God" early in the nineteenth century. The intensity of temperance sentiment has varied widely with time and place and culture, and this variation and its relation to independent variables such as disorderliness have been the primary focus of researchers. The reform has stubbornly persisted, however, in a wide range of social and political environments on a global scale down to the present day. After reviewing the contributions of nearly two thousand American temperance workers, Mark Lender has recently observed that the movement has attracted "a remarkably varied and dynamic mass popular base." Perhaps it would be useful to approach the reform as an adaptive response by society to the real or potential threat that drugs pose to its well-being, even ultimately to its survival, rather than simply and only as a function of industrialization, and so forth.

Whatever an individual's position on the wet/dry spectrum may be and for whatever reasons, society as a whole exhibits a fascination with alcohol-induced behavior that is rivaled only by that with sex. The eighteenth-century compilation by Benjamin Franklin of 228 synonyms for drunkenness has lengthened, so that it now includes at least 2,231 words in the English language alone, more than for any other activity, including the sex act. The nineteenth-century temperance drama *Ten Nights in a Barroom* has become one of the all-time theatrical favorites on a global scale. More than one hundred thousand Kansans have attended its 763 performances in the state since 1960. Clearly there is much to learn about this collective and perpetual human obsession with alcohol-related phenomena. We need to understand more completely both the euphoria produced by drunkenness and the disease of alcoholism, but also to comprehend more fully those who stand with the Cherokee County man who said, "I hate beer and whiskey althow I never tasted neather."[17]

THE PROHIBITION EXPERIENCE in Kansas demonstrates conclusively, as did the Eighteenth Amendment, the futility of attempts to foreclose all avenues of obtaining alcoholic beverages. It became impossible, especially in the post-Volstead environment, to sustain a policy that made the mere possession of liquor a misdemeanor. But the state experience also demonstrates, even more forcefully than does the national one, that legal control measures, mediated through reduced visibility, accessibility, and respectability, can markedly reduce consumption and the deleterious parameters that are linked closely to it.[18]

For a period of approximately twenty years beginning about 1909, Kansas prohibition achieved its highest benefit-to-cost ratio. Strong multipartisan temperance sentiment within its borders, reinforced by growing national approbation beyond, reduced the internal tensions, producing a social and political climate of relative peace and harmony. During the first half of this period, the legal importation of quality liquor for those who wanted it combined with rigorous local enforcement to produce a level of consumption no greater than 15 percent of the national average. Full-fledged raids on bootleggers netted only a few paltry bottles of beer or quarts of whiskey in the towns and a few gallons of hard cider in the countryside.[19]

During this felicitous period, Kansans held a positive image of themselves and enjoyed national approval as the model progressive-prohibition state. If its problems with alcohol were not completely solved, the public seemed pleased enough with the effectiveness of its control strategies. During this period, prohibition met the basic expectations that are normally associated with a successful public policy. But the only constant in life is change.

The greatest irony of Kansas prohibition is that the attainment of the goal that the temperance community had so devoutly sought—namely, national prohibition—led directly to the loss of the state policy. For the first time the Volstead Act of 1920 produced an environment in which the production of relatively low-quality liquor within the state became economically feasible. The development of large-scale production and its associated evils put the drys on the defensive and began to nudge public sentiment in the wet direction for the first time since the mid nineties. For a society that passionately wanted to limit its consumption of alcohol, legal importation from outside the state had created far fewer problems than illegal production from inside.

Rejection of the Eighteenth Amendment by the nation sounded the death knell for the venerable policy in Kansas, though it took another fifteen years to execute the sentence. The drys lost the momentum, the propaganda war, and, ultimately, broad public support. The state policy could thrive in a nation that had not accepted prohibition but not in one that had repudiated it. The "Kansas idea" returned from its national odyssey to slay its progenitors. And Kansans returned to their preoccupation with apology and self-deprecation.

Since 1933, both the state and the nation have lived, moved, and had their being in the long, deep shadow of repeal. Prohibition has been resoundingly discredited as the misguided product of the "fanatical" mind. Everyone and everything linked to the repudiated policy—from Neal Dow and Carry Nation through the WCTU and ASL to the entire state of Kansas—have been marked for ridicule and disparagement. The "dreadful example" of prohibition is held up to those who would advocate more stringent control of nonalcoholic drugs. The "collective memory" of prohibition inclines the public to the view that the consumption of alcohol is virtually a constant—unaffected by advertising, societal attitudes, or legislative acts. For example, an educational TV station recently proclaimed that the enactment of the state's bone-dry law in 1917 had made "nearly everyone" in Kansas a criminal.[20]

The "Imperfect Rectangle" has waged an epic struggle and is still doing so, on a more modest scale, over the issue of liquor by the drink. Prohibition is but the historical phase of the continuing effort to achieve an effective and acceptable public policy to control alcohol abuse. For the nation, prohibition may have been an "experiment," "noble" or otherwise, but for Kansas it represented a long-term, partially successful reform. The policy established a pattern of below-average consumption of alcohol that persists to the present day. The undeniable benefits must be paired with the unmistakable costs, chiefly in the form of increased tensions within the commonwealth and an unwelcome image both within and without.

After a withering review of the state's liquor-control policies, an eastern journalist once asked if the "flat hideousness" and "arid provincialism" of puritan cultures like Kansas were capable of "attracting and permanently interesting the human spirit." Were "a lover of the humane life," someone like

William James, to make a candid appraisal of Kansas' unlovely civilization, he continued, "one knows at once what the verdict would be." But there are those who love her—who see plain, humble Kansas as a past and future "moral leader," helping the nation find workable solutions to the horrendous economic costs of alcohol abuse, which was estimated at $117 billion for 1983. They share the reassuring thought of old Frank Stahl: "What's the matter with Kansas? Kansas is all right. Who's all right? Kansas."[21]

Appendix A

THE PERCENTAGE OF DRY VOTES, BY COUNTY, FOR THE PROHIBITION REFERENDUMS OF 1880, 1934, AND 1948 AND FOR THE LIQUOR-BY-THE-DRINK REFERENDUM OF 1970

County	1880	1934	1948	1970	County	1880	1934	1948	1970
Allen	58	66	53	65	Ford	20	53	39	56
Anderson	51	62	55	62	Franklin	60	70	62	61
Atchison	30	45	43	41	Geary	51	44	34	43
Barber	51	63	49	65	Gove	—	64	44	68
Barton	32	42	28	54	Graham	37	62	51	64
Bourbon	42	63	61	69	Grant	—	59	44	64
Brown	51	68	64	65	Gray	—	59	52	63
Butler	66	60	51	59	Greeley	—	66	55	62
Chase	47	63	55	69	Greenwood	53	59	53	60
Chautauqua	56	64	59	73	Hamilton	—	57	54	63
Cherokee	55	48	48	57	Harper	57	69	64	72
Cheyenne	—	61	60	66	Harvey	57	65	59	62
Clark	—	65	53	73	Haskell	—	62	58	64
Clay	59	71	63	74	Hodgeman	69	60	56	68
Cloud	54	55	46	68	Jackson	49	66	61	66
Coffey	46	71	61	74	Jefferson	43	68	59	58
Commanche	—	70	66	72	Jewell	55	80	72	71
Cowley	79	62	55	67	Johnson	46	54	38	25
Crawford	53	43	39	44	Kearny	—	64	47	64
Decatur	37	63	57	61	Kingman	43	64	54	63
Dickinson	55	63	50	63	Kiowa	—	78	68	76
Doniphan	28	53	62	55	Labette	49	61	48	63
Douglas	63	64	48	41	Lane	—	66	49	67
Edwards	38	56	48	61	Leavenworth	28	29	25	28
Elk	69	66	58	71	Lincoln	46	56	44	61
Ellis	43	27	18	36	Linn	54	72	65	64
Ellsworth	44	36	27	56	Logan	—	63	48	62
Finney	—	57	41	58	Lyon	73	62	47	57

269

County	1880	1934	1948	1970	County	1880	1934	1948	1970
McPherson	70	70	59	69	Rush	51	50	41	63
Marion	55	63	62	71	Russell	40	48	28	53
Marshall	44	54	46	63	Saline	54	48	35	46
Meade	—	63	58	68	Scott	—	59	48	73
Miami	46	57	47	52	Sedgwick	52	40	37	40
Mitchell	53	60	51	62	Seward	—	59	49	60
Montgomery	61	53	47	66	Shawnee	56	48	37	42
Morris	50	69	56	72	Sheridan	59	57	43	61
Morton	—	62	55	63	Sherman	—	58	51	55
Nemaha	51	55	43	61	Smith	60	74	68	69
Neosho	57	63	51	60	Stafford	57	66	57	73
Ness	48	64	51	68	Stanton	—	70	61	70
Norton	54	65	58	69	Stevens	—	65	52	67
Osage	58	66	59	62	Sumner	67	66	57	63
Osborne	54	70	60	73	Thomas	—	60	45	61
Ottawa	58	66	56	68	Trego	65	46	35	57
Pawnee	73	59	52	60	Wabaunsee	39	57	48	62
Phillips	58	69	62	63	Wallace	—	57	57	67
Pottawatomie	51	54	42	57	Washington	41	60	53	65
Pratt	52	65	52	67	Wichita	—	49	43	62
Rawlins	—	49	43	56	Wilson	58	64	54	66
Reno	52	54	46	59	Woodson	59	69	61	64
Republic	59	61	56	67	Wyandotte	33	36	34	30
Rice	63	60	50	67					
Riley	59	65	45	49	Mean	52.0	59.7	50.6	61.3
Rooks	42	64	48	62					

Appendix B

MULTIPLE-REGRESSION ANALYSIS OF DRY VOTES IN PROHIBITORY REFERENDUMS OF 1880, 1934, AND 1948 AND LIQUOR-BY-THE-DRINK REFERENDUM OF 1970

The percentage of dry votes by county was regressed on several independent variables for the prohibitory referendums of 1880, 1934, and 1948 and for the liquor-by-the-drink referendum of 1970. For each statistically significant variable ($P < .05$) the raw (B) and standardized (beta) regression coefficients, simple correlation (r), variance added at step of entry (VA), significance test (F), and probability value (P) are given. The variables entered the equation stepwise and are listed in order of the variance accounted for. R^2 = proportion of the total variance accounted for (sum of VA column).

1880 Referendum

	B	beta	r	VA	F	P
Denomination	.235	.387	.519	.269	13.498	< .001
Politics	.525	.301	.427	.044	7.618	< .01
Amendment vote	.428	.206	.105	.039	4.524	< .05
Constant = − 36.885						

$R^2 = .352$, F = 13.578, 3/75 df, $P < .001$

Measures of voter turnout, voter nativity, and population density did not enter the equation.

1934 Referendum

	B	beta	r	VA	F	P
Denomination	.278	.588	.575	.330	72.727	< .001
Density	.144	.370	.349	.157	28.526	< .001
Politics	.378	.204	.297	.040	8.661	< .01
Constant = 8.948						

$R^2 = .527$, F = 37.532, 3/101 df, $P < .001$

271

1948 Referendum

	B	beta	r	VA	F	P
Denomination	.350	.624	.687	.472	135.699	<.001
Politics (gov.)	.301	.175	.518	.186	4.567	<.05
Density	.059	.165	.409	.027	7.134	<.01
Income	−.003	−.158	−.381	.025	7.150	<.01
Politics (secy. of state)	.236	.157	.471	.011	3.980	<.05

Constant = −1.489

$R^2 = .721$, $F = 51.167$, 5/99 df, $P < .001$

For this referendum, three measures of political affinity were obtained: the votes for governor and for secretary of state entered the equation; the vote for auditor did not. A measure of the churched population (percentage of total denominational membership of the total population) did not enter the equation. This variable had a −.27 correlation with the dry vote and a −.57 correlation with the percentage of evangelicals (denomination).

1970 Referendum

	B	beta	r	VA	F	P
Density	.099	.312	.567	.321	21.641	<.001
Denomination	.323	.496	.520	.200	63.585	<.001
Politics	.413	.267	.501	.084	17.514	<.001
Churched	.208	.253	.337	.049	14.319	<.001

Constant = −4.360

$R^2 = .654$, $F = 47.354$, 4/100 df, $P < .001$

The percentage of churched had a −.20 correlation with the percentage of evangelicals (denomination).

Notes

ACRONYMS USED IN THE NOTES

KCS   *Kansas City Star*
KCT   *Kansas City Times*
KH   *Kansas History*
KHC   *Kansas Historical Collections*
KHQ   *Kansas Historical Quarterly*
KSHS Kansas State Historical Society
TC   *Topeka Capital*
TCJ   *Topeka Capital-Journal*
TSJ   *Topeka State Journal*

Newspapers are from Kansas unless specified otherwise.

PREFACE

1. Jack S. Blocker, Jr., *Retreat from Reform: The Prohibition Movement in the United States, 1890–1913* (Westport, Conn.: Greenwood Press, 1976), p. 5; Robert O'Brien and Morris Chafetz, *The Encyclopedia of Alcoholism* (New York: Facts on File Publications, 1982), p. x.

CHAPTER 1. PROLOGUE

1. *Lawrence Journal*, 26 Aug. 1879.
2. *Weekly Kansas Tribune*, 21 Aug. 1879.
3. Jimmie L. Lewis, "Bismarck Grove, Lawrence, Kansas (1878–1900)" (Master's thesis, University of Kansas, 1968), p. 13.
4. *Weekly Kansas Tribune*, 21 Aug. 1879.
5. *Lawrence Journal*, 23 Aug. 1879.
6. *Topeka Commonwealth*, 26 Sept. 1885; *Lawrence Journal*, 16 Aug. 1879; Otto F. Frederikson, "The Liquor Question in Kansas before Constitutional Prohibition" (Ph.D. diss., University of Kansas, 1931), p. 411.
7. *Temperance Banner*, Sept. 1879.

8. Ibid.

9. *Topeka Commonwealth*, 1 Oct. 1879.

10. *Lawrence Journal*, 17 Aug. 1879.

11. The account of the Bismarck Grove camp meeting is based principally upon the following sources: *Lawrence Journal*, 7-26 Aug. 1879; *Weekly Kansas Tribune*, 21 Aug. 1879; *Temperance Banner*, Sept. 1879; Jim L. Lewis, "'Beautiful Bismarck'—Bismarck Grove, Lawrence, 1878-1900," *KHQ* 35 (1969): 225-56, and "Bismarck Grove," pp. 12-22; O. Frederikson, "Liquor Question in Kansas," pp. 406, 550, 616-31, 702; Edna T. Frederikson, "John P. St. John, the Father of Constitutional Prohibition" (Ph.D. diss., University of Kansas, 1931), pp. 30, 95.

12. Ian R. Tyrrell, *Sobering Up: From Temperance to Prohibition in Antebellum America, 1800-1860* (Westport, Conn.: Greenwood Press, 1979), p. 130.

13. Ibid., p. 111.

14. Norman H. Clark, *Deliver Us from Evil: An Interpretation of American Prohibition* (New York: W. W. Norton, 1976), p. 24.

15. O. Frederikson, "Liquor Question in Kansas," p. 544.

16. John A. Krout, *The Origins of Prohibition* (New York: Alfred A. Knopf, 1925), p. 173.

17. Carroll D. Clark and Roy L. Roberts, *People of Kansas: A Demographic and Sociological Study* (Topeka: Kansas State Planning Board, 1936), p. 208.

18. The chief sources consulted for the summary of the ante-bellum temperance movement include: Tyrrell, *Sobering Up;* W. J. Rorabaugh, *The Alcoholic Republic: An American Tradition* (New York: Oxford University Press, 1979); Krout, *Origins;* D. Leigh Colvin, *Prohibition in the United States: A History of the Prohibition Party and of the Prohibition Movement* (New York: George H. Doran Co., 1926); Ernest H. Cherrington, *The Evolution of Prohibition in the United States of America* (Westerville, Ohio: American Issue Press, 1920); Frank L. Byrne, *Prophet of Prohibition: Neal Dow and His Crusade* (Madison: State Historical Society of Wisconsin, 1961); Paul E. Johnson, *A Shopkeeper's Millennium: Society and Revivals in Rochester, New York, 1815-1837* (New York: Hill & Wang, 1978); Clark, *Deliver Us;* Mark Edward Lender and James Kirby Martin, *Drinking in America: A History* (New York: Free Press, 1982); Joseph R. Gusfield, *Symbolic Crusade: Status Politics and the American Temperance Movement* (Urbana: University of Illinois Press, 1963); Richard Jensen, *The Winning of the Midwest: Social and Political Conflict, 1888-1896* (Chicago: University of Chicago Press, 1971); William G. McLoughlin, *Revivals, Awakenings, and Reform* (Chicago: University of Chicago Press, 1978); Ronald Walters, *American Reformers, 1815-1860* (New York: Hill & Wang, 1978); C. S. Griffin, *The Ferment of Reform, 1830-1860* (New York: Thomas Y. Crowell Co., 1967); Barbara L. Epstein, *The Politics of Domesticity: Women, Evangelism and Temperance in Nineteenth-Century America* (Middletown, Conn.: Wesleyan University Press, 1981); Jed Dannenbaum, *Drink and Disorder: Temperance Reform in Cincinnati from the Washingtonian Revival to the WCTU* (Urbana: University of Illinois Press, 1984); Mark Edward Lender, *Dictionary of American Temperance Biography* (Westport, Conn.: Greenwood Press, 1984); Robert L. Hampel, "Diversity in Early Temperance Reform," *Journal of Studies on Alcohol* 43 (1982): 453-68; Leonard U. Blumberg, "The Significance of the Alcohol Prohibitionists for the Washington Temperance Societies," *Journal of Studies on Alcohol* 41 (1980): 37-77; Sarah E. Williams, "The Use of Beverage Alcohol as Medicine, 1790-1860," *Journal of Studies on Alcohol* 41 (1980): 543-66; Harry Gene LeVine, "Industrialization, Economic Development, and Worker Drinking: Historical and Sociological Observations," in Institute of Medicine, *Legislative Approaches to Prevention of Alcohol-Related*

Problems: An Inter-American Workshop (Washington, D.C.: National Academy Press, 1982), pp. 26-46.

CHAPTER 2. PRELUDE

1. Anonymous, "Letters of New England Clergymen," *KHC* 1 (1881): 193-94; John A. Krout, *The Origins of Prohibition* (New York: Alfred A. Knopf, 1925), pp. 129-30; William H. Carruth, "New England in Kansas," *New England Magazine* 16 (1887): 5-6, 11; Daniel W. Wilder, *The Annals of Kansas, 1541-1885* (Topeka: T. Dwight Thacher, Kansas Publishing House, 1886), p. 47.
2. A. T. Andreas, *History of the State of Kansas* (Chicago: A. T. Andreas, 1883), pp. 313, 325-26, 541, 619, 848, 1371; Otto F. Frederikson, "The Liquor Question in Kansas before Constitutional Prohibition" (Ph.D. diss., University of Kansas, 1931), p. 171; James L. King, *History of Shawnee County, Kansas* (Chicago: Richmond & Arnold, 1905), p. 172; F. W. Giles, *Thirty Years in Topeka* (Topeka: Geo. W. Crane & Co., 1886), pp. 102-4; *KCT,* 22 Oct. 1948 and 30 Apr. 1949.
3. Andreas, *History,* p. 315.
4. Anonymous, "The Topeka Movement," *KHC* 13 (1915): 209, 217.
5. *Herald of Freedom,* 27 Dec. 1856 and 31 Jan. 1857; William Hutchinson, "Sketches of Kansas Pioneer Experience," *KHC* 7 (1902): 405; Spencer H. Givens to Cecil Howes, 28 Apr. 1937, KSHS; Richard Cordley, *A History of Lawrence, Kansas* (Lawrence: E. F. Caldwell, 1895), p. 169; G. W. Martin, "The First Two Years of Kansas," *KHC* 10 (1908): 129.
6. *Herald of Freedom,* 27 Dec. 1856.
7. Ibid., 31 Jan. 1857; G. W. Brown to Maria Hubbell, 15 Apr. 1905, KSHS; Andreas, *History,* p. 326.
8. O. Frederikson, "Liquor Question in Kansas," pp. 166-71; Giles, *Thirty Years,* pp. 102-94; Andreas, *History,* p. 541.
9. Mary Still Adams, *Autobiography* (Los Angeles, Calif.: Buckingham Brothers, 1893), pp. 5, 64, 68-72; Theodosius Botkin, "Among the Sovereign Squats," *KHC* 7 (1902): 428; O. Frederikson, "Liquor Question in Kansas," pp. 172-75; *KCT,* 17 May 1927.
10. Sara T. D. Robinson, *Kansas: Its Interior and Exterior Life* (Boston: Crosby, Nichols & Co., 1856), p. 19; Robert W. Richmond, *Kansas: A Land of Contrasts* (St. Charles, Mo.: Forum Press, 1974), p. 67.
11. Elmer L. Craik, "Southern Interest in Territorial Kansas, 1854-1858," *KHC* 15 (1923): 448; Andreas, *History,* pp. 317, 914, 1530; Leverett W. Spring, *Kansas: A Prelude to the War for the Union* (Boston: Houghton Mifflin & Co., 1885), pp. 44, 47; *Herald of Freedom,* 18 and 25 July and 1 Aug. 1857; Robinson, *Kansas,* pp. 15, 18.
12. Walter L. Fleming, "The Buford Expedition to Kansas," *American Historical Review* 6 (1900): 38-48; Craik, "Southern Interest," pp. 397-98.
13. Thomas H. Gladstone, *The Englishman in Kansas* (New York: Miller & Co., 1857), p. 41.
14. *Kansas City Journal,* 13 Mar. 1901; Richmond, *Kansas,* pp. 74-75.
15. *Herald of Freedom,* 1 Aug. 1857; Samuel J. Reader, "The Letters of Samuel James Reader, 1861-1863," *KHQ* 9 (1940): 36-37; R. G. Elliott, "The Big Springs Convention," *KHC* 8 (1904): 369; Don W. Holter, *Fire on the Prairie: Methodism in the History of Kansas* (n.p.: Editorial Board of Kansas Methodist History, 1969), p. 115.
16. Kansas Territory, House, *House Journal, 1855* (Shawnee Manual Labor School: Public Printer, 1855), p. 264; Kansas Territory, Council, *Council Journal, 1855* (Shawnee Manual Labor School: Public Printer, 1855), p. 76; Kansas Territory,

Legislature, *Statutes of the Territory of Kansas* (Shawnee Manual Labor School: Public Printer, 1855), pp. 322–24, 417–19; Missouri, Legislature, *Revised Statutes of Missouri, 1846* (Jefferson City: Public Printer, 1856), pp. 682–88; Clara Francis, "Prohibition in Kansas," in *History of Kansas: State and People,* ed. William E. Connelley (Chicago: American Historical Society, Inc., 1928), vol. 2, p. 679. For a study of state and federal liquor laws as they relate to Indians see Otto Frovin Frederikson, "The Liquor Question among the Indian Tribes in Kansas, 1804–1881," *Bulletin of University of Kansas, Humanistic Studies* 4 (1932): 437–539.

17. Kansas Territory, *House Journal, 1855,* p. 217; Ian R. Tyrrell, *Sobering Up: From Temperance to Prohibition in Antebellum America, 1800–1860* (Westport, Conn.: Greenwood Press, 1979), p. 280.

18. William R. Bernard, "Westport and the Santa Fe Trade," *KHC* 9 (1906): 564.

19. *Herald of Freedom,* 7 Feb. 1857.

20. Kansas, Legislature, *General Laws of Kansas, 1862* (Topeka: State Printer, 1862), pp. 486–89.

21. Anonymous, "When Kansas Became a State," *KHQ* 27 (1961): 14; Francis, "Prohibition," pp. 685–86.

22. Andreas, *History,* p. 287; Kansas, Legislature, *Session Laws of 1867* (Leavenworth: Bulletin Job Office, 1867), pp. 93–94; Kansas, Legislature, *General Statutes of Kansas, 1868* (Lawrence: Public Printer, 1868), p. 386.

23. Kansas, *General Statutes, 1868,* pp. 399–403, 524; Anonymous, "Biographies of Members of the Legislature of 1868," *KHC* 10 (1908): 265–79; O. Frederikson, "Liquor Question in Kansas," pp. 261–62.

24. John Guthrie, "The Kansas Legislature of 1868," *Agora Magazine* 2 (1893): 237–48; Norman H. Clark, *Deliver Us from Evil: An Interpretation of American Prohibition* (New York: W. W. Norton, 1976), p. 67; Ruth Bordin, *Woman and Temperance* (Philadelphia: Temple University Press, 1981), pp. 6–7.

25. O. Frederikson, "Liquor Question in Kansas," pp. 295–300; Andreas, *History,* p. 649; William F. Shamleffer, "Merchandising Sixty Years Ago," *KHC* 16 (1925): 567–69.

26. Robert R. Dykstra, *The Cattle Towns* (New York: Alfred A. Knopf, 1968), pp. 6–7, 102, 240–48, 253–56, 263–64, 285; Dave Dary, "Those Were the Days, My Friend," *Midway Magazine* of *TCJ,* 30 Aug. 1970; Carol Leonard and Isidor Wallimann, "Prostitution and Changing Morality in the Frontier Cattle Towns of Kansas," *KH* 2 (1979): 34–53; John D. Waltner, "The Process of Civilization on the Kansas Frontier, Newton, Kansas, 1871–1873" (Master's thesis, University of Kansas, 1971), pp. 7, 55, 75–76, 90–104; H. Craig Miner, *Wichita: The Early Years, 1865–80* (Lincoln: University of Nebraska Press, 1982), pp. 48, 105, 109–39; Nyle H. Miller and Joseph W. Snell, *Great Gunfighters of the Kansas Cowtowns, 1867–1886* (Lincoln: University of Nebraska Press, 1967), p. 2.

27. Amory Hunting to Rev. Mr. McVicker, 25 Oct. 1869, KSHS; Francis, "Prohibition," pp. 686–87; O. Frederikson, "Liquor Question in Kansas," pp. 179–85; Andreas, *History,* pp. 325–26, 541; *Kansas Tribune,* 18 Feb. 1856; *Prairie Star,* 31 Jan. and 28 Mar. 1857, KSHS; T. E. Stephens, *Prohibition in Kansas* (Topeka: Kansas Farmer Co., 1902), p. 32.

28. Amory Hunting to Rev. Mr. McVicker, 25 Oct. 1869, KSHS; H. D. Fisher, *The Gun and the Gospel* (Chicago: Kenwood Press, 1896), pp. 214–16; Anonymous, "Kansas Chronology," *KHC* 12 (1912): 422; O. Frederikson, "Liquor Question in Kansas," pp. 261–68, 279, 335–37, 367–68, 372–77, 490–93; *Topeka Commonwealth,* 31 Jan. and 7 Feb. 1872; Francis, "Prohibition," pp. 690–97.

29. *Topeka Commonwealth*, 31 Jan. 1872; O. Frederikson, "Liquor Question in Kansas," pp. 272–78.

30. Independent Order of Good Templars, Grand Lodge of Kansas, *Proceedings of the Annual Session, 1860*, pp. 2, 3, 6–12, *1861*, p. 2, *1871*, p. 7, *1878*, pp. 11, 13, *1880*, p. 7, *1861–83;* Cora Dolbee, "The Fourth of July in Early Kansas (1858–1861)," *KHQ* 11 (1942): 133; *Herald of Freedom*, 1 Aug. 1857.

31. Good Templars, *Proceedings, 1868*, p. 16.

32. Ibid., *1874*, pp. 7, 16, 30, and *1876*, pp. 9, 20, 39; D. Leigh Colvin, *Prohibition in the United States: A History of the Prohibition Party and of the Prohibition Movement* (New York: George H. Doran Co., 1926), p. 90; James C. Malin, *A Concern about Humanity: Notes on Reform, 1872–1912 at the National and Kansas Levels of Thought* (Lawrence: James C. Malin, 1964), pp. 5–11; *Kansas Statesman*, Aug. 1948.

33. Platform of the Temperance party of Kansas, 1874, KSHS; O. Frederikson, "Liquor Question in Kansas," pp. 452–61; Francis, "Prohibition," pp. 694–96.

34. O. Frederickson, "Liquor Question in Kansas," pp. 212–13, 327–37, 372–73, 481–83; Emory Lindquist, "Religion in Kansas during the Era of the Civil War," *KHQ* 25 (1959): 314–23, and "Kansas: A Centennial Portrait," *KHQ* 27 (1961): 29–34; Holter, *Fire on the Prairie*, pp. 114–17.

35. William E. Berger, "A Kansas Revival of 1872," *KHQ* 23 (1957): 368, 372, 381.

36. Bordin, *Woman*, pp. 15–22, 36.

37. Ibid., pp. 26–30; *Topeka Commonwealth*, 28 Feb., 3, 10, 19, and 25 Mar., 1, 7, and 28 Apr. 1874; Wilder, *Annals*, pp. 635, 637; Jed Dannenbaum, *Drink and Disorder: Temperance Reform in Cincinnati from the Washingtonian Revival to the WCTU* (Urbana: University of Illinois Press, 1984), p. 214.

38. O. Frederikson, "Liquor Question in Kansas," pp. 406–9; *Topeka Commonwealth*, 3 Apr. 1874.

39. *Topeka Commonwealth*, 6, 7, 19, 20, and 27 Mar. 1874; O. Frederikson, "Liquor Question in Kansas," pp. 415–31; Stephen Z. Starr, *Jennison's Jayhawkers* (Baton Rouge: Louisiana State University Press, 1973), p. 27.

40. *Fort Scott Monitor*, 18, 20, 21, 25, 26, 27, 28, 29, and 31 Mar. 1874; *Topeka Commonwealth*, 21 and 31 Mar. and 8 Apr. 1874; O. Frederikson, "Liquor Question in Kansas," p. 402.

41. *Topeka Commonwealth*, 8 and 31 Mar. 1874.

42. Ibid., 25 Mar., 7 and 8 Apr. 1874; O. Frederikson, "Liquor Question in Kansas," pp. 387, 389–93; Anonymous ("Kansas"), "Temperance Crusades," two-page manuscript in Kansas WCTU Collection, KSHS, about 1874.

43. Ernest H. Cherrington, ed., *Standard Encyclopedia of the Alcohol Problem* (Westerville, Ohio: American Issue Publishing Co., 1925–30), pp. 359, 1838–40, 1854; James R. Turner, "The American Prohibition Movement, 1865–1897" (Ph.D. diss., University of Wisconsin, 1972), pp. 150–53.

44. *Topeka Commonwealth*, 24 and 31 Oct., 4, 8, 10, 17, 23, and 27 Nov., 1, 5, 7, and 18 Dec. 1877, 29 Jan., 9, 13, 19, 22, and 27 Feb., and 14 July 1878; *Manhattan Nationalist*, 8 Mar. 1878; O. Frederikson, "Liquor Question in Kansas," pp. 518–32; Miner, *Wichita*, pp. 128–29.

45. *Topeka Commonwealth*, 4 and 27 Nov., 1 and 7 Dec. 1877, and 13 Feb. 1878; O. Frederikson, "Liquor Question in Kansas," pp. 521, 529, 531; Wilder, *Annals*, p. 785; Andreas, *History*, p. 382.

46. *Topeka Commonwealth*, 11 Oct. and 4 Nov. 1877, 9, 14, and 19 Feb. 1878; O. Frederikson, "Liquor Question in Kansas," pp. 521–29, 538.

CHAPTER 3. THE AMENDMENT

1. *Manhattan Nationalist,* 10 and 24 May and 19 July 1878; *Topeka Commonwealth,* 1 and 2 Oct. 1879.

2. Edna T. Frederikson, "John P. St. John, the Father of Constitutional Prohibition" (Ph.D. diss., University of Kansas, 1931), pp. 9–30, 42; *Olathe Mirror and News Letter,* 4 May 1876; St. John scrapbooks, no. 14, p. 4, KSHS; Thomas A. McNeal, "The Governors of Kansas," *KHQ* 5 (1936): 75.

3. E. Frederikson, "John P. St. John," pp. 30, 39–47, 53–60.

4. Information relating to the 1878 nomination and the subsequent campaign was obtained chiefly from the *Manhattan Nationalist,* 8 Mar.–29 Nov.; *Kansas* (Troy) *Chief,* 6 June–28 Nov.; *Topeka Commonwealth,* 7 July–10 Nov.; and *Lawrence Daily Tribune,* 1 Aug.–31 Oct.; also *Topeka Commonwealth,* 1 Oct. 1878.

5. "Joshua Rollins Detwiler," biographical circular, vol. 1, KSHS; W. W. Graves, *History of Neosho County Newspapers* (St. Paul, Kans.: St. Paul Journal, 1938), p. 21; Grand Lodge of Kansas, Independent Order of Good Templars, *Proceedings of the Annual Session, 1877,* p. 28; *Temperance Banner,* 20 Aug. and 10 Sept. 1880; 1875 state census, Neosho County, vol. 43, p. 23.

6. J. R. Detwiler, *Prohibition in Kansas,* Kansas prohibition pamphlets, vol. 1, pp. 2–5, KSHS.

7. Good Templars, *Proceedings, 1878,* pp. 11, 20.

8. Ibid., p. 35.

9. Ibid., p. 26.

10. Ibid., pp. 13, 36, 45–46; Detwiler, *Prohibition,* p. 5.

11. *Temperance Banner,* Mar. and Apr. 1879; Detwiler, *Prohibition,* pp. 5–6; J. R. Detwiler to C. E. Faulkner, 17 Feb. 1879, KSHS; Petitions to legislature from Brown, Neosho, and Reno counties, KSHS.

12. Detwiler, *Prohibition,* p. 6; Noah C. McFarland, biographical scrapbook, KSHS.

13. Kansas, Senate, *Senate Journal, 1879* (Topeka: Kansas Publishing House, 1879), p. 33. For recent statements that exaggerate the importance of temperance as an issue in the 1878 campaign, the attractiveness of prohibition for the Republican party, and/or the role of St. John in the legislative passage of the amendment see Norman H. Clark, *Deliver Us from Evil: An Interpretation of American Prohibition* (New York: W. W. Norton, 1976), pp. 73–74, 90; Kenneth S. Davis, *Kansas: A Bicentennial History* (New York: W. W. Norton, 1976), pp. 144–45; Mark Edward Lender, *Dictionary of American Temperance Biography* (Westport, Conn.: Greenwood Press, 1984), p. 430; Don W. Wilson, *Governor Charles Robinson of Kansas* (Lawrence: University Press of Kansas, 1975), pp. 115–17.

14. Otto F. Frederikson, "The Liquor Question in Kansas before Constitutional Prohibition" (Ph.D. diss., University of Kansas, 1931), pp. 581, 585, 590, 602; Clara Francis, "Prohibition in Kansas," in *History of Kansas: State and People,* ed. William E. Connelley (Chicago: American Historical Society, Inc., 1928), vol. 2, p. 701.

15. Kansas, *Senate Journal, 1879,* pp. 88, 94, 266, 348, 390, 405, 407; O. Frederikson, "Liquor Question in Kansas," pp. 585–90, 595, 598–602; Grant W. Harrington, "The Genesis of Prohibition," *KHC* 15 (1923): 228–31.

16. Kansas, *Senate Journal, 1879,* pp. 312, 357, 415; Harrington, "Genesis," p. 229.

17. Kansas, *Senate Journal, 1879,* pp. 415–16; Detwiler, *Prohibition,* p. 7; Harrington, "Genesis," p. 229; O. Frederikson, "Liquor Question in Kansas," p. 596.

18. Kansas, *House Journal, 1879* (Topeka: Kansas Publishing House, 1879), pp. 998–99; Detwiler, *Prohibition*, p. 8; O. Frederikson, "Liquor Question in Kansas," p. 604; *Topeka Commonwealth*, 6 Mar. 1879.

19. Frances Willard, *Woman and Temperance* (Hartford, Conn.: Park Publishing Co., 1883), p. 397; Peter H. Odegard, *Pressure Politics: The Story of the Anti-Saloon League* (New York: Columbia University Press, 1928), p. 114.

20. Harrington, "Genesis," p. 230; Winfred H. Scheib, "The Bride Who Changed History," *Kanhistique*, Feb. 1984, p. 3; Robert W. Richmond, *Kansas: A Land of Contrasts* (St. Charles, Mo.: Forum Press, 1974), p. 169; *Our Messenger*, Mar. 1919; *KCS*, 10 Dec. 1932.

21. Kansas, *House Journal, 1879*, pp. 998–99; *Frankfort Index*, 23 Jan. 1907; *Topeka Commonwealth*, 6 Mar. 1879; O. Frederikson, "Liquor Question in Kansas," pp. 606–8; *KCS*, 24 Oct. 1915; *American Issue* (Kansas ed.), 9 Mar. 1919.

22. In the 3 × 2 test, chi-square is 13.83, df = 2, P < .005. Kansas, *House Journal, 1879*, pp. 998–1000; Daniel W. Wilder, *The Annals of Kansas, 1541–1885* (Topeka: T. Dwight Thacher, Kansas Publishing House, 1886), pp. 840–42.

23. Clark, *Deliver Us*, p. 73; Kansas Census, 1870–1880; U.S., Department of the Interior, *Population of the United States of the Tenth Census (1880)* (Washington, D.C.: Government Printing Office, 1883), pp. 174–84; Carroll D. Clark and Roy L. Roberts, *People of Kansas: A Demographic and Sociological Study* (Topeka: Kansas State Planning Board, 1936), p. 96.

24. D. Leigh Colvin, *Prohibition in the United States: A History of the Prohibition Party and of the Prohibition Movement* (New York: George H. Doran Co., 1926), pp. 39, 101, 103–6, 120; Mark Edward Lender and James Kirby Martin, *Drinking in America: A History* (New York: Free Press, 1982), p. 111.

25. Colvin, *Prohibition*, pp. 25, 137; Ernest H. Cherrington, *The Evolution of Prohibition in the United States of America* (Westerville, Ohio: American Issue Press, 1920), pp. 136, 154.

26. *Temperance Palladium*, 23 Sept. and 4 Nov. 1880; *Topeka Commonwealth*, 1 and 2 Oct. 1879; O. Frederikson, "Liquor Question in Kansas," pp. 633–36; *KCT*, 21 Aug. 1940.

27. *Temperance Palladium*, 2 Sept. 1880; O. Frederikson, "Liquor Question in Kansas," p. 635.

28. *Temperance Palladium*, 20 Nov. 1879 and 4 Nov. 1880; *TC*, 26 Dec. 1926 and 8 Nov. 1983; *TSJ*, 25 and 27 Dec. 1926.

29. *Temperance Palladium*, 16 and 23 Sept. 1880; *Kansas State Journal*, 28 Sept. 1880.

30. Kansas WCTU, *Minutes of the Annual Meeting, 1889*, p. 102; Agnes D. Hays, *The White Ribbon in the Sunflower State* (Topeka: Woman's Christian Temperance Union of Kansas, 1953), pp. 9–10; Susan Metzner Kraft, "Drusilla Wilson: A Friend of Temperance," ms. in KSHS, pp. 1, 5, 12 (see also Kraft, "Drusilla Wilson: A Friend of Temperance," *Heritage of the Great Plains* 13 [Fall 1980]: 11–23); Kansas WCTU, *Minutes, 1882*, p. 11.

31. Kraft, "Drusilla Wilson," pp. 2, 13, 15, 33; Anonymous, *A Brief Sketch of the Lives of Jonathan and Drusilla Wilson* (Plainfield, Ind.: Publishing Association of Friends, 1909), pp. 35–41; *Temperance Palladium*, 2 and 9 Sept. 1880; *KCT*, 24 Aug. 1948.

32. Kraft, "Drusilla Wilson," pp. 2, 17, 20, 23, 24; *Temperance Palladium*, 24 June and 26 Aug. 1880.

33. *Temperance Palladium*, 13 May 1880; *Lawrence Journal*, 7 May 1880.

34. Good Templars, *Proceedings, 1880*, pp. 7, 33.

35. Ibid., pp. 1–10; *Temperance Palladium,* 5 Feb. 1880; J. R. Detwiler, *Constitutional Prohibition of the Liquor Traffic* and *Objections to Constitutional Prohibition of the Liquor Traffic,* both in Kansas prohibition pamphlets, vol. 1, KSHS.
36. *TC,* 1 Mar. 1914; Edward T. James, ed., *Notable American Women, 1607–1950* (Cambridge, Mass.: Belknap Press of Harvard University Press, 1971), vol. 3, p. 652; Ernest H. Cherrington, ed., *Standard Encyclopedia of the Alcohol Problem* (Westerville, Ohio: American Issue Publishing Co., 1925–30), p. 2811; O. Frederikson, "Liquor Question in Kansas," pp. 646–47.
37. Lender and Martin, *Drinking,* pp. 99–109; Clark, *Deliver Us,* pp. 56–57; Hal D. Sears, *The Sex Radicals: Free Love in High Victorian America* (Lawrence: Regents Press of Kansas, 1977), pp. 46–47, 53, 67; Ruth Bordin, *Woman And Temperance* (Philadelphia: Temple University Press, 1981), p. 6.
38. *Topeka Commonwealth,* 24 Jan. 1880; *Atchison Champion,* 1 June 1880; *Temperance Palladium,* 4 Dec. 1879.
39. *Kansas State Journal,* 16 Feb. 1880; *Temperance Palladium,* 29 July 1880 and 19 Feb. 1881; Detwiler, *Objections,* p. 15; O. Frederikson, "Liquor Question in Kansas," pp. 670–71.
40. *Temperance Palladium,* 30 Sept. 1880; *Leavenworth Times,* 2 and 4 Sept. and 6 Nov. 1880.
41. Wilson, *Governor Charles Robinson,* pp. 117–18, 121, 150, 163; O. Frederikson, "Liquor Question in Kansas," pp. 199, 364, 672–73, 684–85; Sears, *Sex Radicals,* p. 44.
42. *Topeka Commonwealth,* 4 June 1880; O. Frederikson, "Liquor Question in Kansas," pp. 673, 680.
43. *Lawrence Journal,* 9 and 18 May 1880; *Topeka Commonwealth,* 9 Nov. 1979, 30 June, 3 and 10 July 1880; *Temperance Palladium,* 8 July 1880.
44. James C. McGinnis, *Prohibition,* Kansas prohibition pamphlets, vol. 1, KSHS, p. 37; Wilson, *Governor Charles Robinson,* pp. 118, 121.
45. Francis, "Prohibition," p. 710; Detwiler, *Constitutional Prohibition,* p. 26; *Topeka Commonwealth,* 1 Mar. 1874 and 9 Nov. 1879; O. Frederikson, "Liquor Question in Kansas," p. 199; *Temperance Palladium,* 27 May 1880.
46. "To the Voters of Kansas," one-page flyer circulated on election eve, Kansas prohibition pamphlets, vol. 1, KSHS; Detwiler, *Constitutional Prohibition,* p. 1; Detwiler, *Objections,* pp. 1–16; *Ford County Globe,* 24 Feb. 1880; *Wichita Weekly Beacon,* 4 Aug., 8 and 29 Sept., 6, 13, 20, and 27 Oct. 1880.
47. Ian R. Tyrrell, *Sobering Up: From Temperance to Prohibition in Antebellum America, 1800–1860* (Westport, Conn.: Greenwood Press, 1979), pp. 263, 280.
48. *Temperance Banner,* 31 Jan., 10 July, and 17 Sept. 1880; *Temperance Palladium,* 27 Nov. 1879 and 23 Sept. 1880; platforms of the Republican, Democratic, and Greenback-Labor parties, 1880; E. Frederikson, "John P. St. John," pp. 106, 108; O. Frederikson, "Liquor Question in Kansas," p. 676.
49. *Temperance Banner,* 13 Mar. 1880; *Lawrence Journal,* 15 and 19 Aug. 1879; *Kansas State Journal,* 16 Jan. 1880; E. Frederikson, "John P. St. John," pp. 100–102, 105.
50. *Kansas State Journal,* 19 and 20 Jan., 31 Aug., and 2 Sept. 1880; E. Frederikson, "John P. St. John," pp. 88, 105, 111–13.
51. *The Nationalist,* Kansas prohibition pamphlets, vol. 2, KSHS; Hill P. Wilson, *Eminent Men of Kansas* (Topeka: Hall Lithographing Co., 1901), p. 97; *Manhattan Nationalist,* 5 Mar., 27 May, 12 Aug., and 16 Sept. 1880; *Lawrence Journal,* 26 Aug. 1879.

52. *Temperance Palladium*, 22 Jan., 17 June, and 28 Oct. 1880; *Temperance Banner*, 26 June 1880; O. Frederikson, "Liquor Question in Kansas," pp. 657-60.

53. O. Frederikson, "Liquor Question in Kansas," pp. 660-66, 700.

54. *Temperance Banner*, 24 Apr., 8 May, and 27 Aug. 1880; *Temperance Palladium*, 22 Apr. and 16 Sept. 1880.

55. *Temperance Banner*, 24 Apr. and 8 May 1880; O. Frederikson, "Liquor Question in Kansas," p. 699.

56. *Temperance Banner*, 24 Sept. 1880; O. Frederikson, "Liquor Question in Kansas," p. 710.

57. *Temperance Palladium*, 23 Sept. 1880; *Temperance Banner*, 24 Sept. 1880.

58. *Temperance Palladium*, 29 July, 28 Oct., and 4 Nov. 1880.

59. Davis, *Kansas*, p. 144. For other recent but undocumented statements on the "powerful" state WCTU see Joanna L. Stratton, *Pioneer Women* (New York: Simon & Schuster, 1981), pp. 254-55; and Arthur M. Schlesinger, Jr., "Introduction," in Stratton, *Pioneer Women*, p. 14.

60. KCTU, *Minutes, 1899*, pp. 71-72; *Temperance Palladium*, 2 and 9 Sept. 1880; *Lawrence Journal*, 26 Aug. 1879; F. G. Adams and W. H. Carruth, *Woman Suffrage in Kansas* (Topeka: Geo. W. Crane Publ. Co., 1888), p. 8; *Our Messenger*, July 1906.

61. *Temperance Palladium*, 23 Sept. 1880; O. Frederikson, "Liquor Question in Kansas," p. 711.

62. Wilder, *Annals*, pp. 931-32; *Temperance Palladium*, 27 May and 28 Oct. 1880.

63. Of the approximately 266,000 eligible voters, 76 percent voted in the election, 66 percent voted on the amendment, and 35 percent voted for the amendment. Political affinity was measured by the vote for secretary of state. The evangelicals included principally Methodists, Presbyterians, Congregationalists, Disciples, and Baptists; the liturgicals included Catholics, Episcopalians, and Lutherans (undifferentiated in 1880 state religious census). Department of Interior, *Population of the United States, Tenth Census, 1880* (Washington, D.C.: Government Printing Office, 1883), pp. 174-84; Secretary of State, *Third Biennial Report* (Topeka: Kansas Publishing House, 1882), pp. 1-5, 7-8, 30-31, 80-81; State Board of Agriculture, *Second Biennial Report* (Topeka: Kansas Publishing House, 1881), pp. 369-72 (source for religious data).

64. Wilder, *Annals*, pp. 902-7, 931-32; *Topeka Commonwealth*, 21 Aug. 1884. The correlation coefficient is +0.11 and is not significant at the .05 confidence level. The proportion of those who voted on the amendment (88 percent) was well above average for constitutional amendments. It was the second-highest percentage among the twelve amendments that voters had approved since 1861 and a much greater total vote than for any prior amendment.

CHAPTER 4. THE AUSPICIOUS EIGHTIES

1. Kansas, *Senate Journal, 1884* (Topeka: State Printer, 1881), pp. 42-43.

2. Thomas A. Lee, "Alfred Washburn Benson," *KHC* 14 (1918): 6, 13; Kansas Judiciary clippings, vol. 1, p. 211, KSHS.

3. Kansas, *House Journal, 1881* (Topeka: State Printer, 1881), pp. 594, 602, 604; Kansas Attorney General, *Report for 1881-82*, p. 67; *TC*, 19 Feb. 1881; Robert M. Wright, *Dodge City: The Cowboy Capital* (Wichita: n.p., 1913), pp. 235-37.

4. *Kansas State Journal*, 19 Feb. 1881; *TC*, 19 and 24 Feb. 1881; *Atchison Champion*, 27 June, 6 and 29 July 1882; *Osage County Chronicle*, 31 Aug. 1882; Edna T. Frederikson, "John P. St. John, the Father of Constitutional Prohibition" (Ph.D. diss., University of Kansas, 1931), pp. 130, 162; David E. Harrell, Jr., "Pardee Butler: Kansas Crusader," *KHQ* 34 (1968): 405-6.

282 NOTES TO PAGES 64-70

5. Kansas, Legislature, *Compiled Laws, 1881* (Topeka: George W. Crane & Co., 1881), pp. 386-88. The original law of 1881, which put the amendment into effect, is called the Benson Law, or Act, after its principal author, though it was rarely identified as such in the contemporary literature.

6. Kansas, *Compiled Laws, 1881*, pp. 386-88; S. O. Thacher, *Prohibition in Kansas*, Kansas prohibition pamphlets, vol. 3, KSHS, p. 16; *Kansas* v. *Fleming*, 32 Kansas 588.

7. "Intoxicating Liquor Cases," 25 Kansas 751.

8. Kansas, *Senate Journal, 1881*, p. 169; *Topeka Commonwealth*, 14 Apr. 1881; *TC*, 2 Mar. 1881.

9. *Ellis County Star*, 31 Mar. 1881; Thacher, *Prohibition*, p. 16.

10. A. T. Andreas, *History of the State of Kansas* (Chicago: A. T. Andreas, 1883), p. 291; *Atchison Champion*, 1 Aug. 1882; Zelma E. McIlvain, "Governor Glick (Kansas) and Prohibition, 1883-1884" (Master's thesis, University of Kansas, 1931), pp. 25, 36; John P. St. John to M. E. Shiel, 18 Sept. 1882, KSHS.

11. Department of the Interior, *Population of the United States at the Tenth Census (1880)* (Washington, D.C.: Government Printing Office, 1883), pp. 60-61, 174-85; Department of Commerce and Labor, *Thirteenth Census of the United States: 1910* (Washington, D.C.: Government Printing Office, 1913), pp. 588-90; *Kansas City Journal*, 1 Sept. 1881; John P. St. John to J. O. Brayman, 13 July 1881, KSHS; J. K. Hudson, ed., *Prohibition in Kansas* (Topeka: Topeka Daily Capital, 1881), pp. 27-31.

12. *Topeka Commonwealth*, 2 July 1881; McIlvain, "Governor Glick," p. 86; Mark Edward Lender, *Dictionary of American Temperance Biography* (Westport, Conn.: Greenwood Press, 1984), pp. 444-45.

13. *Topeka Commonwealth*, 8 July 1881; *Leavenworth Standard*, 26 July 1881; *Abilene Gazette*, 16 Dec. 1881; E. Frederikson, "John P. St. John," pp. 154-55, 160-61.

14. Kansas prohibition clippings, vol. 2, p. 140, KSHS; Atchison County clippings, vol. 2, p. 305, KSHS.

15. *Topeka Commonwealth*, 19 July 1881; E. Frederikson, "John P. St. John," p. 145; *TC*, 21 July 1881; Hudson, *Prohibition*, p. 32.

16. McIlvain, "Governor Glick," p. 76; *TC*, 21 June 1881, 28 and 31 Mar. 1883; *Topeka Commonwealth*, 10 July 1881.

17. Kansas scrapbook, biography, W, vol. 4, Joseph C. Wilson, KSHS; *TC*, 28 and 31 Mar. 1882; *Topeka Commonwealth*, 24 and 26 Aug. 1882 and 6 Dec. 1883.

18. *Kansas* v. *City of Topeka*, 30 Kansas 653, 31 Kansas 459; *Kansas* v. *Wilson*, 30 Kansas 661; *Temperance Palladium*, 8 July 1880; Kansas prohibition clippings, vol. 11, p. 139, KSHS.

19. *Atchison Globe*, 22 Mar. 1884; James L. King, *History of Shawnee County, Kansas* (Chicago: Richmond & Arnold, 1905), pp. 168-71.

20. Nell B. Waldron, "Colonization in Kansas from 1861 to 1890" (Ph.D. diss., Northwestern University, 1933), p. 89; Eleanor L. Turk, "The German Newspapers of Kansas," *KH* 6 (1983): 54; David A. Haury, "German-Russian Immigrants to Kansas and American Politics," *KH* 3 (1980): 227-37; Carroll D. Clark and Roy L. Roberts, *People of Kansas: A Demographic and Sociological Study* (Topeka: Kansas State Planning Board, 1936), p. 210.

21. *Leavenworth Standard*, 3 Aug. 1881; *Atchison Champion*, 2 Aug. 1881; *Topeka Commonwealth*, 16 and 23 July 1881; *TC*, 30 Mar. 1882.

22. *Atchison Champion*, 9 and 11 Mar. 1881 and 21 Jan. 1882.

23. Turk, "German Newspapers," p. 59.

24. Margaret Hill McCarter, "The Measure of a State," *KHC* 10 (1908): 163; Emory Lindquist, *Smoky Valley People: A History of Lindsborg, Kansas* (Lindsborg, Kans.: Bethany College, 1953), pp. 80–81; Waldron, "Colonization," pp. 33, 118.

25. Jacob C. Ruppenthal, "The German Element in Central Kansas," *KHC* 13 (1915): 517.

26. "Prohibitory Amendment Cases," 24 Kansas 499; "Intoxicating Liquor Cases," 25 Kansas 751; Kansas Attorney General, *Report for 1881-82*, pp. 87–91, *Report for 1883-84*, pp. 94–100, *Report for 1885-86*, pp. 151–56, *Report for 1887-88*, pp. 135–39, *Report for 1889-90*, pp. 3–8; McIlvain, "Governor Glick," pp. 45, 64.

27. *State v. Foster*, 32 Kansas 14; *Foster v. Kansas*, 112 U.S. 201; Kansas Attorney General, *Report for 1883-84*, p. 45.

28. *Kansas v. Mugler*, 28 Kansas 181; *Mugler v. Kansas, Kansas v. Ziebold and Hagelin*, 123 U.S. 623, 662; S. B. Bradford, *Prohibition in Kansas and the Kansas Prohibitory Law* (Topeka: Geo. W. Crane Publ. Co., 1889), pp. 11–12; James C. Malin, "Mugler v. Kansas and the Presidential Campaign of 1884," *Mississippi Valley Historical Review* 34 (1947): 274–77.

29. James C. Malin, *Power and Change in Society with Special Reference to Kansas, 1880-1890* (Lawrence: Coronado Press, 1981), pp. 185–87; E. Frederikson, "John P. St. John," pp. 90, 169–71.

30. E. Frederikson, "John P. St. John," pp. 166–67, 179, 200–201, 220–23; *TC*, 10 Aug., 5 Nov., and 1 Dec. 1882; Republican party clippings, vol. 1, pp. 309, 317, KSHS; Shawnee County clippings, vol. 5, pp. 450–54.

31. *TC*, 10 Aug. and 7 Nov. 1882; E. Frederikson, "John P. St. John," pp. 55, 199–201; Malin, *Power and Change*, p. 203; I. O. Pickering, "The Administrations of John P. St. John," *KHC* 9 (1906): 378–94.

32. 1882 Republican Platform; 1882 Democrat Platform; *Wellington Democrat*, 16 Sept. 1882; *TC*, 11 Aug. 1882; Malin, *Power and Change*, pp. 197, 200; E. Frederikson, "John P. St. John," pp. 172, 191.

33. John P. St. John to Frances Willard, 20 Dec. 1881, KSHS; E. Frederikson, "John P. St. John," pp. 183–85, 194, 203.

34. *TC*, 14 and 25 Oct. 1882; E. Frederikson, "John P. St. John," pp. 195–96, 203.

35. Bradford, *Prohibition*, p. 19; Malin, "Mugler," pp. 276–77; David Dary, *Lawrence: Douglas County, Kansas* (Lawrence: Allen Books, 1982), pp. 189–90.

36. John Walruff to L. W. Clay, 22 May 1882, facsimile copy, KSHS.

37. *TC*, 17 Oct. 1882; *Topeka Commonwealth*, 12 Nov. 1881; E. Frederikson, "John P. St. John," pp. 173–74.

38. *Atchison Weekly Champion*, 16 Dec. 1882; *TC*, 1 Dec. 1882; Homer E. Socolofsky, "Kansas," in *Biographical Directory of the Governors of the United States, 1789-1978*, ed. Robert Sobel and John Raimo (Westport, Conn.: Meckler Books, 1979), p. 469; E. Frederikson, "John P. St. John," pp. 208–10; McIlvain, "Governor Glick," p. 23.

39. E. Frederikson, "John P. St. John," p. 211; *Manhattan Nationalist*, 10 Nov. 1882; *TC*, 1 Dec. 1882.

40. McIlvain, "Governor Glick," p. 22; *Topeka Commonwealth*, 11 Jan. 1883; *TC*, 20 Sept. 1883.

41. James Humphrey, "The Administration of George W. Glick," *KHC* 9 (1906): 398; McIlvain, "Governor Glick," pp. 17, 26.

42. Kansas prohibition clippings, vol. 2, pp. 126, 238, KSHS; Humphrey, "Governor Glick," p. 396; *Topeka Commonwealth*, 21 and 23 Aug. 1884.

43. McIlvain, "Governor Glick," p. 23; *TC*, 12 July 1883.

44. McIlvain, "Governor Glick," pp. 101, 102, 115; *Topeka Commonwealth*, 5 Aug. 1884.

45. McIlvain, "Governor Glick," pp. 112-13, 117, 121; Socolofsky, "Kansas," p. 470; *Topeka Daily Journal*, 2 July 1884; *TC*, 2 July 1884.

46. E. Frederikson, "John P. St. John," pp. 234-46, 262; D. Leigh Colvin, *Prohibition in the United States: A History of the Prohibition Party and of the Prohibition Movement* (New York: George H. Doran Co., 1926), pp. 99, 114, 130; St. John scrapbooks, no. 12, p. 3, KSHS.

47. E. Frederikson, "John P. St. John," pp. 250, 254, 258, 261, 263.

48. St. John scrapbooks, nos. 5 and 14 especially, KSHS; Pickering, "Administrations of St. John," p. 393; E. Frederikson, "John P. St. John," pp. 264-69.

49. Walter Young to P. H. Coney, 20 Nov. 1884, Coney Collection, KSHS; John P. St. John scrapbooks, nos. 5, 12, and 14, KSHS; John J. Ingalls, "The Future Relation of the Republican Party to Prohibition in Kansas," *Agora Magazine* 1 (1892): 120; *Topeka Daily Journal*, 7 Nov. 1884; *TC*, 7 and 8 Nov. 1884; *Osage City Free Press*, 13 Nov. 1884; *KCS*, 6 Nov. 1884; Daniel W. Wilder, *The Annals of Kansas, 1541-1885* (Topeka: T. Dwight Thacher, Kansas Publishing House, 1886), p. 1084.

50. *Topeka Daily Journal*, 2 July 1884; *TC*, 20 Nov. 1884; *Topeka Commonwealth*, 20 Nov. 1884; E. Frederikson, "John P. St. John," pp. 240, 262, 271; Wilder, *Annals*, p. 1113.

51. Kansas, *House Journal, 1885* (Topeka: State Printer, 1885), p. 204.

52. Kansas, Legislature, *Session Laws, 1887* (Topeka: State Printer, 1887), p. 255; St. John scrapbooks, no. 8; James P. Jones, *"Black Jack": John A. Logan and Southern Illinois in the Civil War Era* (Tallahassee: Florida State University, 1967), pp. 12, 15, 18-20; N. Dwight Harris, *The History of Negro Servitude in Illinois* (Chicago: A. C. McClurg & Co., 1904), pp. 234-38; E. Frederikson, "John P. St. John," pp. 21-22, 272; Pickering, "Administrations of St. John," pp. 393-94. St. John's name remains on the Kansas map as the seat of Stafford County.

53. Ernest H. Cherrington, ed., *Standard Encyclopedia of the Alcohol Problem* (Westerville, Ohio: American Issue Publishing Co., 1925-30), p. 1852; Terry H. Harmon, "Charles Sumner Gleed: A Western Business Leader, 1856-1920" (Ph.D. diss., University of Kansas, 1973), pp. 151-54; roster of delegates to the Chicago convention, 16 Sept. 1886, Republican State Central Committee, KSHS; *Topeka Commonwealth*, 25 July and 14 Nov. 1886; *TC*, 1 Aug. 1886.

54. Albert Griffin, *An Earnest Appeal* (Topeka: A. Griffin, 1901), pp. 5-6, 23; Wilson, *Eminent Men*, p. 97.

55. James C. Malin, "Was Governor John A. Martin a Prohibitionist?" *KHQ* 1 (1932): 63-73; Socolofsky, "Kansas," p. 470.

56. *Manhattan Nationalist*, 24 Jan. 1884; Atchison County clippings, vol. 2, p. 300, KSHS; *Topeka Daily Journal*, 2 July 1884; *TC*, 16 May 1884.

57. Thomas A. McNeal, "The Governors of Kansas," *KHQ* 5 (1936): 76; Malin, "Was Governor Martin a Prohibitionist?" p. 71; Socolofsky, "Kansas," p. 470; Kansas prohibition clippings, vol. 12, p. 1, KSHS.

58. Malin, *Power and Change*, p. 229; Kansas, *Session Laws, 1887*, chap. 100, p. 142, chap. 166, p. 245, chap. 167, p. 248.

59. Kansas, *Session Laws, 1885*, chap. 169, p. 273, and *Session Laws, 1887*, chap. 165, p. 234, chap. 230, p. 324.

60. Kansas, *Compiled Laws, 1885*, chap. 77a, p. 590, *Session Laws, 1885*, chap. 149, p. 236, and *Session Laws, 1887*, chap. 165, p. 233, chap. 174, p. 256.

61. Bradford, *Prohibition*, p. 4.

62. Wright, *Dodge City*, pp. 143, 148.

63. Robert R. Dykstra, *The Cattle Towns* (New York: Alfred A. Knopf, 1968), pp. 279–80; Nyle H. Miller and Joseph W. Snell, "Some Notes on Kansas Cowtown Police Officers and Gunfighters," *KHQ* 27 (1961): 440–42, and *Great Gunfighters of the Kansas Cowtowns, 1867–1886* (Lincoln: University of Nebraska Press, 1967), pp. 303–8; *Topeka Commonwealth*, 6 Aug. 1885; *TC*, 4 July and 28 Oct. 1885.

64. *TC*, 11 July 1885; Dykstra, *Cattle Towns*, pp. 283–84; Miller and Snell, "Some Notes," p. 442.

65. Attorney General, *Report for 1885–86*, pp. 24–25, *Report for 1887–88*, pp. 10–12, 16–17; *Kansas v. City of Leavenworth*, 36 Kansas 314; Lucian Baker to L. B. Kellogg, 21 Mar. 1889, attorney general's correspondence, KSHS; Bradford, *Prohibition*, pp. 11–16; *Topeka Commonwealth*, 10 Nov. 1886; *TC*, 17 July 1890; Kansas prohibition clippings, vol. 12, p. 1, KSHS.

66. J. L. Abernathy to L. B. Kellogg, 4 Apr. 1889; H. Miles Moore to L. B. Kellogg, 2 Mar. 1889; Lucian Baker to L. B. Kellogg, 21 Mar. 1889—all in attorney general's correspondence, KSHS; S. B. Bradford, *Official Letters Giving Facts and Figures on the Enforcement of the Prohibitory Law*, pamphlet, University of Kansas.

67. C. L. Dutcher to Governor Humphrey, 8 Mar. 1899; F. M. Morgan to L. B. Kellogg, 21 June 1899—both in attorney general's correspondence, KSHS.

68. W. H. Day to L. B. Kellogg, 24 June 1889, attorney general's correspondence, KSHS.

69. Elda A. Jones and Elizabeth Hendricks to L. B. Kellogg, 7 Mar. 1889, attorney general's correspondence, KSHS.

70. Kansas, *House Journal, 1885*, p. 147; James C. McGinnis, *Prohibition*, Kansas prohibition pamphlets, vol. 1, p. 34, KSHS; *North Topeka Mail*, 22 May 1884.

71. Kansas, *Session Laws, 1885*, pp. 237–39, and *Session Laws, 1887*, pp. 236–40; *TC*, 3 Apr. 1885; Sarah E. Williams, "The Use of Beverage Alcohol as Medicine, 1790–1860," *Journal of Studies on Alcohol* 41 (1980): 549–51, 562–63.

72. *Temperance Banner*, 30 July 1880; Kansas Attorney General, *Report for 1885–86*, p. 25; Kansas, *Compiled Laws, 1885*, pp. 590–93, and *Session Laws, 1887*, pp. 256–61; *TC*, 12 Apr. 1885.

73. Kansas WCTU, *Minutes of the 1886 Annual Meeting*, p. 49; Kansas Attorney General, *Report for 1885–86*, p. 26; and Kansas, *Session Laws, 1887*, p. 239.

74. Griffin, *Earnest Appeal*, pp. 12–13; Kansas prohibition clippings, vol. 2, p. 95, KSHS; *TC*, 17 May 1885.

75. Larry Jochims, "Medicine in Kansas, 1850–1900," pt. 2, *Emporia State Research Studies* 30 (1981): 14–15; Kirke Mechem, ed., *The Annals of Kansas, 1886–1925*, vol. 1 (Topeka: KSHS, 1954), p. 14.

76. *Kanhistique*, Feb. 1982, p. 11.

77. Kansas Attorney General, *Report for 1887–88*, p. 12; Jochims, "Medicine," pt. 1, p. 56.

78. *KCS*, 2 Feb. 1901; *Topeka Commonwealth*, 9 Oct. 1877 and 9 Feb. 1878; Jochims, "Medicine," pt. 1, pp. 14–15, pt. 2, pp. 46–57; Williams, "Use of Beverage Alcohol," p. 558; American Academy of Pediatrics, Committee on Drugs, "The Transfer of Drugs and Other Chemicals into Human Breast Milk," *Pediatrics* 72 (1983): 376.

79. Bradford, *Prohibition*, pp. 24, 27–29; Kansas Attorney General, *Report for 1887–88*, p. 9; E. Frederikson, "John P. St. John," pp. 141, 149–52; James A. Troutman, *Prohibition in Kansas* (1883), KSTU pamphlets, vol. 1, KSHS; Bradford, *Official Letters*, pp. 1–8; Kansas prohibition clippings, vol. 12, p. 1; G. H. Prentice, *Constitutional Prohibition: The Best Remedy*, Kansas prohibition pamphlets, vol. 1, p. 20, KSHS; *TC*, 3 Aug. 1886; United States, Commissioner of Internal Revenue, *Annual*

Report, 1889 (Washington, D.C.: Government Printing Office, 1889), pp. 12, 33, 44, 366–69; *Kearney* (Nebraska) *Enterprise,* 16 Oct. 1889.
   80. Kansas Attorney General, *Report for 1889–90,* pp. 36–54.
   81. Harmon, "Charles Sumner Gleed," p. 155; Bradford, *Prohibition,* p. 26; *TC,* 14 Apr. 1889; James A. Troutman, *Prohibition in Kansas: Facts Not Opinions* (Topeka: KSTU, 1890), pp. 7–8.
   82. Bradford, *Prohibition,* p. 24; J. R. Detwiler, *Prohibition in Kansas,* Kansas prohibition pamphlets, vol. 1, p. 19, KSHS; Prentice, *Constitutional Prohibition,* p. 45.
   83. Prentice, *Constitutional Prohibition,* p. 37; Bradford, *Prohibition,* pp. 30–34; *TC,* 3 Aug. 1886; *Troy Chief,* 3 Jan. 1889; *Garden City Sentinel,* 1 Jan. 1888.

CHAPTER 5. FOR GOD AND HOME AND NATIVE LAND

   1. National WCTU, *Minutes of the 1874 Annual Meeting,* pp. 3, 5, 6; Ruth Bordin, *Woman and Temperance* (Philadelphia: Temple University Press, 1981), pp. 5–13, 36–42, 165–73; Janet Z. Giele, "Social Change in the Feminine Role: A Comparison of Woman's Suffrage and Woman's Temperance, 1870–1920" (Ph.D. diss., Radcliffe College, 1961), pp. 26, 32; Barbara L. Epstein, *The Politics of Domesticity: Women, Evangelism and Temperance in Nineteenth-Century America* (Middletown, Conn.: Wesleyan University Press, 1981), pp. 2, 9, 116.
   2. Mrs. H. C. Fields to Frances Willard, 1 June 1880, National WCTU correspondence, 1880–82, roll 12 (microfilm); National WCTU, *Minutes, 1875,* p. 48, *1876,* p. 94, *1887,* pp. 134, 192, 194, *1878,* pp. 78, 116; Kansas WCTU, *Minutes, 1882,* pp. 11–12; Agnes D. Hays, *The White Ribbon in the Sunflower State* (Topeka: Woman's Christian Temperance Union of Kansas, 1953), p. 16; *Kansas Commoner,* 18 Oct. 1884; *Our Messenger,* July 1906.
   3. National WCTU, *Minutes, 1879,* p. 52, *1880,* pp. 103, 125.
   4. Mrs. H. C. Fields to D. Shelton, 13 May 1880, National WCTU correspondence, 1880–82, roll 12 (microfilm).
   5. National WCTU, *Minutes, 1883,* p. 88; Kansas WCTU, *Minutes, 1881,* pp. 8–14; *Topeka Commonwealth,* 1 Nov. 1885.
   6. Kansas WCTU, *Minutes, 1882,* pp. 11–12; *Kansas Commoner,* 18 Oct. 1884; National WCTU, *Minutes, 1881,* p. 95.
   7. *Topeka Commonwealth,* 23 and 26 Sept. 1885; *TC,* 24 Sept. 1885; *Kansas Commoner,* 18 Oct. 1884; Kansas WCTU, *Minutes, 1884,* pp. 32–33, *1889,* p. 57.
   8. *TC,* 26 Sept. 1885, 3 Oct. 1886, 30 and 31 Oct. and 3 Nov. 1888; *Topeka Commonwealth,* 26 Sept. 1885; *Our Messenger,* Oct. 1895; Kansas WCTU, *Minutes, 1889,* p. 57, *1891,* pp. 38–39, *1902,* p. 46; Giele, "Social Change," p. 92.
   9. Kansas WCTU, *Minutes, 1889,* p. 103; *Temperance Palladium,* 20 Nov. 1879 and 2 Sept. 1880.
   10. Kansas WCTU, *Minutes, 1899,* pp. 71–72; *TC,* 30 Sept. 1883; Giele, "Social Change," pp. 103, 106; Epstein, *Politics of Domesticity,* p. 74.
   11. *TC,* 25 Sept. 1885; *Temperance Palladium,* 29 Jan. and 26 Feb. 1880; National WCTU, *Minutes, 1885,* p. 104; Kansas WCTU, *Minutes, 1889,* p. 104; Hays, *White Ribbon,* p. 109.
   12. *Leader,* 5 Sept. 1889; D. C. Milner to G. W. Martin, 17 Feb. 1898; G. W. Martin collection, KSHS; John P. St. John speech, 27 Jan. 1882, Kansas prohibition pamphlets, vol. 1, KSHS; *Kansas State Journal,* 12 Jan. 1880; Epstein, *Politics of Domesticity,* p. 110; Kansas prohibition clippings, vol. 11, pp. 211–15.
   13. Kansas WCTU, *Minutes, 1901,* p. 29; Hays, *White Ribbon,* p. 103.

14. Zelma E. McIlvain, "Governor Glick (Kansas) and Prohibition, 1883–1884" (Master's thesis, University of Kansas, 1931), p. 115.

15. *Topeka Commonwealth*, 26 Sept. 1885; *Our Messenger*, Feb. 1887 and Nov. 1899; Hays, *White Ribbon*, p. 75; Kansas WCTU, *Minutes, 1884*, p. 35; *TC*, 30 Mar. 1924.

16. Kansas WCTU, *Minutes, 1884*, p. 35, and *1889*, p. 56.

17. National WCTU, *Minutes, 1883*, p. 88; Kansas WCTU, *Minutes, 1882*, p. 8, *1889*, p. 104, and *1890*, p. 1; *Our Messenger*, Nov. 1891; Hays, *White Ribbon*, p. 99.

18. Prohibition party clippings, vol. 1, pp. 27–34, KSHS; Kansas WCTU, *Minutes, 1886*, pp. 43–46; *TC*, 29 Sept. and 14 Oct. 1888; *Topeka Commonwealth*, 14 Oct. 1888.

19. Kansas WCTU clippings, vol. 1, p. 211a; *TC*, 3 Oct. 1886; *Topeka Commonwealth*, 24 Sept. 1885; *Our Messenger*, Sept. 1887; National WCTU, *Minutes, 1886*, p. 100.

20. *New York Times*, 8 Apr. 1889; *Our Messenger*, Apr., May, June 1887; Kansas, Legislature, *Session Laws, 1887* (Topeka: State Printer, 1887), pp. 233–34.

21. Kansas, *Session Laws, 1887*, p. 214, and *Session Laws, 1889*, p. 388; National WCTU, *Minutes, 1878*, p. 16, *1889*, p. xci; Kansas WCTU, *Minutes, 1902*, p. 47; *Our Messenger*, Dec. 1889.

22. National WCTU, *Minutes, 1889*, p. xci.

23. Hays, *White Ribbon*, p. 27.

24. Ibid., pp. 28–29; *Our Messenger*, Jan. 1888.

25. *Our Messenger*, Feb. 1888; Kansas WCTU, *Minutes, 1889*, p. 103; Hays, *White Ribbon*, pp. 29–30.

26. Kansas, *Session Laws, 1889*, pp. 226–31; Hays, *White Ribbon*, pp. 31–32; National WCTU, *Minutes, 1889*, p. xci.

27. National WCTU, *Minutes, 1885*, p. 4; Bordin, *Woman*, pp. 135–36; Norman H. Clark, *Deliver Us from Evil: An Interpretation of American Prohibition* (New York: W. W. Norton, 1976), pp. 85–86.

28. National WCTU, *Minutes, 1882*, p. 102, *1884*, p. 75, and *1885*, p. 23; Kansas WCTU, *Minutes, 1882*, p. 29, and *1884*, p. 62.

29. Kansas, *Session Laws, 1885*, p. 273; Kansas WCTU, *Minutes, 1884*, p. 62, and *1885*, pp. 84–86.

30. National WCTU, *Minutes, 1886*, pp. 100, ccxxiv; Kansas WCTU, *Minutes, 1889*, p. 49; *Our Messenger*, July 1891; Laura M. Johns, *An Appeal to Kansas Teachers* (Topeka: Kansas Publishing House, 1889), pp. 1–40; Hays, *White Ribbon*, p. 88.

31. Johns, *Appeal*, pp. 7–8; *Chronicle Monthly Magazine* 2 (Sept. 1894): 3–4; Frances E. Willard and Mary A. Livermore, *American Women* (New York: Mast, Crowell & Kirkpatrick, 1897), p. 420.

32. Hays, *White Ribbon*, p. 88; Bordin, *Woman*, p. 137.

33. National WCTU, *Minutes, 1903*, p. 211; Kansas WCTU, *Minutes, 1885*, p. 91, *1903*, pp. 88–89; *TC*, 14 Aug. 1890; *Our Messenger*, July 1891, Oct. 1892, and June 1902; Clark, *Deliver Us*, p. 86; Clyde L. King, "The Kansas School System—Its History and Tendencies," *KHC* 11 (1910): 453.

34. Bordin, *Woman*, pp. 118–23.

35. Ibid., pp. 118–19; *Temperance Palladium*, 9 Sept. 1880; *Our Messenger*, Dec. 1890; F. G. Adams and W. H. Carruth, *Woman Suffrage in Kansas* (Topeka: Geo. W. Crane Publ. Co., 1888), p. 8; Elizabeth C. Stanton, Susan B. Anthony, and Matilda J. Gage, eds., *History of Woman Suffrage* (Rochester, N.Y.: Susan B. Anthony, 1887), vol. 3, pp. 696–711.

36. Kansas WCTU, *Minutes, 1882*, pp. 26, 29; *Kansas Commoner*, 25 Oct. 1884; *TC*, 3 Oct. 1886. In the early 1890s a Hutchinson suffragist, Henrietta Briggs-Wall,

commissioned local artist W. A. Ford to render a painting that echoed the 1882 WCTU concern of being politically classed with "lunatics, paupers, criminals and Chinese." Entitled *American Woman and Her Political Peers,* the painting depicted the wise and sensitive face of Frances Willard, surrounded by an "Indian, madman, convict, and idiot." The work attracted a great deal of national attention when it was exhibited in Chicago in 1893 at the World's Columbian Exposition. Reproduced on cards, it became a major propaganda piece for the suffragists in the ensuing years. The original is in the KSHS. James R. Kratsas, Mary Ellen Nottage, and John Zwierzyna, "Samples of Our Heritage," *KH* 7 (1984): 94.

37. Adams and Carruth, *Woman Suffrage,* pp. 8-9; Willard and Livermore, *American Women,* p. 420; Kansas WCTU, *Minutes, 1886,* p. 46, and *1887,* p. 30; Giele, "Social Change," p. 84; *Our Messenger,* May 1901; Stanton et al., *History of Woman Suffrage,* vol. 4, pp. 649-51.

38. Adams and Carruth, *Woman Suffrage,* pp. 46-49.

39. Ibid., pp. 13-14; Hays, *White Ribbon,* p. 15.

40. National WCTU, *Minutes, 1888,* p. 37; Adams and Carruth, *Woman Suffrage,* p. 13.

41. Adams and Carruth, *Woman Suffrage,* pp. 12, 50; Kansas, *Session Laws, 1887,* p. 324.

42. *Our Messenger,* Dec. 1887 and Apr. 1888; National WCTU, *Minutes, 1887,* pp. 76-77; Adams and Carruth, *Woman Suffrage,* p. 28 and passim.

43. National WCTU, *Minutes, 1887,* p. 77; Monroe Billington, "Susanna Madora Salter—First Woman Mayor," *KHQ* 21 (1955): 173-83; Karen M. Heady, "On Trial for their Sex," *Kanhistique* 9 (Dec. 1983): 10-11, 13; National WCTU, *Minutes, 1887,* p. 77; Stanton et al., *History of Woman Suffrage,* vol. 4, p. 658.

44. Adams and Carruth, *Woman Suffrage,* pp. 17-18, 45; Kansas WCTU, *Minutes, 1887,* p. 30; Billington, "Susanna Madora Salter," p. 181; Stanton et al., *History of Woman Suffrage,* vol. 4, pp. 662-63.

CHAPTER 6. THE WET NINETIES

1. *Leisy* v. *Hardin,* 135 U.S. 100; D. Leigh Colvin, *Prohibition in the United States: A History of the Prohibition Party and of the Prohibition Movement* (New York: George H. Doran Co., 1926), pp. 531-36; Kansas Attorney General, *Report for 1889-90,* p. 54.

2. *TC,* 15 May 1890 and 12 Aug. 1905; Kansas Attorney General, *Report for 1889-90,* pp. 57-58; Kirke Mechem, ed., *Annals of Kansas, 1886-1925* (Topeka: KSHS, 1954), vol. 1, pp. 105-6.

3. *TC,* 8 and 16 May, 21 June, and 17 July 1890; Mechem, *Annals,* vol. 1, p. 110; Kansas Attorney General, *Report for 1889-90,* p. 58.

4. *TC,* 19 June, 17 and 20 July 1890.

5. *TC,* 9, 16, and 29 May, 15 June, and 17 July 1890; *Leavenworth Times,* 23 May 1890; D. O. McCray, "The Administrations of Lyman U. Humphrey," *KHC* 9 (1906): 423-24; Kansas Attorney General, *Report for 1889-90,* pp. 58-60, 62, 64.

6. *In re Rahrer,* 140 U.S. 545; *TC,* 12 Jan., 7 Aug., and 18 Oct. 1890, and 26 May 1891; McCray, "Administrations of Humphrey," pp. 423-24; Kansas Attorney General, *Report for 1889-90,* pp. 64-65; George Templar, "The Federal Judiciary of Kansas," *KHQ* 37 (1971): 4-5.

7. Peter H. Argersinger, *Populism and Politics: William Alfred Peffer and the Peoples Party* (Lexington: University Press of Kentucky, 1974), p. 42, and "Road to a Republican Waterloo: The Farmers' Alliance and the Election of 1890 in Kansas," *KHQ*

33 (1967): 444; Jack S. Blocker, Jr., "The Politics of Reform: Populists, Prohibition, and Woman Suffrage, 1891-1892," *Historian* 34 (1972): 620; O. Gene Clanton, *Kansas Populism: Ideas and Men* (Lawrence: University Press of Kansas, 1969), p. 100; Robert W. Richmond, *Kansas: A Land of Contrasts* (St. Charles, Mo.: Forum Press, 1974), pp. 174-75; *Leader,* 11 Oct. 1888.

8. Argersinger, *Populism,* pp. 39, 73, 161-62, and "Road," p. 460; Clanton, *Kansas Populism,* pp. 95, 100-101, 153-63, 166, 168, 210; Walter T. K. Nugent, *The Tolerant Populists: Kansas Populism and Nativism* (Chicago: University of Chicago Press, 1963), pp. 46-47, 161-62, 219, 222, and "How the Populists Lost in 1894," *KHQ* 31 (1965): 245-55.

9. Colvin, *Prohibition,* pp. 144-45, 187, 202, 211; James R. Turner, "The American Prohibition Movement, 1865-1897" (Ph.D. diss., University of Wisconsin, 1972), pp. 245, 249, 256-57, 262, 313-14, 326-29, 356-65, 376; Ernest H. Cherrington, *The Evolution of Prohibition in the United States of America* (Westerville, Ohio: American Issue Press, 1920), pp. 176, 180-81; Mark Edward Lender and James Kirby Martin, *Drinking in America: A History* (New York: Free Press, 1982), pp. 111-12.

10. For example, see *Public Opinion* 8 (1889): 108, 165-66, 260-61; *St. Louis Globe-Democrat,* 10 Dec. 1889; *KCT,* 25, 26, and 27 June 1889; *TC,* 24 Mar. and 14 Apr. 1889 and 9 May 1890; G. H. Prentice, *Constitutional Prohibition: The Best Remedy,* Kansas prohibition pamphlets, vol. 1, p. 37, KSHS; Turner, "American Prohibition," pp. 246, 361; Lender and Martin, *Drinking,* p. 111.

11. Charles S. Gleed, "Prohibition and Booms," *Public Opinion* 8 (11 Jan. 1890): 332.

12. Kansas, State Board of Agriculture, *Annual (and Biennial) Reports* (Topeka: State Printer), for *1874,* pp. 250-51, *1875,* pp. 309-12, *1876,* pp. 227-29, *1878,* pp. 396-99, *1880,* pp. 369-72, *1882,* p. 557, *1884,* p. 506, *1886,* p. 112, *1888,* pp. 9-536, *1890,* p. 127, and *1895,* p. 231; United States, Department of the Interior, *Statistics of Churches in the United States, 1890* (Washington, D.C.: Government Printing Office, 1894), pp. 38-43; United States, Bureau of the Census, *Religious Bodies* (Washington, D.C.: Government Printing Office), *1906,* pp. 194-98, 226-30, *1916,* pp. 263-66, 285-87, *1926,* pp. 180-83, 210-14, and *1936,* pp. 212-15, 244-47. The evangelical-pietistical denominations include principally Methodists, Baptists, Presbyterians, Congregationalists, Disciples of Christ, Scandinavian Lutherans, United Brethren, and Friends, plus several small pentecostal groups. The liturgicals include chiefly Roman Catholics, German Lutherans, and Episcopalians and also the much-smaller Eastern Orthodox, Unitarian, Universalist, Spiritualist, Theosophical, and Jewish groups. The dichotomy is based solely on perceived attitudes of the groups toward legislation restricting the consumption of alcoholic beverages—that is, prohibition—not on their theologies.

13. *KCT,* 25, 26, and 27 June and 13 Dec. 1889; *TC,* 11 Aug. 1889, 7 and 12 Mar. 1890.

14. Kansas Republican Resubmission League, *Looking Forward: or Kansas Redeemed* (n.p., 1890), p. 8; Daniel W. Wilder, *The Annals of Kansas, 1541-1885* (Topeka: T. Dwight Thacher, Kansas Publishing House, 1886), pp. 1073-76.

15. Kansas Republican Resubmission League, *Looking Forward,* pp. 6, 8; *TC,* 16 Mar. 1890; Kansas prohibition clippings, vol. 12, p. 3; *TC,* 6 Aug. 1891.

16. Kansas Republican Resubmission League, *Looking Forward,* p. 6; Republican Resubmission Club, *Prosperity and How to Obtain It* (n.p., 1890), pp. 30, 32.

17. *TC,* 30 Mar. and 29 May 1890; *Kingman Leader-Courier,* 29 May 1890; Mechem, *Annals,* vol. 1, p. 105; McCray, "Administrations of Humphrey," pp. 424-25; Charles Willsie, *The Eye-Opener: or the Evil Fruits of the Prohibitory Law in Kansas*

(Wellington, Kans.: C. Willsie, 1890), p. 37; Governor Humphrey, correspondence received, prohibition 1889-92, KSHS.

18. McCray, "Administrations of Humphrey," p. 426; *TC*, 31 Jan. 1892; William F. Zornow, *Kansas: A History of the Jayhawk State* (Norman: University of Oklahoma Press, 1957), p. 199.

19. W. P. Harrington, "The Populist Party in Kansas," *KHC* 16 (1925): 413a.

20. H. B. Schaeffer to J. N. Ives, 10 Nov. 1891, correspondence, attorney general, J. N. Ives, KSHS; Kansas Attorney General, *Report for 1891-92*, p. 31.

21. J. N. Ives to H. B. Schaeffer, 9 Nov. 1891, letterpress books, attorneys general, J. N. Ives, p. 420, KSHS; Schaeffer to Ives, 10 Nov. 1891; C. F. Foley to Ives, 24 Mar. 1891.

22. S. F. White to Ives, 3 June 1891; L. W. DeGreer to Ives, 11 Dec. 1891; A. D. Gilkeson to Ives, 11 and 19 Dec. 1891; *Kanhistique*, Apr. 1985, p. 8.

23. *TC*, 13 Sept. 1894; B. S. Henderson to Ives, 17 Nov. 1891; Ives to Henderson, 8 Oct. 1891, p. 299; Kansas Attorney General, *Report for 1891-92*, p. 36.

24. Ives to Henderson, 15 Oct. (p. 344) and 13 Nov. (p. 445) 1891.

25. Kansas Attorney General, *Report for 1891-92*, pp. 26-31.

26. Ives to A. R. Hill, 20 July 1891, p. 339; D. White to Ives, 7 Mar. 1891; Ives to D. White, 28 Mar. 1891, p. 433.

27. Kansas Attorney General, *Report for 1891-92*, p. 34.

28. Burton J. Williams, *Senator John James Ingalls* (Lawrence: University Press of Kansas, 1972), pp. 1, 4-5, 10, 21-22, 31-32, 122-23, 154.

29. Williams, *Senator Ingalls*, pp. 64-65, 154; Mechem, *Annals*, vol. 1, p. 41; *Leader*, 5 Sept. 1889; *KCT*, 3 July 1883; James C. Malin, *Power and Change in Society with Special Reference to Kansas, 1880-1890* (Lawrence: Coronado Press, 1981), p. 203.

30. John J. Ingalls, "Prohibition and License," *Forum* 7 (1889): 678, 682.

31. John J. Ingalls, "The Future Relation of the Republican Party to Prohibition in Kansas," *Agora Magazine* 1 (1892): 119.

32. *Public Opinion*, 8:260; *Leader*, 5 Sept. 1889; Ingalls to the Rev. W. C. Wheeler, 7 July 1895, Ingalls collection, KSHS; John J. Ingalls, "Kansas—1541-1891," *Harper's Magazine*, Apr. 1893, pp. 708-9; *St. Louis Globe-Democrat*, 10 Dec. 1889; Kansas prohibition clippings, vol. 5, p. 198a, and vol. 10, p. 276.

33. Kansas prohibition clippings, vol. 5, p. 198a.

34. Don W. Holter, *Fire on the Prairie: Methodism in the History of Kansas* (n.p.: Editorial Board of Kansas Methodist History, 1969), p. 121; Republican party platforms, KSHS; *American Issue* (Kansas ed.), May 1898.

35. Kansas Attorney General, *Report for 1895-96*, p. 12; *TC*, 27 July 1894.

36. Anti-Morrill flyer (Oct. 1896), Kansas prohibition pamphlets, vol. 1, KSHS; *American Issue* (Kansas ed.), May 1898; *Junction City Tribune*, 28 Apr. 1892; *Kansas City Gazette*, 2 Jan. 1892; *KCS*, 5 Aug. 1894; *TC*, 31 May 1891; *TSJ*, 21 Dec. 1897; National WCTU, *Minutes of the 1897 Annual Meeting*, p. 192.

37. *TC*, 4 Aug. 1893; *TSJ*, 30 Mar. 1891; *Our Messenger*, Apr. 1891; *Christian Herald*, 4 Jan. 1930.

38. *Issue*, July 1899 and Oct. 1900; M. N. Butler, *The Kansas Klondike and the Leavenworth Inferno* (n.p.: M. N. Butler, 1899), pp. 2, 21; Kansas, Legislature, *Session Laws of 1891* (Topeka: State Printer, 1891), pp. 221-22; *Our Messenger*, Dec. 1900; *TSJ*, 9 June 1899; J. G. Rowland to W. E. Stanley, 6 June 1899, Stanley gubernatorial papers, KSHS.

39. Kansas, Legislature, *General Statutes of 1901*, pp. 521-22; Mechem, *Annals*, vol. 1, pp. 64, 197, 288; *TC*, 16 Aug. 1893; Otto F. Frederikson, "The Liquor Question

in Kansas before Constitutional Prohibition'' (Ph.D. diss., University of Kansas, 1931), pp. 501–5.

40. *TC,* 2, 5, 11, 13, and 19 Aug. 1893; Clad Hamilton, "A Colonel of Kansas," *KHC* 12 (1912): 290; Shawnee County clippings, vol. 21, p. 276; W. L. Hamilton, "The Stag at Eve," *Bulletin of the Shawnee County Historical Society,* no. 40 (Dec. 1963): 49–53.

41. Mechem, *Annals,* vol. 1, pp. 103, 125, 176, 191, 280, 284; Kansas prohibition clippings, vol. 6, p. 21, KSHS.

42. Mechem, *Annals,* vol. 1, p. 118; *Our Messenger,* Apr. 1893; Anti-Morrill flyer (Oct. 1896), Kansas prohibition pamphlets, vol. 1, KSHS; *Topeka Commonwealth,* 18 Aug. 1887; *TC,* 26 Mar. 1889.

43. Kansas, *House Journal, 1897* (Topeka: State Printer, 1897), pp. 297, 571–72, 826; *Our Messenger,* Mar. 1895; Mechem, *Annals,* vol. 1, p. 190.

44. National WCTU, *Minutes, 1892,* p. 224; Kansas WCTU, *Minutes, 1892,* pp. 41–42; *Our Messenger,* Oct. 1892; *TC,* 12 and 18 Nov. 1892.

45. Kansas WCTU, *Minutes, 1893,* pp. 37–38, and *1894,* pp. 39–41; *Our Messenger,* Oct. 1893–Oct. 1894; Wilda M. Smith, "A Half Century of Struggle: Gaining Woman Suffrage in Kansas," *KH* 4 (1981): 83; Susan B. Anthony and Ida H. Harper, eds., *The History of Woman Suffrage* (Rochester, N.Y.: Susan B. Anthony, 1902), pp. 642–47.

46. *TC,* 1 Dec. 1892; Kansas Secretary of State, *Kansas Directory, 1977* (Topeka: Secretary of State, 1977), p. 65.

47. Clanton, *Kansas Populism,* p. 210.

48. *Temperance Banner,* Mar. 1879; *TSJ,* 16 Apr. 1896; Homer E. Socolofsky, "Kansas," in *Biographical Directory of the Governors of the United States, 1789–1978,* ed. Robert Sobel and John Raimo (Westport, Conn.: Meckler Books, 1979), p. 474.

49. *Our Messenger,* Jan. 1896; *TSJ,* 16 Apr. 1896; *TC,* 5 July 1895; *Kansas Temperance Monitor,* 17 Apr. 1896; *Kansas Issue,* July 1900; *Marion Record,* 3 Jan. 1896; Clanton, *Kansas Populism,* p. 190.

50. Kansas Attorney General, *Report for 1887–88,* p. 16; Kansas, *Session Laws, 1887,* pp. 142–49, and *1889,* pp. 267–74; Clanton, *Kansas Populism,* pp. 139, 190, 210, 215, 297; Argersinger, *Populism,* pp. 161–62, 282.

51. Kansas, *Session Laws, 1887,* p. 143; T. E. Stephens, *Prohibition in Kansas* (Topeka: Kansas Farmer Co., 1902), p. 115.

52. McCray, "Administrations of Humphrey," pp. 422–23; *TSJ,* 16 Sept. 1891.

53. *TC,* 31 May 1887; Mechem, *Annals,* vol. 1, pp. 56, 142.

54. *TC,* 13 Nov. 1889; Mechem, *Annals,* vol. 1, p. 112; Kansas, *House Journal, 1891,* p. 1060.

55. Kansas, *House Journal, 1891,* pp. 1051–54; *KCT,* 25, 26, and 27 June 1889; Atchison County clippings, vol. 2, p. 175, KSHS.

56. Kansas, *House Journal, 1891,* pp. 1052–54.

57. Ibid., pp. 1050–63; *TSJ,* 16 Sept. 1891.

58. Kansas, *House Journal, 1891,* p. 1061, and *Special Session Laws, 1898,* pp. 22–23; *Ottawa Journal and Triumph,* 20 Sept. 1894; John P. St. John to G. W. Martin, 19 June 1898, G. W. Martin collection, KSHS; *TSJ,* 2 Feb. 1898; *TC,* 8 and 9 Feb. 1899; *Advocate and News* (Topeka), 9 Feb. 1898.

59. Butler, *Kansas Klondike,* p. 19.

60. *Our Messenger,* Aug. 1895 and Feb. 1896; Stephens, *Prohibition,* pp. 32, 199.

61. Ernest H. Cherrington, ed., *Standard Encyclopedia of the Alcohol Problem* (Westerville, Ohio: American Issue Publishing Co., 1925–30), pp. 1684, 2341; Mark

Edward Lender, *Dictionary of American Temperance Biography* (Westport, Conn.: Greenwood Press, 1984), pp. 319–20, 429–30.

62. *Kansas Issue*, Mar. 1900; *TC*, 1 Dec. 1892.

63. *American Issue* (Kansas ed.), May 1898; *Kansas Issue*, Feb. 1900; *TSJ*, 2 Feb. 1898; *TC*, 30 Jan. 1901; *Advocate and News* (Topeka), 9 Feb. 1898.

64. *Kansas Issue*, Feb., Mar., May–June, and July 1900; *American Issue* (Kansas ed.), May 1898; Kansas WCTU, *Minutes, 1903*, pp. 4, 49–50; Stephens, *Prohibition*, pp. 32, 106–7; *TSJ*, 2 Feb. 1898 and 26 Feb. 1901; *TC*, 8 and 9 Feb. 1899.

65. J. E. Everett to E. K. Miller, 11 Dec. 1902, KSTU correspondence, 1898–1902, KSHS; Stephens, *Prohibition*, p. 76.

66. *Our Messenger*, Oct. 1896 and Oct. 1897; *TC*, 20 July 1895; Stephens, *Prohibition*, p. 32.

67. "Roster of City Workers and Receipts, 1899–1908," papers and records, KSTU, pp. 26–81, KSHS; *Kansas Issue*, July 1899.

68. "Roster," KSTU, pp. 30–35, 38–41, 44–45, 50–51, 56–57.

69. *Kansas Issue*, Aug.–Sept. 1903; W. J. Reese to T. E. Stephens, 21 Apr. 1901; J. W. Hooker to J. E. Everett, 31 May 1902, KSTU correspondence, 1898–1902, KSHS; "Roster," KSTU, pp. 126–39, 150–61.

70. E. T. Scott to J. E. Everett, 5 Dec. 1902, KSTU correspondence, 1898–1902, KSHS.

71. Scott to Everett, 4, 6, and 24 Nov. and 11 Dec. 1902.

72. Scott to Everett, 27 Nov. and 1 Dec. 1902.

CHAPTER 7. MRS. NATION

1. M. N. Butler, *The Kansas Klondike and the Leavenworth Inferno* (n.p.: M. N. Butler, 1899), p. 39.

2. Carry was evidently christened "Carry," but her family and she used "Carrie" until she began to attract public notice, about 1900. She was struck with the cosmic implications of "Carry A. Nation," so she used that form thereafter, although not always consistently. Carry A. Nation, *The Use and Need of the Life of Carry A. Nation* (Topeka: F. M. Steves & Sons, 1908), pp. 28, 31, 35–43, 129; Herbert Asbury, *Carry Nation* (New York: Alfred A. Knopf, 1929), pp. 3–6; Robert L. Taylor, *Vessel of Wrath: The Life and Times of Carry Nation* (New York: New American Library, 1966), pp. 28–36, 62; Carrie Nation scrapbook, p. 101, KSHS.

3. Nation, *Use and Need*, pp. 46–48, 61–82; Asbury, *Carry Nation*, pp. 12–17, 27–34, 37–44.

4. Taylor, *Vessel of Wrath*, p. 85; Nation, *Use and Need*, pp. 93–97, 100; Asbury, *Carry Nation*, pp. 54–55, 59; Carleton Beals, *Cyclone Carry* (New York: Chilton Co., 1962), pp. 79–87.

5. Nation, *Use and Need*, pp. 102–14, 126–36, 140–62, 172–74; Asbury, *Carry Nation*, pp. 64–91, 99–136; *Kiowa News*, 8 June 1900; *TC*, 22, 24, and 25 Jan. 1901; *TSJ*, 22 Jan. 1901; David Nation to A. A. Godard, 20 May 1900, Kansas Attorneys General, correspondence, KSHS.

6. *TC*, 24 and 27 Jan. 1901; *TSJ*, 26 Jan. 1901; *KCS*, 27 Jan. 1901.

7. *KCS*, 29 Jan. 1901.

8. Carrie A. Nation to *TSJ*, ca. 5 Jan. 1902, KSHS; Margaret Whittemore, *One-Way Ticket to Kansas* (Lawrence: University of Kansas Press, 1959), pp. 122–34.

9. John J. Ingalls, "The Future Relation of the Republican Party to Prohibition in Kansas," *Agora Magazine* 1 (1892): 118; *TC*, 13 Feb. 1901.

10. *TC*, 27 Jan. 1901; Asbury, *Carry Nation*, p. 87; E. A. Braniff, "How I Ran out on Carrie Nation," *Commonweal* 47 (19 Mar. 1948): 556.

11. *KCS*, 27 Jan. 1901.

12. Asbury, *Carry Nation*, p. 144; *KCS*, 27 Jan. 1901; *TC*, 27 Jan. 1901.

13. *Kansas Issue*, July 1901; Albert Griffin, *An Earnest Appeal* (Topeka: A. Griffin, 1901), p. 15; *KCS*, 29 Dec. 1900.

14. *TSJ*, 28 Jan. 1901; *KCS*, 28 Jan. 1901; *TC*, 29 Jan. 1901.

15. *KCS*, 30 Jan. 1901.

16. Ibid., 29 Jan. 1901; *TC*, 29 and 30 Jan. 1901; Carrie Nation scrapbook, p. 37, KSHS.

17. *KCS*, 30 Jan. 1901; *TC*, 27 and 31 Jan. 1901.

18. *KCS*, 30 Jan. 1901.

19. Ibid.; Carrie Nation scrapbook, p. 96, KSHS; Braniff, "How I Ran Out," pp. 558-60; *Christian Herald*, 4, 11, and 18 Jan. 1930.

20. *KCS*, 31 Jan. 1901.

21. Ibid.

22. Ibid.; Braniff, "How I Ran Out," p. 558.

23. *KCS*, 2 and 3 Feb. 1901.

24. *TC*, 5 and 6 Feb. 1901; *TSJ*, 5 and 6 Feb. 1901.

25. *TC*, 6 and 9 Feb. 1901; *KCS*, 6 Feb. 1901.

26. *TC*, 8 and 9 Feb. 1901.

27. *Leslie's Illustrated Weekly*, vol. 120 (19 Aug. 1915): 177; *National Cyclopedia of American Biography*, vol. 21 (1913): 110.

28. The Reverend F. W. Emerson, "The Preacher and His Church in Politics," Ministerial Union Series, KSHS; Kansas biographical scrapbook, E, vol. 2-3, pp. 216-23, KSHS.

29. *TC*, 23 Dec. 1913.

30. *Kansas Issue*, Mar. 1902; *TC*, 19 Feb. 1901.

31. Charles M. Sheldon, *Charles M. Sheldon: His Life Story* (New York: George H. Doran Co., 1925), pp. ix-xi.

32. Sheldon, *Charles M. Sheldon*, pp. 245-46; *TC*, 10 and 11 Feb. 1901; *Christian Herald*, 4, 11, and 18 Jan. 1930.

33. *KCS*, 11 Feb. 1901; *Fulcrum*, 15 Feb. 1901.

34. *TSJ*, 11 Feb. 1901; *TC*, 19 Feb. 1901.

35. *TSJ*, 13, 15, and 16 Feb. 1901.

36. *TC*, 17 Feb. 1901; *KCS*, 18 Feb. 1901.

37. *TC*, 17 Feb. 1901; *KCS*, 18 Feb. 1901.

38. *KCS*, 25 Feb. 1901. For a detailed account of the Topeka period as seen by an eastern journalist see the *Utica* (N.Y.) *Globe*, 9, 16, 23, and 30 Mar. and 2 Apr. 1901, KSHS.

39. *KCS*, 17 Feb. 1901; *TC*, 31 Jan., 14 and 16 Feb. 1901; *TSJ*, 13 and 16 Feb. 1901; *Our Messenger*, Apr. 1901; Asbury, *Carry Nation*, pp. 202-8.

40. *Topeka Mail and Breeze*, 15 Feb. 1901; *TC*, 26 Jan. 1901; *TSJ*, 16 Feb. 1901.

41. *KCS*, 8 Feb. 1901; *TC*, 8 Feb. 1901.

42. Kansas, Legislature, *Session Laws, 1901* (Topeka: State Printer, 1901), pp. 416-22; *Our Messenger*, Mar. 1901; *TC*, 7, 14, and 21 Feb. 1901.

43. *TC*, 6 Feb. 1901; *TSJ*, 15 Feb. 1901.

44. *Our Messenger*, Mar. and Nov. 1901.

45. Kansas WCTU, *Minutes of the 1904 Annual Meeting*, pp. 47-48, 59-60, 73-76, and *1918*, pp. 18-21; *Our Messenger*, July and Oct. 1911.

46. *Fulcrum*, 1, 6, and 22 Feb. 1901; Jack S. Blocker, Jr., *Retreat from Reform: The Prohibition Movement in the United States, 1890-1913* (Westport, Conn.: Greenwood Press, 1976), pp. 136-38.

47. *TC*, 19 Feb. 1901.

48. *TSJ*, 23 Feb. 1901.

49. *Wichita Eagle*, 29 Dec. 1900; *TC*, 19 Feb. 1901.

50. *Kansas Issue*, May-June and July 1900, Apr. 1901, May 1902, July 1903, Mar. and May 1904.

51. *Emporia Gazette*, 28 Jan. and 11 Feb. 1901.

52. Alexius H. Baas to John Stewart, 14 Apr. 1901, miscellaneous collection, KSHS; *Our Messenger*, Mar. 1901.

53. Asbury, *Carry Nation*, pp. 221-307; *TSJ*, 10 June 1911; *Kansas Issue*, June 1911.

54. Asbury, *Carry Nation*, pp. 221-307; Taylor, *Vessel of Wrath*, pp. 311-61.

55. Asbury, *Carry Nation*, p. 247. For more-balanced recent treatments see Norman H. Clark, *Deliver Us from Evil: An Interpretation of American Prohibition* (New York: W. W. Norton, 1976), pp. 81-84; Blocker, *Retreat from Reform*, pp. 26-31; Edward Wagenknecht, *American Profile, 1900-1909* (Amherst: University of Massachusetts Press, 1982), pp. 179-87.

56. Nation, *Use and Need*, pp. 140, 167, 253.

57. *TSJ*, 13 Mar. 1901.

58. Dorothy J. Caldwell, "Carry Nation, a Missouri Woman, Won Fame in Kansas," *Missouri Historical Review* 63 (1969): 485; Agnes D. Hays, *The White Ribbon in the Sunflower State* (Topeka: Woman's Christian Temperance Union of Kansas, 1953), pp. 48-49, 83; *TC*, 27 Jan., 8 Feb., and 26 Mar. 1901.

59. *TC*, 15 Feb. 1901; Charles S. Gleed, "Law Enforcement in Kansas," *Outlook* 67 (30 Mar. 1901): 744.

60. Beals, *Cyclone Carry*, p. 344; *TC*, 27 Apr. 1901.

61. Beals, *Cyclone Carry*, p. 193.

62. *KCS*, 19 Feb. 1901; *TSJ*, 18 and 26 Feb. 1901.

CHAPTER 8. A GLORIOUS VICTORY

1. *TSJ*, 20, 24, and 25 Mar. 1902.

2. *TC*, 15 Feb. 1903; *TSJ*, 14 Feb. 1903; *KCS*, 18 Feb. 1903.

3. Harold C. Evans, "Custer's Last Fight," *Kansas Magazine*, 1938, pp. 72-74; Robert Taft, "The Pictorial Record of the Old West," pt. 4: "Custer's Last Stand—John Mulvany, Cassilly Adams and Otto Becker," *KHQ* 14 (1946): 384-85; *TSJ*, 9 and 11 Jan. 1904, 29 July 1905, and 14 Feb. 1940.

4. Myra W. McHenry, *John Marshall, a Dangerous Man and Should Be Exposed—What I Know about Him*, Kansas biographical pamphlets, vol. 8 (20 Feb. 1909), KSHS; Carrie Nation scrapbook, p. 153, KSHS; *TSJ*, 7 and 9 Feb. 1907; *Wichita Eagle*, 19 and 20 June 1939.

5. *Kansas Issue*, July 1905; Kirke Mechem, ed., *The Annals of Kansas, 1886-1925* (Topeka: KSHS, 1954), vol. 1, p. 422.

6. *State v. Stark*, 63 Kansas 529; *Coppedge et al. v. Goetz Brewing Co.*, 67 Kansas 851; S. S. Jackson to W. E. Stanley, 11 Feb. 1901, gubernatorial papers; J. K. Codding to E. C. Hadley, 20 Oct. 1908, Hadley papers, KSHS.

7. *Attention! Prohibition Voters of Kansas*, pamphlet of Kansas Prohibition party, 1904, KSHS; political party platforms, 1900-1904; *TC*, 19 Apr. 1901.

8. *TSJ*, 26 May 1902.

9. Michael J. Brodhead and O. Gene Clanton, "G. C. Clemens: The 'Sociable Socialist,'" *KHQ* 40 (1974): 480–83; *State* v. *City of Topeka*, 30 Kansas 653, 31 Kansas 452; *State* v. *Wilson*, 30 Kansas 661.

10. *Kansas Issue*, Oct. 1905; Brodhead and Clanton, "G. C. Clemens," p. 500.

11. Brodhead and Clanton, "G. C. Clemens," p. 500; Shawnee County clippings, vol. 21, p. 169.

12. *Kansas Issue*, May 1902 and Aug. 1905; *TC*, 7 Sept. 1905; *Topeka Herald*, 10 Dec. 1906.

13. *TC*, 7 Sept. 1905; Shawnee County clippings, vol. 21, p. 82; *Kansas Issue*, May 1905.

14. *TSJ*, 23 Sept. 1908; *TC*, 16 Oct. 1906.

15. Carrie Nation scrapbook, p. 18, KSHS; *New York Sun*, quoted in *TC*, 28 Jan. 1899.

16. Robert M. Crunden, *Ministers of Reform: The Progressive Achievement in American Civilization, 1889–1920* (New York: Basic Books, 1982), pp. ix–x, 276–78; Daniel T. Rogers, "In Search of Progressivism," *Reviews in American History* 10 (Dec. 1982): 113–32; James H. Timberlake, *Prohibition and the Progressive Movement, 1900–1920* (Cambridge: Harvard University Press, 1963), see especially pp. 2–10, 40–47; John C. Burnham, "New Perspectives on the Prohibition 'Experiment' of the 1920's," *Journal of Social History* 2 (1968): 53–55.

17. Charles E. Hill, "Progressive Legislation in Kansas," *KHC* 12 (1912): 69; Walter R. Stubbs, "'Mob Rule' in Kansas," *Saturday Evening Post*, 11 May 1912, p. 6; Robert S. La Forte, *Leaders of Reform: Progressive Republicans in Kansas, 1900–1916* (Lawrence: University Press of Kansas, 1974), passim.

18. *Kansas Issue*, Feb. 1905; *Marion Record*, 3 Jan. 1886; *TC*, 20 Mar. 1900; Michael J. Brodhead, "The Early Career of E. W. Hoch, 1870–1904" (Master's thesis, University of Kansas, 1962); La Forte, *Leaders*, pp. 35–45; Homer E. Socolofsky, "Kansas," in *Biographical Directory of the Governors of the United States, 1789–1978*, ed. Robert Sobel and John Raimo (Westport, Conn.: Meckler Books, 1979), pp. 478–79.

19. *Kansas Issue*, Oct. 1905; *TC*, 12 May 1906.

20. *Kansas Issue*, June and Aug. 1905.

21. C. R. Carpenter to E. W. Hoch, 27 Sept. 1905, Hoch gubernatorial papers; *KCS*, 5 May 1905; *TSJ*, 26 Apr. 1905.

22. Shawnee County clippings, vol. 21, p. 172; E. W. Hoch to F. G. Severance, 3 June 1908, Hoch gubernatorial papers; Kansas Attorney General, *Report for 1905–6*, p. 24; *Kansas City Journal*, 26 Feb. 1906; *Kansas Issue*, Mar. 1906; *TSJ*, 8 and 13 Feb. 1906; *TC*, 8 Mar. 1906.

23. *Kansas Scrap-Book*, biography, Ti–Ty, vol. 4, pp. 169, 209; *Assistant Attorney General Trickett's Address*, at KSTU convention, 5 Feb. 1907, Kansas prohibition pamphlets, vol. 3, KSHS; *Kansas Issue*, Dec. 1906.

24. C. W. Trickett, *The Cleansing of a Large City*, Kansas prohibition pamphlets, vol. 3, p. 6, KSHS; Trickett, *Address*, pp. 1–20; Kansas Attorney General, *Report for 1905–6*, pp. 23–24; *Topeka Herald*, 6 Feb. 1907.

25. *State* v. *Rose*, 74 Kansas 262 and 78 Kansas 601; Kansas Attorney General, *Report for 1905–6*, pp. 24–25; *TC*, 14 May 1905 and 3 Apr. 1907.

26. *State* v. *City of Pittsburg*, 77 Kansas 848 and 80 Kansas 710; *State* v. *Wilcox*, 78 Kansas 597; *State* v. *City of Coffeyville*, 78 Kansas 599; *State* v. *City of Wichita*, 96 Pacific 1118; *State* v. *Harsha*, 80 Kansas 93; *State* v. *City of Hutchinson*, 80 Kansas 795; Kansas Attorney General, *Report for 1907–8*, pp. 21–22, *Report for 1909–10*, p. viii; *Kansas Issue*, May 1906 and Apr. 1907; *TC*, 3 and 4 Apr. 1907.

27. *Kansas Issue*, Apr. and Dec. 1907; *TC*, 7 May 1907.

28. *State* v. *Anheuser-Busch*, 76 Kansas 184; *State* v. *Lemp*, 79 Kansas 705; Kansas Attorney General, *Report for 1907–8*, pp. 22–24.

29. Kansas Attorney General, *Report for 1907–8*, p. 28; T. E. Stephens, *Prohibition in Kansas* (Topeka: Kansas Farmer Co., 1902), p. 117; *Kansas Issue*, July 1907.

30. *Topeka Herald*, 13 Aug. 1904; *TC*, 13 Oct. 1906 and 20 July 1907; *Christian Herald*, 4 Jan. 1930.

31. *TC*, 2 June 1907; *TSJ*, 23 Sept. 1908; United States Commissioner of Internal Revenue, *Annual Reports for 1901 through 1909* (Washington, D.C.: Government Printing Office).

32. *Wichita Eagle*, 17 Feb. 1946; *TC*, 20 Dec. 1908; *Kansas Issue*, Dec. 1908.

33. Kansas Legislature, *Session Laws of 1909* (Topeka: State Printer, 1909), pp. 302–5; Kansas, *Senate Journal, 1909* (Topeka: State Printer, 1909), p. 10; Kansas Attorney General, *Report for 1907–8*, pp. 28–29; *Kansas Issue*, Nov. 1908.

34. G. W. Ogden, "Lifting the Curse from Kansas," *Hampton's Magazine* (Summer 1909): 371–80; J. K. Codding and E. W. Hoch, "Prohibition in Kansas," *Annals of the American Academy of Political and Social Science* 32 (Nov. 1908): 567–73; Stubbs, "Mob Rule," p. 6.

35. E. W. Hoch, "The Success of Prohibition in Kansas," *Annals of the American Academy of Political and Social Science* 32 (Nov. 1908): 575; Kansas, *Senate Journal, 1905*, p. 18.

36. *Kansas City Journal*, 25 May 1909; *KCS*, 16 May 1909.

37. *TC*, 20 May 1909.

38. *State* v. *Topeka Club*, 82 Kansas 756; *Kansas City Journal*, 1 July 1909; W. L. Hamilton, "The Stag at Eve," *Bulletin of the Shawnee County Historical Society*, no. 40 (Dec. 1963): 49–52; *Kansas Issue*, Jan. 1910; *TSJ*, 14 and 24 July 1909.

39. 82 Kansas 756; *TSJ*, 14 July 1909.

40. Kansas, *Session Laws, 1909*, pp. 302–5, and *1911*, pp. 250, 412–16.

41. W. C. Dills to W. R. Stubbs, 21 July 1911, Stubbs gubernatorial papers; prohibition files, Stubbs gubernatorial papers, passim; Kansas Attorney General, *Report for 1911–12*, pp. 18, 47; *TC*, 16 June, 18 July, and 15 Nov. 1911; *TSJ*, 15 June 1911.

42. W. I. Branin to E. W. Hoch, 25 Oct. 1907, Hoch gubernatorial papers; C. A. Calkins to W. R. Stubbs, 26 July 1909, Stubbs gubernatorial papers; anonymous to E. W. Hoch, 19 July 1906, Hoch gubernatorial papers; Kansas WCTU, *Minutes, 1911*, p. 54.

43. W. I. Branin to Hoch, 25 Oct. 1907; W. R. Stubbs to C. A. Calkins, 16 Aug. 1909, Stubbs gubernatorial papers; prohibition files, Stubbs gubernatorial papers, passim.

44. H. C. Ericcson to W. R. Stubbs, 18 Apr. 1911, Stubbs gubernatorial papers; prohibition files, Stubbs gubernatorial papers, passim.

45. Testimony of E. E. Sapp, 14 July 1911, pp. 2, 5, Stubbs gubernatorial papers.

46. *Kansas Issue*, Feb. 1911; Socolofsky, "Kansas," pp. 479–80; La Forte, *Leaders*, pp. 107–15.

47. *TC*, 21 July 1911; *KCS*, 20 Aug. 1911; *TSJ*, 4 Oct. 1911; Stubbs gubernatorial papers, June–July 1911.

48. Stubbs to Dawson, 1 July and 3 Oct. 1911, Dawson to Stubbs, 7 July, 2 and 4 Oct. 1911—all in Stubbs gubernatorial papers.

49. *State* v. *Dawson*, 86 Kansas 180, 181, 187.

50. Kansas WCTU, *Minutes, 1905*, p. 20, *1909*, p. 44, *1912*, p. 43, and *1913*, p. 26.

51. *Kansas Issue*, Nov. 1907 and Dec. 1910; Mary Sibbitt to A. D. Wilcox, 23 July 1901; KSTU papers and records, KSHS; *Our Messenger*, Oct. 1907.

52. *Our Messenger*, Nov. 1906, Sept. 1912, and Jan. 1913.

53. Kansas, *Session Laws, 1915*, p. 401; Kansas WCTU, *Minutes, 1906*, p. 31, and *1913*, pp. 65–66; *Our Messenger*, Dec. 1912, Mar. 1913, June 1914, Aug. 1915, Jan. and Aug. 1916.

54. Kansas WCTU, *Minutes, 1905*, p. 29, *1906*, p. 32, and *1916*, p. 49; *Our Messenger*, Mar. 1909 and Jan. 1916.

55. Kansas WCTU, *Minutes, 1906*, p. 31, *1909*, p. 46, *1911*, p. 76, and *1915*, p. 48.

56. *TC*, 10 Oct. 1917.

57. Ibid., 1 Mar. 1953; *KCT*, 22 May 1930; Agnes D. Hays, *The White Ribbon in the Sunflower State* (Topeka: Woman's Christian Temperance Union of Kansas, 1953), pp. 78–79; Kansas WCTU, *Minutes, 1914*, p. 18; *Our Messenger*, July 1914, Sept. 1915, May 1916, and Sept. 1931.

58. *TC*, 12 Oct. 1917.

59. Kansas WCTU, *Minutes, 1905*, p. 74, and *1911*, p. 73; Ida Husted Harper, ed., *The History of Woman Suffrage* (New York: National American Woman Suffrage Association, 1922), pp. 193–206.

60. *Our Messenger*, Sept. 1912; Minnie J. Grinstead to Lucy B. Johnston, 17 June 1911, Lucy P. Johnston papers, KSHS.

61. *Our Messenger*, Feb. 1911, Sept. 1912, and July 1918; Kansas WCTU, *Minutes, 1911*, pp. 86–87; Harper, *History of Woman Suffrage*, pp. 195–96, 205; Kansas, *Senate Journal, 1911*, p. 235.

62. Lucy B. Johnston to D. B. Mitchell, 14 May 1912, Johnston papers, KSHS; Kansas WCTU, *Minutes, 1911*, p. 75, and *1912*, pp. 113–15; *Our Messenger*, Aug. 1912; Martha B. Caldwell, "The Woman Suffrage Campaign of 1912," *KHQ* 12 (1943): 301; Harper, *History of Woman Suffrage*, pp. 197–201.

63. Lucy B. Johnston, "Report of Kansas Campaign for Political Liberty, 1911–12," pp. 2–3, 21 Nov. 1912, Johnston papers, KSHS; Wilda M. Smith, "A Half Century of Struggle: Gaining Woman Suffrage in Kansas," *KH* 4 (1981): 83–84, 86–87, 89.

64. Kansas, *Session Laws, 1927*, p. 556; *Kansas American*, 5 Aug. 1903; Harper, *History of Woman Suffrage*, p. 201.

65. Kansas WCTU, *Minutes, 1916*, pp. 59–60.

66. C. H. Matson, "How Prohibition Works in Kansas," *Outlook* 74 (22 Aug. 1903): 981–84; *TC*, 26 Apr. and 12 May 1906; T. A. McNeal, "Prohibition in Kansas," *Kansas Magazine* (1934): 20–23.

67. George H. Hodges to C. Sheldon, 20 Jan. 1914; Hodges to C. C. Butler, 20 Jan. 1913; Hodges to L. Mitchner, 2 June 1913; L. M. Mitchner to S. T. Seaton, 25 Mar. 1913—all in Hodges gubernatorial papers, KSHS; Socolofsky, "Kansas," pp. 480–81; Mark Edward Lender, *Dictionary of American Temperance Biography* (Westport, Conn.: Greenwood Press, 1984), pp. 231–32.

68. Governor's secretary to N. Arbuckle, 13 Aug. 1913; governor's secretary to J. H. Courtuer, 14 Nov. 1913; Hodges to G. W. Wadsworth, 21 Apr. 1913—all in Hodges gubernatorial papers, KSHS.

69. Executive clerk to C. L. Hatfield, 14 Sept. 1914; Hodges to E. C. Dinwiddie, 11 Sept. 1914; Hodges to B. F. Workman, 5 Dec. 1914; Hodges to C. M. Sheldon, 12 Jan. 1914—all in Hodges gubernatorial papers; 1914 state political party platforms.

70. E. W. Hoch to N. A. Porter, 19 Mar. 1908, Hoch gubernatorial papers, KSHS; *Kansas Issue*, Mar. 1911; *Our Messenger*, June 1914; *TSJ*, 18 Nov. 1913; *Collier's*, 27 June 1914.

71. O. C. Curtis to Arthur Capper, 15 Dec. 1915, Capper gubernatorial papers; *TC*, 20 July 1916; Norman H. Clark, *The Dry Years: Prohibition and Social Change in*

Washington (Seattle: University of Washington Press, 1965), p. 112; many items throughout the Hoch, Stubbs, Hodges, and Capper gubernatorial papers to and from out-of-state correspondents.

72. M. B. Platt to Hodges, 8 Sept. 1914, Hodges gubernatorial papers, KSHS; *TC*, 22 Dec. 1916; *Congressional Record*, 64th Cong., 2d sess., vol. 54, pt. 1, pp. 539, 541; Kansas, *Session Laws, 1915*, pp. 500–501.

73. *State* v. *Cairns*, 64 Kansas 782; Kansas, *Session Laws, 1885*, pp. 243–44; Kansas Attorney General, *Report for 1889–90*, p. 66.

74. *State* v. *Cairns*, 64 Kansas 788; *State* v. *Hickox*, 64 Kansas 650; *Delamater* v. *South Dakota*, 205 U.S. 93; *Kansas Issue*, Feb. 1910.

75. *Kansas Issue*, Dec. 1903, Mar. 1907, Dec. 1908, and June 1909.

76. *Congressional Record*, 64th Cong., 2d sess., vol. 54, pt. 1, p. 641; *Kansas City Journal*, 28 June 1909; *TC*, 11 June 1907, 16 June 1911, and 12 May 1916; *TSJ*, 24 Jan. and 11 May 1916; *Atchison Globe*, 25 Apr. 1916; *KCT*, 24 Jan. 1916.

77. A. Faulconer to W. R. Stubbs, 8 Dec. 1911; G. W. Wickersham to President W. H. Taft, 14 Apr. 1910; Stubbs to county attorneys and sheriffs, 31 Jan. 1912; Stubbs correspondence, 1909/10—all in Stubbs gubernatorial papers; *TC*, 25 Apr. 1916.

78. Stubbs to A. B. Moffat, 1 Mar. 1909, Stubbs gubernatorial papers; *Kansas Issue*, Oct. 1909.

79. Trego County attorney to Capper, 7 Dec. 1915; Ellsworth County attorney to Capper, 7 Dec. 1915; M. Schoonover to Capper, 11 Jan. 1916—all in Capper gubernatorial papers, KSHS; *TC*, 19 Dec. 1915.

80. Osage County attorney and Rush County attorney to Capper, 7 Dec. 1915, Capper gubernatorial papers; A. Faulconer to Stubbs, 8 Dec. 1911, Stubbs gubernatorial papers.

81. Trego County attorney and Stafford County attorney to Capper, 7 Dec. 1915, Capper gubernatorial papers.

82. *TC*, 20 Oct. 1915; J. Kovar to Stubbs, 12 Feb. 1910, Stubbs gubernatorial papers.

83. N. L. Bossing to Stubbs, 21 Aug. 1912, Stubbs gubernatorial papers.

84. S. E. Bear to Hodges, 9 Nov. 1914, Hodges gubernatorial papers.

85. Kansas, *Session Laws, 1913*, pp. 428–30.

86. Franklin County attorney to Capper, 8 Dec. 1915, Capper gubernatorial papers.

87. United States Commissioner of Internal Revenue, *Annual Reports for 1881 through 1919* (Washington, D.C.: Government Printing Office).

88. B. B. Reimer to Hodges, 31 Oct. 1913; W. J. Moore to Hodges, 27 Oct. 1913; F. M. Holcomb to Hodges, 28 Oct. 1913—all in Hodges gubernatorial papers; *TSJ*, 8 July and 23 Oct. 1913 and 14 Jan. 1916; *TC*, 4 Apr. 1915; *St. Louis Globe-Democrat*, 21 Mar. 1915; *Kansas Issue*, Apr. 1914. In the sources cited, importation was reported on a total-population basis. It has been adjusted to a drinking-age basis for comparative purposes in the text.

89. *TC*, 25 Mar. 1917; *KCS*, 25 Mar. 1917; *Wichita Eagle*, 25 Mar. 1917; *Kansas Issue*, Dec. 1916; *TC*, 22 Dec. 1916; *Congressional Record*, 64th Cong., 2d sess., vol. 54, pt. 1, p. 641; W. J. Rorabaugh, *The Alcoholic Republic: An American Tradition* (New York: Oxford University Press, 1979), pp. 232–33. The original Blackmar report has not been located; the results are known from newspaper accounts and the *Congressional Record*. Blackmar reported the data on a total-population basis.

90. County attorneys' responses to request for information from Governor Capper on 6 Dec. 1915; responses of Bourbon, Rush, and Wallace county attorneys, Capper gubernatorial papers.

91. Responses of Lane, Wallace, and Ness county attorneys, ibid.

92. *Rhodes* v. *Iowa,* 170 U.S. 412.

93. Purley A. Baker and S. E. Nicholson, *Inter-State vs. State Control of the Liquor Traffic* (n.p.: ASL of America, 1910), Kansas prohibition pamphlets, vol. 3, KSHS; *Our Messenger,* June 1910; *TC,* 28 Jan. 1913; *U.S. Statutes,* vol. 37, pt. 1, pp. 699–700.

94. Hodges to C. M. Sheldon, 12 Jan. 1914, Hodges gubernatorial papers; *Clark Distilling Co.* v. *Western Maryland Railway Co.,* 242 U.S. 311; *TSJ,* 9 Jan. 1917.

95. Baker and Nicholson, *Inter-State,* p. 2; *TSJ,* 26 May 1902.

96. *TSJ,* 13 Jan. 1917.

97. *TC,* 12, 18, and 20 Feb. 1917; *TSJ,* 9 Jan. 1917; Kansas, *Session Laws, 1917,* pp. 283–86.

98. *TSJ,* 23 Feb. 1917; *Kansas Issue,* Feb. 1917; *Our Messenger,* Mar. 1917.

99. *State National Prohibition Convention,* auspices of the Anti-Saloon League of America, Kansas Department, 18–20 June 1917, Topeka, in Prohibition party pamphlets, KSHS.

CHAPTER 9. THE FEDERAL ERA

1. D. Leigh Colvin, *Prohibition in the United States: A History of the Prohibition Party and of the Prohibition Movement* (New York: George H. Doran Co., 1926), p. 435.

2. Ibid., p. 447; Andrew Sinclair, *Era of Excess: A Social History of the Prohibition Movement* (New York: Harper & Row, 1964), pp. 154–56, 163–64.

3. Colvin, *Prohibition,* pp. 450–51; Norman H. Clark, *Deliver Us from Evil: An Interpretation of American Prohibition* (New York: W. W. Norton, 1976), pp. 122–24; Peter H. Odegard, *Pressure Politics: The Story of the Anti-Saloon League* (New York: Columbia University Press, 1928), pp. 78, 163; John Kobler, *Ardent Spirits: The Rise and Fall of Prohibition* (New York: G. P. Putnam's Sons, 1973), p. 206; K. Austin Kerr, "Organizing for Reform: The Anti-Saloon League and Innovation in Politics," *American Quarterly* 32 (1980): 52; S. J. Mennell, "Prohibition: A Sociological View," *Journal of American Studies* 3 (1969): 170; *American Issue* (Kansas ed.), 25 Aug. 1917.

4. Sinclair, *Era of Excess,* pp. 157–58.

5. Arthur Capper to J. Frank Hanly, 5 Oct. 1918, Capper gubernatorial papers, box 11; Capper's secretary to V. G. Hinshaw, 9 Jan. 1918, Capper gubernatorial papers, box 14; Colvin, *Prohibition,* p. 449.

6. J. Frank Hanly and Oliver W. Stewart, eds., *Speeches of the Flying Squadron* (Indianapolis, Ind.: Hanly & Stewart, n.d.), p. 9.

7. Clifford S. Griffin, *The University of Kansas: A History* (Lawrence: University Press of Kansas, 1974), p. 382; *Kansas Issue,* Jan. 1914; *TC,* 29 May and 23 Nov. 1917.

8. Harry M. Chalfant, "The Anti-Saloon League—Why and What?" *Annals of the American Academy of Political and Social Science* 109 (1923): 279; Kerr, "Organizing for Reform," pp. 37–53; Jack S. Blocker, Jr., *Retreat from Reform: The Prohibition Movement in the United States, 1890–1913* (Westport, Conn.: Greenwood Press, 1976), pp. 159, 160, 166; Colvin, *Prohibition,* p. 393; Clark, *Deliver Us,* pp. 93–117; Odegard, *Pressure Politics,* passim.

9. Robert Norris to E. W. Hoch, 30 Oct. 1905, Hoch gubernatorial papers; Margaret Whittemore, *One-way Ticket to Kansas* (Lawrence: University of Kansas Press, 1959), pp. 122–23 and passim; Blocker, *Retreat from Reform,* pp. 141, 157; *Kansas Issue,* May, Nov., and Dec. 1914; *TC,* 12 May 1906; *TSJ,* 17 Jan. 1917.

10. *Kansas Issue,* Jan. 1917; *TC,* 5 and 20 Dec. 1916; *TSJ,* 17 Jan. 1917.

11. *Kansas Issue,* Jan. and Feb. 1917.

12. *Vigliotti* v. *Pennsylvania,* 258 U.S. 403; *U.S.* v. *Lanza et al.,* 260 U.S. 377; Sinclair, *Era of Excess,* pp. 192–97, 216–17.

13. United States, *Statutes*, vol. 41, pt. 1, pp. 305-23; *New York Times*, 16 and 17 Jan. 1920.

14. Kansas, *Session Laws of 1927* (Topeka: State Printer, 1927), p. 247; Anti-Saloon League of America, *Yearbook for 1927* (Westerville, Ohio: Anti-Saloon League of America, 1927), p. 92; Sinclair, *Era of Excess*, p. 192.

15. *State v. Macek*, 104 Kansas 745.

16. *State v. Peterson and Martin*, 107 Kansas 641; *State v. Van Oster*, 119 Kansas 874; *Van Oster v. Kansas*, 272 U.S. 465; Kansas, *Session Laws, 1919*, pp. 294-96.

17. *State v. Jackson*, 121 Kansas 715.

18. Wickersham Commission, *National Commission on Law Observance and Enforcement* (Washington, D.C.: Government Printing Office, 1931), vol. 4, p. 477; *State v. Finch*, 128 Kansas 665.

19. *Crabb v. Dental Examiners*, 118 Kansas 516.

20. *In re Sanford*, 117 Kansas 750; *State v. Bieber*, 121 Kansas 536.

21. Kansas prohibition clippings, vol. 9, pp. 291, 299, 306, KSHS; Kansas Attorney General, *Report for 1917-18*, p. 7; *Wichita Beacon*, 5 Dec. 1920; Colvin, *Prohibition*, p. 446.

22. R. R. Nelson to H. J. Allen, 17 Feb. 1919; H. J. Allen to R. R. Nelson, 20 Feb. 1919, Allen gubernatorial papers.

23. Kansas prohibition clippings, vol. 9, pp. 285, 340, 348, KSHS; *American Issue* (Kansas ed.), 13 July 1918.

24. Kansas prohibition clippings, vol. 9, pp. 322, 324, 326, 327, KSHS; *TC*, 26 Nov. 1919.

25. Kansas, *Session Laws, 1923*, p. 193; *TSJ*, 17 Dec. 1921.

26. Hugh F. Fox, "The Consumption of Alcoholic Beverages," *Annals of the American Academy of Political and Social Science* 109 (1923): 138; Clark Warburton, *The Economic Results of Prohibition* (New York: Columbia University Press, 1932), pp. 106-7; Alfred G. Hill, "Kansas and Its Prohibition Enforcement," *Annals of the American Academy of Political and Social Science* 109 (Sept. 1923): 134; *Lawrence Journal-World*, 12 Sept. 1984; Herman Feldman, *Prohibition: Its Economic and Industrial Aspects* (New York: D. Appleton & Co., 1930), pp. 127, 278-80.

27. William G. Shepherd, "Kansas, the Beer State," *Collier's*, 26 Jan. 1929, pp. 8-9, 40; Walter W. Liggett, "Holy Hypocritical Kansas," *Plain Talk* 6 (Feb. 1930): 140; Vance Randolph, "Wet Words in Kansas," *Kansas Magazine* (1934): 92-93; *TC*, 26 Apr. 1931.

28. Warburton, *Economic Results*, p. 107; Randolph, "Wet Words," pp. 91-93; Sinclair, *Era of Excess*, pp. 201-4; Kobler, *Ardent Spirits*, pp. 266-72; Kansas prohibition clippings, vol. 9, p. 299, KSHS; J. C. Furnas, *The Life and Times of the Late Demon Rum* (New York: G. P. Putnam's Sons, 1965), pp. 332-34; Charles Merz, *The Dry Decade* (Garden City, N.Y.: Doubleday, Doran & Co., 1931), pp. 51-65.

29. Ernest A. Dewey, "Cocktails in Kansas," *Commonweal* 11 (5 Feb. 1930): 385; Kirke Mechem, ed., *The Annals of Kansas, 1886-1925*, vol. 2 (Topeka: KSHS, 1956), pp. 288, 304, 307, 323, 329, 351, 380; *Wichita Beacon*, 6 Dec. 1920; *TSJ*, 15 May 1922; *TC*, 14 June 1929; Randolph, "Wet Words," p. 93.

30. Liggett, "Holy Hypocritical Kansas," p. 140; John Jones, "Kansas Dry?" *Literary Digest* 123 (10 Apr. 1937): 7; William A. Brandenburg, Jr., "A History of Liquor Prohibition in Crawford County, Kansas" (Master's thesis, Kansas State Teachers College, Pittsburg, 1931), p. 28; *Kansas Repealist*, July 1933; *TC*, 14 June 1929; *KCS*, 28 June 1930; *Pittsburg Headlight*, 2 May 1933; Randolph, "Wet Words," pp. 91-93.

31. *State v. Carl*, 120 Kansas 733; Brandenburg, "History," p. 20.

32. George S. Hobart, "The Volstead Act," *Annals of the American Academy of Political and Social Science* 109 (1923): 92; Sinclair, *Era of Excess*, pp. 208-9.

33. *Kansas v. Miller*, 92 Kansas 995; *Bowling v. Illinois Bankers Life Assoc.*, 141 Kansas 377; William G. Shepherd, "Kansas by Ginger!" *Collier's*, 26 July 1930, pp. 12-13, 48, 50; *Wichita Beacon*, 8 and 26 May 1930; *TC*, 27 Aug. 1930; *New York Times*, 27 and 30 July 1930.

34. John B. Madden, *Just Who Is Stabbing Prohibition in Kansas!* pp. 27-30, pamphlet, Kansas Collection, Kansas University; Wickersham Commission, *National Commission*, vol. 4, pp. 487-89; *Chicago Tribune*, 28 and 29 Apr. 1929; *KCT*, 9 June 1931.

35. Liggett, "Holy Hypocritical Kansas," p. 141; *Chicago Tribune*, 29 Apr. 1929; *TSJ*, 17 Sept. 1929; *Wichita Beacon*, 18 Sept. 1929.

36. Madden, *Just Who Is Stabbing?* pp. 26-27; *Wichita Beacon*, 13 May 1930; *KCS*, 1 June 1930.

37. Madden, *Just Who Is Stabbing?* pp. 12-27, 32-35; *KCS*, 1 and 4 June 1930 and 17 May 1931; *KCT*, 9 June 1931; *Wichita Beacon*, 13, 14, 15, and 17 May, 1, 4, and 15 June 1930. In the two years after the Gorges case, Madden had a number of clashes with his colleagues and superiors in the Prohibition Bureau and in other law-enforcement agencies. At various times he accused Prohibition Commissioner Woodcock, District Administrator Wark, Deputy Administrator Going, Special Agents Chief Duncan, U.S. District Attorney Brewster, and Kansas Attorney General Smith of incompetence and/or dishonesty. Madden, an Irish Catholic, received constant support in his difficulties from several leading Protestant ministers (see Madden, *Just Who Is Stabbing?* pp. 37-72).

38. Arthur Capper, "Speaking about Kansas," a one-page ASL pamphlet, 1917, Kansas Collection, Kansas University; *American Issue* (Kansas ed.), 15 Dec. 1917.

39. Liggett, "Holy Hypocritical Kansas," p. 139; *Christian Science Monitor*, 6 Sept. 1934.

40. Martha B. Bruere, *Does Prohibition Work?* (New York: Harper & Brothers, 1927), pp. 118-24, 301-2, 305-12.

41. Prohibition clippings, Kansas State Library, p. 52; Mabel Walker Willebrandt, *The Inside of Prohibition* (Indianapolis, Ind.: Bobbs-Merrill, 1929), p. 186. The highest-ranking woman in the federal government throughout the twenties, Mabel Elizabeth Walker had been born in a "sod dugout" near Woodsdale in Stevens County in 1889. A maternal uncle had been killed in the Stevens county-seat "war" a few months before her birth. Her family left Kansas when she was still a child, and eventually she settled in California. Before the end of the twenties she had become "the most famous and controversial woman in America" (Dorothy M. Brown, *Mabel Walker Willebrandt* [Knoxville: University of Tennessee Press, 1984], pp. xi, 3, 5).

42. James C. Carey, *Kansas State University: The Quest for Identity* (Lawrence: Regents Press of Kansas, 1977), p. 147; *KCS*, 14 Apr. 1929; J. H. Barnett, "College Seniors and the Liquor Problem," *Annals of the American Academy of Political and Social Science* 163 (1932): 130-46.

43. *Literary Digest* 74 (9 Sept. 1922): 11, and 113 (30 Apr. 1932): 6; Sinclair, *Era of Excess*, p. 313.

44. Wickersham Commission, *National Commission*, summary, p. iii; *American Issue* (Kansas ed.), 21 Jan. 1922; Sinclair, *Era of Excess*, pp. 362-68.

45. Wickersham Commission, *National Commission*, vol. 1, pp. 49-59, vol. 4, p. 474, summary, p. 41; *TSJ*, 12 Feb. 1930; Sinclair, *Era of Excess*, p. 197.

46. Wickersham Commission, *National Commission*, vol. 4, pp. 479-80, 491.

47. United States Commissioner of Internal Revenue, *Annual Reports for Fiscal Years Ended June 30, 1921 and 1922* (Washington, D.C.: Government Printing Office);

United States, Treasury Department, Bureau of Prohibition, *Statistics Concerning Intoxicating Liquors* (Washington, D.C.: Government Printing Office), for fiscal years 1923 through 1933; Wickersham Commission, *National Commission,* vol. 4, pp. 549, 755, 817. Adjustment for population size was made using the mean of the 1920 and 1930 censuses.

48. United States, Treasury Department, *Statistics,* for 1923 through 1933; Wickersham Commission, *National Commission,* vol. 4, p. 479; *TC,* 15 June 1930.

49. Kansas WCTU, *Minutes of the 1919 Annual Meeting,* pp. 41–43; *Our Messenger,* Mar. 1920.

50. Kansas WCTU, *Minutes, 1919,* pp. 41–43; and *1927,* p. 33; *Our Messenger,* May 1919 and Jan. 1927.

51. Kansas WCTU, *Minutes, 1928,* p. 49, and *1931,* p. 52; *Our Messenger,* Apr. 1931; *TC,* 29 Sept. 1918 and 12 Oct. 1919.

52. *Kansas Prohibition Herald,* 1 Feb. 1929; Anti-Saloon League of Kansas, *Third Annual Report* (Topeka: ASL of Kansas, 1920), p. 2; Odegard, *Pressure Politics,* p. 272.

53. *American Issue* (Kansas ed.), 8 Mar. 1919.

54. Ibid., 6 Mar. 1920.

55. *KCS,* 6 Oct. 1929.

56. *Lawrence Journal-World,* 26 Oct. 1929; *TC,* 11 May 1927 and 1 Feb. 1928.

57. *Kansas Prohibition Herald,* 1 Feb. 1929; *KCS,* 8 May 1927; *TC,* 13 June 1927.

58. W. G. Clugston, *Rascals in Democracy* (New York: Richard R. Smith, 1941), pp. 192–93; Anti-Saloon League of America, *Yearbook for 1921,* p. 185; *American Issue* (Kansas ed.), 4 May 1918 and 11 Dec. 1920.

59. A. L. Stewart to F. S. McBride, 12 Dec. 1925, F. Scott McBride papers, roll 5, Ohio Historical Society, microfilm; *TC,* 11 Dec. 1925; *TSJ,* 15 Dec. 1925 and 22 Jan. 1926; *Kansas City Journal Post,* 12 Dec. 1925.

60. Joseph A. McClellan to F. S. McBride, 12 and 19 Dec. 1925; McBride to McClellan, 22 Dec. 1925, F. Scott McBride papers, roll 5, Ohio Historical Society, microfilm; Clugston, *Rascals in Democracy,* pp. 191–206; Odegard, *Pressure Politics,* pp. 240–43; *TC,* 11 May 1927; *Kansas City Journal Post,* 6 July 1927; *Chicago Tribune,* 23 Apr. 1929; Marko L. Haggard, "Prohibition, a Political Factor in Kansas" (Master's thesis, University of Kansas, 1948), pp. 285–86.

61. David E. Kyvig, *Repealing National Prohibition* (Chicago: University of Chicago Press, 1979), pp. 3, 9, 72, 88, 144–45, 163; Leslie Wallace, "The Kansas Optimist," *Outlook,* 27 Jan. 1932, p. 109.

62. Herbert Asbury, *The Great Illusion: An Informal History of Prohibition* (New York: Greenwood Press, 1968), p. 316; Kyvig, *Repealing,* pp. 53–54, 58, 66–67; Sinclair, *Era of Excess,* p. 344.

63. J. C. Burnham, "New Perspectives on the Prohibition 'Experiment' of the 1920's," *Journal of Social History* 2 (1968): 61, 65, 67; Kyvig, *Repealing,* pp. 46, 118–21, 126; Sinclair, *Era of Excess,* pp. 343–44.

64. Asbury, *Great Illusion,* p. 332.

65. *Chicago Tribune,* 23, 25, 28, and 29 Apr. 1929.

66. Dewey, "Cocktails," p. 386.

67. Charles B. Driscoll, "Kansas in Labor," *American Mercury* 16 (1929): 346; Frank Doster, "The Prohibition Craze," *Plain Talk* 1 (1927): 27.

68. Liggett, "Holy Hypocritical Kansas," p. 130; prohibition clippings, Kansas State Library, pp. 23–26.

69. Liggett, "Holy Hypocritical Kansas," p. 132; Francis W. Schruben, *Kansas in Turmoil, 1930–1936* (Columbia: University of Missouri Press, 1969), pp. 23–24.

70. *KCS,* 19 and 20 Sept. 1929.

71. Liggett, "Holy Hypocritical Kansas," pp. 129–41; *Plain Talk* 6 (May 1930): 639; *TSJ*, 12 Feb. 1930.

72. Liggett, "Holy Hypocritical Kansas," p. 136; *KCS*, 23 Feb. 1930.

73. Mark Keller and Carol Gurioli, *Statistics on Consumption of Alcohol and on Alcoholism* (New Brunswick, N.J.: Journal of Studies on Alcohol, Inc., 1976), p. 5; Warburton, *Economic Results*, pp. 24, 107; Burnham, "New Perspectives," p. 59; Joseph R. Gusfield, "Prohibition: The Impact of Political Utopism," in *Change and Continuity in Twentieth Century America: The 1920's*, ed. John Braeman, Robert H. Bremner, and David Brody (Columbus: Ohio State University Press, 1968), pp. 276–77; Anti-Saloon League of America, *Yearbook for 1930*, pp. 86–89. The more-useful estimates of national consumption include those of the AAPA (Warburton), the Prohibition Bureau (Sanford), the World League against Alcoholism (Corradini), and the liquor industry (Fox). Warburton (*Economic Results*, pp. 86, 89) estimated the national consumption of alcohol during the Volstead period from the correlation of consumption with the combined death rates from alcoholism and cirrhosis of the liver in the preceding decade. Applying his regression formula to the Kansas death rates, a value of 0.25 gallons of absolute alcohol per capita of the drinking-age population is obtained for 1922, the lowest for this period. The Kansas value is 18 percent of Warburton's national estimate for 1922. These alcohol-related mortality rates may lag one or more years behind the consumption rates.

CHAPTER 10. THE DEPRESSION YEARS

1. Kansas, *House Journal, 1931* (Topeka: State Printer, 1931), pp. 10–11.

2. Harry H. Woodring to Ida B. Malloy, 9 June 1932, and Woodring to Lillian Mitchner, 19 May 1932, Woodring gubernatorial papers; Andrew Sinclair, *Era of Excess: A Social History of the Prohibition Movement* (New York: Harper & Row, 1964), pp. 375–86.

3. Woodring to A. S. Colvin, 21 May 1932; prohibition correspondence, 1931/32, Woodring gubernatorial papers; Keith D. McFarland, *Harry H. Woodring* (Lawrence: University Press of Kansas, 1975), pp. 56, 75–76, 247; *TC*, 14 and 15 May 1932.

4. *KCS*, 3 Dec. 1932; David E. Kyvig, *Repealing National Prohibition* (Chicago: University of Chicago Press, 1979), p. 172; Sinclair, *Era of Excess*, pp. 389–91.

5. Kansas WCTU, *Minutes, 1933*, pp. 91–92; *TSJ*, 21 Feb. and 8 Mar. 1933.

6. Kansas WCTU, *Minutes, 1933*, pp. 91–92; Kansas, *Senate Journal, 1933*, p. 525, and *House Journal, 1933*, pp. 709–10; *TSJ*, 14 Mar. 1933.

7. *Pittsburg Headlight*, 3 May 1933; *Kansas Repealist*, May and June 1933; *KCT*, 28 Apr. 1933; *TSJ*, 19 May 1933.

8. *TSJ*, 5 Apr. 1933; *KCT*, 16 Aug. 1932.

9. *TSJ*, 5 Apr. 1933; *Kansas Repealist*, May and June 1933; Jay E. House, "When I Was Mayor," *North American Review* 228 (1929): 526.

10. *Kansas Repealist*, June and July 1933; *KCT*, 16 Aug. 1932.

11. *New York Times*, 6 Dec. 1933; Kyvig, *Repealing*, p. 174.

12. Kansas WCTU, *Minutes, 1933*, p. 45.

13. *St. Louis Post-Dispatch*, 3 Apr. 1983; *St. Louis Globe-Democrat*, 2 Apr. 1983; *KCT*, 7 Apr. 1933; United States, *Statutes*, vol. 48, pt. 1, pp. 16–20.

14. *New York Times*, 6 July 1933; *KCS*, 26 Mar. 1933; *KCT*, 28 Apr. and 24 June 1933.

15. *KCT*, 24, 26, and 27 June, 14 July 1933; *New York Times*, 6 July 1933; *Wichita Eagle*, 24–30 June 1933.

16. *State* v. *Owston*, 138 Kansas 173; *KCT*, 27 June and 14 July 1933.

17. *Intoxicating Liquor Cases*, 25 Kansas 524; *State* v. *Miller*, 92 Kansas 994; *State* v. *Owston*, 138 Kansas 173; *TSJ*, 11 July 1933.

18. *New York Times*, 15 July 1933; *Kansas City Kansan*, 15 July 1933; Roland Boynton to W. S. Schoen, 21 Nov. 1934, attorney general's files on intoxicating liquor.

19. Prohibition clippings, Kansas State Library, pp. 107-9; *Christian Science Monitor*, 13 July 1935; *Emporia Gazette*, 3 Aug. 1933; *TSJ*, 21 July 1933; *KCT*, 2 July and 9 Nov. 1934.

20. Kansas, *House Journal, 1933 Special Session*, pp. 128, 204, 218-19; *Kansas City Journal Post*, 29 Oct. 1933; Kansas WCTU, *Minutes, 1934*, p. 60; *Our Messenger*, Dec. 1933; Robert S. Bader, *The Great Kansas Bond Scandal* (Lawrence: University Press of Kansas, 1982), pp. 68-75.

21. Donald R. McCoy, *Landon of Kansas* (Lincoln: University of Nebraska Press, 1966), p. 164; Kansas, *House Journal, 1933 Special Session*, p. 127; Kansas WCTU, *Minutes, 1934*, p. 60.

22. Kansas, *Session Laws, 1933 Special Session*, p. 167; *TC*, 18 Nov. 1933; *KCT*, 16 Oct. 1934.

23. *Our Messenger*, July, Oct., Nov., and Dec. 1934; Kansas WCTU, *Minutes, 1934*, p. 27; *Christian Science Monitor*, 20 Sept. 1934.

24. *TSJ*, 5 Apr. 1933; *Kansas Repealist*, June 1933; *Our Messenger*, Oct. 1934; *KCT*, 8 Nov. 1934; Marko L. Haggard, "Prohibition, a Political Factor in Kansas" (Master's thesis, University of Kansas, 1948), p. 50.

25. Republican and Democratic state party platforms, 1932 and 1934; Haggard, "Prohibition," p. 49; *TC*, 29 Oct. 1934; Kansas prohibition clippings, vol. 11, p. 88; McCoy, *Landon*, pp. 49-51, 107; *Emporia Gazette*, 13 Oct. 1934; *KCT*, 8 Nov. 1934.

26. Kansas Secretary of State, *Biennial Report, 1933-34* (Topeka: State Printer, 1934), p. 113; *TSJ*, 21 Jan. 1935 and 15 Apr. 1937; *KCS*, 5 Jan. 1935 and 30 Nov. 1936; *Emporia Gazette*, 7 Nov. 1934; Haggard, "Prohibition," p. 51.

27. Kansas Secretary of State, *Report for 1933-34*, pp. 102-3, 112-13, 134-35; United States, Department of Commerce, Census Bureau, *Fifteenth Census of the United States: 1930*, Population Bulletin, 2d. ser.: *Kansas* (Washington, D.C.: Government Printing Office, 1931), pp. 25-31, and *Religious Bodies: 1936* (Washington, D.C.: Government Printing Office, 1941), vol. 1, pp. 755-58.

28. Walter Johnson, *William Allen White's America* (New York: Henry Holt & Co., 1947), pp. 219-20, 357-60; W. A. White, "As Kansas Sees Prohibition," *Collier's* 78 (3 July 1926): 23; W. A. White to Gabriel Wells, 26 Feb. 1927, in *Selected Letters of William Allen White, 1899-1943*, ed. Walter Johnson (New York: Henry Holt & Co., 1947), pp. 266-67; Frank C. Clough, *William Allen White of Emporia* (New York: McGraw-Hill, 1941), p. 164.

29. W. A. White, "A Dry West Warns the Thirsty East," *Collier's* 70 (2 Sept. 1922): 3-4, 18-19; White, "Kansas Sees," p. 23; W. A. White to C. G. Christgau, 29 July 1926, *Selected Letters*, pp. 262-63.

30. *KCT*, 4 May 1932; *New York Times*, 15 June 1932.

31. *Emporia Gazette*, 1 Aug. and 8 Nov. 1933.

32. Ibid., 21, 25, and 28 Sept., 3, 30, and 31 Oct., 2, 5, 16, and 20 Nov. 1934.

33. Ibid., 9 Nov. 1934.

34. *Our Messenger*, Dec. 1924. No primary source has been located for the aphorism, widely attributed to White, that "Kansans would vote dry so long as they could stagger to the polls." An identical and undocumented quip has been attributed to Will Rogers with respect to Oklahoma (Jimmie L. Franklin, *Born Sober* [Norman: University of Oklahoma Press, 1971], p. 189).

35. Kansas, *House Journal, 1935* (Topeka: State Printer, 1935), pp. 213-17, 521, 556, 565, and *Senate Journal, 1935*, pp. 239, 299, 401-3; *Our Messenger*, Jan. and Aug. 1935, Feb. and Aug. 1936; *TSJ*, 14 Feb. 1935; *KCS*, 10 Mar. 1935; *KCT*, 1 July 1935.

36. Hubert Kelley, "These Dry States," *American Magazine* 120 (July 1935): 81; *University Daily Kansan*, 12 July 1935.

37. W. A. White, "Kansas and Prohibition," *Kansas Magazine*, 1937, p. 52; *KCS*, 30 Nov. 1936.

38. *KCT*, 11 Feb. and 12 Mar. 1937; Kansas, *House Journal, 1937*, pp. 273-75, 545, 586, and *Senate Journal, 1937*, pp. 411-12, 416, 458.

39. Kansas, *House Journal, 1937*, pp. 740-42, and *Senate Journal, 1937*, pp. 416, 458, 628; *KCS*, 30 Nov. 1936; *KCT*, 12, 17, 26, and 27 Mar. 1937.

40. U.S. Brewers Association, *Brewers Almanac* (New York: U.S. Brewers Association, annually).

CHAPTER 11. REPEAL

1. *KCS*, 28 Nov. 1937 and 22 Oct. 1946; *TC*, 8 June 1938 and 4 Feb. 1939; *TSJ*, 28 July 1938; *Our Messenger*, Jan. 1944 and Mar. 1945; W. E. Connelley, ed., *A Standard History of Kansas and Kansans* (Chicago: Lewis Publishing Co., 1919), pp. 1963-64.

2. *Our Messenger*, Mar. and Apr. 1937 and Oct. 1938.

3. Kansas WCTU, *Minutes, 1941*, p. 19, and *1943*, p. 16; *Our Messenger*, Mar. 1939 and Jan. 1943; *KCT*, 17 Feb. 1939 and 14 Nov. 1945; *KCS*, 5 Mar. 1941 and 9 Feb. 1943; *TSJ*, 27 Feb. 1941; *TC*, 15 June 1942; Marko L. Haggard, "Prohibition, a Political Factor in Kansas" (Master's thesis, University of Kansas, 1948), pp. 97-114.

4. *Indianapolis Brewing Co.* v. *Liquor Control Commission*, 305 U.S. 394; U.S., *Statutes* (1936), vol. 49, pt. 1, pp. 1928-30; Kansas, *Session Laws, 1935*, pp. 242-44, and *1939*, pp. 299-301.

5. C. V. Beck to J. B. Carter, 29 June 1936, file 21, Kansas attorneys general's opinions, KSHS; *TC*, 27 Apr. 1937 and 19 Feb. 1941; *KCT*, 2 Apr. 1938 and 21 Dec. 1940; *KCS*, 1 July 1939.

6. *KCT*, 10 Nov. 1945.

7. *KCS*, 11 Nov. 1945; *KCT*, 10 Nov. 1945; *Wichita Beacon*, 25 Nov. 1945.

8. *KCT*, 13 Nov. 1945.

9. *KCS*, 10 Nov. 1945; United States, Commissioner of Internal Revenue, *Annual Report, 1945* (Washington, D.C.: Superintendent of Documents, 1945), p. 62.

10. *KCT*, 15, 16, 17, 20, and 21 Nov. 1945.

11. David E. Kyvig, *Repealing National Prohibition* (Chicago: University of Chicago Press, 1979), p. 188; *KCS*, 6 Sept. 1937.

12. W. B. Vorhees to A. Schoeppel, 8 Jan. 1944; Schoeppel gubernatorial papers, box 36; Clarence Woodbury, "What Happened to Kansas," *American Magazine* 147 (Jan. 1949): 119; *TC*, 27 Aug. and 9 Oct. 1948; *KCT*, 29 Oct. 1948; Frank Carlson interview by Lawrence A. Yates, 15 June 1976, p. 10, Kansas Collection, University of Kansas.

13. Keith D. McFarland, *Harry H. Woodring* (Lawrence: University Press of Kansas, 1975), pp. 234, 246-48.

14. *TSJ*, 19 Feb. 1946.

15. Ibid., 23 Feb. 1946; *KCT*, 5 Apr. 1946; *KCS*, 17 Apr. 1946.

16. *Time Magazine*, 9 Sept. 1946, p. 26; *TSJ*, 19 and 25 Feb. 1946; McFarland, *Harry H. Woodring*, pp. 243-48.

17. *KCS*, 17 Apr. and 1 Aug. 1946; *KCT*, 26 Aug. 1946.

18. State Democratic party platforms, 1936–46; Haggard, "Prohibition," p. 173; *TC*, 4 and 28 Aug. 1946.

19. State Republican party platforms, 1936–46; Committee of 100,000 to A. Schoeppel, 26 Aug. 1946, Schoeppel gubernatorial papers, box 54; *TC*, 26 and 27 Aug. 1946; Carlson interview, 15 June 1978, p. 10.

20. *TC*, 17 June and 23 Aug. 1946; Homer E. Socolofsky, "Kansas," in *Biographical Directory of the Governors of the United States, 1789–1978*, ed. Robert Sobel and John Raimo (Westport, Conn.: Meckler Books, 1979), pp. 493–94; Haggard, "Prohibition," pp. 185, 189; Kansas Director of Alcoholic Beverage Control, *Biennial Reports*.

21. *TSJ*, 17 Jan. 1947; Haggard, "Prohibition," pp. 198–200. For a detailed legal analysis of the possible meanings of "open saloon" in the years subsequent to repeal see Barkley Clark, "Wyatt Earp and the Winelist: Is a Restaurant an 'Open Saloon?' " *Journal of the Kansas Bar Association* 47 (1978): 63–80.

22. Kansas, *House Journal, 1947*, p. 45, and *Senate Journal, 1947*, p. 48; Haggard, "Prohibition," pp. 193–94; *Wichita Eagle*, 24 Jan. 1947; Carlson interview, 15 June 1976, pp. 11, 17.

23. Kansas, *House Journal, 1947*, pp. 45–47, and *Senate Journal, 1947*, pp. 48–49.

24. Kansas, *Session Laws, 1947*, p. 382.

25. Haggard, "Prohibition," pp. 194–95, 211; E. F. Arn to Mrs. A. J. Dodd, 23 Jan. 1947, file 21, attorney general's opinions, KSHS; correspondence in box 13, Carlson gubernatorial papers.

26. Anonymous to A. Schoeppel, 29 Nov. 1945, and J. E. Addington to Legislative Council, 14 Nov. 1945—both in box 36, Schoeppel gubernatorial papers.

27. A. M. Benjamin to A. Schoeppel, 17 Nov. 1945; H. Quakenbush to Schoeppel, 1 Dec. 1945; "Your Friend and Booster" to Schoeppel, 17 May 1945; G. C. Hall to Schoeppel, 3 Dec. 1945—all in box 36, Schoeppel gubernatorial papers.

28. Mrs. E. L. Granger to Schoeppel, 19 Nov. 1945, box 36; M. Hamm to Schoeppel, 20 Feb. 1945, box 34; W. M. Horton to Schoeppel, 19 Nov. 1945, box 36—all in Schoeppel gubernatorial papers.

29. A. Schoeppel to Mrs. E. W. Kelly, 17 Dec. 1945, and Schoeppel to J. E. Schaefer, 5 Dec. 1945, box 36, Schoeppel gubernatorial papers, *TC*, 8 Apr. 1948.

30. *KCS*, 24 Jan. and 5 Oct. 1946; *KCT*, 11 Oct. 1946; C. Benge to Schoeppel, 2 Sept. 1946, box 54, Schoeppel gubernatorial papers.

31. *Kansas Business Magazine*, Mar. 1949; Socolofsky, "Kansas," pp. 495–96; *Wichita Eagle*, 10 Dec. 1947.

32. Kansas, *Session Laws, 1947*, p. 365; United States, Commissioner of Internal Revenue, *Reports, 1946, 1947, 1948;* E. F. Arn to Mrs. M. E. Rickard, 19 Feb. 1947, file 21, attorney general's opinions, KSHS; Kansas Attorney General, *Report for 1947–48*, pp. 7–8; *TC*, 18 Mar. 1948.

33. *Wichita Eagle*, 8 Aug. 1948; *TSJ*, 2 Dec. 1947 and 15 Jan. 1948; *TC*, 3 and 4 Dec. 1947; *KCT*, 30 Dec. 1947, 6 Mar. and 10 July 1948; *KCS*, 18 Jan. 1948.

34. *Time Magazine*, 12 Jan. 1948, p. 18; C. Small, "Kansas Staggers to the Polls," *Collier's*, 28 Aug. 1948, p. 68; *TSJ*, 29 Dec. 1947; *Ottawa Herald*, 3 Jan. 1948.

35. *KCT*, 30 Dec. 1947; *TSJ*, 29 Dec. 1947.

36. *KCT*, 7 Jan. 1948; *TSJ*, 2 Oct. 1948.

37. F. Carlson to Mrs. Glenn G. Hays, 12 Feb. 1947; J. J. Ballinger to Carlson, 18 Jan. 1947; A. S. Kern to Carlson, 5 Mar. 1947; N. E. Schneider to Carlson, 26 Mar. 1947—all in box 13, Carlson gubernatorial papers; Carlson interview, 15 June 1976, p. 24; *TSJ*, 15 Jan. 1948; *TC*, 8 Apr. 1948; *Sunflower Seeds*, May 1948, KSHS. Arn went on to become a justice of the Kansas Supreme Court (1949/50) and governor (1951–55).

38. *TSJ*, 6 July 1947; *KCT*, 14 Sept. 1946.
39. *TSJ*, 10 and 12 July 1946; *KCS*, 5 Oct. 1946; *KCT*, 3 Jan. 1948.
40. *TSJ*, 1 Oct. 1948.
41. *Chicago Tribune*, 5 Dec. 1945, 2 and 12 Oct. 1946, 4 and 5 Dec. 1947, and 8 Dec. 1948; *KCT*, 10 July 1948; *Topeka Magazine*, Oct. 1946, p. 3; *Time Magazine*, 9 Sept. 1946, p. 26; *Baltimore Sun*, 27 Feb. 1946; *TSJ*, 12 July 1946; *Abilene Reflector-Chronicle*, 9 Oct. 1948; J. E. Schafer to Schoeppel, 10 Dec. 1945, box 34, Schoeppel gubernatorial papers; interview with a former bootlegger, 11 Mar. 1985.
42. *Dry Rot*, pamphlet of KLCC, Kansas prohibition pamphlets, vol. 5, KSHS; Distilled Spirits Institute, *Apparent Consumption of Distilled Spirits, 1934-1967* (Washington, D.C.: Distilled Spirits Institute, 1968); United States, Department of Commerce, Bureau of the Census.
43. For elaboration regarding national and state drinking practices see notes 7 and 8 of chap. 12. *Ottawa Herald*, 3 Jan. 1948; *Life Magazine*, Oct. 1946, p. 31; *TSJ*, 30 Oct. 1947; *Christian Herald*, 18 Jan. 1930; Mark Keller and Carol Gurioli, *Statistics on Consumption of Alcohol and on Alcoholism* (New Brunswick, N.J.: Journal of Studies on Alcohol, Inc., 1976), p. 3.
44. Kansas State Board of Health, Division of Vital Statistics, *Vital Statistics of Kansas, 1900-1946;* Alcohol Epidemiologic Data System, *Cirrhosis of Liver Mortality* (Rockville, Md.: National Institute of Alcohol Abuse and Alcoholism, 1980), *Data Reference Manual*, sec. 2, p. 2.1-3; Anti-Saloon League of America, *Yearbook for 1930* (Westerville, Ohio: Anti-Saloon League of America, 1930), pp. 86-87; E. M. Jellinek, "Recent Trends in Alcoholism and in Alcohol Consumption," *Quarterly Journal of Studies on Alcohol* 8 (1947): 26; E. M. Jellinek and Mark Keller, "Rates of Alcoholism in the United States of America, 1940-1948," *Quarterly Journal of Studies on Alcohol* 13 (1952): 52, 57; Distilled Spirits Institute, *Apparent Consumption*, p. 40; U.S. Brewers Association, *Brewers Almanac*.
45. *KCS*, 21 Jan. 1948; Haggard, "Prohibition," p. 323.
46. Woodbury, "What Happened," pp. 21, 115-16.
47. *Dry Rot*, KLCC pamphlet; *An Examination of "Dry Rot,"* American Business Men's Research Foundation, Kansas prohibition pamphlets, vol. 5, KSHS; *Our Messenger*, Apr. 1948; Haggard, "Prohibition," pp. 234-39; *TC*, 8 and 30 Apr., 2 May 1948; *Wichita Eagle*, 6 Aug. 1948.
48. *Hutchinson News-Herald*, 8 July 1948; *Wichita Eagle*, 6 Aug. 1948; Woodbury, "What Happened," p. 119.
49. *KCS*, 2 Oct. 1948; Woodbury, "What Happened," p. 116.
50. *TC*, 25 Oct. 1948; *Our Messenger*, Dec. 1948.
51. *Hutchinson News-Herald*, 8 July 1948.
52. *Would You Sell Your Vote for a Few Cents Worth of Beer?* United Dry Forces pamphlet, Kansas prohibition pamphlets, vol. 5, KSHS; *TC*, 14, 15, and 19 Oct. 1948; Woodbury, "What Happened," p. 118.
53. *KCT*, 29 Sept. and 8 Oct. 1948; *Wichita Eagle*, 14 May 1948.
54. *Emporia Gazette*, 7 Oct. 1948.
55. Kansas WCTU, *Minutes, 1939*, p. 38, *1947*, p. 33, and *1948*, p. 31; Woodbury, "What Happened," p. 21; Haggard, "Prohibition," pp. 249, 287, 291; *TC*, 13 Oct. 1948.
56. *TC*, 9 and 30 Oct. 1948; *Wichita Eagle*, 25 Oct. 1948; Kansas WCTU, *Minutes, 1949*, p. 28; *Our Messenger*, May 1948; *Sunflower Seeds*, Oct. 1948.
57. *Newsweek*, 30 Aug. 1948, pp. 21-22; *TSJ*, 9 Sept. 1948; *TC*, 15 Aug. 1948; *KCS*, 22 Aug. 1948; F. Carlson to W. Mayberry, 10 Aug. 1948, box 36, Carlson gubernatorial papers.

58. *TC*, 13, 23, 25, 28, and 30 Oct. and 10 Dec. 1948; *Wichita Eagle*, 25 Oct. 1948.

59. O. M. Yoder to A. Schoeppel, 4 Mar. 1945, box 34, Schoeppel gubernatorial papers; N. Fine to F. Carlson, 22 Jan. 1947, box 13, Carlson gubernatorial papers; short phrases chiefly from box 13, Carlson gubernatorial papers.

60. H. Davis to F. Carlson, 9 Jan. 1947, box 13, Carlson gubernatorial papers.

61. *Wichita Eagle*, 25 Oct. 1948; *KCT*, 28 Oct. 1948; *Topeka Capital-Journal*, 13 Jan. 1985.

62. *Wichita Eagle*, 29 Oct. 1948.

63. State political party platforms for 1948; *TC*, 1 Sept. 1948.

64. W. P. Lambertson, *Vote Dry in the Primary, Too*, Kansas prohibition pamphlets, vol. 4, KSHS; *Cloakroom*, 5 July 1947, in G. T. Davies to F. Carlson, 18 Dec. 1947, box 22; Carlson to E. Abels, 18 Nov. 1947, box 9; Carlson to J. A. Miller, 16 July 1948, box 36; Carlson to T. A. Miller, 22 Oct. 1948, box 36; C. D. Walker to Carlson, 30 Oct. 1948, box 36; Carlson to Walker, 11 Nov. 1948; Carlson to L. R. Templin, 11 Nov. 1948, box 36—all in Carlson gubernatorial papers; Carlson interview, 15 June 1976, pp. 3-4, tape 2.

65. *TC*, 8 Apr., 4 and 9 Oct. 1948; *TSJ*, 24 May 1948; *KCT*, 28 and 29 Oct. 1948.

66. *TC*, 9 and 30 Oct. 1948; *KCT*, 2 Nov. 1948; *TSJ*, 21 Oct. 1948; *Wichita Eagle*, 31 Oct. 1948; Kansas Secretary of State, *Biennial Report for 1947-48*, pp. 95-96.

67. Kansas State Board of Agriculture, *Biennial Report, 1933-1934* and *1947-1948;* Kansas Secretary of State, *Biennial Report, 1947-48*, pp. 77-78, 81-84, 95-96; United States, Department of Commerce, Census Bureau, *Census of Population: 1950* (Washington, D.C.: Government Printing Office, 1952), vol. 2, pt. 16: *Kansas*, pp. 11-12, 112-15; National Council of Churches, *Churches and Church Membership in the United States* (New York: National Council of Churches, 1957), ser. C, nos. 29 and 30.

CHAPTER 12. IN CONCLUSION

1. W. G. Clugston, *Rascals in Democracy* (New York: Richard B. Smith, 1941), pp. 183, 187.

2. Kenneth S. Davis, "That Strange State of Mind Called Kansas," *New York Times Magazine*, 26 June 1949, p. 52, "What's the Matter with Kansas?" *New York Times Magazine*, 27 June 1954, p. 12, and *Kansas: A Bicentennial History* (New York: W. W. Norton, 1976), p. 145; Milton S. Eisenhower, "The Strength of Kansas," *Kansas Magazine*, 1950, pp. 9-15; Karl A. Menninger, "Bleeding Kansans," *Kansas Magazine*, 1939, pp. 3-6; Francis W. Schruben, *Kansas in Turmoil, 1930-1936* (Columbia: University of Missouri Press, 1969), p. 26; O. Gene Clanton, *Kansas Populism: Ideas and Men* (Lawrence: University Press of Kansas, 1969), p. 210; Marko L. Haggard, "Prohibition, a Political Factor in Kansas" (Master's thesis, University of Kansas, 1948), pp. 288-89.

3. *KCT*, 26 Mar. 1937; Davis, *Kansas*, p. 145; political party platforms, 1880-1948. In 1984, one of the major parties simply told its county chairmen to consult the 1970 results of the liquor-by-the-drink referendum and to support the majority position.

4. *Our Messenger*, Sept. 1909.

5. Peter Gay, *Style in History* (New York: Basic Books, Inc., 1974), p. 44.

6. For comment on White's aphorism see note 34 of chap. 10. E. M. Jellinek, "Recent Trends in Alcoholism and in Alcohol Consumption," *Quarterly Journal of Studies on Alcohol* 8 (1947): 29-30.

7. Harold A. Mulford and Donald E. Miller, "The Prevalence and Extent of Drinking in Iowa, 1961," *Quarterly Journal of Studies on Alcohol* 24 (1963): 47; for additional figures on postrepeal national drinking patterns see Mark Keller and Carol Gurioli, *Statistics on Consumption of Alcohol and on Alcoholism* (New Brunswick, N.J.: Journal of Studies on Alcohol, Inc., 1976), p. 3; Robert O'Brien and Morris Chafetz, *The Encyclopedia of Alcoholism* (New York: Facts on File Publications, 1982), pp. 74, 217; *TCJ*, 23 Mar. 1985; Raymond G. McCarthy, ed., *Drinking and Intoxication* (New Haven, Conn.: Yale Center of Alcoholic Studies, 1959), pp. 182-204; Don Cahalan, Ira H. Cisin, and Helen M. Crossley, *American Drinking Practices* (New Brunswick, N.J.: Rutgers Center of Alcohol Studies, 1969), pp. 1-260.

8. Dean R. Gerstein, "Alcohol Use and Consequences," in *Alcohol and Public Policy: Beyond the Shadow of Prohibition,* ed. Mark H. Moore and Dean R. Gerstein (Washington, D.C.: National Academy Press, 1981), p. 193; a regression of percentage of abstention on per capita alcohol consumption, based on fourteen pairs of post-Volstead national observations, predicts an abstention rate of 57 percent for Kansas in 1914 with 95 percent confidence limits of 47-67.

In the mid 1950s, comparable surveys of high-school students in Nassau County, New York, Racine County, Wisconsin, and twenty-four eastern and central Kansas counties reported abstention rates of 14, 36, and 50 percent respectively. In the Kansas sample, abstainers represented 44 percent of the Sedgwick County students, 50 percent of those living in communities of 1,000 to 25,000, and 60 percent of those living in communities of less than 1,000 and in rural environments. The study also reported evidence that the prevalence of drinking 3.2 beer, especially among boys, was significantly affected by the law that restricted purchase to those eighteen years of age and older (Marston M. McCluggage, E. Jackson Baur, Charles K. Warriner, and Carroll D. Clark, "Summary of Essential Findings in the Kansas Study," in McCarthy, *Drinking and Intoxication,* pp. 211-18).

A 1977 Kansas survey reported that 47 percent of the adults said that alcohol had not been used in their parents' home. This implies an individual abstention rate of 50 to 70 percent. The five counties (Johnson, Leavenworth, Sedgwick, Shawnee, and Wyandotte), whose wet majorities accounted for the repeal victory in 1948, are reported in the survey as all being above the state average in usage of from one to four of five types of alcoholic beverages and below average in none (Kenneth A. Martinez, Larry L. Havlicek, and Herman D. Lujan, "Comprehensive Study of Drug and Alcohol Use in Kansas: Present Patterns, Attitudes, and Changes in Use," report to the State of Kansas, Department of Social and Rehabilitation Services, Alcohol and Drug Abuse Section, pp. IV-2, C-37.

9. Walter Johnson, *William Allen White's America* (New York: Henry Holt & Co., 1947), p. 219; Keith D. McFarland, *Harry H. Woodring* (Lawrence: University Press of Kansas, 1975), p. 249; Menninger, "Bleeding Kansans," p. 4.

10. Rhoda T. Tripp, comp., *The International Thesaurus of Quotations* (New York: Thomas Y. Crowell, 1970), sec. 438.15.

11. *TCJ*, 14 Jan. and 15 Nov. 1984.

12. Robert W. Richmond, *Kansas: A Land of Contrasts* (St. Charles, Mo.: Forum Press, 1974), p. 232; G. H. Hodges to W. H. Scott, 16 Dec. 1914, Hodges gubernatorial papers.

13. Data for the USA were obtained from Keller and Gurioli, *Statistics on Consumption,* p. 5; E. M. Jellinek, "Recent Trends," p. 8; United States, Department of Commerce, *Statistical Abstract of the United States* (Washington, D.C.: Government Printing Office, annually). Data for the nation and for Kansas came from the U.S. Brewers Association, *Brewers Almanac* (New York: U.S. Brewers Association, annually); Distilled Spirits Council, *Annual Statistical Review* (Washington, D.C.: Distilled

Spirits Council, annually); Wine Institute, *Annual Wine Industry Statistical Survey* (San Francisco, Calif.: Wine Institute, annually). U.S. values for the 1918–30 period follow Warburton and Fisher: Clark Warburton, "Prohibition," in *Encyclopedia of the Social Sciences*, ed. R. A. Seligman, vol. 12 (1937), p. 507; Irving Fisher and H. Bruce Broughman, *The Noble Experiment* (New York: Alcohol Information Committee, 1930), pp. 265, 277, 285, 289.

Through 1973 the drinking-age population was taken as that fifteen years of age and older; from 1974, as fourteen and older. The average percentage of alcohol by volume in beer has been assumed as 5.0 through 1919 and 4.5 subsequently; in spirits, as 45 through 1971, 43 through 1976, and 41.1 subsequently; in wine, as 18 through 1951, 17 through 1968, 16 through 1971, 14.5 through 1976, and 12.9 subsequently (following Keller and Gurioli and the National Institute on Alcohol Abuse and Alcoholism).

14. Kansas State Department of Health and Environment, *Annual Summary of Vital Statistics;* Keller and Gurioli, *Statistics on Consumption,* pp. 13, 15; United States, Department of Health and Human Services, Alcohol Epidemiologic Data System, *County Alcohol Problem Indicators, 1975–1977* (Rockville, Md.: National Institute on Alcohol Abuse and Alcoholism, 1981), sec. 3, pp. 3.2-74 and 3.2-75; O'Brien and Chafetz, *Encyclopedia of Alcoholism,* p. 319.

15. For the raw data see app. A. Similar results with respect to the correlation of evangelicals with the dry vote were obtained in a quantitative study of the Ohio vote in 1883: George G. Wittet, "Concerned Citizens: The Prohibitionists of 1883 Ohio," in *Alcohol, Reform and Society,* ed. Jack S. Blocker, Jr. (Westport, Conn.: Greenwood Press, 1979), pp. 134–36; Kansas Secretary of State, *Election Statistics, 1970* (Topeka: State Printer, 1970), pp. 78–79, 122–23; United States, Department of Commerce, Census Bureau, *1970 Census of Population* (Washington, D.C.: Government Printing Office, 1973), *Characteristics of the Population,* vol. 1, pt. 18: *Kansas,* pp. 17–18; Douglas W. Johnson, Paul R. Picard, and Bernard Quinn, *Churches and Church Membership in the United States, 1971* (Washington, D.C.: Glenmary Research Center, 1974), pp. 76–84.

16. For the various theories regarding the national movement see the references in note 18 of chap. 1 and notes 3 and 6 of chap 9. John C. Burnham, "New Perspectives on the Prohibition 'Experiment' of the 1920's," *Journal of Social History* 2 (1968): 56.

17. John Shaw to A. Capper, 22 Jan. 1916, box 7, Capper gubernatorial papers; *St. Louis Post-Dispatch,* 25 Aug. 1982; Harry G. Levine, "The Vocabulary of Drunkenness," *Journal of Studies on Alcohol* 42 (1981): 1038–51; Mark Edward Lender, *Dictionary of American Temperance Biography* (Westport, Conn.: Greenwood Press, 1984), p. xii; *TCJ,* 5 June 1985.

18. Moore and Gerstein, *Alcohol and Public Policy,* pp. 62–64.

19. *TSJ,* 23 and 24 May, 30 June 1913.

20. Paul Aaron and David Musto, "Temperance and Prohibition in America: A Historical Overview," in Moore and Gerstein, *Alcohol and Public Policy,* p. 127; Robert H. Hohner, "The Prohibitionists: Who Were They?" *South Atlantic Quarterly* 68 (1969): 491–93.

21. Albert J. Nock, "Prohibition and Civilization," *North American Review* 204–12 (1916): 407–12; James R. Shortridge, "Introduction to the Paperback Edition," in Federal Writers Project, *The WPA Guide to 1930s Kansas* (Lawrence: University Press of Kansas, 1984), p. 2; Research Triangle Institute, "Economic Costs to Society of Alcohol and Drug Abuse and Mental Illness," report of June 1984, p. G-16; *Kansas Issue,* 11 Mar. 1911; *Wall Street Journal,* 25 June 1984; *Time Magazine,* 20 May 1985.

Selected Bibliography

No systematic study of Kansas prohibition, or even a major segment of it, has been published. Primary and secondary materials are widely scattered through a broad range of sources. Citations in full are given for each when it first appears in the notes. These secondary sources were useful for background.

BOOKS AND DISSERTATIONS

Ashbury, Herbert. *The Great Illusion: An Informal History of Prohibition.* New York: Greenwood Press, 1968.

Blocker, Jack S., Jr. *Retreat from Reform: The Prohibition Movement in the United States, 1890–1913.* Westport, Conn.: Greenwood Press, 1976.

———, ed. *Alcohol, Reform and Society.* Westport, Conn.: Greenwood Press, 1979.

Bordin, Ruth. *Woman and Temperance.* Philadelphia: Temple University Press, 1981.

Byrne, Frank L. *Prophet of Prohibition: Neal Dow and His Crusade.* Madison: State Historical Society of Wisconsin, 1961.

Cherrington, Ernest H. *The Evolution of Prohibition in the United States of America.* Westerville, Ohio: American Issue Press, 1920.

———, ed. *Standard Encyclopedia of the Alcohol Problem.* Westerville, Ohio: American Issue Publishing Co., 1925–30.

Clark, Norman H. *Deliver Us from Evil: An Interpretation of American Prohibition.* New York: W. W. Norton, 1976.

Colvin, D. Leigh. *Prohibition in the United States: A History of the Prohibition Party and of the Prohibition Movement.* New York: George H. Doran Co., 1926.

Crunden, Robert M. *Ministers of Reform: The Progressive Achievement in American Civilization, 1889–1920.* New York: Basic Books, 1982.

Dannenbaum, Jed. *Drink and Disorder: Temperance Reform in Cincinnati from the Washingtonian Revival to the WCTU.* Urbana: University of Illinois Press, 1984.

Dykstra, Robert R. *The Cattle Towns.* New York: Alfred A. Knopf, 1968.

Epstein, Barbara L. *The Politics of Domesticity: Women, Evangelism and Temperance in Nineteenth-Century America.* Middletown, Conn.: Wesleyan University Press, 1981.

Furnas, J. C. *The Life and Times of the Late Demon Rum.* New York: G. P. Putnam's Sons, 1965.

Griffin, C. S. *The Ferment of Reform, 1830–1860.* New York: Thomas Y. Crowell Co., 1967.

Gusfield, Joseph R. *Symbolic Crusade: Status Politics and the American Temperance Movement.* Urbana: University of Illinois Press, 1963.

Harper, Ida Husted, ed. *The History of Woman Suffrage.* New York: National American Woman Suffrage Association, 1922.

Jensen, Richard. *The Winning of the Midwest: Social and Political Conflict, 1888–1896.* Chicago: University of Chicago Press, 1971.

Johnson, Paul E. *A Shopkeeper's Millennium: Society and Revivals in Rochester, New York, 1815–1837.* New York: Hill & Wang, 1978.

Kobler, John. *Ardent Spirits: The Rise and Fall of Prohibition.* New York: G. P. Putnam's Sons, 1973.

Krout, John A. *The Origins of Prohibition.* New York: Alfred A. Knopf, 1925.

Kyvig, David E. *Repealing National Prohibition.* Chicago: University of Chicago Press, 1979.

Lender, Mark Edward. *Dictionary of American Temperance Biography.* Westport, Conn.: Greenwood Press, 1984.

————, and Martin, James Kirby. *Drinking in America: A History.* New York: Free Press, 1982.

McLoughlin, William G. *Revivals, Awakenings, and Reform.* Chicago: University of Chicago Press, 1978.

Merz, Charles. *The Dry Decade.* Garden City, N.Y.: Doubleday, Doran & Co., 1931.

Odegard, Peter H. *Pressure Politics: The Story of the Anti-Saloon League.* New York: Columbia University Press, 1928.

Rorabaugh, W. J. *The Alcoholic Republic: An American Tradition.* New York: Oxford University Press, 1979.

Sinclair, Andrew. *Era of Excess: A Social History of the Prohibition Movement.* New York: Harper & Row, 1964.

Timberlake, James H. *Prohibition and the Progressive Movement, 1900–1920.* Cambridge: Harvard University Press, 1963.

Turner, James R. "The American Prohibition Movement, 1865–1897." Ph.D. diss., University of Wisconsin, 1972.

Tyrrell, Ian R. *Sobering Up: From Temperance to Prohibition in Antebellum America, 1800–1860.* Westport, Conn.: Greenwood Press, 1979.

Walters, Ronald. *American Reformers, 1815–1860.* New York: Hill & Wang, 1978.

Wickersham Commission. *National Commission on Law Observance and Enforcement.* Washington, D.C.: Government Printing Office, 1931.

ARTICLES

Aaron, Paul, and Musto, David. "Temperance and Prohibition in America: A Historical Overview." In *Alcohol and Public Policy: Beyond the Shadow of Prohibition,* edited by Mark H. Moore and Dean R. Gerstein, pp. 127–81. Washington, D.C.: National Academy Press, 1981.

Blumberg, Leonard V. "The Significance of the Alcohol Prohibitionists for the Washington Temperance Societies." *Journal of Studies on Alcohol* 41 (1980): 37–77.

Burnham, John C. "New Perspectives on the Prohibition 'Experiment' of the 1920's." *Journal of Social History* 2 (1968): 51–68.

Chalfant, Harry M. "The Anti-Saloon League—Why and What?" *Annals of the American Academy of Political and Social Science* 109 (1923): 279–83.

Gusfield, Joseph R. "Prohibition: The Impact of Political Utopism." In *Change and Continuity in Twentieth-Century America: The 1920's,* edited by John Braeman, Robert H. Bremner, and David Brody, pp. 257-308. Columbus: Ohio State University Press, 1968.

Hampel, Robert L. "Diversity in Early Temperance Reform." *Journal of Studies on Alcohol* 43 (1982): 453-68.

Hohner, Robert H. "The Prohibitionists: Who Were They?" *South Atlantic Quarterly* 68 (1969): 491-505.

Kerr, K. Austin. "Organizing for Reform: The Anti-Saloon League and Innovation in Politics." *American Quarterly* 32 (1980): 37-53.

LeVine, Harry Gene. "Industrialization, Economic Development, and Worker Drinking: Historical and Sociological Observations." In Institute of Medicine, *Legislative Approaches to Prevention of Alcohol-Related Problems: An Inter-American Workshop,* pp. 26-46. Washington, D.C.: National Academy Press, 1982.

Rogers, Daniel T. "In Search of Progressivism." *Reviews in American History* 10 (Dec. 1982): 113-32.

Williams, Sarah E. "The Use of Beverage Alcohol as Medicine, 1790-1860." *Journal of Studies on Alcohol* 41 (1980): 543-66.

Index

314

Prohibition Emergency Committee, 224, 228, 231
Prohibition party (national), 29, 76, 92, 192, 250
Prohibition Ridge, 2
Protestants, 249
Public Opinion, 110
Purchasing liquor, 179

Quakers, 8, 11, 51
Quantrill's Raid, 20
Quapaw Indians, 23
Quindaro, 16, 18

Raids, 233, 240
Railroads, 23
Randolph, A. M. F., 35
Rastall, Fanny H., 95, 98, 99, 103
Rastall, John E., 95
Red Hot Street, 23
Reed, Clyde, 213, 225
Reed, James, 179
Reeder, Andrew, 16
Religious composition, 110-111
Reno County, 60, 202, 242
Repeal, 225, 245, 252
Republic County, 131
Republican National Convention (1932), 226
Republicans, 250, 256
Resubmission, 88, 112-113, 123, 158, 177
Reynolds, E. B., 34
Rhode Island, 109
Rice, John H., 48
Richardson, A. M., 46
Riley County, 131
Ritchie, John, 17, 21
Robinson, Charles, 17, 48, 53-54, 68, 73, 159, 248, 263
Robinson, Sara T. D., 18, 59
Roman Catholic, 11, 69, 249
Rooney, Ed, 234
Roosevelt, Franklin Delano, 217, 236
Roosevelt, Theodore, 78
Root, Joseph P., 25
Rose, W. W., 163, 172
Rossville, 182
Ruppert, Jacob, 221
Rush, Benjamin, 8
Rush County, 231
Russell, 16, 233
Russell, Frank U., 231
Russell County, 233, 240, 242

St. John, Rev. Eugenia Schultz, 128
St. John, John, 1, 6, 35, 37, 39, 47, 55, 71, 92-93, 108, 159, 191, 222
St. John County, 77

St. Louis Globe Democrat, 77
St. Mary's Silver Coronet Band, 4
Salina, 119, 164
Saloon axing, 17-18, 145-146
Salter, Susanna Madora, 104
Sandy, Harry, 183
Santa Fe Railway, 68-69
Santa Fe Road, 22
Sapp, Edward E., 169
Saratoga (saloon), 24, 32
Saturday Evening Post, 149
Scandinavian Lutherans, 11, 30, 70
Scandinavians, 11
Schlitz (company), 164
Schmidt, C. B., 69
Schoeppel, Andrew F., 234, 236, 238-239
Schuyler's Saloon, 33
Scientific Temperance Instruction (STI), 99
Scotch, 11
Scotch-Irish, 11
Scott, Angelo, 246
Scott, Charles, 162
Scott, Edgar T., 132
Searchlight, 157
Second Great Awakening, 10
Sedgwick County, 60, 201, 240, 242
Senate Saloon, 22, 142
Seward County, 132
Sharon, M. J., 29
Shawnee County, 60, 182
Shawnee Methodist Mission, 20
Sheldon, Charles M., 129, 136, 144, 165, 191
Shipping of liquor, 180
"Short pledge," 9
Shouse, Jouett, 211
Shultz, A. L. ("Dutch"), 210
Sibbitt, Rev. Mary ("Mollie") Ferguson, 94, 129, 173
Sibley, Frank, 67
Sicilians, 168
Six Sermons on the Nature, Occasions, Signs, Evils and Remedy of Intemperance (Beecher), 8
Slavs, 168
Smasher's Mail, 151
Smith, Al, 212, 225
Smith, Mrs. M. B., 93
Smith, William A., 194
Snow, Francis, 32
Socialist party, 250
Society of Friends. *See* Quakers
Sons of Temperance, 12
South Dakota, 109
Spencer, Charles F., 126
Spencer, Sue, 17
Stahl, Frank M., 136, 142, 165, 181, 192, 268

Wilson Act of 1890, 107, 185
Wine, 198; communion, 186
Winfield, 68, 119, 146
Wisconsin, 203
Woman's Christian Temperance Union
 (WCTU), 5, 31, 48, 59, 79, 93–94, 96,
 107, 116, 123, 133, 142, 172, 232
"Woman's Crusade," 31, 33, 62, 90
Woman suffrage, 21, 29, 64, 69, 72–73, 80,
 99, 102, 108–109, 113, 176
Women, 16, 28, 32, 59, 81, 153–154. *See
 also* under individual names
Women's Organization for National Prohibi-
 tion Reform, 211
Wood, Leonard, 203
Wood, Sam,
Wood, Mrs.

Woodbine, 123
Woodcock, Amos W. W., 205
Woodring, Harry H., 217, 235, 256
Woodson County, 131
Wooster, Lorraine ("Lizzie"), 207
World War I, 190
Wright, Bob, 64
Wyandotte Constitution, 116
Wyandotte Convention, 21
Wyandotte County, 18, 34, 60, 67–68, 163,
 181, 184, 240, 242

Yates Center, 131

Zinc, 168